Looking for forms or applications?
Download the most recent versions at
USPA.ORG/DOWNLOADS

2023-2024 USPA INSTRUCTIONAL RATING MANUAL

©2022 United States Parachute Association®. All rights reserved. May not be reproduced without the express permission of USPA.

Note: This manual may be used as a valid textbook for USPA rating courses held through November 2024.

uspa.org/downloads

- ✓ forms
- ✓ most current electronic version
- ✓ mid-cycle change documents

United States Parachute Association

5401 Southpoint Centre Blvd.,
Fredericksburg, VA 22407

(540) 604-9740 (phone)
(540) 604-9741 (Fax)
uspa.org

If found, please return to:

Name:

Address:

City, State, Zip:

Phone:

Email:

Cover photo by James Foran | D-40087

Instructors Amber Wright (left) and Eddie Glasset see AFF student Steve Lobin through his deployment at Skydive San Diego in Jamul, California.

WARNING

IMPORTANT NOTICE

SPORT PARACHUTING OR SKYDIVING IS A POTENTIALLY DANGEROUS ACTIVITY THAT CAN RESULT IN INJURY OR DEATH. EACH INDIVIDUAL PARTICIPANT, REGARDLESS OF EXPERIENCE, HAS FINAL RESPONSIBILITY FOR HIS OR HER OWN SAFETY.

THE FOLLOWING INFORMATION IS PRESENTED AS A MEMBERSHIP SERVICE BY THE UNITED STATES PARACHUTE ASSOCIATION (USPA). USPA MAKES NO WARRANTIES OR REPRESENTATIONS AND ASSUMES NO LIABILITY CONCERNING THE VALIDITY OF ANY ADVICE, OPINION OR RECOMMENDATION EXPRESSED IN THIS MATERIAL. ALL INDIVIDUALS RELYING ON THIS MATERIAL DO SO AT THEIR OWN RISK.

An individual's safety can be enhanced by exercising proper precautions and procedures. This manual contains some of the knowledge and practices that, in the opinion of USPA, will promote the safe enjoyment of skydiving. The UNITED STATES PARACHUTE ASSOCIATION is a nonprofit, voluntary membership organization of the participants and supporters of the sport of parachuting. The sport is also referred to as skydiving. USPA has no involvement in the conduct or operations of any skydiving center, parachute center, or drop zone. **USPA, AS A PRIVATE, NON-REGULATORY ORGANIZATION WHICH HAS NO LEGAL AUTHORITY TO REGULATE OR CONTROL INDIVIDUALS OR CORPORATIONS, CANNOT BE HELD LIABLE FOR ANY JUMP OR TRAINING OPERATIONS THAT RESULT IN INJURY OR DEATH TO ANY PARTY.** Regardless of any statements made in any USPA publications, USPA has neither been given nor has it assumed any duty to anyone. USPA has no obligation to anyone concerning his or her skydiving activities. All references by USPA to self-regulation refer to each individual person regulating or being responsible for him or herself. USPA issues various licenses, ratings, awards, and appointments and provides various types of information, advice, and training but does not authorize anyone in any capacity to act for USPA as an agent or representative in connection with the regulation or control of skydiving operations.

It is the responsibility of each student to ask whatever questions are necessary for him or her to have a thorough understanding of the actions and procedures that he or she must perform in order to make a safe jump. Each skydiver has the responsibility to exercise certain practices and perform certain actions to maintain safety for himself or herself and for other people.

USPA MAKES NO WARRANTIES, EXPRESSED OR IMPLIED, AS TO THE INFORMATION SET FORTH IN THIS MANUAL. PEOPLE RELYING THEREON DO SO AT THEIR OWN RISK.

> This manual provides procedures to address many foreseeable situations, but each situation is different. Deviations from these recommendations does not imply negligence.

CONTENTS

- v — 1: Coach and Instructor Qualities
- vi — 2. USPA Hierarchy
- vii — 3: Introduction
- viii — 4: How to Administer a USPA Rating Course (Course Examiners Only)
- x — 5: Pre-Course Training for Rating Candidates
- xi — 6: Protest Procedures

13 Coach Rating Course
- 14 — 1. Introduction and Orientation
- 16 — 2. Rules, Liability, and the USPA Rating Structure
- 19 — 3. Document Layout
- 20 — 4. Basic Instructional Methods
- 25 — 5. First-Jump Course: General Sections
- 27 — 6. Basic and Group Freefall Skills Training
- 34 — 7. Equipment
- 35 — 8. Conducting a Coached Jump
- 37 — 9. Observation and Debriefing Strategies
- 40 — 10. Problem Solving
- 41 — 11. Candidate Evaluation
- 46 — Coach Rating Course Ground Evaluation Checklist
- 47 — USPA Coach Rating Course (Ground) Scoring and Criteria Examples
- 48 — USPA Coach Rating Course (In-Air) Scoring and Criteria Examples

49 AFF Instructor Rating Course
- 50 — 1. Introduction and Orientation
- 52 — 2. The Integrated Student Program
- 60 — 3. AFF Method
- 67 — 4. Instructor's Duties
- 70 — 5. Demonstration and Ground Practice for Evaluations
- 71 — 6. Candidate Practice and Evaluation
- 75 — AFF Instructor Rating Course Ground Evaluation Checklist
- 76 — Sample Evaluation Form
- 77 — Scoring and Criteria examples

79 IAD and Static-Line Instructor Rating
- 80 — 1. Introduction and Orientation
- 82 — 2. The Integrated Student Program
- 90 — 3. IAD and Static-Line Methods
- 94 — 4. Instructor's Duties
- 97 — 5. Demonstration and Ground Practice for Evaluations
- 98 — 6. Candidate Evaluation
- 102 — IAD, Static-Line and Tandem Instructor Rating Course Ground Evaluation Checklist
- 103 — Sample Evaluation Form
- 104 — Scoring and Criteria Examples

107 Tandem Instructor Rating Course
- 108 — 1. Introduction and Orientation
- 111 — 2. The Integrated Student Program
- 119 — 3. Tandem Method
- 125 — 4. Instructor's Duties
- 130 — 5. Demonstration and Ground Practice for Evaluations
- 132 — 6. Candidate Evaluation
- 134 — Tandem Instructor Rating Course Ground Evaluation Checklist
- 135 — Sample Evaluation Form
- 136 — Scoring and Criteria Examples

139 Examiner Rating Course
- 140 — 1. Introduction and Orientation
- 145 — 2. Conducting Presentations
- 147 — 3. Presentation Methods
- 149 — 4. Application Methods
- 150 — 5. Feedback Methods
- 151 — 6. Training Aids
- 152 — 7. Methods of Evaluation for Ground and Air Skills
- 153 — 8. Facilitation Methods
- 157 — 9. Psychology and Goal Setting
- 159 — 10. Motor Skills Evaluation Methods
- 161 — 11. Video Analysis Workshop
- 162 — 12. Situational Leadership
- 163 — 13. Administrative Duties of the Examiner and the S&TA
- 164 — 14. Examiner Administrative Responsibilities
- 165 — 15. Conflict Resolution

167 Appendix A: Lesson Planning

171 Appendix B: Exams

USPA VALUES STATEMENT

USPA is committed to promoting an atmosphere that allows our sport to be safe, inclusive and fun. We advocate for the dignity and well-being of all individuals and respect diverse traditions, heritages and experiences. We value inclusivity and reject discrimination based on race, ethnicity, gender, sexual orientation, religious belief or any other attribute not related to performance or merit. USPA affirms its vision of a safe and healthy skydiving environment free of violence and any form of discrimination, including sexual or racial harassment.

For additional information, refer to the USPA Policy Regarding Discrimination and Harassment in Governance Manual Section 1-9.

1: Coach and Instructor Qualities

USPA expects its rating holders, who are representatives of the sport and are in positions of leadership, to uphold the principles spelled out in the USPA Values Statement.

INSTRUCTIONAL RATING HOLDER CODE OF CONDUCT

Responsibility to the Profession

Act in a professional manner, with honesty, integrity, and ethical conduct while interacting with all students, members, and the public. Exercises principles of good judgment for the safety of yourself and others. Avoid impropriety and misconduct and commit to the USPA Values Statement.

Responsibility for Competence

Act as role models and embrace the concept of leadership in teaching and mentoring in all aspects of training. Ensure that all documents and records associated with the privileges of the rating are accurate, complete, and submitted in a timely manner. Take responsibility to maintain and update their professional skill sets, content knowledge, and competency on an ongoing basis.

Responsibility to Students and Members

Respect diverse traditions, heritages, and experiences and reject discrimination based on race, ethnicity, gender, sexual orientation, disability, religious belief, or any other attribute not related to performance or merit.

Responsibility to follow the Rules

Comply with applicable BSRs, FARS, IRM content, and with timely reporting of incidents on the USPA Confidential Incident Report.

QUALITIES

To succeed as a USPA instructional rating holder, each candidate needs to possess a generous measure of seven qualities: good attitude, experience, proficiency, knowledge, judgment, responsibility, and professionalism.

ATTITUDE

Your attitude must display the highest degree of professionalism and dedication. You must be prepared to put all of your effort into getting the job done properly. This often means setting your personal feelings and desires aside. A good attitude means dealing with adversity in a positive and cheerful manner. It also means maintaining high standards of personal appearance and hygiene.

EXPERIENCE

Experience, both as a jumper and as an instructor, is the best teacher to prepare you for the responsibility of this job. You can gain general experience only by going out and jumping; but no specific number of jumps ensures that you have an adequate amount of experience. You must be successful in your own skydiving prior to attempting to become a USPA instructional rating holder. It requires experience to exercise good judgment and to anticipate events before they happen.

PROFICIENCY

You need a high degree of proficiency and skill to get the job done safely. This means you must develop a keen sense of awareness and quick reactions. You must stay abreast with new techniques and methods that will enhance your skill.

KNOWLEDGE

You can not teach something that you don't know yourself. You need a thorough knowledge of the program and the specific methods of instruction used by the other instructional staff members at your school. You must be thoroughly familiar with the equipment used at the drop zone and with the procedures used in your aircraft and by your pilot.

JUDGMENT

You exercise good judgment by using your experience and knowledge to make decisions. You need good judgment to keep everything in proper perspective. You use it to make prudent decisions that have long-term goals and overall success as the priority. You use good judgment to decide if your student is fully prepared to make a planned jump. You also use it to execute the correct procedure, rapidly, in an emergency.

RESPONSIBILITY

Responsibility is the requirement, both legally and morally, to conduct the training and jumping of your students in a safe and competent manner. You must ensure that they understand the situation that confronts them and that they are aware of how to handle it. You are responsible for ensuring that they receive the caliber of instruction that they have purchased. You also have a responsibility to yourself and to the DZ not to endanger yourself physically or legally, regardless of what happens.

PROFESSIONALISM

You must really believe in your work if you are to do your best. Although the word "professionalism" is widely used, it is rarely defined. In fact, no single definition encompasses all of the qualities of a true professional.

1. Professionalism exists when a service is performed for someone for the common good.
2. Professionalism is achieved only after extended training and preparation.
3. True performance as a professional is based on study and research.
4. Professionalism presupposes any intellectual requirement. The professional must be able to reason logically and accurately.
5. Professionalism requires the ability to make good judgments. The professional cannot limit his actions and decisions to standard patterns and practice.
6. Professionalism demands a code of ethics. The professional must be true to himself and those he serves. Students will quickly detect anything less than a sincere performance, which immediately destroys the teacher's effectiveness.

If you have not developed these qualities, then go out and work on them. If you do have these qualities, then you should continue to develop and improve them.

Achieving these qualities once is not enough either. Every time you work with a student you must ask yourself, "Am I currently proficient?" "Am I using good judgment?" and so on. It is your responsibility to maintain your proficiency and regain your currency after a layoff from jumping, before instructing or jumping with students.

2. USPA Hierarchy

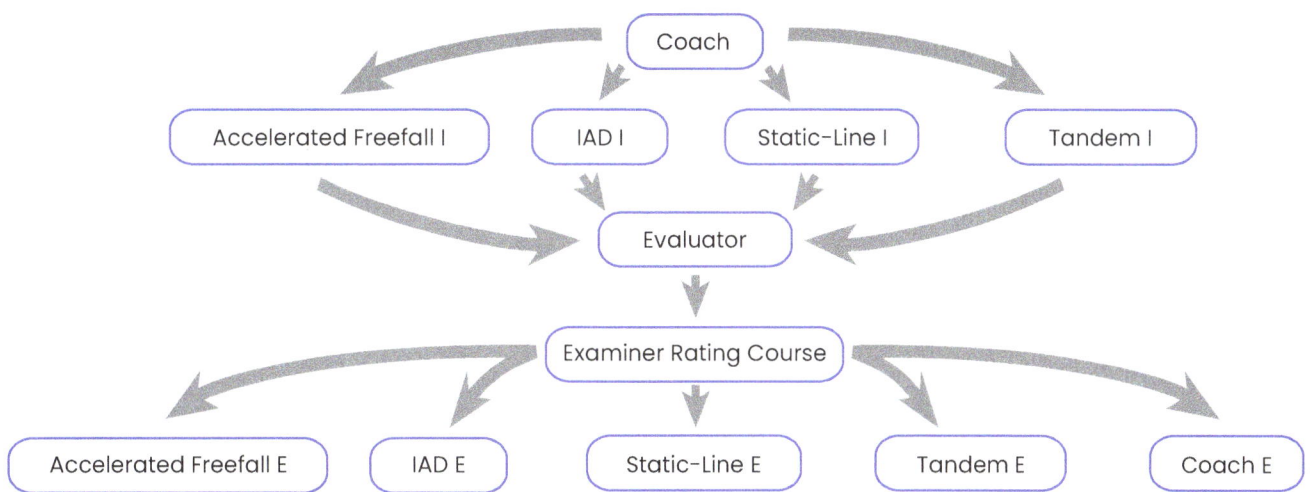

A. USPA RATING STRUCTURE

1. USPA rating hierarchy
   a. USPA Coach
      (1) Includes basic instructional methods that apply to all other ratings
      (2) Provides a solid foundation of skills and knowledge in order to prepare for the USPA Instructor rating
   b. USPA Instructor
      (1) USPA Accelerated Freefall (AFF)
      (2) Instructor-Assisted Deployment (IAD)
      (3) Static Line
      (4) Tandem
   c. USPA Coach Examiner and Examiner
      (1) Coach
      (2) AFF
      (3) IAD
      (4) Static Line
      (5) Tandem
2. Appointments
   a. The Regional Director, a member of the elected USPA Board of Directors, appoints S&TAs as liaisons between USPA members, drop zone management, USPA Headquarters, and the USPA Regional Director.
   b. Examiners
      (1) USPA Instructors may qualify as Examiners for method specific instructional rating courses
      (2) In some cases, Examiners require additional qualifications described in the Introduction and Orientation section of each instructional rating course outline.
      (3) Examiners may appoint other qualified USPA Instructors or Examiners as evaluators to assist in their courses.

B. ELECTED OFFICIALS

1. The USPA Board is comprised of 23 members:
   a. 14 regional directors
   b. Eight national directors (directors-at-large)
   c. A representative appointed by the National Aeronautical Association and who has full voting privileges
2. The board elects the officers from among its members.
3. The board operates via a committee system, which includes the USPA Safety & Training Committee.
   a. headed by the S&T Chair (appointed by the USPA President), who appoints committee members from among other elected board members and non-voting advisors
   b. studies program and policy proposals as assigned by the president
   c. recommends additions, changes, deletions, and waivers to policies for full board vote

C. USPA HEADQUARTERS STAFF

1. The USPA Executive Committee hires an Executive Director, an employee who reports to the president.
2. The Executive Director hires the headquarters staff, including the staff Director of Safety & Training, who—
   a. reports to the Executive Director
   b. coordinates and administers safety & training programs, including the license, instructional rating, and PRO rating programs
   c. oversees the maintenance of the USPA instructional program documents
   d. coordinates mass communications to USPA instructional rating holders

3: Introduction

A. PURPOSE AND SCOPE

The USPA Instructional Rating Manual (IRM) provides the necessary course outlines and all related support materials for both candidates and examiners of USPA instructional courses. All the USPA courses for USPA Coach and USPA Instructor in any of the four first-jump methods—AFF, instructor-assisted deployment, static line, and tandem—are included. Please note that IAD and static-line, while requiring different equipment, follow the same course outline.

One book serves several purposes.
Some of the text is written to the candidate, some to the course examiner, and some serves as a reference to the rating holder. Where practical, who's being addressed is indicated.

Additional course materials needed.
To successfully complete the USPA instructional rating courses, the candidates and course examiners will also need a current Skydiver's Information Manual. Additionally, USPA Tandem Instructor rating candidates and course examiners will need the manufacturer's equipment manual.

All courses are included.
Each IRM booklet contains enough applications and forms—answer sheets, practical evaluation forms, etc.—so its owner can take all the USPA instructional rating courses without buying another copy of the manual. Someone taking the USPA Coach Rating Course today can use the same book for the AFF, IAD, Static-Line, and Tandem Instructor Rating Courses for up to two years.

Document expiration
At the beginning of each rating course, the course examiner will check each rating candidate's copy of the IRM and SIM to make sure they are no more than two years old at the start of the course. (Check the version date on the title page.) Both are updated annually. Candidates with versions more than two years old would find it difficult to follow the class and pass newer rating examinations. Important information and rules may have changed.

Outline formatting
The IRM is structured into outline format for easy reference by candidates and course examiners, as well as for revision by the USPA Safety & Training Committee and USPA Headquarters. Outline form also makes the book more useful as a reference during the open-book final exams.

Reference only
The IRM course outlines merely list the concepts to be discussed. It is up to the course examiner and rating candidates to take it from there. The trained course examiner knows how far to develop each concept. Naturally, some ideas and discussions deserve more attention than others.

Redundancy among course outlines
Some information that is shared by all the courses is presented once only in the IRM. However, to make it easier for course examiners and candidates to follow the outlines, sometimes the same information is included in more than one course. It would be nice to have a common course outline for all instructors, for example, followed by the method-specific portions. However, constructing the program in this manner proved too unwieldy.

Wherever possible for currently rated USPA Instructors seeking new method-specific ratings, the course outlines steer clear of previous, redundant training. What remains serves as a good update or review.

B. HOW TO USE THIS MANUAL (CANDIDATES)

As soon as you get this manual, write your name on the front in permanent marker and fill out all the owner and "return if lost" information at the beginning.

If your examiner is using the online course manager to notate your progress in the course, you can find your online proficiency card by clicking on the name of the course in your Education page of your profile. You can work on pre-requisite activity even before you are enrolled in a course through a link (view my pre-reqs for rating courses) on your Education page.

If your examiner is using paper (pdf) proficiency cards, find the corresponding card online at uspa.org/downloads. Fill out all your name and address information on only the card for the USPA instructional course you are planning to take. This will prevent anyone else from using your card once you begin collecting signatures for requirements. Keep the card in a safe place until you have completed it and are ready to hand it to your course examiner (Your course examiner is required to send the card for you.)

Know the requirements for your rating.
Overview the sections pertaining to your course to help you get an idea of the material that will be covered. Determine the requirements for your rating found in the "Introduction and Orientation" section of each course outline and listed on the proficiency card for your rating. All the proficiency requirements for the rating are included on the proficiency card, and the outline provides further details. You must complete all the requirements listed in the outline and on the proficiency card to qualify for your rating.

The proficiency card is the rating application.
Various rating requirements are completed before the start of the course, during the course, or after the course is over. Your course examiner will tell you which requirements you should complete ahead of time and which may be completed during or after the course.

For qualifications required prior to the course, discuss the section in the IRM on Instructor Administrative Notes, "Pre-Course Training for Rating Candidates" with a USPA Instructor at your school to begin preparing for your rating course. Please make sure to arrive at the course with the pre-course requirements complete, or you may be asked to participate at another, later course. It is your responsibility to know what you need before you arrive.

How to propose changes to this manual
Corrections and comments on this manual are welcome and should be forwarded to headquarters. USPA relies on its instructional rating holders to point out problems and errors or to suggest improvements to the program. Submit your suggestions and comments to the Director of Safety & Training at headquarters. Refer to the title page to get contact information for USPA.

Keep in touch.
Periodically, USPA publishes the "USPA Professional." Once you obtain a USPA instructional rating, USPA will automatically send it to you via email. It is also posted for everyone at the USPA website. You can find past editions of the newsletter archived there, as well.

Additionally, articles and announcements for rating holders regularly appear in *Parachutist* magazine. Especially look at the end of the monthly rating course schedule for rating holder updates and reminders.

Please try to keep abreast of new information for rating holders through these valuable resources. Make sure USPA always knows your current residence and email address.

1-4 HOW TO ADMINISTER A USPA RATING COURSE

4: How to Administer a USPA Rating Course (Course Examiners Only)

A. COURSE EXAMINER DUTIES

1. Know the material to be presented.
   a. Assist at a complete USPA instructional rating course of the type you plan to conduct.
   b. Be thoroughly familiar with the USPA Integrated Student Program.
   c. Read and understand the relevant outlines in each new edition of the IRM and the SIM prior to conducting a course.
2. Schedule the course and maintain communication with all candidates prior to the start of the course.
3. Courses must be scheduled and conducted separately. Each course must be held at a USPA Group Member drop zone, or USPA must receive a course permit payment not to exceed the Category 3 Group Member fee in a calendar year.
   a. Some examiners may elect to schedule a Coach Rating course followed immediately by an instructor rating course.
   b. Each course must be run separately, including the classroom, ground evaluations and air evaluations.
   c. Combining or merging any of the rating courses in any way is not permissible.
4. Set and collect any course fees.
   a. Consider all materials and rating fees (if collected at the course).
   b. USPA rating candidates should be prepared to pay adequately for professional training to further their jumping careers.
   c. Course fees should be sufficient to encourage the examiner to conduct the course completely and effectively.
5. Register the course with USPA Headquarters (if desired).
   a. To be announced in *Parachutist*, a course must be registered with headquarters at least 45 days before the start of the course.
   b. Announcements on the USPA website may allow for a shorter lead time.
6. Use current documents.
   a. Each candidate must possess:
      (1) a complete, original printed version of the IRM (photocopies are not authorized) or the electronic PDF file having an edition date within two years of the start of the course
      (2) a recent copy of the SIM
   b. The course examiner should have current copies of both manuals on hand for candidates who don't.
7. Arrange for all ground support.
8. Coordinate with the drop zone hosting the course to ensure that classroom facilities and other learning aids are adequate and available.
9. Familiarize and orient candidates to the training facility and course procedures.
10. Coordinate course staff.
    a. classroom sessions
    b. ground evaluation demonstrations and evaluations
    c. air evaluations
11. Refer to the candidate qualifications in the "Introduction and Orientation" section of each course syllabus and verify that each candidate qualifies for the rating at the start of the course.
    a. license
    b. age
    c. time in sport (tandem)
    d. minimum freefall time (AFF candidates)
    e. previous rating, as required
12. Begin lessons on time.
13. Be present and attentive for the entirety of the specific course.
14. Follow the course outline and conduct the course according to USPA policy.
15. Include the "Instructor Administrative Notes" section for candidates applying for their first method-specific rating.
16. Documentation
    a. Whether you use online or paper proficiency cards, verify completion of the Proficiency Card and sign as the course examiner when the course is complete.
    b. Online Course Manager (OCM) must be used to track all USPA courses. Candidate and course status must be updated to received credit for the course.
    c. Encourage the candidates to fill out the feedback form that will be on their education page on the USPA website once their status is changed in the Online Course Manager
    d. If paper forms are used, retain a copy for at least two years after the course dates.
    e. Forward to headquarters:
       (1) USPA Rating Application and Proficiency Card if not done online
       (2) copy of acceptable medical certification for USPA Tandem Instructor applicants
       (3) any rating fees due
    f. If paper proficiency cards are submitted by email, request an email verification from USPA Headquarters to verify that the proficiency cards have been received for processing, and retain the email in your records.

B. RESOURCE ALLOTMENT

1. One air skills evaluator minimum should be engaged for every three candidates.
2. Recommend that USPA Coach candidates complete their first-jump course requirements prior to the start of the course.
   a. to learn a first-jump-course course syllabus
   b. provides supervised teaching practice prior to the ground training evaluations
3. Refer to the retesting procedures included at the end of the evaluation section of each course outline.

C. EVALUATORS

1. Examiners who have taught five or fewer method-specific rating courses must use Evaluators who have evaluated in more than five rating courses of the same method.
2. Refer to each USPA instructional course outline for evaluator qualifications and attendance requirements.
3. Designated evaluator
   a. A designated evaluator (method-specific) may conduct a qualifying evaluation jump with a rating holder who cannot meet the annual rating renewal

requirements or whose rating has expired for less than one year.

    b. With the permission of the course examiner, a Designated Evaluator may assist a candidate in finishing the course evaluations without direct supervision of an examiner for:

        (1) ground evaluations once the candidate has completed at least fifty percent of ground evaluations for that course

        (2) air evaluations once the candidate has completed at least fifty percent of the air evaluations for that course

    c. To qualify as a designated evaluator, an instructor must (all the following)—

        (1) have worked as an evaluator for a minimum of three method-specific courses

        (2) attend the entire classroom portion of a method-specific Rating Course every two years

        (3) be recommended in writing by the Rating Course Examiner and confirmed by Headquarters

D. HEADQUARTERS RESPONSIBILITIES

1. Accept registration of each course in advance (if submitted).
2. Maintain information on the date, location, and course examiner contact information for each course.
3. Process all rating applications, fees, forms, and the After-Action Report.
4. Notify the appropriate parties of any errors or deficiencies.
5. Maintain a registry of all instructional rating holders and course examiners.
6. Maintain this program and its related documents.

1-5 PRE-COURSE TRAINING FOR RATING CANDIDATES

5: Pre-Course Training for Rating Candidates

A. SCOPE AND PURPOSE

1. This section serves as a guide to current USPA Instructors who are preparing candidates for rating courses.
2. USPA Instructors may train and supervise jumpers who are preparing for various rating courses, including verifying certain pre-course requirements on the proficiency card for that rating.
3. Once each requirement has been satisfactorily completed, the supervising USPA Instructor signs off that section of the course candidate's USPA Proficiency Card.
4. Only USPA Examiners may submit candidate rating proficiency cards and required course documentation for the candidates in their rating courses to USPA Headquarters for processing.
5. An appropriately rated USPA Instructor must directly supervise all candidate training of actual students (see SIM definition of "Direct Supervision").

B. VERIFYING PROFICIENCY REQUIREMENTS

USPA COACH

1. Review the outline for the "Basic Instructional Method" portion of the Coach Rating Course outline.
2. Involve USPA Coach rating candidates in the solo first-jump course to develop the candidate's skills in observation, correction, and communication.
3. While conducting the solo first-jump course, the USPA Instructor directly supervises and evaluates the candidate for the following until satisfactory—
   a. follows the solo first-jump-course syllabus
   b. breaks the information into manageable chunks and presents them in a logical sequence
   c. adheres to the 90-20-8 course management principles
   d. applies the principles of preparation, presentation, application, and evaluation to the lessons
   e. answers questions accurately or consults the correct staff member
4. Observe the candidate for satisfactory conduct of the following:
   a. freefall skills training from Categories F, G and H
   b. equipment check
   c. spotting
   d. debriefing skills

ALL USPA INSTRUCTOR RATINGS

1. Each candidate assists with the method-specific portions of at least one first-jump course in the method for the rating sought until familiar with all procedures.
2. The candidate must hold a current rating in another method-specific discipline or satisfy the following requirements:
   a. demonstrate the ability to teach the Exit and Freefall, Canopy, and Emergency Procedures sections of Categories E and F, which are not evaluated during the USPA Instructor Rating Course.
   b. emergency procedure training:
      (1) aircraft, including engine out, parachute equipment entanglement, fires, catastrophic damage, forced landings
      (2) freefall, including instability, instrument failure, collisions, student loss of altitude awareness
      (3) equipment, including all parachute malfunctions and premature container opening in the aircraft
      (4) landings, including all obstacles and high-wind procedures
   c. Basic canopy flight planning and ground-to-air canopy instruction (radio, etc.)
   d. Spotting training (participate in spotting training for Categories E and F)

USPA AFF INSTRUCTOR

Each candidate assists with the pre-jump ground preparation (Exit and Freefall, Canopy, and Emergency Procedure Review) in Categories C and D of the ISP syllabus, which are included in the ground training and air skills evaluations of the AFF course.

USPA IAD AND STATIC-LINE INSTRUCTOR

1. Each candidate assists with the pre-jump ground preparation in Categories B and C of the ISP (Exit and Freefall, Canopy, and Emergency Procedure Review) for at least two solo students or simulated students.
2. Equipment
   a. Each candidate (either method) conducts five jumps with B-licensed jumpers who have made at least 100 jumps—
      (1) static-line: using an actual static line or a line rigged like a static line (but does not have to open the container on exit)
      (2) IAD: instructor candidate deployment, using a live pilot chute
   b. Static-line candidates receive instruction on direct bag and pilot-chute assist static-line rigging.
3. Only an appropriately rated USPA Instructor is authorized to handle the deployment device and conduct jumps with IAD and static-line students.

USPA TANDEM INSTRUCTOR

No method-specific pre-course activities required

6: Protest Procedures

A. INTRODUCTION

1. No system is perfect, and a candidate who feels unfairly scored may protest a score.
2. Errors may occur when an evaluator does not score a candidate in accordance with the guidelines.
   a. in the "Practice and Evaluation" section of this course
   b. in the verbal or videotaped briefing presented before an evaluation
3. Pointing out a discrepancy to the evaluator being questioned during the critique will usually resolve the question.
4. When a question remains in the candidate's mind, the following procedure allows a timely and accurate review of a score.

B. PROCEDURES

1. Clarify the scoring points with the evaluator being questioned during or as soon as possible after the critique to determine exactly why the score was assigned.
2. If still not satisfied with the reason given for the score, speak with the course examiner within four hours of receiving the score; either—
   a. The course examiner resolves the question immediately.
   b. A more formal procedure will be followed.
3. Formal protest
   a. Within four working hours of the candidate's first contact with the course examiner regarding the matter, the candidate provides a written statement explaining the reason the score is being protested.
   b. The course examiner asks the evaluator being questioned to prepare a written statement identifying the scoring criteria.
   c. The evaluator provides the written statement within four working hours.
   d. Four hours from receiving both the evaluator's and the candidate's statements, the course examiner will seek any additional information necessary to make a decision and provide a written reply to the candidate's inquiry.
4. Protests will be available for review by any of the persons involved in the course but will be kept by the course examiner.
5. In the event that a score given on the evaluation by the course examiner is challenged, it will, if possible, be reviewed by the next most experienced evaluator at the course.
6. Decisions made by the course examiner will stand
   a. Comments about those or other decisions may be made to USPA's Director of Safety & Training at—

   Director of Safety & Training
   U.S. Parachute Association
   5401 Southpoint Centre Blvd.
   Fredericksburg, VA 22407

   b. A copy of each protest will be forwarded to the USPA Safety & Training Committee.

COACH RATING COURSE

C-1 INTRODUCTION AND ORIENTATION

1. Introduction and Orientation

A. WHAT IS A USPA COACH?

1. USPA Coach is the first of three instructional ratings USPA administers, followed by Instructor and Examiner.
2. A USPA Coach may—
   a. conduct training in the non-method-specific portions of the skydiving ground school.
      (1) equipment familiarization as it pertains to the first jump
      (2) basic canopy control
      (3) parachute emergency procedures
      (4) landings and landing emergencies (obstacles)
      (5) aircraft emergencies for students cleared to freefall self-supervision and who have completed the Category E aircraft briefing in the USPA Integrated Student Program
   b. teach the general portions of transition training for students changing from tandem to solo methods
   c. conduct group freefall skills training and jumps with students who have been cleared by a USPA Instructor
   d. make gripped exits with students during group freefall skills jumps
   e. train and supervise the ISP Category F thru H canopy dive flows
   f. supervise currency jumps with licensed skydivers
   g. supervise static-line and IAD students beginning in Category C after each student demonstrates a successful clear and pull
      (1) All ground training must be performed by an appropriately rated instructor.
      (2) The student must be trained by an instructor to independently handle aircraft emergencies.
      (3) The coach may only observe the jumps using the same rules and guidelines for freefall with students that apply to static line and IAD instructors.
3. All student training and currency jumps with a USPA Coach are conducted under the supervision of a current and appropriately rated USPA Instructor.
4. Candidates who have met all the following requirements may attend the USPA Coach Course:
   a. reached the age of 18 years
   b. issued a USPA B license
   c. completed at least 100 jumps
5. Candidates who have completed the following requirements may earn the USPA Coach rating:
   a. completed the USPA Coach Proficiency Card
   b. satisfactorily completed a USPA Coach Rating Course

B. THE NATURE OF THE COURSE

1. Strategy
   a. This course teaches effective methods for training adults to skydive.
   b. Candidates learn to apply those methods to a restricted portion of the USPA Integrated Student Program.
      (1) the non-method-specific portions of the skydiving first-jump course
      (2) All skills in Categories F-H
      (3) Static-line or IAD student supervision in the aircraft, during climb out and exit, and freefall observation following a stable clear and pull in Category C
2. Course length: Development of the course using various formats and materials show that course length is typically three full days.
   a. regardless of class size
   b. one evaluator per three course candidates

C. WHO MAY CONDUCT THIS COURSE?

1. A Coach Examiner who has conducted at least one USPA Coach Course within the past 24 months
2. Continues to meet all of the requirements to qualify as a course evaluator

D. WHAT IS REQUIRED TO PASS THIS COURSE?

1. Prior to this course each candidate must correctly answer at least 80% of the questions on an open-book-written examination covering the following:
   a. FAR 105 (SIM Section 9-1)
   b. USPA Basic Safety Requirements and waivers (SIM Section 2-1)
   c. this syllabus
   d. any related readings included in the USPA Coach Rating Course
   e. portions of the USPA Integrated Student Program (SIM Section 4)
      (1) Category A, Solo General Section
      (2) all sections of Categories F-H
2. Before, during, or after the course a supervising USPA Instructor observes and evaluates each candidate during the required first-jump courses and portions of courses for coaching skills and communication ability.
3. During the course
   a. a supervising USPA Instructor observes each candidate conduct training sessions from the ISP syllabus that USPA Coaches are qualified to teach:
      (1) sample lessons from the general sections of the first-jump course
      (2) freefall portions of Categories F-H
   b. The candidate performs at least two satisfactory evaluation jumps, including freefall training.
   c. The candidate is evaluated on his or her debriefing skills.
   d. commencement of privileges
      (1) The privileges of any instructional rating will commence upon successful completion of the rating course and will be valid for 15 days with a candidate logbook endorsement by the coach examiner.
      (2) The rating must be processed at headquarters to be considered valid after the 15-day grace period expires.

E. RENEWING AN EXPIRED COACH RATING

1. Ratings expire with USPA memberships. Persons with an expired USPA Coach rating (up to two years) must:

   a. make at least one satisfactory USPA Coach Rating Course evaluation jump with a Coach course Designated Evaluator or Examiner acting as a student, to include all jump preparation, supervision during the jump and debriefing

   b. having taught or assisted with the entire general portion of at least one first-jump course

   c. attend a USPA rating renewal seminar

   d. pass the coach course written exam with a score of at least 80 percent

2. Persons with an expired coach rating of more than two years must requalify by successfully passing the USPA Coach Rating Course.

F. CONVERTING A NON-USPA COACH RATING TO A USPA COACH RATING

1. A jumper with a current Coach or Instructor rating from a non-U.S. skydiving federation may convert that rating to a USPA Coach Rating by completing a USPA Coach Course, excluding the first-jump-course training on the Coach Rating Course Proficiency Card.

G. KEEPING A USPA COACH RATING CURRENT

1. USPA Coaches may annually renew their ratings with their USPA membership by paying the annual rating renewal fee and providing documentation, signed by a USPA Instructor, S&TA, Examiner or member of the USPA Board, for the following:

   a. that the rating was initially earned within the current membership cycle (renewal fee and signature required), in which case the annual minimum coach jump number (15) does not apply.

   b. having taught or assisted with the entire general portion of at least one first-jump course.

   c. made at least 15 coaching jumps in the last 12 months.

   d. participated in an annual rating renewal seminar (see SIM glossary for definition).

   e. or, having met the renewal requirements for an expired USPA Coach rating.

2. A skydiver may not certify his or her own rating renewal requirements.

3. Renewing an instructor rating automatically renews a coach rating.

H. COURSE OVERVIEW

1. Introduction and orientation (this section)
2. Rules, liability, and the USPA rating structure
3. Document layout
4. Basic instructional method
5. First-jump course general sections
6. Group freefall skills training and evaluation
7. Equipment
8. Conducting a coached jump
9. Observation and debriefing strategies and evaluation
10. Problem solving
11. Candidate evaluation

C-2 RULES, LIABILITY, AND THE USPA RATING STRUCTURE

2. Rules, Liability, and the USPA Rating Structure

2-1: RULES OF SKYDIVING

A. ETHICAL CONSIDERATIONS

1. USPA instructional rating holders must know the rules and abide by them when conducting training jumps.
2. All USPA rating holders must maintain an impartiality toward every student while performing their duties.
3. Students must know when they are receiving reliable information.
4. Breach of the rules can result in disciplinary action.

B. SKYDIVING RULES PERTINENT TO COACHING

1. Review clouds and visibility requirements (FAR 105.17).
2. Review the USPA Basic Safety Requirements with special attention to the following points:
   a. A student remains a student until issued a USPA A license and must be supervised by the appropriate USPA rating holder until then.
   b. All student training is supervised by an appropriately rated USPA Instructor.
      (1) must be readily available
      (2) responsible for satisfactory completion of the training
      (3) definitions of "direct supervision" and "supervision" in the SIM
   c. All student jump operations must be completed (landed) by sunset.
   d. All solo students must comply with wind limits until licensed.
      (1) round reserve—10 mph
      (2) ram-air reserve—14 mph
   e. All solo students and A-license holders must deploy by 3,000 feet AGL.
   f. Landing areas for students and A license holders must be clear of obstacles for a radius of at least 100 meters (200 meters in diameter).
   g. Unless waivered, student equipment requirements apply until the student obtains a USPA A license (review requirements in the BSRs).
3. Review waivers to the BSRs with special attention to the following points:
   a. An S&TA or Examiner may file waivers to certain BSRs pertaining to students.
      (1) use of non-USPA-rated coaches
      (2) wind limits
      (3) drop zone size requirements
      (4) flotation devices
   b. The waiver must be on file with the Regional Director and USPA Headquarters and reviewed annually.

C. RESPONSIBILITIES FOR BSR COMPLIANCE

1. The USPA Group Member drop zone or school owner is responsible for administering the school's training programs in compliance with the BSRs.
2. The USPA rating holder is responsible to conduct all student jumps in compliance with the BSRs, regardless of the location of the jump.
3. Students are also responsible for following the BSRs.

D. EQUALITY ISSUES

Rating holders should understand federal and state laws pertaining to gender, race, religion, and national origin.

   a. The provisions of the Federal grant assurances at publicly funded airports require equal treatment of all clients, regardless of differences, and all businesses on the airport are subject to those terms.
   b. State and local laws may apply to the discriminatory treatment of individuals by a business or club on private property.

E. AFTER-JUMP ACTIVITIES

1. Protect students from misinformation outside the classroom environment.
2. Explain that extracurricular conversations with experienced jumpers may contain unreliable or misleading information for their current level of understanding.

F. DISCIPLINARY ACTIONS

1. Actions or behavior that specifically violate the BSRs or otherwise jeopardize skydiving can result in disciplinary action from the USPA Board of Directors, including suspension or revocation of ratings or membership.
2. A USPA Regional Director, S&TA or Examiner may temporarily suspend USPA ratings. (RD may suspend for 60 days; S&TA or Examiner may suspend for 30 days.)
3. Review USPA Governance Manual, Section 1-6.

2-2: LIABILITY CONCEPTS (READING)

Skydivers, like everyone else, are obliged to conduct themselves within the law. When supervising a jump for another person, it is especially important that every portion of the jump operation, from training to packing to the aircraft ride to the actual jump comply with the applicable laws.

Secondly, and of equal importance, are liability concerns. A skydiving instructor can minimize personal liability exposure by observing all laws and industry standards, most of which are contained in USPA's Skydiver's Information Manual. As a USPA rating holder, you should understand the extent and nature of your potential liability exposure, as well as how to reduce it.

THE FEDERAL AVIATION REGULATIONS

The Federal Aviation Administration (FAA) is responsible for the safety of the flying public and people on the ground who could be affected by an aviation accident. The safety of the skydiver is not as much of a concern to the FAA as is the safety of someone whom a skydiver could hit. You might notice that this philosophy pervades the Federal Aviation Regulations (FARs).

In the U.S., the FARs are the laws of the sky. Most of the FARs that apply to skydivers are contained in FAR 65, Certification: Airmen Other Than Flight Crewmembers, which includes information about parachute riggers; FAR 91, General Operating and Flight Rules (various sections); and most importantly, FAR 105, Parachute Jumping. All of FAR 105 is included in the SIM, as are pertinent sections of Sections 65, 91, and other FARs.

When someone reports a violation of an FAR, the FAA requires that it be investigated. For example, if someone on the ground reports to the FAA seeing a skydiver jump through a cloud, an inspector from the closest FAA Flight Standards District Office must investigate and file a report on the incident.

First, the FAA inspector asks for further details in writing from the observer. If the inspector believes an FAR has been violated, the investigation continues. The inspector may choose to inform the accused party that an investigation is underway but is not required to do so.

If, after completing the initial investigation, the inspector believes that a violation has occurred, he or she sends the file to the FAA regional headquarters, where it is turned over to the legal department. The legal department continues the investigation and may issue a notice of violation. Once that happens, the FAA prosecutes under federal administrative law proceedings, which differ from the criminal justice system.

If the accused are found guilty, an appeal may be possible through the National Transportation Safety Board. Failing that, the guilty parties may be forced to pay a fine. If any one of them holds an FAA certificate, such as a pilot or a rigger, that certificate can be suspended or revoked. The FAA may find several parties guilty, such as the pilot and the jumper in the case of a cloud violation.

Typically, investigation into a jump operation begins only after an accident. FAA and NTSB investigators will first look for violations of any FARs that may have contributed to the accident. Was the individual's reserve in date? Was the pilot properly rated to fly jumpers in that plane? Was the plane maintained according to FAA standards? Were alcohol or drugs involved? Was the main parachute packed according to regulations?

The best way to avoid an FAA investigation is to comply with the FARs and to develop a reputation for consistently complying with them.

Although rare, it is also possible to be prosecuted for criminal negligence or manslaughter for bad performance as a skydiving instructor. At least one individual has gone to jail as a result of criminal negligence where a student was killed.

STATE AND LOCAL LAWS

Few states still carry laws on the books specifically about skydiving. More frequently found are local airport rules, which may fall under city or county codes or under the transportation or aviation laws of the state. In the case of a federally funded airport, which includes most airports with paved runways and runway lighting, the FAA expects the owner—usually a city, town, or county—to create and enforce rules that contribute to a safe airport environment. These rules often address skydiving.

LIABILITY

FARs and state and local regulations are written laws. When one is violated, the accused is found guilty or not guilty. Liability, on the other hand, is more difficult to determine.

Exactly what is liability? Liability goes hand in hand with responsibility. If a person is responsible for an operation, that person is liable for the consequences if something goes wrong. Just as responsibility can be shared, so can liability.

Naturally, it is most desirable to place the liability on the skydiver who is actually making the jump. From the instructor skydiver's perspective, that means making certain that every person who jumps from an airplane is capable of preserving his or her own life and avoiding injuries. Each skydiver should be made ultimately responsible for the outcome of his or her jump.

In the case of an AFF, IAD, or static-line, each student is taught to open the main parachute, how to use the reserve if the main fails, and how to steer and land the parachute. Each tandem student should also be trained how and when to operate the drogue release handle and how to read the altimeter.

Most skydiving injuries occur on landing, so solo skydiving students learn canopy control, obstacle avoidance, priorities for landing and hard landing procedures prior to the first jump. In tandem jumping, the parachutist in command typically handles most decisions.

USPA BSRS AND RECOMMENDATIONS

The key to avoiding accidents and the liability that may be incurred from an accident is close adherence to industry standards. The majority of skydivers have agreed upon many aspects of skydiving procedures and instruction. For example, very few people dispute the minimum pull altitudes or that students should wear automatic activation devices. These are considered industry standards.

The USPA Basic Safety Requirements contain the elemental standards for skydiving and skydiving instruction. In the case of a student accident where any BSRs were violated, the staff members who

RULES, LIABILITY, AND THE USPA RATING STRUCTURE — C-2

made the bad call could find themselves in serious trouble. Conversely, strict adherence to the BSRs helps to protect the staff and management in case someone gets hurt.

There are certain exceptions where a deviation from a BSR is permitted. Waivers to the BSRs and procedures for obtaining a waiver are described in SIM Section 2-2.

The USPA recommendations provide additional protection. The SIM describes USPA's first choice on many procedures that may vary because of locale, equipment, individual experience or expertise, or other reasons.

A deviation from USPA recommendations does not necessarily imply negligence, but the alternative procedure should have a very good justification and it should be documented. No waiver from USPA is needed to deviate from a recommendation, but the rationale should be strong enough to defend the DZ owner or staff member in court in the event of a lawsuit.

THE LIABILITY LAWSUIT

You won't need a comprehensive lesson in liability law to be an effective skydiving instructor, but understanding some of the common tactics used by plaintiffs' attorneys may help you to realize how important it is to avoid a lawsuit.

In many states, the concept of "joint and several" liability causes the lawsuit to be brought against anyone even remotely connected with a jump operation, including the drop zone owner, property owner, coach, instructor, aircraft owner, pilot, aircraft mechanic, equipment manufacturer, rigger, radio coach, USPA, and others.

If the lawsuit succeeds, the responsibility to pay may fall on the person with the most ability to pay—the one with the most assets—regardless of who was most a fault. You could become financially responsible for a mistake made by someone else on your staff, even though you were only remotely involved.

The lawsuit will often be brought at the last possible date before the statute of limitations expires, typically two or three years. The trial, if it goes that far, may not occur for another year after that. The goal is that the defense witnesses will have forgotten the details of the incident or

C-2 RULES, LIABILITY, AND THE USPA RATING STRUCTURE

The best way to avoid a lawsuit is to avoid an injury.

cannot be found. For that reason, it is best to immediately document every detail of any injury on the drop zone and obtain written statements from any possible witnesses.

It is considered bad practice, but some plaintiffs will bring a lawsuit in hopes of gaining a quick settlement from the defendants, who would otherwise have to pay even more in legal fees, win or lose.

The best way to avoid a lawsuit is to avoid an injury. No lawsuit can succeed unless some harm has been done to the plaintiff.

THE LIABILITY WAIVER

Most drop zones require that each participant complete a release of liability, or "waiver." It has proven valuable to prevent many frivolous lawsuits brought by people who don't want to take responsibility for their own actions. The release must be written by a lawyer qualified to practice law in the state where the drop zone operates. To be effective, it must be executed, or filled out and signed, according to the lawyer's instructions.

The ability of the liability release to protect you is limited by state law and the circumstances of your actions leading up to the accident. Even the most carefully crafted waiver cannot prevent someone from filing a lawsuit and may not help if the staff acted irresponsibly.

INSURANCE

There are two clear schools of thought on insurance to cover a skydiving center in the event of a lawsuit. One says that insurance is good protection for the drop zone owner who has accumulated assets and equity related to running the business. The second says that insurance invites lawsuits from less-scrupulous people who would not otherwise sue, knowing there would be little gain.

Insurance may not be commercially available to cover all aspects of your skydiving center's operations.

RISK MANAGEMENT

Adherence to industry standards, good equipment, careful supervision of the programs, use of a waiver, proper procedures after an accident, and insurance—or lack thereof—all work together to create what is known as risk management. The goal is to prevent an accident and to minimize the effects an accident has on the business and the individual staff members involved.

The bottom line is, if you're careful and stick to the rules, people are less likely to get hurt and to sue you.

2-3: USPA RATING STRUCTURE

A. USPA RATING HIERARCHY

1. USPA Coach
    a. includes basic instructional methods that apply to all other ratings
    b. prepares future USPA Instructor rating holders for rating courses and evaluations
2. USPA Instructor
    - Accelerated Freefall (AFFI)
    - Instructor-Assisted Deployment (IADI)
    - Static Line (SLI)
    - Tandem (TI)
3. USPA Coach or Examiner
    - AFF (AFFE)
    - Coach (CE)
    - IAD (IADE)
    - Static Line (SLE)
    - Tandem (TE)

B. APPOINTMENTS

1. The regional director, a member of the elected USPA Board of Directors, appoints S&TAs as liaisons between USPA members, drop zone management, USPA Headquarters, and the USPA Regional Director.
2. Course directors and Examiners
    a. USPA appointed course directors before the Examiner rating was restructured in 2008.
    b. Course director appointments were replaced by Coach and Examiner ratings.
    c. In some cases, Examiners require additional qualifications described in the Introduction and Orientation section of each instructional rating course outline.
    d. Examiners may appoint other qualified USPA Instructors or Examiners as evaluators to assist in their courses.

C. ELECTED OFFICIALS

1. The USPA Board is comprised of 23 members:
    a. 14 regional directors
    b. eight national directors (directors-at-large)
    c. a representative appointed by the National Aeronautical Association and who has full voting privileges
2. The board elects USPA's officers from among its members.
3. The board operates via a committee system, which includes the USPA Safety & Training Committee.
    a. headed by the S&T Chair (appointed by the USPA President), who appoints committee members from among other elected board members and non-voting advisors
    b. studies program and policy proposals as assigned by the president.

D. USPA HEADQUARTERS STAFF

1. The USPA Executive Committee hires an executive director, an employee who reports to the president.
2. The executive director hires the headquarters staff, including the staff director of safety & training, who—
    a. reports to the executive director
    b. coordinates and administers safety & training programs, including the license, instructional rating, and PRO rating programs
    c. oversees the maintenance of the USPA instructional program documents
    d. coordinates mass communications to USPA instructional rating holders

3. Document Layout

A. SKYDIVER'S INFORMATION MANUAL

1. The Skydiver's Information Manual contains four sections of primary importance to students and USPA Coaches:
   a. USPA Basic Safety Requirements, Section 2
   b. Integrated Student Program (ISP) syllabus, Section 4
   c. General Recommendations, especially Sections 5 and 6
   d. Federal Aviation Regulations and FAA Advisory Circulars pertinent to skydiving, Section 9
2. Each student should have a SIM.
3. USPA Coaches should study and understand:
   a. Category A
      (1) solo equipment orientation
      (2) freefall position
      (3) main deployment (freefall only)
      (4) canopy skills
      (5) landing training
      (6) landing problems
      (7) equipment problems
      (8) equipment emergency procedures
   b. Category E freefall and training and the aircraft briefing
   c. Categories C through H freefall and canopy training
4. All topics in exit, freefall, canopy, and emergency procedure review should be taught prior to the first jump in each category.
5. In Categories A (first-jump course) and Categories F through H, the outline specifies which portions may be taught by a USPA Coach under an appropriately rated USPA Instructor's supervision.
6. At the end of each ISP category are recommended canopy and freefall dive flows.

B. INTEGRATED STUDENT PROGRAM OVERVIEW

1. The USPA Integrated Student Program is a complete and detailed outline recommended by USPA to train students from the first jump through the A license.
2. The ISP integrates all USPA-recognized methods for teaching skydiving, particularly in the early portion of the training: harness hold (USPA Accelerated Freefall), instructor-assisted deployment, static line, and tandem.
3. Schools using the ISP outline or its equivalent can easily track a student's performance and interchange the various training methods to make the most effective use of their training resources.
   a. There are eight categories of advancement, A-H.
      (1) Categories A-D focus on basic skydiving survival skills and are very closely supervised.
      (2) During Categories E through H, students become more independent and supervision requirements are relaxed.
      (3) Categories G and H concentrate on group freefall skills and to prepare a student to jump without supervision and the USPA A license.
   b. Each category following Category A, the first-jump course, is divided into six skills and knowledge sets.
      (1) exit and freefall
      (2) canopy
      (3) emergency procedure review
      (4) equipment
      (5) rules and recommendations
      (6) spotting and aircraft
   c. Each student, except those making tandem jumps, should complete training in the freefall, canopy, and emergency review sections prior to making a jump in any category.
      (1) Some freefall dive flows require the freefall and emergency procedure training and review for the student to safely perform them.
      (2) The canopy dive flows require canopy training first so the student can understand what to practice.
      (3) The student becomes more independent and less supervised as he progresses and may require the information in these three areas when encountering new experiences during jumps in that category.
   4. An oral quiz follows each category.
      a. It may be given after the student completes the last jump in the category or serve as a review preceding training in the next category.
      b. The USPA Instructor conducting the A license check dive draws from the quiz questions for the oral testing portion of the license review.
   5. The USPA written A-License Exam is required in addition to the oral quiz.
      a. A USPA Instructor, S&TA or Examiner may administer the official USPA A License written exam.
      b. The study guide for the exam can be found in Appendix C of the Skydiver's Information Manual.
      c. A score of 75% or higher is required to pass the written exam.
      d. An oral exam of at least 20 questions taken from the category quizzes is also administered by a USPA Instructor, S&TA or Examiner as a requirement for the USPA A license.

C. THE A LICENSE APPLICATION

1. Official USPA document (not a student's logbook)
2. Two versions:
   a. A License Progression Card (four page)
      - for use with the ISP
      - progressive performance record
      - each category recommended to be completed prior to advancing to the next
   b. A License Proficiency Card (two page) for DZs using alternative training programs

D. THE FLIGHT PLANNER

1. Helps students plan each jump and reinforce training by applying it to their jumps
2. Informs the USPA Coach and Instructor that the lesson plan and emergency procedure review have been completed
3. Category G and H students should complete the entire Flight Planner, to include calculating the opening point and determining the jump run.
4. A sample flight planner is included in Appendix A of this manual.

C-4 BASIC INSTRUCTIONAL METHODS

4. Basic Instructional Methods

4-1: LEARNING THEORY

A. OVERVIEW

1. This section and the next section teach the candidate to apply known teaching and training techniques to skydiving instruction.
2. Discussions include
   a. students' motivation for skydiving
   b. characteristics of a good coach
   c. psychology of learning and training
   d. effective presentation strategies
   e. involving the student's senses
   f. effective debriefing strategies

B. WHY PEOPLE JUMP—MOTIVATION

1. It is evident that skydiving students are highly motivated to learn.
   a. Jumping and jump training are expensive.
   b. Participants must devote a great deal of time to go skydiving.
   c. Knowing that failure in this sport can be dangerous motivates students to pay attention and learn.
   d. Skydivers must overcome a natural fear not to jump, which shows that skydiving students must be very committed to making a jump.
2. Some personal motivations to participate in skydiving—
   a. affiliation: a desire to belong to a social or elite activities group
   b. sensation: the thrill and rush of skydiving
   c. achievement: a sense of accomplishment, particularly in an activity that requires overcoming natural fears
   d. self-actualization: the sense of personal fulfillment
3. The skydiving instructor uses the skydiving student's high level of motivation to his or her advantage for making the lesson more effective.
4. The skydiving instructor recognizes intrinsic versus extrinsic student motivations to help students set achievable goals and over come challenges.

C. CHARACTERISTICS OF A GOOD TEACHER

1. As teacher
   a. assesses each student's current abilities and determines the starting point for the lesson
   b. helps the student set goals
   c. ensures that learning takes place
   d. compares the student's performance to the goals
2. As leader and role model
   a. sets a good example
   b. maintains a positive image
   c. practices professionalism
   d. acts as a motivator

D. APPLYING SPORTS PSYCHOLOGY

1. The student's self image is crucial to his ability to learn.
   a. What is self-image? (discussion)
   b. How does self-image affect performance?
      (1) negative v. positive attitude during a performance
      (2) negative v. positive assessment of performance
   c. How can the teacher affect the student's self-image?
      (1) praise (example)
      (2) derision or mocking (example)
2. Goal setting: SMART (specific, measurable, achievable, relevant, timely)
   a. Specific—The training should be straightforward and designed to achieve the intended outcome.
   b. Measurable—There should be a means of gauging the student's short and long term progress (i.e., advancement criteria).
   c. Achievable—Meaningful goals will improve the chance for success and reinforce a positive self-image.
      (1) short-term goals: setting specific, measurable goals will enable the student to verify success and see progress toward achieving the long-term goal.
      (2) long-term goals: trackable, relevant goals will enable the student to chart a path showing that consistent progress is (or isn't) being made
   d. Relevant—The training should focus on the short and long term goals of the student, building from simple to complex.
   e. Timely—The short and long term goals need to be scheduled with a realistic timetable that provides enough time to achieve each of the goals but still keep the training focused
3. Present correct material only.
   a. The teacher's demonstration must be correct.
   b. The teacher must closely monitor the student's initial practice (hands on) to initiate good habits from the beginning.
   c. Practice does not make perfect—practice makes permanent, therefore; "Practicing perfectly makes perfect permanent."
   d. Tell students what to do, rather than what not to do.
4. Introduce cue words during the practice to connect the student's verbal understanding to muscle response (for example, when docking, "legs out, grips, elbows up, altitude").
5. Correct by referring back to the proper action
   a. example: "Good legs out position, now fly all the way to the grips with arms neutral."
   b. example to avoid: "No, not like that, don't reach for grips"
6. Positive post-jump and debrief (more on this later)

E. CHARACTERISTICS OF THE LEARNING PROCESS

1. The difference between learning and performance
   a. learning: acquiring knowledge and understanding
   b. performance: acquiring skills (motor learning)
2. Role of the left brain and the right brain
   a. left brain: analytical, verbal
   b. right brain: imagery, physical

Example: Have the group name the colors of the words (not read the words) printed on the inside back cover of this

BASIC INSTRUCTIONAL METHODS — C-4

manual. This exercise demonstrates the conflict language (left brain) presents over concept (right brain).

3. Primacy-recency curve

   a. Students tend to remember the first two points and some of the last points of the lesson.

   Example: Recite in monotone a string of seven random numbers between 100 and 1,000 and have the students repeat back the numbers as a group.

   b. The curve can be manipulated by emphasis or association.

   Example: Recite another string of seven random numbers between 100 and 1,000 with emphasis on selected ones by shouting one, whispering another, adding a tag ("357 magnum"), or by making a sudden motion, and have the students repeat back the numbers as a group. Compare the results.

   c. applying primacy and recency; examples

      (1) first-jump course

         (i) Begin with instruction on the operation handles (most important).

         (ii) End with equipment emergency procedures (most complicated and high importance of outcome).

      (2) equipment emergency procedure training

         (i) Begin with how to deploy the reserve (most important).

         (ii) End with how to respond to two canopies out (most complicated).

4. Most adults can take in seven learning points, plus or minus two, in one group or session.

   Example: Recite a phone number and get the students to recite it back ten seconds later. Then repeat with an 11-digit serial number. Compare the results

5. 90:20:8 Rule

   a. Learning sessions should last no more than 90 minutes.

   b. The class should change location or pace at least every 20 minutes.

   c. The coach should involve the student through active participation (questions, reading out loud, engaging in an example) at least every eight minutes.

   d. One example is called "think-pair-share."

      (1) Single out one student and ask him to repeat what you have just explained.

      (2) Once the singled out student repeats the information, ask another student if that is correct.

      (3) Ask the class a question and have one student tell another student the answer.

      (4) The instructor then gives the correct answer and asks the class who in the classroom had the correct answer.

      (5) Corrections can be made at this point if needed.

   e. Each 20-minute segment should contain no more than seven independent learning points.

   f. Present the seven points with regard to the primacy-recency curve.

   g. Use low-attention, low-retention periods of the primacy-recency curve for physical practice.

   h. These principles should apply to USPA instructional rating courses, also.

6. Teaching similar tasks at the same time interferes with learning either one, for example:

   a. centerpoint turn and side-slide

   b. pulling a ripcord and pulling a cutaway handle mounted near each other

   c. clearing end-cell closure (holding down the brakes) and bringing down a slider (pumping the brakes)

   d. landing a ram-air main and a round reserve

7. Keep it short, simple, and specific (KISSS).

F. **PRINCIPLES OF PSYCHO-MOTOR LEARNING**

1. Three stages of learning motor skills

   a. cognitive (left brain)

      (1) the mental, or thinking, phase

      (2) easy to overload the student during this phase (small learning blocks required)

      (3) slow explanation and demonstration required

      (4) student struggling to figure out the sequence of components and what is required to perform

      (5) student primarily using the left brain during this phase

   b. practice (moving concepts from the left brain to actions generated in the right brain)

      (1) The student begins practice; the teacher is close enough to ensure perfect practice (hands on).

      (2) The teacher's feedback should reinforce the student's senses.

      (3) Corrections should be immediate and specific using sensory or tactile applications, rather than verbal.

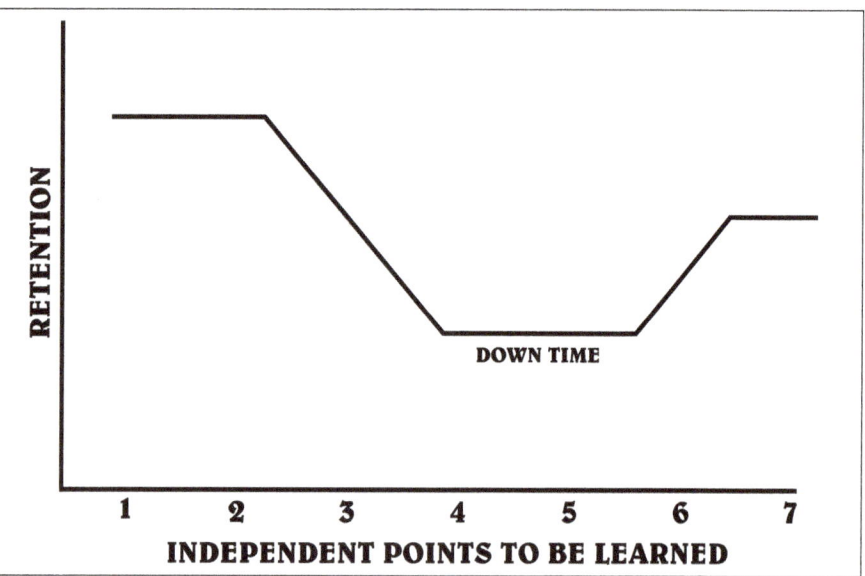

C-4 BASIC INSTRUCTIONAL METHODS

    (4) The teacher uses positive feedback and cue words to guide and encourage the student.

  c. autonomous

    (1) The autonomous phase, or flow, is achieved through repetition and practice.

    (2) The student is in right-brain activity during this phase.

    (3) Because the left brain is relatively freed-up, student can become overly self-critical during this phase, so the teacher should focus the student on action, rather than verbal analysis.

    (4) Student responses to questions or input should be action, rather than verbal, indicating the shift to right brain.

    (5) Work toward achieving an automatic flow.

2. Lecture is the least effective means of teaching motor skills; people remember 20 percent of what they hear but 80 percent of what they do.

G. SHORT- AND LONG-TERM MEMORY

1. Evaluating retention

   a. Retention is highest when the coach provides modeling, meaning and practice for the student.

   b. Information stored only in short-term memory begins to fade within 30 seconds after the item is last recalled and applied (phone number example).

   c. Retention an hour after the last exposure or application indicates storage in long-term memory.

2. Distributive practice: Skills need to be practiced at repeated intervals to be committed to long-term memory and to restore and maintain peak proficiency (see distributive practice diagram).

3. Discussion: What implications do these facts about short-term and long-term memory have for—

   a. skills testing in the first-jump course?

   b. a marginal performance in the first-jump course?

   c. refresher training on emergency procedures?

4-2: TEACHING SKYDIVING EFFECTIVELY

A. LESSON DESIGN

1. Preparation

   a. Scope of the lesson: explaining what will be taught in the lesson and how long it is expected to take.

   b. Objective and purpose: stating the goals/objectives

      (1) lets students know what they will learn and how they will show they have learned it

      (2) lets students know why they should learn the material, how it fits into their goals, and why it is important

   c. Lesson plan: a logical, point-by-point building sequence for the activity being trained

   d. Organization of the training session

      (1) schedule – time needed for proper training

      (2) location

      (3) controlled environment

      (4) training aids

      (5) assistance and USPA Instructor supervision, as required

2. Presentation

   a. explanation: overview of what skills the student is expected to learn (goal setting) in this lesson and why, including how they will be tested

   b. demonstration: perfect example of how the skill is to be performed

3. Application

   a. trial and practice, the student tries the new skill and is closely guided at first to ensure perfect practice (hands on)

   b. use of cue words to move the skill from a concept in the left brain to an action coming from the right brain

   c. sufficient repetition

      (1) minimum of 25 times for each skill to build a habit (more is often required)

      (2) rest period prior to a second practice session, as necessary

   d. uninterrupted practice once the skill is being performed correctly

      (1) Explain all concepts sufficiently prior to beginning any practice.

      (2) If further explanation becomes necessary, interrupt the lesson, move to another topic or take a break and re-start the lesson later.

      (3) The student should demonstrate a perfect practice two times.

4. Evaluation

   a. Test to see that learning has occurred by—

      (1) the student's correct demonstration of the skill when presented with a scenario; for example, "Nothing has come off your back. What will you do?" (training for a total malfunction).

      (2) oral questions, which should require the student to perform an action (preferred) or give a brief explanation, rather than a "yes" or "no" answer

      (3) written exam

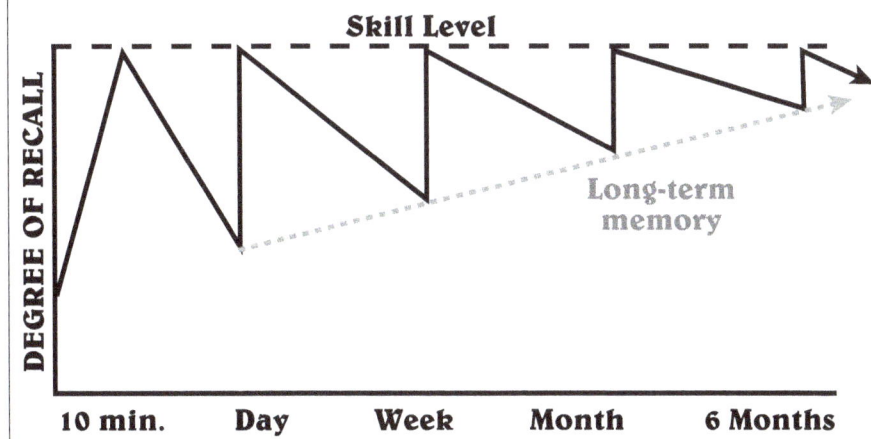

This graph demonstrates the importance of recurrent training to place a skill into long-term memory. Source: Madeline Hunter (1982), presented in Sousa, David A. How the Brain Learns. (2001). p. 100. Thousand Oaks, California: Corwin Press, Inc.

BASIC INSTRUCTIONAL METHODS — C-4

    (4) specific performance objectives

  b. Have the student recap the lesson, including the stated objectives and the resulting student performance.

  c. Record the training and progress (logbook or A License Progression Card), for the next coach or instructor.

B. PRESENTATION STRATEGIES

1. Whole-part-whole

   a. Describe and demonstrate the entire activity to be trained and tested in the lesson (whole).

   b. Break the lesson into seven (plus or minus two) manageable, related information bits and teach them (part).

   c. Recombine the bits into the correct order before beginning the application (practice).

   d. Practice until autonomous (whole).

2. When a skill is broken down into its parts, there are a number of strategies in which we can present these parts. Your knowledge and ability to use these strategies allows you to be flexible in your teaching approach and enables you to cater more to the needs of the student. The different strategies of ordering the parts are as follows:

   a. Forward-backward and chaining. This is when the parts are taught one at a time in either chronological order (forward chaining) or in reverse order (backward chaining). Backward chaining is starting from the final action and working backwards to the first action. A good example of backward chaining is teaching the landing pattern from the flare backwards to the 1,000 foot entry point.

   b. Shaping. This is when you take a skill and initially train a simplified version of that skill. Once this simple version is learned, we add on more joint usage or detail. A good example of this would be tracking where initially we are simply looking for a flat forward motion in a straight line, then add a reverse arch and finally a more streamline/narrow position for speed.

   c. Simple to complex. Otherwise known as the building block method. A simple part is picked first and then followed up with adding increasingly more difficult parts. For example, teaching a rear float exit prior to teaching a floater track exit.

   d. Known to unknown. Prior to beginning your coaching with a student take time to ask what other sports or activities they may have participated in that may relate to the skill for the up coming lesson. Also ask the student to "show me" what they know about the lesson so you can build on what they already know.

3. Example of whole-part-whole, chaining, and spiking using BOC hand deployment instruction from the first-jump course for students who have already learned the basic freefall position:

   a. Whole: Demonstrate the entire deployment sequence in real time, using cue words—arch, reach, grab, throw, check!"

   b. Parts: Break the sequence into no more than seven distinct smaller sections and explain and demonstrate the entire sequence slowly and in order (forward chaining).

   c. Reorder or emphasize some parts of the sequence, according to importance to increase retention. For example you may teach the pull sequence as follows:

     (1) locating and throwing the pilot chute (right hand only; standing up; no arch yet)

     (2) left hand for balance (standing up; no arch yet)

     (3) reaching from the correct body position (previously learned arch) while standing

     (4) throwing from the correct position while standing (practice until correct)

     (5) checking for deployment while standing

     (6) location or extraction problems (lost handle, hard pull)

   d. Whole: Combine the actions back in the correct order to begin practice while standing and then lying down.

C. TEACHING AND LEARNING TOOLS

1. Sensory input

   a. Use all the available senses (cite examples for each).

     (1) sight

     (2) feeling

     (3) sound

   b. Emotion, especially positive emotion, associated with learning improves retention.

     (1) happiness

     (2) humor (distracting when overdone)

     (3) pride, as from praise and recognition

     (4) fear (somewhat effective for retention, but not conducive to getting the student to return)

2. Provide a relaxed, non-threatening training environment.

   a. physical environment: sound (including background noise), temperature, lighting, overall comfort

   b. reasonable privacy (to reduce self-consciousness while the student learns and practices)

   c. teacher's appearance and hygiene

   d. positive presentation and feedback

   e. fostering class cooperation and support

   f. nutrition and hydration

     (1) When working in a learning environment, the brain consumes as much as 20 percent of the body's caloric intake.

     (2) It is important to stay hydrated.

3. Realistic simulation helps the student perform the skill under stress, for example, adding confusion during simulations of malfunctions.

4. Training aids (discussion)

   a. advantages

   b. limitations

5. Summary of effective training and practice. How you practice will make a big difference in performance. To effectively practice, start by making the practice as realistic as possible. If the skill to be learned is falling belly to earth (prone), then practice it as such.

   a. Perfect practice makes perfect permanent.

   b. When practicing, do so as correctly as possible to develop the proper kinesthetic feel and mental pictures. Always practice the correct technique.

   c. Select training aids for realism.

   d. Utilize all senses possible: feel, sight and inner balance.

   e. Choose a comfortable learning environment.

C-4 BASIC INSTRUCTIONAL METHODS

f. Practice new skills individually, then build on or link them together, KISSS.

g. Introduce new skills only once the previous ones have been learned and/or memorized

h. When rehearsing multiple or complex skills, layer or stage the information from simple to complex or SHAPE the skill.

i. Use repetition, the more times you repeat the skill (autonomous), the more natural and comfortable it will become. It will also reduce the overall stress during the jump.

j. Prior to jumping, rehearse the entire sequence until memorized to the point of anticipation.

k. Rehearse with full concentration and focus.

l. Respect the holding times and physical and mental limits of the individuals or mental and physical fatigue.

D. SAMPLE TRAINING TOPICS

1. Landing approach strategy (candidates should already be familiar with landing pattern training in Category A):

    a. preparation

    (1) Find a place to walk out a simulated landing pattern that's in view of the target and DZ landmarks.

    (2) Use a DZ photo or other visual aid to help the student imagine the view from under canopy.

    b. presentation (use the illustrations in the SIM)

    (1) Explain and demonstrate the projected glide distance from a pre-planned altitude (e.g., 300 feet) for a student canopy on a calm day.

    (2) Show the student how that relates to a base leg of the same distance flown from twice the altitude (using 600 feet in this example).

    (3) Show the student the planned pattern entry point abreast of the target beginning at 1,000 feet.

    (4) Explain how to adjust the base leg if arriving at the planned base-to final corner of the pattern at the wrong altitude, high and low.

    (5) Walk a simulated left-hand pattern, including the arm motion for making the turns.

    c. application

    (1) Have the student follow the instructor walking the pattern.

    (2) Have the student walk the pattern without assistance.

    d. evaluation

    (1) Ask the student to show a pattern with a different wind direction.

    (2) Ask the student to demonstrate how to handle arriving at the planned base-to-final turning point with too little altitude; again with too much altitude.

2. Malfunction procedures

    a. preparation

    (1) Set up the training harness.

    (2) Gather the malfunction photos or other visual aids.

    (3) Turn the music down, etc.

    b. presentation (assume that the simulated student has been trained for routine canopy problems, such as line twist, stuck slider, end-cell closure, etc.)

    (1) Explain the various malfunctions using the visual aids.

    (2) Demonstrate the correct reserve procedures for the various malfunctions.

    c. application

    (1) Guide the student through the correct procedures.

    (2) Allow the student to practice until familiar with the procedures.

    d. evaluation: Have the student react to the malfunctions as presented, using the visual aids.

5. First-Jump Course: General Sections

5-1: FIRST-JUMP COURSE STRATEGIES

A. USE THE ISP OUTLINE OR AN EQUIVALENT

1. The Category A outline for the first-jump course provides a complete outline, according to the principles in the USPA Integrated Student Program.
2. Drop zones may use their own first-jump course outline, as long as all students are taught an effective method of meeting their Category A advancement criteria.
3. A USPA Coach who is teaching the non-method-specific (general) portions of the first-jump course under the supervision of a USPA Instructor should adhere to a detailed outline, such as the one contained in the ISP.
4. The Category A solo first-jump course outline is laid out in sequence so the general portions can be taught first by a USPA Coach, who then turns the class over to a USPA Instructor in that student's training method.
5. Tandem jumps may be conducted as a skydiving orientation or as Category A training using the tandem method.

5-2: CATEGORY A, FIRST-JUMP COURSE

At this time, the USPA Coach examiner should review the applicable portions of the Category A first-jump course from the ISP with the candidates.

A. EQUIPMENT

1. The student should know the location of all operation handles he or she may be expected to use.
2. Using terms the student will hear throughout the course and the jump, the instructor describes a correct parachute opening in the three significant stages that determine the response from the jumper.
   a. activation (container opening) for AFF students
      (1) procedure for stable activation of the main parachute practiced until smooth and exact
      (2) activation of an actual main parachute while wearing the equipment the student is expected to jump
      (3) importance of deploying at the correct altitude over the importance of deploying while stable
   b. deployment
   c. inflation
3. Students should know that the instructor is responsible for checking the equipment at these three points:
   a. choosing the correct system and preflighting it
   b. putting the equipment on the student, adjusting it properly, and performing a complete pre-boarding equipment check
   c. checking that the equipment is ready to jump before the student exits the aircraft
4. Students should help with operation handle protection, but the primary responsibility during the first jump rests with the instructor.
5. The student should be familiar with any other equipment operation he or she is expected to perform independently (personal items, equipment recovery and return, etc.).
6. The student should know that the responsibility for the equipment shifts from the instructor to the student later in the student's progression.
7. Discussion

B. RELAXED FREEFALL POSITION

1. All students can be taught the basic freefall body position together and then broken out later for method-specific exit training.
2. Use a body position that allows for relaxed fall and the ability to see the altimeter easily, focusing primarily on the hips and leg position.
3. Discussion

C. CANOPY

1. Introduce the student to the canopy in terms that will be used throughout the course and during radio instruction.
2. Canopy training should be based on flying a specific, pre-planned pattern into a clear landing area.
   a. This portion of the training is best taught in the landing area with an aerial photograph.
   b. Refer to the canopy training outline and illustrations in Category A of the ISP syllabus for this portion of the lesson.
3. The student should fly a straight final approach to avoid collisions (avoid S-turns).
4. The student should remain upwind in a pre-planned holding area until ready to enter the landing pattern at 1,000 feet.
5. If unable to make the planned landing area, decide on a clear alternate landing area by 2,000 feet and apply the planned pattern to the new area.
6. Students should be taught to look for traffic before turning.
7. Discussion

D. LANDINGS

1. This section is best taught using a practical landing trainer, where the student simulates parachute landings.
2. Teach the student a prepare-to-land position that will enable an easy transition into a proper PLF.
3. The student should learn all types of obstacle landings with emphasis on obstacles the student might encounter at that DZ.
4. Round reserve techniques may be omitted from the course if all the school's student equipment is equipped with ram-air reserves, but a note on the type of reserve should be entered in the log of each student's jump ("RAM").
5. Students with prior tandem experience using special tandem landing techniques need to know that those techniques are not correct for a hard landing when jumping solo; introduce and demonstrate the PLF.
6. Landing priorities (from the first-jump course syllabus)
   a. Land with the wing level and flying in a straight line.
   b. Land in a clear and open area, avoiding obstacles.
   c. Flare to at least the half-brake position.
   d. Always be prepared to make a PLF.
7. Discussion

E. EQUIPMENT EMERGENCIES

1. A USPA Coach or higher rating holder should assist and critique the jumper throughout all ground training.
2. A watch or training altimeter may be used during parachute emergency drills to help the student develop time awareness.

C-5 FIRST-JUMP COURSE: GENERAL SECTIONS

3. The harness trainer should be equipped with a cutaway handle and a reserve ripcord handle, each of which can actually be pulled.
4. Teach the school procedures for all parachute situations the student may encounter (follow the Category A Emergency Procedure outline).
5. Discussion

5-3: FJC TRAINING STANDARDS

A. ASSESSING BY SPECIFIC OBJECTIVES

1. All first-jump ground training should be specific and oriented to measurable goals (Specific, Measurable, Achievable, Relevant, Timely).
2. Each student should meet the goals prior to making a jump.
3. Students should be correct and consistent in demonstrating their ability to perform the tasks of the ground training in preparation for their parachute jump.
4. This section provides sample performance criteria for use in the first-jump course to help determine a student's aptitude for a solo skydive.

B. EQUIPMENT KNOWLEDGE

1. Can find and operate main deployment, cutaway and reserve activation handles (or SOS handle)
2. Understands the use of the altimeter in freefall and under canopy
3. Knows to expect three complete equipment checks

C. APTITUDE FOR THE FREEFALL POSITION

1. Able to arch sufficiently to lift both shoulders and knees off a flat surface and hold for ten-second intervals without straining
2. During arch practice, controls both legs and arms with symmetry and extends both legs slightly
3. AFF: demonstrates the correct deployment and practice deployment procedures, including cue words (e.g., "arch, reach, touch!") and symmetrical movement
4. AFF: Understands and responds correctly to freefall hand signals

D. UNDERSTANDING OF CANOPY DESCENT

1. Understands canopy descent strategies well enough to solve contrived descent problems from opening to 1,000 feet:
   a. too close to the planned pattern entry point at too high an altitude—face upwind
   b. more than halfway down, but not yet halfway back—steer downwind and plan an alternate landing area
2. Can solve contrived landing approach problems (e.g., ISP model):
   a. too high at the planned 600-foot point—arc the base leg
   b. too low at the planned 600-foot point—cut the corner for the planned 300-foot point
   c. on final approach at 100 feet and running with the wind – Keep going straight with wing level
3. Knows the landing priorities (wing level, clear area, flare)

E. LANDING AND LANDING EMERGENCY DRILLS

1. Prior to jumping, demonstrates a proper PLF until satisfactory.
   a. Feet and knees together
   b. Flared position with the hands together in the front of the hips to prevent wrist and hand injuries
   c. Chin to chest to help prevent neck injuries
   d. Allow feet to make contact with the ground first
   e. Maintain PLF position throughout the entire landing roll
   f. As both feet touch the ground:
      (1) Lean into the direction of the landing to roll down one side of the body.
      (2) Lay over the side of one calf.
      (3) Continue to roll to the thigh on the same side.
   g. Continue rolling on to that hip (side of the butt).
   h. Roll diagonally across the back to the opposite shoulder
   i. Allow the body to continue rolling and absorb the energy of the fall
2. Demonstrates the correct procedure for each landing hazard at or near the planned drop zone.
   a. power lines
   b. water
   c. trees
   d. buildings
   e. other hazards specific to the drop zone

F. EQUIPMENT PROBLEMS AND EMERGENCY DRILLS

1. Responds correctly to questions about how to handle an open parachute in the aircraft with the door open and closed.
2. Demonstrates the following in the training harness:
   a. response to lost deployment handle, hard extraction
   b. how to clear a pilot chute hesitation (main or reserve)
   c. within five seconds, the correct response to contrived partial and total malfunction situations, including looking at the emergency handle(s)
   d. correct response to line twists, slider up, and end-cell closures and addresses them in that order (in case they are experienced simultaneously)
   e. the correct response to all three two-canopy-out scenarios discussed in Category A

G. REMEDIES

When a USPA Coach encounters a student who has difficulty in meeting the first-jump training performance objectives, he or she should immediately notify the supervising USPA Instructor of the difficulty.

H. DISCUSSION

1. How does the first-jump course at the home drop zones of the candidates differ from or compare to Category A training in the ISP?
2. Why?

5-4: PRACTICAL EXERCISES AND GUIDED PRACTICE

1. Course staff demonstrates correct training techniques for basic skydiving skills by conducting full mock training sessions to be used for ground training.
   a. equipment for first jumpers
   b. relaxed freefall position and deployment
   c. canopy flight for beginners
   d. landings
   e. equipment emergencies
2. Candidates practice training sessions under course staff supervision.
3. Count acceptable practical exercises towards the guided practice training sessions required to pass the USPA Coach Rating Course and log them on the USPA Coach Proficiency Card

6. Basic and Group Freefall Skills Training

A. USPA COACH'S FREEFALL TRAINING DUTIES

1. USPA Coaches are authorized to supervise students in a static-line or instructor-assisted-deployment program beginning with Category C.
   a. Ground training for Categories C-E must be conducted by an appropriately rated instructor.
   b. A Coach may supervise IAD and static-line students in the aircraft beginning with Category C.
   c. A Coach may be able to effectively observe a student making short freefalls (up to ten seconds) from the airplane.
   d. A Coach may jump with IAD and static-line students making longer freefalls to observe and critique for retraining during the debrief.
2. The last three categories of the Integrated Student Program prepare the student to jump safely and effectively in groups.
   a. group exits
   b. group flying skills
   c. breakoff procedures
3. Students who complete Category H should be ready for
   a. the USPA A license checkout with a USPA Instructor
   b. independent skydiving at most drop zones
   c. jumping at off-site DZs that meet the A-license landing area criteria (non-demos)

B. CATEGORY C: FIVE- AND TEN-SECOND DELAYS

1. Three jumps minimum are recommended, including a qualifying IAD or static-line jump the same day as the first freefall.
   a. stable clear-and-pull not to exceed five seconds
   b. two ten-second freefalls
2. Relaxed freefall position ("altitude, arch, legs, relax")
   a. "Altitude" means the student must read the altimeter and understand the altitude; or students on freefall in the IAD or static-line progression performing short delays need to know their altitude by the count in seconds from exiting the aircraft.
   b. "Arch" means to push the hips forward slightly and smoothly and to keep them there.
   c. "Legs" means to pay attention to the leg position and place both legs in the correct position, probably extending them slightly.
   d. "Relax" means to take a breath and relax the muscles that aren't needed for the correct body position.
3. Heading control
   a. Heading control may be passive ("altitude, arch, legs, relax").
   b. The instructor should introduce active heading control (turn method), but the student must understand that a correct body position is necessary for effective active heading control.
   c. The student's objective is hover control using a coordinated and trimmed body position to maintain balance in freefall.
4. Introduction to wave-off (ten-second freefalls)
   a. teaches the student the wave-off signal early
   b. helps protect instructors who may follow the student on future jumps
   c. trains for safety on future group freefall jumps
5. Introduce the altimeter as a back-up to counting and looking at the ground.
6. At least two successful ten-second freefalls are recommended before advancing.
   a. control within five seconds of exit
   b. reasonable heading control
7. Recommended minimum deployment is 4,000 feet, particularly for students making ten-second freefalls and reaching deployment altitude at near-terminal velocity.
8. Pull priorities
   a. Pull
   b. Pull at the correct altitude
   c. Pull while stable
9. Review the Category C advancement criteria and the freefall dive flow recommendations from the ISP.
10. The Coach Examiner demonstrates a complete lesson on the relaxed freefall position to the course candidates.

C. CATEGORY D: FREEFALL TURNS

1. The lesson on turning should emphasize the importance of a neutral body position prior to initiating a turn.
2. A simple technique for changing heading, such as upper body turns only, will increase confidence and improve chances for success; after the student has completed the A-license program, techniques for center-point turns can be easily added.
   a. multiple 90-degree turns only on the first jump where turns are attempted
      (1) reduces student stress and workload
      (2) increases confidence in heading control prior to initiating bigger turns, leading to greater success
      (3) reduces the likelihood of uncontrolled spins
   b. 180- and 360-degree turns, once 90-degree turns have been mastered
   c. In the event of lost heading control (spin), the student should recover lost control with "altitude, arch, legs, relax," before initiating opposite turn input.
   d. If the turn is sluggish or seems to go opposite the direction intended, the student should, provided altitude allows—
      (1) return to neutral arch
      (2) relax
      (3) extend legs
      (4) attempt the turn again
3. Maneuvers should be finished by 5,000 feet.
4. The coach may accompany the student to observe heading control whenever practical.
   a. A USPA Coach seeing a student in danger of a low pull should immediately get clear and deploy his or her own parachute by 3,500 feet.
   b. Any student who is being accompanied by a USPA Coach should be told to deploy immediately upon seeing the Coach's parachute begin to open.
   c. A USPA Coach may not assist with the deployment of a student in freefall.

C-6 BASIC AND GROUP FREEFALL SKILLS TRAINING

5. Review the importance of deployment at the correct altitude, regardless of stability.
6. Introduce alternate altitude references, e.g., looking at the ground, cloud bases, mountaintops, etc.
7. Increase exit altitude gradually as the jumper exhibits comfort with longer freefalls.
8. The student should begin this category with a 15-second freefall.
9. Four jumps are recommended.
10. Recommended minimum deployment altitude is 4,000 feet.
11. The candidates review the Category D freefall dive flows with the CE.
12. The Coach Examiner demonstrates a complete lesson on freefall turns to the course candidates.

D. CATEGORY E: RECOVERY FROM INSTABILITY

1. The student should attempt a stable unpoised exit.
2. Students begin this category directly supervised by a USPA Coach or Instructor until they can demonstrate reliable recovery from instability.
   a. Each student shows the ability twice to recover stability and altitude awareness within five seconds following an intentional disorienting maneuver.
   b. The first maneuver attempted should be a barrel roll, which has a natural recovery mode from back-to-earth fall.
   c. Recovery within five seconds (twice) is required to clear the student to freefall self-supervision.
3. Once any student has demonstrated stability recovery, he or she may self-supervise in freefall (requires the sign-off of a USPA Instructor).
4. Once signed off, the student should be supervised by a USPA instructional rating holder aboard the aircraft, who—
   a. is responsible and available for all training, spotting supervision, equipment choice, exit order, group separation on exit, and pre-jump equipment checks
   b. is encouraged to jump with and observe the student
   c. may make gripped exits
5. Once a student has qualified for freefall self-supervision, that student's previous training discipline is recognized only for the purpose of currency training (see SIM Section 5 on currency training).
6. Students may self-assess for the heading control required for the A license check dive (back loop within 60 degrees of the initial heading).
7. Three jumps are recommended in Category E for all students.
8. Hazards of aerobatics
   a. erratic fall rate and altimeter readings (chest mount, etc.)
   b. disorientation (altitude, arch, legs, relax)
   c. equipment considerations
9. The candidates review the Category E freefall dive flow with the CE.
10. The Coach Examiner demonstrates a complete lesson on teaching barrel rolls, front loops and back loops to the course candidates.

E. CATEGORY F: TRACKING AND CLEAR AND PULLS

1. Tracking
   a. The goal of a tracking maneuver is to gain as much horizontal separation from the center of a formation of skydivers as possible, while losing as little altitude as possible.
   b. Priorities
      (1) heading-directional control should be the first priority, along with altitude awareness
      (2) pitch-working to flatten the track and conserve altitude is the next priority
      (3) distance/speed-refining the track for maximum distance and speed is the final priority
      (4) directional control-legs should extend and stay wide for steering and more stability
      (5) dipping a shoulder in the desired direction is a common method used for heading control.
      (6) stopping the track-extending arms forward and down, and dropping knees slightly to slow the track before main canopy deployment.
   c. The student should continue to refine the tracking position on every jump, working towards a narrower body position and de-arched torso for maximum speed and minimum loss of altitude.
   d. Key teaching and observation points
      (1) Extend legs fully
      (2) Knees remain the same width as the neutral "box" position
      (3) Flatten torso to a slight de-arched position
      (4) De-arch lower back, roll pelvis into the thighs
      (5) Roll shoulders forward and down to a cupped position
      (6) Sweep arms out 90 degrees to the torso
      (7) Press hands down below the hips
   e. Teaching method
      (1) The Coach first demonstrates the tracking position to the student
      (2) The student then begins in a neutral position (also called the boxed position).
      (3) Tracking is taught in two stages:
         (i) Stage 1: Initiate the track from neutral by extending both legs fully, flattening the body to the floor and bringing the arms to the sides at a 90 degree position. (Goal is to move forward in a straight line without diving).
         (ii) Stage 2: Add POWER to the track by slowly pushing the hands, elbows, shoulders, and toes on the floor and slightly de-arch. (Goal is to cup air and conserve the most altitude during the track)
      (4) As the student practices the physical moves for tracking, the coach reinforces the training with key words
         (i) First command is "Neutral, track 1." While watching for the correct arm, leg and torso positions
         (ii) Second command is "2." While watching for the student to press against the floor with arms and legs and de-arch slightly.
         (iii) The student holds the pressing position for a count of five, then the Coach commands "Neutral", and 'Relax." Wait 10 seconds, then start the cycle again. This is repeated 10 times, with the first five performed with eyes open and the second done with eyes closed.
   f. The Coach Examiner demonstrates a complete lesson on tracking to the course candidates

2. Clear and pulls

Students learn to perform successful clear and pulls to simulate a low altitude emergency exit or pre-planned low-altitude jumps

   a. Use a familiar, stable exit technique
   b. emphasize presentation into the relative wind and orientation of deployment to the relative wind
   c. The first clear and pull is performed from 5,500 feet, once proficient at 5,500 feet the exit is repeated from 3,500 feet
   d. The coach demonstrates a clear and pull to the student
   e. The student practices the exit until smooth and confident
   f. The Coach Examiner demonstrates a complete lesson on clear and pulls to the course candidates

F. CATEGORIES G AND H EXITS

1. Climb-out and set-up
   a. Purpose
      (1) shortens the group climb-out and set-up times so multiple groups can exit on the same pass
      (2) reduces potentially dangerous equipment contact with the door or other jumpers
      (3) Improves stability on exits which increases working time on training jumps.
   b. Phases for all exits
      (1) "Set up" is climbing out to the "ready" position.
      (2) "Launch" is the action to turn and present to the aircraft heading.
      (3) "Flyaway" is the time right after the launch, watching the aircraft in a neutral body position.
   c. Key teaching points for all exits
      (1) "Balanced" is your balance in the door which will affect stability
      (2) "Tightness" refers to closeness to the coach in the door, which will affect separation
      (3) "Timing" is the precise timing of "go" as a group, which affects separation
      (4) "Presentation" is the action to place the body into the airflow, which affects stability.
   d. Exit count
      (1) Regardless of the positions of the coach and student or who is giving the exit count, the coach must control the exit timing.
      (2) Students may balk in the door or perform the count incorrectly, which can lead to a large separation if the coach lets go of the airplane but the student does not.
      (3) The Coach must always design an exit that allows for control of the exit timing.
      (4) If the student is initiating the count, the coach should plan to leave on the movement of the student, not trusting that the student will leave at the end of the count.
      (5) if the coach is giving the count, the coach should be prepared to remain on the airplane until the student has committed to the exit.
   e. Exit priorities
      (1) Aircraft heading. The student should hold the correct body position for three to five seconds after launch to establish stability and orientation before beginning to maneuver.
      (2) Neutral box body position
      (3) Relax
      (4) Identify the coach. After establishing a stable heading in the line of flight, the student should then look for the coach, who should be in position beside the student.
   f. Teaching method
      (1) Finish training the exit before moving on to the freefall skills
      (2) Use whole-part-whole strategies to teach the exit, breaking the exit into the set-up, launch and flyaway as the parts of the lesson

2. Rear float exit (for left side door exit) - Key teaching and observation points
   a. Climb outside the plane to rear portion of the door
   b. Turn torso to present directly to line of flight
   c. Trail the outside leg
   d. Crouch slightly without compromising balance (feeling heavy)
   e. Drop down on exit (lazy exit)
   f. Neutral box is the flyaway position. Apply A/C heading, box, relax, look for coach.
   g. Cue words: "Ready, Set, Drop"

3. Front float exit (for left side door exit) - Key teaching and observation points
   a. Climb outside the plane to front portion of the door
   b. Turn torso to present directly to line of flight
   c. Trail the outside leg
   d. Launch is more dynamic and powerful
   e. Launch is up and away from fuselage
   f. Neutral box is the flyaway position. Apply A/C heading, box, relax, look for coach.

4. Diving exit (for left side door exit) - Key teaching and observation points
   a. For a left side door, left foot forward to edge
   b. Crouched down over foot with weight forward
   c. Right leg back and poised for balance
   d. Left elbow/arm dropped to left knee
   e. Right elbow/arm raised up above head
   f. Drop down over the left foot with a very lazy launch
   g. Keep chest and hips presented square to the relative wind
   h. Bring legs into the neutral box for the flyaway position. Apply A/C heading, box, relax, look for coach. It is just like a rear float exit except 90 degrees off heading (perpendicular to the relative wind.
   i. Exit is passive just dropping through the door. (prevents student from doing a 360 degree turn on the hill)

5. Cessna Exits
   a. If the drop zone primarily uses a Cessna 182 or 206 airplane, the student should be trained for each of the available exit positions
   b. Setup, launch, and flyaway considerations from side door aircraft also apply to a Cessna strut type exit

6. The Coach Examiner demonstrates a complete lesson on each exit.

G. CATEGORY G: FORWARD AND BACKWARD MOVEMENT WITH GRIP TAKING

1. Neutral Position
   a. Success in all maneuvers needed for group flying start with a strong neutral body position. The neutral position must be reinforced in order to progress in Categories F, G, & H.

C-6 BASIC AND GROUP FREEFALL SKILLS TRAINING

  b. Key teaching and observation points
     (1) Relaxed with limp hands
     (2) Slight arch through torso
     (3) Lift head/chin as high as possible
     (4) Knees at shoulder width or slightly wider
     (5) Feet slightly extended beyond 90-degrees
     (6) Elbows equal height with shoulders, in a straight line from elbow to elbow
     (7) 90-degree angles at shoulders and elbows
  c. Teaching method
     (1) Using a creeper or table, demonstrate the neutral "box" position, then have the student switch places with you
     (2) Say "box" or "neutral," look for observation points and make corrections as necessary
     (3) Have the student hold the position for 10 seconds, then rest for 10 seconds
     (4) The student will do 10 repetitions, five with eyes open and five with eyes closed
     (5) Avoid talking during the repetitions. Make hands on corrections during hold times
     (6) Any verbal explanations should be done during rest times
2. Forward movement
  a. Purpose: To gain the ability to smoothly start and stop forward motion In order to build formations for group skydives.
  b. Key teaching and observation points
     (1) Start from the neutral box position
     (2) Only the lower legs move
     (3) The knees must remain at their original neutral box width
     (4) Extend legs to full range of motion locking the knees during practice
  c. Teaching method
     (1) demonstrate Forward movement
     (2) the legs should be extended and retracted smoothly
     (3) during forward movement leg extension, the knees remain the same width as in the box position
     (4) the wider the spread, the better the directional control
     (5) ensure independent movement of the arms and the legs. (i.e. Arms remain neutral with no movement when legs are extended)
     (6) explain that full extension may not be needed to perform a final approach
     (7) place the student on a creeper for the following static training
     (8) say "neutral" or "box," then "forward," look for observation points and make corrections as necessary
     (9) have the student hold the "forward" position for 10 seconds, then say "neutral" or "box" "relax" to rest for 10 seconds
     (10) it is important that the student start and stop each movement in the neutral box position
     (11) the student will do 10 repetitions, five with eyes open and five with eyes closed.
     (12) avoid talking during the repetitions and make hands-on corrections during hold times
     (13) Use hand signals to reinforce the command words, such as the "legs out" signal when you say "forward"
     (14) Perceptual training: holding the student's feet and moving them forward on a creeper will be done during Start-Coast-Stop training.
     (15) any verbal explanations should be done during rest times
3. Backward movement
  a. Backward movement is primarily used to slow and stop forward movement
  b. Key teaching and observation points
     (1) with the student on a creeper, start from the neutral box position
     (2) initiate backward movement in a two-stage process
        (i) first, extend arms straight out keeping hand at original box width
        (ii) second, roll shoulders down cupping upper body
     (3) lower arms should be angled upward at about 45 degrees, forearms are just above the ground
     (4) legs remain in neutral position for stability.
  c. Teaching method
     (1) say "neutral" or "box," then "backward," look for key observation points and the two-stage process.
     (2) have the student hold the "backward" position for 10 seconds, then say "neutral" or "box," then "relax" to rest for 10 seconds.
     (3) it is important that the student start and stop each movement in the neutral box position.
     (4) the student will do 10 repetitions, five with eyes open and five with eyes closed.
     (5) avoid talking during the repetitions, make hands on corrections during hold times, and any verbal explanations should be done during rest times.
     (6) the full range of leg or arm motion may not be necessary for effective backwards motion.
  d. The coach controls any fall rate changes during the forward and backward motion skydives.
4. Docking/Grip Taking
  a. Grip taking priorities
     (1) fly on level all the way to the grips
     (2) fly in your slot
     (3) take the grips
  b. Key teaching and observation points
     (1) start by taking the grip, thumb under and fingers over the wrist
     (2) check elbows are back to neutral
     (3) extend the feet slightly into the wind for positive pressure
     (4) open hands or "palm" when inward pressure is felt.
     (5) this ensures that the a neutral position is maintained during the dock, allowing the jumper to fall straight down
  c. Teaching method:
     (1) demonstrate taking grips by walking forward several feet, then while taking the grips on your student say " grips, elbows, feet, palms."
     (2) allow your student to feel the forward pressure
     (3) allow the student to practice this for five repetitions with no specific hold times. Walking forward demonstrates an

average approach speed in freefall.
- (i) once the grips are taken, it is important to ensure a neutral position, falling straight down while docked.
- (ii) depending on the speed of the approach and whether a backwards motion or flare move was needed to stop the forward motion, the student may be arriving on grips in a position other than the box.
- (iii) use the Cue words "grips, elbows, feet, palms" to ensure the student returns to neutral after taking the grips.
- (4) for more realistic training, place the student a creeper with his feet against a firm surface (such as a wall).
- (5) move forward on a creeper and present wrist grips to the student.
- (6) allow the student to take correct grips by applying the "grips, elbows, feet, palms" principles.
- (7) during the "feet" phase of the exercise, have the student gently push their feet against the wall.
- (8) This effort will create positive pressure on the grips. (Note: the coach should be braced in a position so the students pressure does not move the coach)

5. Start, Coast, Stop (SCS)
   a. All maneuvers in skydiving will have increased precision and performance using the SCS method of training. Start is the initiation of a movement, Coast is in the neutral box position, Stop is the equal and opposite movement of Start. For example in this section SCS equals Forward, Coast and Backward movements.
   b. Key teaching and observation points for Forward.
      (1) explain each phase of SCS
      (2) explain that the coast phase is used as the assessment time
      (3) perform static practice first to confirm correct body positions
      (4) provide correct physical responses (force) to student inputs during perceptual drills on creeper (i.e., pushing forward when student extents legs to start position)
      (5) Watch timing of moving from coast (neutral box) to stopping position
      (6) Explain that a well-timed coast may not require a stop action
   c. Teaching method
      (1) on a creeper have the student start in the box position, then say start (for forward), Coast (for neutral box), then Stop (for backward action).
      (2) complete five repetitions with three second holds in each position.
      (3) allow 10 second rests between repetitions.
      (4) on a creeper, roll the student to a target (wall or other creeper). As the student presses out with his legs push him forward.
      (5) Only respond to the student's actions (If the student does not provide legs out input, he will not move forward).
      (6) Watch for all three phases of SCS. If a coach is the target on another creeper, watch for stop phase and grip taking actions (grips, elbows, feet, palms).
      (7) practice until student displays anticipation and smoothness.

6. The Coach Examiner demonstrates a complete lesson on forward, backward, grip taking and start-coast-stop.

H. CATEGORY G: ADJUSTING FALL RATE FOR DOWN AND UP MOVEMENT

1. Purpose - To gain the ability to get level with the formation prior to docking. Getting level first prevents collisions from above and below with other jumpers on approach.
2. Downward movement - key teaching and observation points
   a. push hips forward
   b. begin from neutral box
   c. relax back into the arch
   d. apply breathing
3. Downward teaching method
   a. have the student practice the spill body position while kneeling
   b. the coach should brace the students lower back for support
   c. kneel behind or place a hand in the student's lower back and have them lean back against the support while relaxing into a full arch
   d. encourage the student to look backwards during the arch, identifying some reference point to gauge their success.
   e. the more the student trusts the coach the more relaxed they will be. Pulsing is a sign that the student needs to relax or "let go" more allowing the coach to completely take his weight.
   f. the student should do 10 repetitions, five with eyes open and five with eyes closed. Hold times should not exceed five seconds.
4. Upward movement - key teaching and observation points
   a. initiate from lower spine
   b. crunch knees down and widen them out
   c. de-arch elbows down through the shoulders cupping the chest
   d. stretch arm forward similar to backward movement
   e. the body should be lifted off of the floor
   f. feet remain neutral or very slightly extended
   g. arms are slightly pushed forward and pushing down
   h. head remains up
5. Upward teaching method
   a. the cup body position should be performed in two stages
      (1) first with the student kneeling on the mat
      (2) second laying flat on the mat
   b. first, have the student flatten the spinal arch and initiate a reverse arch in the lower back, curving the spine upward (like a mad cat).
   c. De-arching the lower back can be best achieved by rotating the pelvis down into the hamstrings. (like sucking your belly button to your spine)
   d. the shoulders and hips should be equal in height. The head should remain in the up position as this is upward movement during the final approach to docking (not low recovery position).
   e. the legs should remain in the neutral box position or only slightly extended.
   f. the arms should also be slightly extended to counter any forward motion.
      (1) the arm position during the horizontal practice is not completely realistic.

C-6 BASIC AND GROUP FREEFALL SKILLS TRAINING

    (2) the arms position should be refined during the vertical drill to be wider and more forward.

  g. this drill should always start and finish in the box body position.

  h. the student should do five repetitions in the vertical position with 10 second holds and 10 second rests.

  i. the five repetitions are repeated in the horizontal position, with five second holds and 10 second rests.

  j. cue words are "cup," "spine" or "de-arch."

6. Start, coast, stop (SCS) up and down – key teaching and observation points

  a. Train and practice only cup – box – spill for SCS

  b. Objective is to stop on level with the formation or coach

  c. Only hold the spill for half a second

  d. Practice on raised creeper or table and student must wait for signal to start. (When Coach is in position above student, he gives a thumbs up to tell the student to start)

  e. Use hand signals to help develop visual cues, such as the thumb down signal presented as the student arches harder

7. Start, coast, stop teaching method

  a. review the SCS principles with the student.

  b. complete both the static and perceptual drills in the same training session

  c. the static drill is performed on a bean bag or mat

    (1) have the student move from one position to the next (hold both the cup and coast positions for three seconds, and spill for half a second)

    (2) confirm each body position is correct during each of the phases

    (3) complete five repetitions with 10 second rest times

  d. the perceptual drill is performed on a table

    (1) the coach places his hands as far above his head as possible, simulating being above the student in freefall

    (2) the coach gives a thumbs up to signal the student to start (cup).

    (3) as the student shows you the correct cupping position, begin bringing your hands down and end up on level with the student by the time they show you the stop

    (4) watch for all three SCS phases. The stop (spill) should come exactly at your eye level

    (5) the drill should be done from approximately 15 feet away

    (6) remind the student that this is a very visual skydive

    (7) the goal is to maintain a 15 foot distance between the Coach and the student during the freefall

    (8) The Coach Examiner demonstrates a complete lesson on down and up movement with SCS drills. Start with downward movement first.

    (9) If there is any unintentional forward or backward movement during the up and down movement it should be corrected.

      (i) If the student sees he is moving forward while going up, he can extend his arms to stop the forward motion and check that legs are neutral

      (ii) If he sees he is moving backward while going down, he can extend his legs back out to neutral to stop the backward motion

      (iii) If the student does not correct the horizontal distance, the coach must make the correction and make note of it for the debrief after the jump

8. The Coach Examiner demonstrates a complete lesson on down and up movement with SCS drills. Start with downward movement first.

I. CATEGORY H: DIVING

1. Purpose - To gain the ability to smoothly dive down to a formation using SCS and stopping on level with the formation prior to moving forward to dock.

2. Key teaching and observation points

  a. legs fully extended

  b. knees at box width

  c. head up

  d. body arched

  e. arms swept back just past 90 degrees

  f. hands above the hips spilling air

3. Teaching method

  a. Have the student lay on a creeper or mat.

    (1) start in the neutral box position

    (2) say Delta and watch for full leg extension first, maintaining the arch, then arms sweeping back

    (3) the legs should lead the arms. Hold the students feet and as he gives the leg input lift the legs.

    (4) a wide body stance helps maintain stability and directional control.

    (5) remind the student if he is having trouble moving in a straight line, he needs to widen his knees and bring his arms closer to 90 degrees in relation to his torso

  b. Start, coast, stop - stair-step approach

    (1) this is a series of starts and coasts that is used to maintain control while diving to the formation

    (2) remember the coast is the assessment phase. The student will need to start into the delta, then coast to assess both his vertical and horizontal distance to the formation, then start again

    (3) the student will do several starts and coast until he is level with the formation approximately five to 20 feet away in the final approach zone

    (4) the student will then use forward motion to close the distance and take grips.

  c. Flaring for the stop

    (1) this is a combination of the full de-arch used to stop downward motion and full backward motion used to stop forward motion

    (2) to initiate the Flare, push arms forward, while de-arching and slightly dropping the knees

    (3) the longer the coast phase, the less aggressive the stop will need to be

    (4) this also helps to ensure ending up on level with the formation at the end of a dive.

  d. The student will use his previously learned skills to accomplish arriving on level 5-20 feet from the formation

  e. If during the coast phase of a dive the student sees he is close, but high, he should be trained to use downward motion to get level

BASIC AND GROUP FREEFALL SKILLS TRAINING — C-6

    f. if the student sees he is level but far away, he should be trained to track to close the distance while conserving altitude

4. Safety considerations
   a. the student should always keep the formation and the approach path in sight during the dive
   b. The student should keep an option to turn off to one side of the formation to prevent an impending collision
   c. when jumping with larger groups, diving to a position to one side or the other can interfere with the approach of another jumper
5. The Coach Examiner demonstrates a complete lesson on diving

J. BREAK-OFF SEQUENCE

1. Students must learn to initiate a break-off sequence that ensures a deployment in clear airspace at the correct altitude
2. Breakoff - key teaching and observation points
   a. The student turns 180 degrees from the center point of the formation
   b. Track on heading
   c. Flare (stop)
   d. One big, deliberate wave to signal deployment
   e. Pull at the assigned altitude
3. Break-off teaching method
   a. One effective break-off method uses the "count of eight"
      (1) the student begins to count to eight in one second intervals as the turn for tracking is initiated
      (2) the student counts two, three and four while tracking
      (3) the track is stopped with a flaring technique at the count of five
      (4) wave-off is initiated at six
      (5) the pull is initiated at seven, with deployment starting by eight
      (6) practice the break-off sequence until smooth
   b. Explain to the student that count of eight never goes away, however as he becomes a more proficient tracker he will gain more speed and distance, and lose less altitude during that same eight seconds
   c. The count of eight will require a break-off at least 1,500 feet above the planned deployment altitude
   d. Students must break off high enough to provide tracking practice and to meet the advancement criteria of 50 feet for Category G and 100 feet for Category H
   e. Recommended opening altitudes are 3,500 feet for Category G and 3,000 feet for Category H
4. Freeflying groups require higher break-off altitudes.
   a. Freeflying's faster fall rates mean greater altitude loss during break-off procedures.
   b. Jumpers in fast-fall positions must dive steeply until clear of any jumpers above before beginning an effective flat track with a slower descent rate (i.e., similar to diving for a coin at the bottom of a pool.)
   c. The student should review the break-off procedures for group freefall and freeflying outlined in Section 6 of the Skydiver's Information Manual
5. The Coach Examiner demonstrates a complete lesson on the break-off sequence.

C-7 | EQUIPMENT

7. Equipment

A. USPA COACH EQUIPMENT RESPONSIBILITIES

1. By Category G, the student should be independently responsible for equipment selection and gearing up safely.
   a. Students may require assistance.
   b. A USPA Coach should direct any questions about a student's equipment selection to the supervising USPA Instructor.
2. The USPA Coach should set an example by conducting an equipment check for the student on each jump and have the student check the coach's equipment, as well.
3. Good equipment checks add safety to every jump.
4. AADs and audible altimeters are recommended for USPA instructional rating holders when making training jumps with students.

B. EQUIPMENT CHECKS

1. Conduct equipment checks in an organized sequence for consistency and to prevent errors.
   a. top to bottom, back to front or in another logical order
   b. hands on, eyes following hands
2. Verify that the student conducts an equipment check prior to suiting up.
3. Conduct a full check on the student prior to boarding.
4. Conduct a third check on the student prior to exit.
5. Items to check prior to gearing up
   a. personal items available and suitable for the jump
   b. size of harness, main, and reserve suitable for student's size and experience
   c. reserve in date and sealed
   d. correct assembly of three-ring release
   e. condition of harness webbing and hardware
   f. condition of container, including pin and riser covers and stiffeners
   g. condition and calibration of automatic activation device, including scheduled service (FAR 105.43.c)
   h. routing and assembly of reserve static line
   i. seating of reserve pin, handle in pocket and movement of cable
   j. main deployment system
   k. check personal equipment ("SHAGG")

      Shoes—tied, no hooks
      Helmet—fit and adjustment
      Altimeter—set for zero
      Goggles—tight and clean
      Gloves—lightweight and proper size

6. Items to check prior to boarding
   a. in the front
      (1) three-ring assembly (and reserve static line)
      (2) leg and chest straps for assembly and correct routing, adjustment, and no twists
      (3) main, cutaway, and reserve handles
   b. pin check back of system, top to bottom
      (1) AAD
      (2) RSL
      (3) reserve ripcord cable
      (4) seal
      (5) reserve pin
      (6) main pin and cable (ripcord)
      (7) bridle routing and collapsible indicator, if applicable (hand deploy)
      (8) main deployment handle
   c. check personal equipment again (SHAGG)
7. Items to check prior to exit
   a. leg and chest straps
   b. AAD
   c. RSL
   d. reserve ripcord cable
   e. reserve pin
   f. main pin and cable (ripcord)
   g. bridle routing and collapsible indicator, if applicable (hand deploy)
   h. main deployment handle
   i. helmet snapped and tight
   j. altimeter operating
   k. goggles on and tight
   l. gloves on (if worn)

C. PRACTICE

Candidates gear up and practice equipment checks on each other using actual drop zone student gear.

8. Conducting a Coached Jump

8-1: COACH PROCEDURES

A. PREPARATION

1. Introduction
   a. The coach takes the initiative to find the student and introduce himself or herself.
   b. Most students appreciate learning a moderate amount of their coach's skydiving history as part of the introduction.
2. Consult with a USPA Instructor—
   a. to verify that the student is prepared for the assigned freefall training and to jump
   b. to verify emergency procedure review complete
   c. to determine what training is appropriate for the next jump
   d. If observing a Category C-E static-line or IAD jump, verify an instructor has completed the ground training for the skydive.
3. Determine the student's physical readiness for the jump.
   a. recent activities (SCUBA, partying, exercise, etc.)
   b. health
      (1) cold, sinus, etc.
      (2) medication
      (3) injuries
      (4) nutrition and hydration
4. Review the lesson and jump, and identify the phases.
   a. preparation and training for the skydive
   b. skydiving equipment
   c. in-flight and during the skydive
   d. after the jump

B. QUALIFICATION AND PREPARATION

1. Determine that the student has the correct equipment needed to make the jump.
   a. parachute
   b. shoes, helmet, altimeter, goggles, gloves (SHAGG)
   c. jumpsuit suitable for the dive plan
      (1) The student should generally wear a tight suit, unless there is an obvious need to slow the student's fall rate.
      (2) The coach should wear a suit appropriate for the student's fall rate.
2. Determine that the student knows the weather forecast, wind conditions, and the current spot (Flight Planner).

C. JUMP PLANNING AND TRAINING

1. The USPA Coach may conduct all the freefall training ahead for the entire category or only the skills to be accomplished on the next jump.
2. Design the exit.
3. Train and practice the physical movements needed on the exit and freefall.
4. Plan the breakoff.
   a. The student chooses the breakoff altitude necessary to meet the tracking distance requirements.
   b. The USPA Coach advises on the feasibility of the planned breakoff altitude.
5. Review the canopy flight plan.
6. Dirt dive the entire jump sequence in real time until smooth and exact.

D. VIDEO AND CAMERA

1. Video has proven to be an effective training and marketing aid, but the supervising USPA Instructor must qualify the videographer and supervise the briefing with the USPA Coach.
2. Minimum experience qualifications:
   a. 300 group freefall skydives
   b. 50 jumps flying camera with experienced jumpers
3. Brief the camera flyer: Refer to the Skydiver's Information Manual, Section 6, for camera flyer recommendations, particularly those pertaining to student jumps.
4. The USPA Coach should correct any camera flyer actions that cause concern or report them to the supervising USPA Instructor.

E. MANIFEST, BOARD, AND JUMP

1. Provide the correct information to manifest, but involve the student in manifesting for the load.
2. Perform a complete pre-boarding equipment check on the student.
3. Plan seating to allow the student to spot with the coach observing.
4. Review the dive plan at 4,000 feet prior to exit.
5. Conduct the pre-exit equipment check.

F. SPOTTING, EXIT, AND FREEFALL

1. Verify that the student knows the correct spot before boarding.
2. If necessary, remind the student to observe the weight and balance limits of the aircraft during climb-out procedures.
3. Make sure the student gets into a correct spotting position to view the area below the aircraft; coach as necessary.
4. Observe that the student begins the climb-out over the correct location and according to the pre-planned time or distance between groups.
5. The coach assists with the climb-out and exit.
6. Coaches can observe static-line and IAD students performing Category C five and 10-second delays while remaining in the door of the airplane.
7. The coach leads and observes the freefall portion of the skydive.
8. The coach observes the student execute the planned breakoff without a signal (unless necessary) and track.
9. Whenever possible, the coach observes the student's canopy descent and landing.

G. CANOPY DESCENT AND LANDING

1. Observe the wave-off and deployment; on Category H, the student should look above while waving off.
2. Observe the student's pattern, final approach, and landing distance from the target.
   a. Unassisted landings within 65 feet of a planned target logged during any category may be counted toward program requirements.
   b. At least two cumulative landings within 65 feet are recommended to complete Category G, and a total of five are required for the USPA A license.

H. POST JUMP

1. Verify that the student has landed safely and returned to the operations center.

C-8 | CONDUCTING A COACHED JUMP

   a. All equipment accounted for and put away.
   b. The student knows the debrief plan.
   c. The debrief process contains the following steps:
      (1) Ask student to restate the goals
      (2) Ask student to state things that went well
      (3) Ask student to state things that need improvement
      (4) Ask student how to improve
      (5) Discuss new goals for next jump
   d. Review the video, if available.
   e. Provide any necessary corrective training.
   f. Conduct or overview the training for the next jump.
   g. Record the jump.
      (1) student's logbook
      (2) A-license application card
      (3) DZ master log
2. Once all freefall advancement criteria for that Category have been met, recommend the student to the supervising USPA Instructor for advancement (Category quiz and sign-up for the next jump in the category or the A-license check dive).

8-2: LOGGING THE JUMP (READING)

Some Instructors can remember every student's name and what happened on every jump. Others get so busy, they can't even remember the details from two training jumps back. Your student's recollection of the events of the skydive, especially during the first few jumps, is often patchy. One of your jobs as a rating holder is to keep accurate records of your students' progress.

The methods vary from school to school, but the goal is the same: Jump records must provide the next coach or instructor with enough information to know where to begin the next lesson. All records should be complete, accurate, legible, and positive.

WHAT TO LOG

Your students will count on you to keep the important events from getting mixed up with those that are not so important. Especially during a student's early training, you need to log completely and in detail. Log in sequence any significant information about pre-jump equipment handling, the ride to altitude, spotting, exit, in-air performance and awareness, opening, canopy ride, and landing.

Think about any details the next USPA Coach or Instructor will need to review, for example, the student's climb-out.

Log anything unusual, such as a fast or slow fall rate or special equipment requirements so the next coach isn't surprised. Notes on a slightly weak or remarkably good performance help the next coach know how much to challenge that student on the next jump.

To count toward license requirements, the log entry must include the following (according to the SIM): jump number, date, location, exit altitude, freefall length (time), type of jump, landing distance from target, equipment used, and verifying signature. Log entries for licenses need to be in chronological order and written in an "appropriate log." Most commercially sold logbooks have marked spaces for all the necessary information, although some don't include a space for accuracy.

BE ACCURATE AND POSITIVE

Even the best students leave some room for improvement on the next jump, and the logbook needs to show where additional training is needed. To be effective at coaching your student, keep your observations and corrections positive—both verbally and in your record keeping.

Take the example of a student who exited with a good arch but whose leg and head position need improvement. The log entry could read one of two ways:

"Arch OK, head down, legs on butt."

or—

"Great arch! Extend your legs and look at the plane."

Both entries accurately describe the student's performance to the next coach, but which one makes the student happier? Which one gives the student clear corrections? Most students skydive to improve their self image in one way or another. A positive log entry will help your students attain that goal.

Make your log entries clear and legible so the student may benefit from them, too. The best entries are written in small, easy-to-read text with a minimum of abbreviations and buzz words. Use short, but complete phrases written in plain language. Consider the following two log entries:

"CO OK., slow. Good ck- in-out and count. COA to main-side only. PRCPs too fast, missed RC Good COA. #2. 5-5 late, Inst. assist pull, CC good, s-up."

and—

"Good climb-out; practice for speed. Good communication for launch. Make practice pulls slow and exact. Great improvement on second altitude check. Anticipate pull altitude. Assisted with pull. Nice job steering. Stood up!"

In the second sample log entry, not only can the student understand as well as the instructor what is written, but that entry includes clear and specific instructions on how to correct the problem. (The sloppy first altitude check got fixed on the second try—why mention it?)

Also, the first sample entry tells the story of the instructor rescuing the bungling student at pull time; but in the second entry, the student performs well enough to help the instructor with the pull. Either way, the next instructor knows who was supposed to deploy the parachute and who actually did. Doesn't entry number 2 go much easier on the student's ego?

WHO SHOULD LOG

Generally, a USPA Coach or Instructor makes each logbook entry for the student immediately following the jump. However, to meet the Basic Safety Requirements, at least a USPA Instructor must sign entries that clear the student to perform additional tasks.

Special briefings for night and water jumps should be signed by a USPA Instructor, S&TA, or Examiner.

DZ MASTER LOG

Some schools keep a master log of all student jumps in addition to or instead of individual logs for students. A master log makes it easier to monitor the effectiveness of the overall program and locate problem areas. A DZ master log of student jumps makes it easy for a student to reconstruct the information missing from a lost logbook.

PERSONAL LOG

To renew your USPA instructional rating each year, you will need to show log entries of your student training activities. You may present renewal requirement to a USPA S&TA, Examiner, or Board member.

Some skydivers enjoy logging more that others. For a USPA instructional rating holder, it's all part of the job.

9. Observation and Debriefing Strategies

A. INTRODUCTION AND PURPOSE OF SKILL ANALYSIS

1. A coach divides a skill into small, manageable parts, and analyzes the performance as a sum of the parts (whole-part-whole).
   a. Recognize the most important areas for improvement.
   b. Communicate to the student effectively how to improve those areas.
2. In this section, the course examiner explains how to apply motor skills observation strategies to skydiving actions and how to effectively debrief with a student.
3. If available, the class should observe videos of student jumps in Categories D, E, G and H to apply what they have learned in this section.

B. BASIC BIOMECHANICS

1. The center of the body (trunk) takes priority.
2. Movement of the torso is the most effective against the air.
3. The extremities follow in importance and effectiveness.
4. Example: tracking (Category F freefall outline)

C. PRE-OBSERVATION PLAN

1. Identify the purpose of the skill.
2. Break the skill into phases: initiation, intermediate steps, completion—for example, in teaching diving with start-coast-stop or dive-neutral-stop.
3. Identify the key elements of each phase: physical movement, associated activities (altitude checks, breathing, etc.)
4. The characteristics of each phase must be fully understood in order to provide an accurate evaluation.
5. The evaluator must establish a plan based on the specific type of motion being evaluated.

D. OBSERVATION PLAN

1. Key elements to observe.
2. Choose a scanning strategy
   a. Ground sessions can be more effectively viewed from a slight distance to allow for scanning all parts of the body.
   b. Close, hands-on ground training is often necessary, but can make it difficult to scan the entire body.
   c. In the air, the evaluator must remain in place, which in some cases will also limit the ability to see the entire body.
   d. Use of outside video during freefall training jumps can help capture the necessary angles for use as an effective debrief following the skydive.
   e. Canopy control is best observed from the target area using a video camera to film the landing while in front of and to one side of the candidate for the best view of the landing flare.
3. Scanning strategy.
4. Number of observations.

E. POSITION PLANNING

1. Establish the most valuable position for the planned observation for each stage of the ground training or the skydive.
2. Position will change based on the type of training jump and the altitude.
3. Videographers must be briefed to understand the required positioning and break-off procedures.

F. DECIDE ON THE NUMBER OF REPETITIONS OR THE EXPECTED MANEUVER TO OBSERVE

1. May be difficult to predict for skydiving maneuvers
2. Exit altitude and type of maneuver will largely determine the number of repetitions that can realistically be expected.
3. Different views may be required during various stages of the freefall for air skills evaluations, depending on the maneuver.

G. WHEN OBSERVING OR HOW TO APPLY

1. Use whole-part-whole strategy.
   a. Review the entire performance.
   b. Break the performance down to phases of all the specific parts such as exit, freefall, practiced maneuvers, break-off procedure, deployment and canopy descent.
   c. Make a note of any areas that need improvement.
2. Identify problems or weaknesses.
   a. Take note of any trends that continue throughout the skydive.
   b. In general, the skydive should improve overall from start to finish.
   c. Skydivers will often self-correct errors through repetition.
   d. If errors are eliminated as the skydive advances, there is no need to focus on the error during the debrief.
   e. Try to choose two to three major points of improvement to review, but no more than five.
3. Correct the skill that needs to be addressed using a positive manner.
   a. The whole-part-whole method of evaluation allows the evaluator to point out as many correct aspects of the performance as possible.
   b. The exact cause of the deficiency can then be examined and corrected, rather than focusing on elements which are performed correctly already.
4. Practice again, training with the correct actions to strengthen the diffident skill.

H. CATEGORY G AND H AIR SKILLS

1. Climb-out and exit
   a. Verify that the student places hands, feet, and torso into the exit pre-position as practiced; coach as necessary during climb-out.
   b. Look for conscious breathing before exit to relax; coach as necessary while in the set-up position.
   c. Observe the student's hips to know when to exit, regardless of his or her count.
   d. Look for the correct presentation to the relative wind.
      (1) hips first, then observe leg and arm control
      (2) student facing into the relative wind until establishing control (usually two to three seconds)
      (3) legs neutral during flyaway
      (4) conscious breathing after exit to aid relaxation; coach as necessary (AFF "relax" signal)
2. Forward motion to dock
   a. The student should initiate forward motion and maintain heading control using legs.

C-9 OBSERVATION AND DEBRIEFING STRATEGIES

- b. Docks should be positive; instructor controls separation and docking force.
- c. Once docked, the student should reduce tension by extending both legs and lifting both elbows to increase the arch across the chest.

3. Fall-rate control
   - a. For fast fall, look for
     - (1) a rounded belly
     - (2) all extremities relaxed (legs and arms may be slightly extended)
   - b. For slow fall, look for a change in the student's body position in two places only.
     - (1) sternum (shoulders) cupped
     - (2) legs slightly extended

4. Diving
   - a. Look for the student to use the slow-fall position on the wind immediately upon exit to arrest the aircraft's forward throw.
   - b. Look for level recognition and fall rate control during the dive, evidenced by a smooth approach.
   - c. Evaluate fall rate for arrival at a point 10-20 feet out and level.
   - d. Evaluate dive and final approach for start-and-stop principles.
   - e. Watch for final approach and docking techniques to be performed as practiced on previous jumps.

5. Breakoff and tracking
   - a. Evaluate for completion of the turn on heading before beginning the delta.
   - b. Look for legs straight and knees locked with the student on heading (maintained within ten degrees) before smoothly sweeping both arms back.
   - c. Observe the student's torso for a flat or concave belly, indicating a flat track.
   - d. Observe the position of the student's arms, which should be on plane with or slightly below the hips.
   - e. Look for shoulder extension (difficult to observe).
   - f. Remain in place to gauge the distance flown in the track before deployment.

I. REVIEW OF CATEGORY G AND H VIDEOS OF STUDENT JUMPS (IF AVAILABLE)
   1. Course staff demonstrates skill-analysis using video-taped basic drill skydives (optional).
   2. Candidates practice skill-analysis using video-taped skydives (optional).

J. DEBRIEFING STRATEGY
   1. Debriefing
      - a. The debrief is where Coach facilitates the learning process by encouraging the student to recognize their achievements and what they did correctly as well as help them realize what is needed to move forward in their skill development
      - b. The student must become more aware of their strengths and weaknesses and take responsibility for their training
      - c. The debrief process contains the following steps:
        - (1) Ask the student to restate the goals
        - (2) Ask the student to state things that went well
        - (3) Ask the student to state things that need improvement
        - (4) Ask the student how to improve
        - (5) Discuss and set new goals for the next jump
      - d. Restate the goals
        - (1) The student will most likely focus on the negative parts of the jump
        - (2) Restating the goals helps them open up their minds to the rest of the tasks whether it be the exit, break-off or canopy control tasks
      - e. Things that went well
        - (1) Ask the student what went well on the jump, what he did well
        - (2) The student will naturally want to focus on the negative; by having him state what he did well on the jump, it starts the debrief on a positive note
        - (3) This process will need to be repeated on several jumps before the student typically starts to enter the debrief on a positive note stating what they liked about their performance then noting what they need to improve on
      - f. Things that need improvement
        - (1) Ask the student what needs improvement
        - (2) This lets you know if the student is aware of his errors
        - (3) If the student overlooks a part of the skydive that should have been recalled, play through the video again and ask him how he felt about performing the skill to see if it jogs his memory
        - (4) If it does not, this is the Coach's opportunity to restate the goals of the jump and provide guidance on how to improve
      - g. How to improve
        - (1) Ask this question to the student
        - (2) The student should have a good idea of what he needs to work on
        - (3) If the student cannot see the answer, this is the opportunity for the Coach to review the correct techniques and assist him to see what is needed
        - (4) Patience and good listening skills of the Coach will help the student take charge of his learning and become further committed to his goals
      - h. Make new goals
        - (1) Ask the student what he would like to do on the next jump
        - (2) If the goals and expectations of each jump are clear, the student should be quite realistic about his performance
        - (3) If the environment has been set that "mistakes are OK" the student should have a realistic assessment of what he needs to do on the next jump, even if it means repeating the same jump
        - (4) The Coach's role during the debrief should be one of a facilitator
        - (5) Asking questions and directing the student to the right information through self-realization will be of greater benefit to the student

K. DEMONSTRATION

Course staff demonstrates correct debriefing technique during a mock debrief of a contrived student performance.

L. DEBRIEF PRACTICE (CONTRIVED PERFORMANCE)

Each candidate conducts a successful debrief session of a contrived student performance.

C-10 | PROBLEM SOLVING

10. Problem Solving

A. SPOTTING

1. If during ground preparations, the student chooses a spot downwind of the target—
   a. The student may have confused the winds aloft report or the wind sock as indicating where the wind is blowing to, instead of blowing from.
   b. Use practical evidence to help the student to understand the process more easily, for example, stand outside and feel the wind, then look at the windsock.
2. If the student appears inattentive on jump run—
   a. Explain that it's more effective to find a problem early on jump run than very close to climb-out.
   b. Remind the student to look for other aircraft during jump run.
3. If the student begins to climb out too early, be prepared to prevent the student from an early climb-out, and point out straight down, if sufficient time remains.
4. If the student has missed the climb-out point, be prepared to prompt the student to climb out at a no-later-than point on the ground to allow the student to learn from a minor spotting error.

B. ALTITUDE MONITORING

1. Responsibilities
   a. The coach is responsible for gaining sufficient separation for a safe deployment.
   b. The student must pull at the planned altitude, regardless of the Coach's actions.
2. The student should look at an altimeter—
   a. every four to five seconds
   b. after every maneuver
   c. whenever having difficulty with a maneuver
3. The student initiates breakoff at the planned altitude.
   a. Teach the student that if the coach waves his or her arms, it means to break off and track to deployment altitude; if the coach deploys, it means that the student should also deploy.
   b. If the student fails to break off at the planned altitude, wave off, but remain in place to observe tracking.
   c. If the student fails to turn and track after the wave-off, the coach should turn and track for sufficient separation and deploy by 3,500 feet.
   d. Under no circumstances should a USPA Coach assist with a student's deployment.

C. DEBRIEF

1. If the student has a negative attitude in the debrief, stop them and continue to ask the student to report at least one positive aspect of his or her performance and build on the success. Every time the student begins to talk about something negative say "STOP! We are only discussing things that went well." It takes some students several jumps to initiate a debrief with positive statements on their own. Keep forcing the positive first!
2. If the student needs improvement in a great number of points of the skydive: As long as safety is not an issue, focus on only the most important points to improve and limit the debrief retraining to those two or three points.
3. Use skill analysis and the goals of the jump to list as many positive points of the jump as possible. Use the positive points to show the jump was a success even though points of improvement exist. For example, "Your climb-out, set up, balance, and timing of the count were all excellent! On the flyaway you need to present to the relative wind in a neutral body position to improve stability." This example points out four positive points of the exit and two points of improvement. The more detailed the analysis of the jump, the easier it is to show the success.
4. If a student has multiple or very serious safety issues on one jump, request the intervention of a USPA Instructor.

11. Candidate Evaluation

A. INTRODUCTION

1. This section of the course is to be presented to the candidates with all evaluators for that course present.
   a. serves as the evaluator's briefing
   b. reassures the candidates that they are fully informed of all evaluation criteria and instructions
   c. provides a dialog and rapport between candidates and evaluators before testing begins
2. The Coach Rating Course includes four practical evaluation sections.
   a. general portions of the first-jump course
   b. group freefall skills
   c. candidate in-air observation and supervision
   d. debriefing
   e. b., c., and d. may be conducted separately or combined
3. The course also includes a written exam.
   a. open-book format
   b. must be taken before the course begins
   c. 80% correct score required
   d. If the test must be administered during the course, a score of 100% is required.

B. GENERAL

1. To ensure standardized procedures, each evaluation should be conducted in generally the same manner and to the same standards of performance.
2. Training evaluation teams
   a. For first-jump course and group freefall skills training evaluations, the course examiner divides the candidates into teams of two, supervised by an evaluator.
   b. The teams should stay together during the practical evaluations and alternate acting as student and coach.
3. For the in-air observation and supervision evaluation(s) only, evaluators will portray students participating in a training jump.

C. AREAS TO BE EVALUATED

GROUND TRAINING

1. The candidates and evaluators should be briefed together, following the applicable portions of the outline in the Candidate Evaluation section of this course.
2. Each candidate is expected to follow the ISP outlined for the Category G-1 and G-2. The candidate must pass with a score of 75% with no automatic unsatisfactory.
3. Lesson design and presentations for Category G-1 and G-2 include:
   a. preparation – lesson plans prepared, training aids available, and suitable teaching environment available
   b. explanation and demonstration on all required items
   c. student trial and practice – (vertical and horizontal training)
   d. review and evaluation – check on learning concepts (feedback, questions, testing etc.)
   e. the use of whole part whole (why it's important, expectations, criteria to pass, breakdown of parts, recombine parts and practice until autonomous)
4. Ground training concepts and topics to be evaluated. Each candidate is evaluated on subject areas and sub-subject areas listed below:
   a. introduction
      (1) name
      (2) background
   b. student
      (1) motivations
      (2) physical condition: medical, vision, hearing, age, weigh, dental, scuba, injuries, blood donations, prescription and non-prescription drugs and alcohol
      (3) USPA membership, waiver, etc.
      (4) appropriate clothing (pocket, Jewelry)
      (5) non-jump background
      (6) logbook
      (7) video (if available)
      (8) student's opinion of their performance of last jump
      (9) procedure to prepare for jump (time frame, etc.)
   c. skydive
      (1) state measurable goals clearly and succinctly (concept, flow-emphasis on breakoff and pull altitude)
      (2) relate goals to prior knowledge
      (3) relate goals to future goals (emphasis on safety)
      (4) accurate physical demonstration or video, if available, with minimal details to give big picture lesson and training environment preparation
      (5) thorough, complete, and correct information presented using standard resources
      (6) effective use of trial and practice with sufficient repetition
      (7) attention to detail of student's performance with on the spot correction, using hand signals when possible
      (8) goals and skills broken into parts/details, with sufficient student practice for each
      (9) skills master individually, then combined in logical order
      (10) asked questions to check for deeper understanding
      (11) present scenarios to check deeper application
      (12) "show me" for review skills
      (13) "demo-do" for new skills
      (14) utilized strategies fitting for content
      (15) real-time dirt dives without interruption or prompting until autonomous
      (16) realism
   d. training aid use
      (1) aircraft mock-up
      (2) vertical trainer
      (3) horizontal trainer (body position and techniques must always be correct)
      (4) real time use (e.g., clock altimeter)
   e. canopy Control (10-15 minutes)
      (1) use of DZ photo or flight planner; walk in field

C-11 CANDIDATE EVALUATION

- (2) exit point and holding
- (3) landing pattern for the day and Canopy Dive Flow
- (4) landing procedure: flare height, stall recovery
- (5) effect of low turn

f. meeting Student (20-Minute Call)
- (1) equipment (ordinate with supervising USPA instructor)
- (2) pre-jump equipment check (student and instructor)
- (3) pre-boarding supervision
- (4) full-dress rehearsal at mock-up or aircraft
- (5) boarding

g. climb to altitude
- (1) helmet and seat belt
- (2) view of airport from aircraft
- (3) deployment and breakoff altitude review (at correct altitude)
- (4) student mental rehearsal
- (5) student verbal rehearsal with instructor
- (6) verify student's spotting (coach is responsible for the spot)
- (7) supervision during pre-exit and climb out

h. opening to landing
- (1) observe canopy control (if possible)
- (2) set good example

i. debriefing (10 -15 minutes)
- (1) use of appropriate area (aircraft, mockup, etc.)
- (2) student's view first
- (3) student's perceptions correct
- (4) coach's perceptions thorough and accurate
- (5) proper review of video, if used
- (6) emphasis on positive
- (7) advancement/non-advancement decision
- (8) corrective training
- (9) introduction of objectives for next level (if advanced) and flow of dive
- (10) paperwork, logbook entry and A-license proficiency card

5. Debrief and Observation

    a. Schedule (either)
    - (1) The candidate uses the evaluator's performance on an in-air observation and supervision evaluation dive to prepare and conduct a debrief; limit 15 minutes.
    - (2) The evaluator presents the candidate with a student performance scenario, which the candidate uses to prepare and conduct a debrief; limit 15 minutes.

    b. Count successful sessions toward the practical teaching evaluations required to pass the USPA Coach Rating Course and log them on the USPA Coach Proficiency Card.

IN-AIR OBSERVATION AND SUPERVISION

1. In this section, the coach rating candidate demonstrates the ability to observe, evaluate, and correct the evaluator, acting as a student, for category G1 and G2 evaluation jumps.

    a. Category G-1 dive flow:
    - (1) floater exit (front, center, or rear) grips optional, evaluated using set up, launch and fly-away
    - (2) forward movement, evaluated using start coast stop
    - (3) docking
    - (4) break off
    - (5) tracking review

    b. Category G-2 dive flow:
    - (1) floater exit (front, center, and rear) or inside exit, evaluated using set up, launch and fly-away
    - (2) fall rate (fast fall and slow fall)
    - (3) breakoff
    - (4) tracking review

    c. Category G canopy dive flow (included on both dive flow presentations)
    - (1) check altitude, position, and traffic
    - (2) make a sharp, controlled 90-degree turn
    - (3) reverse the toggle position aggressively and make a controlled 180-degree turn
    - (4) check altitude, position, and traffic - repeat to no lower than 2,500 feet, in case of line twist
    - (5) coach measures the student's landing distance from a planned target

2. The evaluator commits some or all of the following errors, which the candidate should correct immediately:

    a. spotting:
    - (1) (before boarding) planning an opening point downwind of the drop zone (from "misreading" the winds-aloft report or wind sock)
    - (2) attempting to observe jump run with his or her head inside the aircraft
    - (3) inattention to the plane's progress on jump run
    - (4) attempted early or late climb-out

    b. Climb-out: The evaluator attempts to climb into a position other than the one practiced, and the candidate corrects (with evaluator cooperation).

3. The evaluator commits some or all of the following errors, which the candidate should observe, recognize, and correct later during the debrief.

    a. exit and freefall
    - (1) premature or late exit
    - (2) incorrect presentation to relative wind, resulting in momentary loss of stability (three seconds or less)
    - (3) focusing on the coach too early, resulting in momentary loss of stability (three seconds or less)
    - (4) legs retracted
    - (5) for diving exit, inattention to slow fall presentation to the relative wind

    b. docking
    - (1) poor or reverse arch across the chest (elbows down)
    - (2) legs retracted

    c. fall rate control
    - (1) fast fall—retracting legs or arms; knees down; extending legs while retracting arms
    - (2) slow fall—overextension of arms or legs; head back and looking up; bent forward at the waist (rather than sternum)

    d. freefall turns
    - (1) buffeting while turning
    - (2) overshooting or undershooting the intended heading
    - (3) spinning

    e. breakoff: ignoring the breakoff altitude and/or the coach's wave-off

f. tracking
  (1) initiating forward movement with the arms without extending both legs (may additionally result in poor heading control and distance)
  (2) arch in torso (may additionally result in insufficient distance)
  (3) arms above the hips (may additionally result in insufficient distance)
  (4) attempting to initiate forward movement before establishing the correct heading (resulting in heading more than ten degrees off planned heading or erratic heading control)
  (5) If the evaluator breaks off, he or she tracks (with or without errors) and does or does not pull at the specified altitude.
g. canopy skills
  (1) S-turns on final approach
  (2) incorrect or indiscernible landing pattern
  (3) landing well more than 20 meters of the planned target

D. GROUND RULES

1. Prior to each evaluation session, the evaluator will conduct a briefing with the candidate for all subjects of the evaluation process, to include—
   a. a brief review of the evaluation procedures
   b. comprehensive and detailed explanation of the scoring criteria
   c. the level of performance expected
   d. specific safety and scoring reminders
   e. for air skills evaluations, the equipment to be used on the actual jump with that evaluator, including instructions to ignore specific equipment preferences of the evaluator not ordinarily found on students (hook knife, etc.)
   f. an opportunity for the candidates to ask questions about the skydive and the evaluation procedure
2. Each candidate is expected to follow the ISP outline for the jump to be trained.
3. The candidate works with a partner, preferably a candidate in the course, to be trained while the evaluator takes notes.
4. The evaluator may call a "time out" during any part of the ground or air evaluation, but the candidates may not, except for safety reasons.
   a. The evaluator should call time-outs only when necessary.
   b. The evaluator will allow time for the candidate to regroup following a time-out.

E. DIVE FLOWS

1. Evaluation jump 1 and 2: Use the dive flow for Category G, Dive Plan 1, 2 or 3 in the Integrated Student Program.
2. Evaluation jump 2 option: Use the dive flow for Category D-IAD and static-line 90-degree turns
   a. Conduct the jump from full altitude.
   b. Available as an optional evaluation jump for coach candidates who plan to work with students in IAD or static line training programs.

F. IN-AIR OBSERVATION AND SUPERVISION EVALUATION JUMP PROCEDURES

1. At the 20-minute call, the person acting as student and candidate arrive fully rigged and ready to jump, although the evaluator may present common errors for the candidates to discover during the pre-boarding equipment check.
2. Evaluator's equipment
   a. Evaluators will wear standard student accessory equipment, including clear goggles or visor, shoes, and hard helmet.
   b. All rigging problems must be determined during the pre-boarding equipment check.
   c. Under no circumstances will an evaluator attempt to board an aircraft with mis-rigged equipment or exit an aircraft with contrived equipment problems.
   d. The evaluator may present non-safety equipment problems to be caught during the pre-exit check aboard the aircraft.
3. Scenarios will be drawn from an ordinary skydiving school environment, considering that the freefall skills student is expected to be responsible for the following (but may need to be reminded or assisted by the USPA Coach):
   a. equipment selection and inspection prior to rigging up
   b. aircraft procedures, including seat belt use, seating priorities, and observing balance procedures on jump run
   c. spotting, with the USPA Coach as an informed observer

CANDIDATE EVALUATION | C-11

   d. independent exit and freefall stability (evaluator should demonstrate reasonable control)
   e. deployment
   f. canopy control
   g. post-jump equipment management
4. Evaluators should make the evaluation scenarios both challenging and a learning experience for the candidates.
   a. Evaluator challenges will provide opportunities for the candidates to observe problems in freefall for subsequent review and correction.
   b. The evaluator may not correct or assist the candidates during the evaluations with the exception of discrepancies that might compromise safety on that jump.
5. Observation and assistance with the student's aircraft spotting will be included in the practical (in-aircraft) evaluation of freefall evaluation jumps.
6. During the evaluation, the candidate may be presented with a loss-of-altitude awareness scenario, which may require the candidate to wave the student off and get clear and deploy by 3,500 feet. In this case, the student (evaluator) remains in freefall until the candidate deploys, in order to determine the deployment altitude of the candidate. If the candidate fails to deploy at 3,500 feet, the student (evaluator) must deploy immediately, provided there is sufficient horizontal separation.
7. The in-air observation and supervision evaluation begins at the 20-minute call for the load; continues through pre-boarding, climb-out, the jump, canopy descent, and the return of the jumpers to the packing area, and ends either—
   a. at that point
   b. when combined with a debriefing evaluation, when the candidate completes the debrief of the evaluator acting as the student
8. At the end of each evaluation session, the evaluator will debrief the candidate on the performance.
   a. reinforcement of areas where the candidate was successful
   b. where possible, provide instruction, including demonstration and practice, to correct deficiencies

C-11 CANDIDATE EVALUATION

   c. assignment and necessary explanation of the scoring for that evaluation

G. COACH EVALUATION SCORING

GROUND TRAINING

1. Each candidate must obtain a score of 75% in the following ground training sessions.
   a. two sessions from the first-jump course topics
   b. Category G, Dive Plan 1 and 2 ground training
   c. debriefing
2. Ground training sessions are evaluated according to the correct application of the Basic Instructional Methods section of this course and shown on the USPA Coach Ground Training Evaluation Form.
   a. preparation of the lesson
      (1) breaking the lesson into manageable, related parts
      (2) recombining the parts into a meaningful practice flow
   b. clear and accurate explanation
   c. accurate demonstration
   d. sufficient supervision for correct practice
   e. accurate evaluation of the student's mastery of the lesson
3. Mandatory scores of unsatisfactory
   a. failure to perform training using the preparation, presentation, application, evaluation method
   b. insufficient repetition during practice
   c. insufficient correction and positive feedback for the student to acquire the skills

STUDENT SUPERVISION

1. Each candidate is responsible for the supervision of their student
   a. In the classroom while working around training aids
   b. Near landing areas, taxiways, runways and other potentially hazardous areas of an airport
   c. Selecting appropriate equipment for the skydive
   d. Ensuring the student's equipment is in good working order and properly fitted
   e. While approaching and boarding aircraft
   f. During the climb to altitude, climb-out, exit and freefall
   g. After landing until the student is back in the hangar with equipment removed
2. Scoring of supervision will not count towards the freefall portion of the evaluation
3. Each candidate must earn satisfactory scores in student supervision for each evaluation jump
4. For any score of unsatisfactory, the candidate must demonstrate proficiency in the missed area on the next evaluation jump
5. If the candidate has completed the air evaluations but still needs to correct a deficiency in student supervision, the course staff will use a contrived student scenario to test the candidate
6. Mandatory scores of unsatisfactory
   a. Failure to safely supervise a student during any part of the ground training, boarding of the aircraft, ride to altitude or return from the landing area
   b. Failure to check the simulated student's equipment before boarding or before exiting the aircraft
   c. Missed major rigging errors, including but not limited to—
      (1) missing altimeter or goggles
      (2) misrouted three-ring release system or improperly routed RSL (depending on the severity)
      (3) improperly routed or threaded chest strap or leg straps
      (4) unsuitable parachute assembly
      (5) altimeter not zeroed

IN-AIR OBSERVATION AND SUPERVISION

1. Each candidate must score at least 75% on two air-skills evaluation jumps.
2. The candidate must observe at least half of the problems presented by the evaluator in each of the following portions of the skydive:
   a. pre-boarding equipment check
   b. aircraft supervision and spotting
   c. pre-exit equipment check
   d. exit and climb-out
   e. group freefall skills
   f. breakoff
   g. tracking
   h. canopy descent and landing
3. Unsafe performance
   a. The evaluator must advise the course examiner of any performance which, in the evaluator's opinion, creates a safety hazard during an evaluation jump.
   b. The course examiner may recommend additional training for the candidate or that the candidate not continue with the in-air practical evaluation of the course at this time.
4. Mandatory scores of unsatisfactory
   a. bad spot where the simulated student would not be able to return to a safe landing area
   b. jump in violation of FAA cloud clearance minimums
   c. Out of position in freefall. (More than 20 feet vertically or horizontally for more than 10 seconds on Category D or G evaluations, more than 100 feet vertical or horizontal for Category H dive and dock evaluations.)
   d. breakoff
      (1) An automatic unsatisfactory is scored for failure to recognize breakoff altitude and signal the evaluator by waving off within 500 feet below the planned altitude.
      (2) The candidate's wave-off in response must be accomplished within 500 feet of the planned break-off altitude, and the candidate must be clear by at least 200 feet horizontally and deploy by 3,500 feet if the evaluator fails to track.
   e. failure to respond to evaluator inaction at breakoff and to get clear and deploy by 3,500 feet
   f. collision with the evaluator
   g. other

Note: "Other" is not meant as an open or broad interpretation of the reasons for a score of Unsatisfactory; rather, it is reserved for unforeseeable situations that in the judgment of the evaluator and the course examiner would compromise the safety of an evaluator or a real group freefall skills student.

5. Group freefall debriefing skills
   a. The candidate must score at least 75% on at least one debriefing session.
   b. The candidate is evaluated in the following skill categories:
      (1) restatement of the goals of the jump

CANDIDATE EVALUATION | C-11

(2) reinforcement of properly executed skills

(3) recognition of the evaluator's errors

(4) correction according to the observation strategies outlined in this course

(5) retraining according to the correct order of the lesson (preparation, presentation, application, evaluation)

(6) verbal skills: use of positive coaching statements

H. RETESTING

1. Candidates must succeed within the following evaluation limits:
   a. four ground training sessions in Category A
   b. four ground training sessions in group freefall skills
   c. four in-air observation and supervision evaluation jumps
   d. four debriefing evaluations

2. A candidate who earns a mandatory score of Unsatisfactory during the equipment check prior to boarding may continue scoring on that jump and be retested on a subsequent equipment check.

3. A candidate who fails to obtain all the required scores of Satisfactory will be required to wait fourteen (14) days or a detailed plan is discussed by the Examiner and the candidate which is executed within the time frame decided upon by both parties before attending or retesting at another USPA Coach Rating Course. The disqualified candidate may act as a stand-in student for ground evaluations as approved by the attending Examiner.

4. Evaluations of debriefing sessions may be contrived for candidates who have completed both in-air observation and supervision evaluations successfully but have not performed a satisfactory debriefing.

5. Written exam retesting
   a. Each candidate will be provided a second opportunity to pass the test during the course.
   b. Failure to answer 100% of the questions correctly on the second attempt will require the candidate to study, retake the classroom portion of a future USPA Coach Rating Course, and pass the written exam at that course.

6. Retesting fees: All retesting and re-evaluation fees are at the discretion of the course examiner.

7. All portional retesting must be accomplished within 12 months of the failed course, or the candidate must retake the complete course.

COACH RATING COURSE
GROUND EVALUATION CHECKLIST

1. **Introduction (5-10 minutes)**
   a. **coach**
      - [ ] name
      - [ ] background
   b. **student**
      - [ ] motivations
      - [ ] physical condition: medical, vision, hearing, age, weight, dental, scuba, injuries, blood donations, prescription and non-prescription drugs, alcohol
      - [ ] appropriate clothing (pockets, jewelry)
      - [ ] non-jump background
      - [ ] logbook
      - [ ] video (previous, this jump?)
      - [ ] student's subjective evaluation
      - [ ] procedure to prepare for jump (time frame, etc.)
   c. **skydive**
      - [ ] tie-in to previous experience
      - [ ] introduce objectives (emphasis on breakoff and pull altitude)
      - [ ] brief description (concept, flow)
      - [ ] demonstration and video, if available

2. **New Training (15 minutes)**
   a. **instructional strategy**
      - [ ] lesson and training environment prepared
      - [ ] explanations and demonstrations correct
      - [ ] effective mix of explanation and demonstration with trial and practice
      - [ ] on-the-spot correction, using hand signals when possible
      - [ ] performance objectives explained thoroughly and properly
      - [ ] each objective explained and demonstrated individually, with student trial and practice for each
      - [ ] skills mastered individually, then combined
      - [ ] effective mix of vertical and horizontal training
      - [ ] real-time dirt dives without coaching
      - [ ] realism
   b. **training aid use**
      - [ ] aircraft mock-up
      - [ ] vertical trainer
      - [ ] horizontal trainer (body position and techniques must be correct at all times)
      - [ ] real time use (e.g., clock altimeter)

3. **Meeting Student (20-Minute Call)**
   - [ ] equipment (coordinate with supervising USPA Instructor)
   - [ ] pre-jump equipment check (student and instructors)
   - [ ] pre-boarding supervision
   - [ ] full-dress rehearsal at mock-up or aircraft
   - [ ] boarding
   - [ ] pre-boarding equipment check

4. **Climb to Altitude**
   - [ ] helmet and seat belt
   - [ ] view of airport from aircraft
   - [ ] deployment and breakoff altitudes reviewed (at correct altitudes)
   - [ ] student verbal rehearsal with coach
   - [ ] student mental rehearsal
   - [ ] pre-exit gear check
   - [ ] spotting
   - [ ] supervision during pre-exit and climb-out

5. **Opening to Landing**
   - [ ] observe canopy control (if possible)
   - [ ] set good example

6. **Debriefing (10-15 minutes)**
   - [ ] use of appropriate area (aircraft, mock up, etc.)
   - [ ] walk and talk
   - [ ] student's view first
   - [ ] student's perceptions correct
   - [ ] coach's perceptions thorough and accurate
   - [ ] proper review of video, if used
   - [ ] emphasis on positive
   - [ ] advancement/non-advancement decision
   - [ ] corrective training
   - [ ] introduction of objectives for next level (if advanced) and flow of dive
   - [ ] paperwork, log entry

USPA COACH RATING COURSE (GROUND) SCORING AND CRITERIA EXAMPLES

Jump Preparation	Teaching Environment	Quiet setting, lights, temperature, etc.
	Knowledge of Topic	Confidence and correct explanation
	Lesson Plan	Follows design format
	Use of time Allotted	Time management skills
Explanation And Demonstration (Presentation)	Whole-Part-Whole	Method of training
	Clear Explanation	Ensures understanding by target audience
	Correct Demonstration	Accurate, precise, close to perfect
	Short, Simple, Specific	KISSS principle of explaining
Student Trial And Practice (Application)	Skill Phases Taught in a Logical Order	Self explanatory
	Training Aid Use	Proper training aids to support effectively used
	Attention to Detail of Students Practice	Present and attentive
	Positive Delivery of Needed Corrections	Specific and immediate
	Focused: Correct Hold/Rest Times	Changes pace and helps retention
	Later Correction Techniques Emphasis on Physical	Specific and immediate
	Uninterrupted Practice	Correct and close to perfect as possible (no corrections at this time should be necessary)
	Sufficient Repetition	Near perfect performance by the student (feedback)
Review (Evaluation)	Goals Reviewed and Compared to Performance	By the student and candidate
	Appropriate Use of Questions	Self explanatory
	Positive Manner and Content	Self explanatory
General Instructor Ability	Provides Positive Motivation for Learning	Upbeat, relaxed, non-threatening
	Correct Information	Stayed on topic

USPA COACH RATING COURSE (IN-AIR) SCORING AND CRITERIA EXAMPLES

Jump Preparation	Students Flight Plan	If it applies can be uspa format or dz format. minimum of a specific and accurate pattern
	Correct Equipment . (Simulated)	Select for proper fit, wing load, etc.
Equipment Checks	Three Required	Pre-flight (observed), before boarding, before exiting. the evaluator cannot enter an aircraft mis-rigged
Supervision	Guidance for Boarding and Climb	Loading sequence according to dz, protecting handles, helmet on, under supervision, direct seat belts, etc.
Climb To Altitude	Mental and Verbal Review	Verbal after altimeter cross check and mental for visualization
	Spotting Observation	At least look over shoulder and ensure location, cloud clearance, traffic, etc.
Climb-Out And Exit	Assist as Necessary	Facilitate the setup/launch and able to observe.
Exit And Freefall	In Position	Based on category, must be able to observe, give signals (if needed), be the "base", etc.
Altitude Awareness	Breakoff Signal (If Needed)	Physical wave prompt by the candidate to get the student to track away (within 500 ft of planned alt)
	Loss of Altitude Awareness Protocol	Candidate turns and tracks away for safety and deploys by 3,500 ft AGL to observe student canopy control
Canopy Observation	If Possible	Based on candidates opening altitude and type of main canopy. Should at least observe the students approach and landing procedures
Debrief And Review	Student First Then Coach	Collect all the facts and help student determine what actually occurred
	Positive	What did the student like best? 2-3 points
	Limited Improvement Points	What 2-3 things would the student like to improve
	Correct Retraining	Based on student and coach agreements physical corrective retraining on the items of improvement
Automatic Unsats	Bad Spot Or Clouds	Landing off the DZ due to improper exit point or falling through a cloud
	Out of Position in Freefall (no student learning possible)	For Category G candidate is more than 20 ft vertical or horizontal for more than 10 seconds, for Category H candidate is more than 100 ft vertical or horizontal (to much separation for student to "dive" safely)
	Hard Collision	The student is stable and the candidate collides with the student creating instability
	Not Clear and Open By 3,500 ft After Evaluator	The candidate must gain at least 200 ft of horizontal separation from the student not vertical
	Missed Breakoff Signal	If needed at breakoff altitude, Category G 5,500 ft AGL, Category H 5,000 ft AGL
	Low Deployment	Not clear and open by 3,500 ft. AGL for Category G or 3,000 ft. AGL for Category H.
	Other	Safety actually deploying the student's main or reserve canopy, pulling the student's cutaway handle, candidate deploys within 50 ft. of the student, missed major rigging error, etc.

AFF INSTRUCTOR RATING COURSE

A-1 INTRODUCTION AND ORIENTATION

1. Introduction and Orientation

A. WHAT IS A USPA ACCELERATED FREEFALL (AFF) INSTRUCTOR?

1. The USPA Instructor is the one of three instructional ratings USPA administers, preceded by USPA Coach and followed by Examiner.
2. A USPA AFF Instructor may—
    a. exercise all privileges of the USPA Coach rating
    b. conduct AFF-type jumps, the AFF first-jump course, and transition training to AFF
    c. conduct training in the general portions of any first-jump course
    d. train and supervise jumps with non-method-specific students
    e. conduct the A-license quiz and check dive
    f. verify certain USPA license applications, according to the requirements in SIM Section 3
    g. supervise a USPA Coach in training students and making currency jumps with licensed skydivers
    h. Supervise static-line and IAD students beginning in Category C after a successful clear-and-pull.
3. Supervision (BSRs)
    a. All student training is conducted under the supervision as required by an appropriately rated USPA Instructor (refer to the BSRs).
    b. All general, non-method-specific student training and jump supervision may be conducted by any USPA Instructor, but method-specific training and jumps (AFF, IAD, static-line, and tandem) require a USPA Instructor who holds that method-specific rating.
4. Candidates who have met all the following requirements may attend the USPA AFF Instructor Rating Course:
    a. reached the age of 18 years
    b. holds or has held any USPA instructional rating
    c. must have held a USPA Coach or Instructor rating for at least 12 months, or have at least 500 jumps
    d. issued a USPA C license
    e. logged six hours of freefall time
5. Candidates who have completed the following may earn the USPA AFF Instructor Rating:
    a. completed the USPA AFF Instructor Proficiency Card (applicable portions completed within the previous 12 months)
    b. successfully proven ability by successfully completing the written and practical AFF evaluation process with a USPA AFF Examiner

B. AFF TRAINING BACKGROUND

1. Unsanctioned harness-hold training had been done prior to its adoption by USPA
    a. a jump with talk show host Johnny Carson, in 1968, with Bob Sinclair acting as instructor
    b. remedial jumps for static-line progression students with instability problems
    c. the U.S. Army Parachute Team and the Military Freefall School
2. Harness-hold training wasn't feasible until the concurrent adaptation of—
    a. modern automatic activation devices
    b. instructors well trained in the method
    c. modern student piggyback equipment for students in the late '70s, of which USPA Instructor Ken Coleman, working with Strong Enterprises, was an innovator
3. The Accelerated Freefall method of harness-hold training was developed in the late 1970s under the leadership of Coleman as an alternative to static-line training.
4. USPA approved and adopted Coleman's Accelerated Freefall program in October 1981 and began issuing AFF ratings later that year.
5. Other harness-hold progression programs have since been developed under different names.
6. USPA outlines its recommendations for harness-hold training under the name USPA Accelerated Freefall in the USPA Integrated Student Program.

C. THE NATURE OF THE COURSE

1. This course may be conducted—
    a. as an initial USPA Instructor rating course for USPA Coaches
    b. as a shorter transition course for—
        (1) current USPA Instructors rated in another method
        (2) instructors who hold a harness-hold rating issued by another FAI-member country
2. Course and testing arrangements
    a. The host coordinates with an instructor examiner for scheduling of an AFF Instructor Rating Course
    b. The course host negotiates fees and accommodations with the instructor examiner.
3. Each candidate is required to arrive at this course with all prerequisites completed, as specified on the AFF Instructor Rating Course Proficiency Card.
4. The course will cover the USPA Integrated Student Training Program—
    a. as it applies to AFF training
    b. subsequent training and jumps to the A license
    c. transition from another training discipline
5. Candidates may make a series of practice training evaluations and jumps with the course staff prior to actual evaluations.
6. Schedule for the camp format AFF Instructor Rating Course
    a. The classroom training portion of this course is expected to be conducted over a minimum period of two days.
    b. The practice and evaluation portion is conducted subsequently over a period of several additional days (typically, nine days total for classroom and evaluation are scheduled).
7. The schedule for abbreviated and other courses are according to the preparation requirements of the candidates, class size, and the instructor examiner's and facility's schedule.

D. WHO MAY CONDUCT THIS COURSE?

1. An AFFE who has maintained currency as follows: conducted at least one USPA AFF Instructor Rating Course and attended a standardization meeting within the past 24 months
2. Continues to meet all of the requirements to qualify as a course evaluator (listed in Section E, "How to become a USPA AFF Examiner.")

E. CONVERTING A NON-USPA AFF RATING TO A USPA AFF RATING

1. A jumper with a current AFF Instructor rating from a non-U.S. skydiving federation may convert that rating to a USPA AFF Instructor Rating by completing a USPA AFF course,

INTRODUCTION AND ORIENTATION — A-1

excluding the first-jump-course training on the AFF Instructor Rating Course Proficiency Card.

F. PROCEDURES FOR RENEWING AN EXPIRED AFF RATING

1. Ratings expire with USPA memberships. Persons with an expired USPA AFF rating (up to two years) must:
   a. Satisfactorily conduct at least one complete AFF evaluation jump with an AFF Examiner or evaluator (under the supervision of an AFF Examiner) acting as a student, to include all jump preparation, supervision during the jump and debriefing.
   b. Pass the General USPA Instructor and AFF Instructor written exams with a score of at least 80 percent
   c. Attend a USPA rating renewal seminar
   d. Conducted training or complete review training in Category A for AFF
2. Persons with an expired AFF rating of more than two years must requalify by successfully passing the AFF rating course.
3. A skydiver may not verify his or her own rating renewal requirements.
4. Renewing an instructor rating automatically renews a coach rating.

G. WHAT IS REQUIRED TO PASS THIS COURSE?

1. Practical: Candidates for the USPA AFF Instructor rating will be evaluated during the course for their ability to—
   a. understand the course material
   b. conduct effective ground training, using other candidates as stand-in students
   c. safely prepare, supervise, and perform in-air training of students making AFF jumps with AFF evaluators acting as students
2. Written: Prior to attending the course, each candidate must correctly answer at least 80% of the questions on an open-book written examination covering the following:
   a. this syllabus
   b. the complete ISP syllabus
   c. the USPA Basic Safety Requirements
   d. SIM Section 5
   e. FARs
3. Commencement of privileges
   a. The privileges of any instructional rating will commence upon successful completion of the rating course and will be valid for 15 days with a candidate logbook endorsement by the instructor examiner.
   b. The rating must be processed at USPA Headquarters to be considered valid after the 15-day grace period expires
4. Currently rated instructors attending this course do not need to meet the first-jump course requirements. The method-specific first-jump course topics will be covered in detail during the course by the examiner.

H. KEEPING AN AFF INSTRUCTOR RATING CURRENT

1. USPA AFF Instructors may annually renew their ratings with their USPA membership by paying the annual rating renewal fee and providing documentation of any of the following:
   a. that the rating was initially earned within the current membership cycle (renewal fee and signature required) in which case the annual minimum AFF jump number (15) does not apply.
   b. that the applicant has met the annual rating renewal requirements by performing all of the following within the previous 12 months:
      (1) acted as instructor on at least 15 AFF student jumps
      (2) attended a USPA rating-renewal seminar (see SIM glossary for definition)
      (3) conducted training or complete review training in Category A for AFF, having taught or assisted with at least one entire first-jump course
      (4) acquired the signature of a current S&TA, Examiner, or member of the USPA Board of Directors on the renewal application to verify that the renewal requirements were met
   c. or, having met the renewal requirements for an expired rating
2. Persons with an expired AFF rating of more than two years must requalify by successfully passing the USPA AFF Rating Course.
3. A skydiver may not verify his or her own rating renewal requirements.
4. Renewing an instructor rating automatically renews a coach rating.

I. COURSE OVERVIEW

1. USPA's Integrated Student Program for AFF students
   a. the first-jump course
   b. first-jump course performance standards
   c. Categories B-E, basic skydiving skills
   d. group skydiving skills
2. AFF method
3. Problem solving
4. General instructor's duties
5. Jump preparation and equipment checks
6. Demonstration and practice sessions
7. Evaluation section

A-2: THE INTEGRATED STUDENT PROGRAM

2. The Integrated Student Program

2-1: ISP OVERVIEW

1. The USPA Integrated Student Program is a complete and detailed outline recommended by USPA to train students from the first jump through the A license.
2. The ISP integrates all USPA-recognized methods for teaching skydiving, particularly in the early portion of the training: harness hold (USPA Accelerated Freefall), instructor-assisted deployment, static line, and tandem.
3. Schools using the ISP outline or its equivalent can easily track a student's performance and interchange the various training methods to make the most effective use of their training resources.
   a. There are eight categories of advancement, A-H.
      (1) Categories A-D focus on basic skydiving survival skills and are very closely supervised.
      (2) During Categories E through H, students become more independent and supervision requirements are relaxed.
      (3) Categories G and H concentrate on group freefall skills and to prepare a student to jump without supervision and the USPA A license.
   b. Each category following Category A, the first-jump course, is divided into six skills and knowledge sets.
      (1) exit and freefall
      (2) canopy
      (3) emergency procedure review
      (4) equipment
      (5) rules and recommendations
      (6) spotting and aircraft
   c. Each student, except those making tandem jumps, should complete training in the freefall, canopy, and emergency review sections prior to making a jump in any category.
      (1) Some freefall dive flows require the freefall and emergency procedure training and review for the student to safely perform them.
      (2) The canopy dive flows require canopy training first so the student can understand what to practice.
      (3) The student becomes more independent and less supervised as he or she progresses and may require the information in these three areas when encountering new experiences during jumps in that category.
4. An oral quiz follows each category.
   a. It may be given after the student completes the last jump in the category or serve as a review preceding training in the next category.
   b. The USPA Instructor conducting the A license check dive draws from the quiz questions for the oral testing portion of the license review.

2-2: THE ISP FIRST-JUMP COURSE FOR AFF

1. The course staff and candidates discuss the first-jump course using the Category A outline in the ISP.
2. The number of students in the first-jump course should be appropriate for the number of staff available to facilitate the course.

A. EQUIPMENT

1. The student should know the location of all operation handles he or she may be expected to use.
2. Using terms the student will hear throughout the course and the jump, the instructor describes a correct parachute opening in the three significant stages that determine the response from the jumper.
   a. activation (container opening)
      (1) procedure for stable activation of the main parachute practiced until smooth and exact
      (2) activation of an actual main parachute while wearing the equipment the student is expected to jump
   b. deployment
   c. inflation
3. Equipment responsibilities
   a. The USPA Instructor is primarily responsible for choosing the correct system and preflighting it.
      (1) putting the equipment on the student, adjusting it properly within the hangar
      (2) performing a complete pre-boarding equipment check
      (3) checking that the equipment is ready to jump before the student exits the aircraft
   b. Students are responsible for—
      (1) making sure the instructor checks the equipment at these three points
      (2) all equipment as the student progresses through the program
4. Students are taught to protect the parachute system operation handles, but monitoring the equipment throughout the jump operation is a primary duty of the instructor(s).
5. The student should know that the responsibility for the equipment shifts from the instructor to the student later as the student progresses.
6. The student should be familiar with any other equipment operation he or she is expected to perform independently (personal items, equipment recovery and return, etc.).
7. Discussion

B. EXIT

1. Prior to exit, the student should be responsible to check that the instructor has performed the final in-aircraft equipment check, including radio when used.
2. Set-up: Following the instructors' commands, the student moves into a position on the aircraft that—
   a. allows the instructors to control the student (maximum grips) throughout the climb-out and exit
   b. provides the student with the best advantage for launching into the relative wind
3. The student should exhibit at least reasonable control during climb-out and exit before advancing.

C. FREEFALL (FLOW OF THE DIVE)

1. First-jump students should expect a momentary period of sensory overload, lasting three to five seconds, after which they can begin the freefall dive plan.
2. Circle of Awareness (CoA) for harness-hold students
   a. Heading: The student selects a prominent heading reference towards the horizon.
   b. Altitude: The student focuses on the altimeter and really reads it.
   c. Reserve-side instructor: The student makes eye contact with

the reserve-side instructor and waits for possible corrective signals followed by a smile and nod, meaning "OK!"

d. Main-side instructor: The student makes eye contact with the main-side instructor, looking for signals and affirmation.

D. HAND SIGNALS

1. Presenting hand signals
   a. All hand signals are performed with one hand and must be placed in plain view of the student, generally no closer than 12 inches from the student's face and held for a minimum of three seconds.
   b. The instructor may need to get the attention of the student first.
2. Suggested signals are shown in the Skydiver's Information Manual, Appendix A.
3. Limit hand signals to those six or seven that may be required based on observation during the student's training.
   a. For example, perfecting a student's arm position may be of low relative importance during the first jump compared to a poor arch or a tendency toward an incorrect leg position observed in training.
   b. Additional hand signals can be introduced during subsequent training.

E. CANOPY

1. Opening altitude is recommended by 4,500 feet to deal with pull-time problems and to increase canopy learning time.
2. Introduce the student to the canopy in terms that will be used throughout the course and during radio instruction.
3. Canopy training should be based on flying a specific, pre-planned pattern into a clear landing area.
   a. This portion of the training is best taught in the landing area with an aerial photograph.
   b. Refer to the canopy training outline and illustrations in Category A of the ISP syllabus for this portion of the lesson.
4. Students should be taught to look for traffic before turning.
5. The student should remain upwind in a pre-planned holding area until ready to enter the landing pattern at 1,000 feet.
6. If unable to make the planned landing area, decide on a clear alternate landing area by 2,000 feet and apply the planned pattern to the new area.

7. Final approach
   a. The student should fly a straight final approach to avoid collisions.
   b. S-turns should be avoided, except when clear of all traffic, but may be valuable in an off-field landing.
8. Discussion

F. LANDINGS

1. This section is best taught using a practical landing trainer, where the student simulates parachute landings.
2. Teach the student a prepare-to-land position that will enable an easy transition into a proper PLF.
3. The student should learn all types of obstacle landings with emphasis on obstacles the student might encounter at that DZ.
4. The student should learn the priorities of landing.
5. Round reserve training and backward PLFs may be omitted from the course if all the school's student equipment is equipped with a ram-air reserve, but a note on the type of reserve should be entered in the log of each student's jump ("RAM").
6. Students with prior tandem experience using special tandem landing techniques need to know that those techniques are not correct for a hard landing when jumping solo; introduce and demonstrate the PLF.
7. Discussion

G. EQUIPMENT EMERGENCIES

1. A USPA Coach or higher rating holder should assist and critique the jumper throughout all ground training.
2. A watch or training altimeter may be used during parachute emergency drills to help the student develop time awareness.
3. The harness trainer should be equipped with a cutaway handle and a reserve ripcord handle, each of which can actually be pulled.
4. Teach the school procedures for all parachute situations the student may encounter (follow the Category A emergency procedure outline).
5. Prior to any jump in Category A, solo students should review all emergency procedures on that day.
   a. A second complete emergency procedure review performed during Category A on another day can count toward one of the two complete reviews (one scheduled in Category B) required for the USPA A license.
   b. In the ISP program, the same review can be applied towards the emergency procedure review session in Category B.
   c. Training for main deployment problems (ripcord or hand deployment) must be included for any crossover student previously trained only for IAD or static line.

H. AIRCRAFT EMERGENCIES

The appropriately rated USPA Instructor must train first-jump or crossover students for aircraft emergency procedures specific to AFF.

I. ADDITIONAL STUDY

1. First-jump students who wish to return should be introduced to the SIM and encouraged to study all aspects of the sport that will eventually fall under their responsibility.
2. The "Book Stuff" recommended reading in ISP Category A introduces the students to the FARs and other recommendations in preparation for the oral quiz.
   a. Instructors can inform students of the seat belt requirements while boarding, and the student can study the rule from the SIM.
   b. Canopy descent
      (1) Jumpers who make a solo canopy descent assume the responsibility to land in an open area clear of persons and property on the ground even on the first jump.
      (2) AFF students have the advantage of being able to follow their instructors.
3. Introduction of the oral quiz (which can also serve as a review prior to the next jump)—
   a. establishes the student's responsibility to acquire the supporting knowledge of the sport
   b. helps generate discussion about aspects of skydiving that the student will need to understand as an A-license holder

J. REVIEW CATEGORY A QUIZ

A-2 | THE INTEGRATED STUDENT PROGRAM

2-3: FJC TRAINING PERFORMANCE STANDARDS FOR AFF STUDENTS

A. ASSESSING BY SPECIFIC OBJECTIVES

1. All first-jump ground training should be specific and oriented to measurable goals.
2. Students should be correct and consistent in demonstrating their ability to perform the tasks of the ground training in preparation for their parachute jump.
3. This section provides sample performance criteria for use in the first-jump course to help determine a student's aptitude for a solo (AFF, IAD, or static-line) jump.

B. EQUIPMENT KNOWLEDGE FOR AFF STUDENTS

1. Can find and operate all handles
2. Understands the use of the altimeter in freefall and under canopy
3. Knows to expect three complete equipment checks

C. CLIMB-OUT AND EXIT (AT THE MOCK-UP)

1. Understands and can perform the climb-out, set-up, count, and launch following the instructor's commands
2. Demonstrates sufficient strength, agility, and mental faculties during practice to perform the tasks
3. Aircraft emergency review
   a. Procedures for not exiting
   b. Procedures for reserve deployment exit
   c. Procedures for main deployment exit

D. APTITUDE FOR FREEFALL

1. Able to arch sufficiently to lift both shoulders and knees off a flat surface and hold for ten-second intervals without straining
2. During arch practice, controls both legs and arms with symmetry and extends both legs slightly
3. Recites and understands the pull priorities: pull, pull at proper altitude, and pull with stability.
4. Understands the responses to AFF freefall emergencies
   a. loss of stability
   b. loss of altitude awareness
   c. loss of one or both instructors

E. UNDERSTANDING OF CANOPY DESCENT

1. Understands canopy descent strategies well enough to solve contrived descent problems from opening to 1,000 feet:
   a. too close to the planned pattern entry point at too high an altitude—face upwind
   b. more than halfway down, but not yet halfway back—plan an alternate landing area
2. Can solve contrived landing approach problems (e.g., ISP model):
   a. too high at the planned 600-foot point—arc the base leg
   b. too low at the planned 600-foot point—cut the corner for the planned 300-foot point
   c. on final approach in a downwind direction, use only slight corrections to continue steering to a clear area with the wing level, and prepare to make a parachute landing fall following the landing flare

F. LANDING AND LANDING EMERGENCY DRILLS

1. Prior to jumping, demonstrates a proper PLF
2. Recites and understands the landing priorities: wing level, avoid obstacles, flare at least to half brakes
3. In the training harness, demonstrates the correct procedure for each landing hazard at or near the planned drop zone:
   a. power lines
   b. water
   c. trees
   d. buildings
   e. other hazards specific to the drop zone

G. EQUIPMENT PROBLEMS AND EMERGENCY DRILLS

1. Responds correctly to questions about how to handle an open parachute in the aircraft.
2. Demonstrates in the training harness—
   a. response to lost deployment handle, hard extraction
   b. how to clear a pilot chute hesitation (main or reserve)
   c. within five seconds, the correct response to contrived partial and total malfunction situations, including looking at the emergency handle(s)
   d. correct response to line twists, slider up, and end-cell closures and addresses them in that order (in case they are experienced simultaneously)
   e. the correct response to all three two-canopy-out scenarios discussed in Category A

H. REMEDIES

1. Students who do not meet these standards may—
   a. review the deficient sections of the first-jump course until demonstrating a satisfactory performance
      (1) Review on the same day if the student shows improvement during the review.
      (2) Because of the taxing nature of a solo first-jump course, some students may perform better after reviewing deficiencies another day.
   b. transfer to another discipline that doesn't require the deficient skill
   c. be discouraged from engaging in skydiving

2-4: CATEGORIES B-E, BASIC SKYDIVING SKILLS

The course staff and candidates discuss the Category B-E outline in the ISP.

CATEGORY B

A. EXIT AND FREEFALL

1. Category B serves primarily a confidence builder for the returning student.
   a. increased body awareness
   b. relaxed performance from exit through deployment
2. The student should demonstrate increasing comfort with the climb-out, set-up, and exit.
3. Relaxed freefall position ("altitude, arch, legs, relax").
   a. "Altitude" means the student must read the altimeter and understand the altitude.
   b. "Arch" means to push the hips forward slightly and smoothly and to keep them there.
   c. "Legs" means to pay attention to the leg position and place both legs in the correct position, probably extending them slightly to 45 degrees.

THE INTEGRATED STUDENT PROGRAM | **A-2**

d. "Relax" means to take a breath and relax the muscles that aren't needed for the correct body position.
4. Leg extensions and team turns help the student to understand freefall control and gain overall body awareness.
5. Reinforce the importance of an altitude check between each maneuver, when having difficulty with a maneuver, or every five seconds, whichever comes first.
6. One jump minimum is recommended in Category B.
7. With the instructor examiner, candidates review the Category B advancement criteria and the freefall dive flow from the ISP.

B. CANOPY

1. With the instructor examiner, candidates review the Category B advancement criteria and the canopy dive flow from the ISP.
2. AFF, students deficient in canopy skills may benefit from IAD, static-line, or tandem training, which places fewer demands on the student during each jump.
3. Tandem training provides a canopy instructor present on each jump.
4. Students should remain in those programs until meeting these simple objectives.

C. EMERGENCY PROCEDURE REVIEW

1. Because so much information is presented during the first-jump course, many students soon forget a great deal of their emergency procedure training.
2. The emergency procedure section of Category B serves several function.
   a. review of first-jump course emergency procedures
   b. review for all returning first-jump solo students who did not get to jump on the day of their course (log as the first or Category B emergency procedure review on the USPA A license application)
   c. review for students and experienced jumpers making currency skydives (adjust the cutaway decide-and-act altitude according to that jumper's license level)
3. Tandem students already trained in emergency procedures on another day should review them on the same day prior to making any jump in Category C.

D. EQUIPMENT

1. How a parachute opens
   a. to differentiate between malfunctions requiring only a reserve deployment and those requiring a cutaway before reserve deployment
   b. easily taught while packing or unpacking a parachute
2. Reviewing equipment retrieval at this point facilitates packing operations later for the staff.

E. RULES AND RECOMMENDATIONS

1. To make informed decisions about the safety of his or her own jumps, each student should be made aware of the pertinent BSRs.
2. Knowing the rules helps the student understand why the DZ won't allow jumps when conditions exceed the BSR limits for student operations.

F. SPOTTING AND AIRCRAFT

1. Review handle protection as a responsibility of the student.
2. Familiarize the student with the compass orientation and length of the runway in preparation for upcoming training in spotting.
3. Teaching aircraft traffic patterns early will help prevent student-aircraft conflicts on final approach and on the runway.

G. METHOD TRANSITION STUDENTS (TO AFF)

1. Review "Transitions" in the introduction to Category B.
2. Who may teach the transition course:
   a. A USPA AFF Instructor may teach the aircraft procedures, climb-out, exit, freefall, freefall communications, freefall emergencies, and aircraft emergencies.
   b. A USPA Coach or a USPA Instructor rated in another discipline may teach the remaining, general portions of the transition course for former tandem students.

H. REVIEW CATEGORY B QUIZ

CATEGORY C

A. EXIT AND FREEFALL

1. Two jumps minimum are recommended.
   a. one jump with two AFF Instructors
   b. one jump with a single AFF Instructor
2. Differences in exit with a single instructor
   a. more vertical
   b. may turn
3. On a single-instructor Category C jump and at the instructor's discretion, a student who is comfortable immediately after exit may be released, followed by the instructor flying to a no-contact facing 2-way.
4. Heading control
   a. Heading control may be passive ("altitude, arch, legs, relax").
   b. The instructor should introduce active heading control (turn method), but the student must understand that a correct body position is necessary for effective active heading control.
   c. The student's objectives are hover control using a coordinated and trimmed body position to maintain balance in freefall.
5. Introduction to wave-off (transition students)
   a. teaches the student the wave-off signal early
   b. helps protect instructors who may follow the student on future jumps
   c. trains for safety on future group freefall jumps
6. Pull priorities
   a. Pull.
   b. Pull at the correct altitude.
   c. Pull while stable.
7. Advancement criteria (instructor examiner reviews with candidates)
   a. Category C advancement criteria and the freefall dive flow recommendations from the ISP
   b. BSR advancement criteria for students making AFF-type jumps

B. CANOPY

1. Introduction to wing loading (ISP syllabus)
   a. The wing-loading exercise is especially important for drop zones with higher performance student canopies.
   b. Each student should be referred to the canopy manufacturers' websites to study recommended wing-loading.
2. Flaring
   a. Review of the concept that flaring momentarily converts forward speed to lift (from Category A).
   b. The discussion continues with the concept of the jumper swinging forward and momentarily increasing the canopy's angle of attack.

A-2 THE INTEGRATED STUDENT PROGRAM

c. The student should understand that flaring the canopy produces these results.

   (1) Pulling on the tail increases the amount of air the tail deflects to produce additional lift.

   (2) The additional drag abruptly slows the forward speed.

   (3) As the jumper swings forward, the nose raises and the momentary increased angle of attack causes the canopy to attempt to climb.

d. A canopy enters a dynamic stall when the jumper swings back under the canopy, the nose lowers, and the canopy begins a slight dive.

e. The canopy enters a full stall when the tail is held below the nose and the canopy begins to fly backwards.

f. Maintaining maximum lift (prior to stall or sink) provides a softer landing, even when significant forward speed remains.

g. Review of early flare and stall recovery actions are critical canopy survival skills and must not be overlooked.

3. Effects of higher winds

   a. Students who have exhibited good pattern flying skills in Categories A and B are introduced to—

      (1) turbulence

      (2) off-field landings

      (3) collapsing the canopy in winds (introduction for most students)

   b. The effects of a downwind landing are potentially greater, so downwind landing technique is discussed.

      (1) Flare according to height, not ground speed.

      (2) Flare normally to maximize lift and minimize final ground speed.

      (3) PLF

4. The student should by this time be able to fly a proper landing pattern with minimal assistance.

5. Landings: Students should understand when it is safe and unsafe to attempt a stand-up landing.

6. Candidates review the Category C canopy dive plan with the instructor examiner.

C. EMERGENCY PROCEDURE REVIEW

1. Remind the student that he or she must deploy at the correct altitude, regardless of stability.

2. Modification of emergency procedure for loss of both AFF Instructors: If altitude aware, in control and relaxed (AIR), continue the freefall until the assigned deployment altitude.

3. Stability recovery

   a. altitude, arch, legs, relax

   b. if caught on back, roll-out-of-bed technique

   c. if still out of control, think "AIR: Altitude aware, In control, and Relaxed."

      (1) The student must know his altitude at all times.

      (2) The student can use up to five seconds to regain control if altitude permits.

      (3) The student should be relaxed to help ensure a smooth freefall.

      (4) If still not in control, the student should deploy the main canopy.

4. Review in detail all aspects of preventing an open container in the aircraft and the associated emergency procedures.

5. Discuss in detail all aspects of landing off the intended DZ.

   a. selecting a suitable landing area

   b. anticipating and avoiding turbulence in the area

   c. other jumpers in the pattern

   d. procedures for returning without damaging property and equipment

6. Review landing priorities.

D. EQUIPMENT

1. The instructor introduces the student to equipment in more detail, including the AAD, RSL, and the strategy for the equipment check before rigging up.

   a. The introduction can be performed as the student is preparing to gear up for the jump.

   b. The student will check his or her equipment, supervised by a USPA Instructor.

2. Details about the three-ring system, AAD, and RSL are included in future categories; this is only an introduction.

3. Because of the introduction to the AAD and RSL in Category C, discussions on them can be postponed from the first-jump course.

E. RULES AND RECOMMENDATIONS

1. BSRs for student equipment

2. FARs for parachute packing (FAR 105.43)

3. state and local regulations

4. drop zone neighbor relations (with DZ manager)

F. SPOTTING AND AIRCRAFT

Planning a landing pattern for a day with moderate winds

G. METHOD TRANSITION STUDENTS

Review "Transitions" in the Introduction to Category C.

H. REVIEW CATEGORY C QUIZ

CATEGORY D

A. EXIT AND FREEFALL

1. The lesson on turning should emphasize the importance of a neutral body position prior to initiating a turn.

2. A simple technique for changing heading, such as upper body turns only, will increase confidence and improve chances for success; after the student has completed the A license program, techniques for center-point turns can be easily added.

   a. multiple 90-degree turns only on the first jump

      (1) reduces student stress and workload

      (2) increases confidence in heading control prior to initiating bigger turns, leading to greater success

      (3) reduces the likelihood of uncontrolled spins

   b. 180- and 360-degree turns, once 90-degree turns have been mastered

   c. In the event of lost heading control (spin), the student should recover lost control with "altitude, arch, legs, relax," before initiating opposite turn input.

   d. If the turn is sluggish or seems to go opposite the direction intended, the student should, provided altitude allows—

      (1) return to neutral arch

      (2) relax

      (3) extend legs

      (4) attempt the turn again

3. Release

   a. As soon as stability has been established, the instructor should release the student and move to the front.

   b. Once the student has demonstrated the ability to exit stable and comfortably without assistance, the instructor may train the student for an unassisted (no-grips) exit.

4. No new maneuvers should be initiated below 6,000 feet.
    a. Maneuvers should be finished by 5,000 feet.
    b. At 6,000 feet, the student should signal that maneuvers are finished (head shake "no").
    c. If the student initiates maneuvers below 6,000 feet, the instructor should be prepared to signal (head shake "no"), and the student responds in kind.
5. Review the importance of deployment at the correct altitude, regardless of stability.
6. Introduce alternate altitude references, e.g., looking at the ground, cloud bases, mountain tops, etc.
7. Two jumps minimum are recommended.
8. Recommended minimum deployment altitude is 4,000 feet.
9. The candidates review the Category D freefall dive flows with the Examiner.

B. CANOPY

1. Introduction of rear riser steering and flaring
    a. back-riser steering with brakes on for evasive maneuvers immediately after opening
    b. steering with brakes off to evaluate controllability with a disabled toggle
    c. flaring to be able to decide whether a canopy can be landed safely with disabled controls
2. It is not recommended that a student practice an actual landing using rear risers to flare.
3. Students should practice all maneuvers above 1,000 feet with frequent traffic and position checks.
4. Landing within 50 meters with minimal assistance is recommended before advancing.
5. The candidates review the Category D canopy dive flow with the Examiner.

C. EMERGENCY PROCEDURE REVIEW

1. Because of the lower planned deployment altitude, students should by now demonstrate the ability to rapidly recognize and respond to equipment malfunctions.
    a. Category D includes the last formal training harness review of parachute malfunctions with an instructor as required for the A license, although the student should continue to self-review each new day of jumping (at least every 30 days).
    b. Review the cutaway decide-and-act altitude (2,500 feet).
2. Various categories of the ISP provide the instructor the opportunity to review emergency procedures taught in the first-jump course and discuss them in greater detail.
3. When possible, emergency procedure review topics coincide with other related concepts from that category.
4. Detailed building or structure landing review, including disconnecting the RSL.

D. EQUIPMENT

1. The student should be calculating wing loading on both canopies (USPA Flight Planner) prior to each jump.
2. Introduce the AAD and three-ring release in detail.
    a. The student should operate the AAD.
    b. Ask the student to study the AAD owner's manual.
    c. Explain three-ring assembly and operation in detail.
    d. The student will disconnect and service the three-ring assembly in Category H.
3. Demonstrate a jumper equipment self-check and ask the student to perform it in the aircraft, followed by a check of the back of the rig by the instructor.
4. Discuss outerwear.

E. RULES AND RECOMMENDATIONS

The student should memorize the cloud clearance requirements from FAR 105.17 sufficiently to pass the Category D quiz and, later, the oral quiz as part of the USPA A-license check dive.

F. SPOTTING AND AIRCRAFT

1. The student should lead the pattern planning.
2. Introduction to spotting
    a. basic procedure overview
    b. looking straight down is the proper technique for observing the ground track of the aircraft
3. Technique for determining straight down
4. Coordinating spotting training with other jumpers
    a. In most aircraft, it is easy for the student to spot from the door, then move into position for a later exit.
    b. Experienced jumpers may need encouragement when introducing the modified pre-exit procedures.
    c. Coordinate and practice the procedures prior to takeoff.

G. METHOD TRANSITION STUDENTS

Review "Transitions" in the introduction to Category D.

H. REVIEW CATEGORY D QUIZ

CATEGORY E

A. EXIT AND FREEFALL

1. The student should attempt a stable unpoised exit.
2. AFF students begin this category supervised by an AFF Instructor until they can demonstrate reliable recovery from instability.
    a. Each student shows the ability twice to recover stability and altitude awareness within five seconds following an intentional disorienting maneuver.
    b. The first maneuver attempted should be a barrel roll, which has a natural recovery mode from back-to-earth fall.
    c. Recovery within five seconds (twice) is required to clear the student to freefall self-supervision.
3. Once any student has demonstrated stability recovery, he or she may self-supervise in freefall (requires the sign-off of a USPA Instructor).
4. Once signed off, the student should be supervised by a USPA instructional rating holder aboard the aircraft, who—
    a. is responsible and available for all training, spotting supervision, equipment choice, exit order, group separation on exit, and pre-jump equipment checks
    b. is encouraged to jump with and observe the student
    c. may make gripped exits
5. Once a student has qualified for freefall self-supervision, that student's previous training discipline is recognized only for the purpose of currency training (see SIM Section 5 on currency training).
6. Students may self-assess for the heading control required for the A license check dive (back loop within 60 degrees of the initial heading).
7. Three jumps are recommended in Category E for all students.
8. Hazards of aerobatics

A-2 THE INTEGRATED STUDENT PROGRAM

a. erratic fall rate and altimeter readings (chest mount, etc.)

b. disorientation (altitude, arch, legs, relax)

c. equipment considerations

9. The candidates review the Category E freefall dive flow with the Examiner

B. CANOPY

1. Instructor's level of understanding

   a. Candidates for the USPA Instructor rating should have a working knowledge of the aerodynamic principles of a ram-air canopy.

   b. During the course, discussion on these topics led by knowledgeable individuals is encouraged.

2. By Category E, the student should now have sufficient canopy experience to recognize the results of different flare entries (review the "nine flares" discussion in the Canopy outline in Category E).

3. The goal is for the student to learn how to assess the flare on any new or unfamiliar canopy before landing.

4. The student learns to evaluate the result of the flare by recognizing a dynamic stall following a flare on landing and to adjust flare height, flare rate, and flare depth for the next landing.

5. The candidates review the Category E canopy dive flow with the Examiner.

C. EMERGENCY PROCEDURE REVIEW

Two canopies out: Review the "Two Canopies Out" discussion in SIM Section 5-1.

D. EQUIPMENT

1. The student should be performing a pre-flight inspection on the equipment (USPA Flight Planner checklist) prior to each jump.

2. Characteristics of different canopy designs (overview)

3. A person with appropriate knowledge should introduce the student to the open parachute canopy, identifying and naming all the significant parts in preparation for packing.

E. RULES AND RECOMMENDATIONS

1. Detailed discussion on winds pertinent to the student's increased level of experience and to prepare the student to make informed decisions as a USPA A license holder

2. Discussion with pilot on portions of FAR 91 applicable to jump operations (Section 9 of the SIM)

F. SPOTTING AND AIRCRAFT

1. Category E aircraft Briefing

   a. interaction between jumpers and aircraft control

   b. reading a winds-aloft report

   c. spotting procedures

2. The USPA Instructor should be sure the student has been trained for independent action in all aircraft emergency procedures (Category E aircraft briefing) before clearing the student to freefall self-supervision.

3. Technique for determining opening point by averaging the speed and direction of winds forecast at opening altitude and read at the surface on the drop zone

G. REVIEW CATEGORY E QUIZ

2-5: GROUP SKYDIVING SKILLS

1. The last three categories of the Integrated Student Program prepare the student to jump safely and effectively in groups:

   a. tracking

   b. group exits

   c. group flying skills

   d. breakoff procedures

   e. flying the canopy in groups

2. Students who complete Category H should be ready for

   a. the USPA A License checkout with an appropriately rated USPA Instructor

   b. independent skydiving at most skydiving centers

   c. jumping at off-site DZs that meet the A-license landing area criteria (non-demos)

3. The exit and freefall sections of Categories F through H are included in the USPA Coach Rating Course syllabus.

CATEGORY F

A. EXIT AND FREEFALL

1. Tracking

   a. Emphasize legs fully extended as the primary means of movement.

   b. Demonstrate shoulder steering using a creeper or similar training aid.

   c. Make heading control the primary objective (over speed).

   d. This training will lead toward developing a better flat track during Categories G and H.

2. Two tracking dives minimum are recommended in Category F.

3. Clear and pull: Students trained in the AFF method should gain confidence with a stable exit and pull at a higher altitude (5,500 feet) before attempting the actual clear and pull at 3,500 feet.

4. The candidates review the Category F freefall dive flow with the Examiner.

B. CANOPY

1. Encourage students to become familiar with braked flight and braked landings to prevent the mistake of making a low single-toggle turn when presented with the need for a low heading change.

   a. sudden recognition of an obstacle

   b. returning from a long spot and misjudging the final turn (frequently committed error)

   c. being cut off by another jumper in the landing area

2. Use of brakes or rear risers to increase glide

   a. Anticipate loss of the tailwind nearer the ground and keep an alternate landing area in mind between the jumper's position and the target.

   b. Different canopies exhibit different flight characteristics with brake or rear riser input.

3. Anticipate a much broader landing pattern and longer final approach when flying in brakes with some canopies.

4. It is important for the USPA Instructor to understand and experience these aspects of canopy flight, particularly how they apply to the canopy the student is jumping.

5. The candidates review the Category F canopy dive flow with the Examiner.

C. EMERGENCY PROCEDURE REVIEW

Detailed power-line avoidance and landing review

D. EQUIPMENT

1. Focus on packing

2. Equipment check on another jumper (with that jumper's permission)

E. RULES AND RECOMMENDATIONS

The USPA Instructor needs to familiarize students with the existence of USPA currency recommendations in SIM Section 5.

F. SPOTTING AND AIRCRAFT

1. The student should be calculating the opening point on each jump (USPA Flight Planner).
2. Averaging the winds aloft to determine the jump run and exit point (effective only in routine conditions)
3. Separating groups according to distance across the ground
4. A dedicated spotting training and practice flight has shown to be an effective method of familiarizing students with spotting.

CATEGORIES G AND H

The course staff and candidates discuss the Category G and H outline in the ISP.

A. CANOPY

1. Category G
    a. Performance turns teach the student necessary information about his or her canopy.
        (1) how to keep the center of lift and pressure in the center of the canopy during turn entry and exit and avoid a collapse or line twist
        (2) the limits of control on that canopy with that student's weight before it develops line twists or collapses from over control
        (3) how to test the limits of any new or unfamiliar canopy
        (4) potential consequences of high-performance maneuvers near the ground
    b. Review collision avoidance, focusing on the group skydiving environment, including rights of way and the importance of avoiding a collision, regardless of the rules and courtesies.
2. Category H
    a. Front risers provide a potential third set of controls.
    b. Some jumpers will not be able to take advantage of front riser control, but should realize their limits compared to other jumpers.
    c. Emphasize front riser safety: The canopy must be returned to straight and level flight in time for landing.

B. EMERGENCY PROCEDURE REVIEW

1. Category G
    a. A USPA Instructor reviews in detail the procedures for responding to an imminent canopy collision and what to do in the event of an entanglement.
    b. A canopy formation specialist makes a good resource for teaching this topic.
2. Category H (USPA Instructor or Examiner)
    a. training for an unintentional water landing
    b. training for an unplanned low turn under canopy

C. EQUIPMENT

1. Category G
    a. The student continues to focus on packing, and should pack one parachute without assistance prior to advancing to Category H.
    b. An FAA rigger or an instructor should conduct the wear and maintenance seminar outlined in this Section of the ISP syllabus, including a review of the FARs concerning maintenance personnel.
2. Category H
    a. three ring disassembly, maintenance, and reassembly
    b. discussion of stow band choice (review)
    c. replacement and adjustment of a main closing loop

D. RULES AND RECOMMENDATIONS

1. Category G: repack cycle (review) and rigger maintenance
2. Category H: general review of the oral quizzes for the A license check dive

E. SPOTTING AND AIRCRAFT

1. Category G
    a. The student should be calculating the spot, including the exit point, for each jump in routine winds (USPA Flight Planner).
    b. Jumpers need to be responsible for knowing the kinds of weather that can get them into trouble.
    c. The instructor or pilot should review the various means of finding weather forecasts.
2. Category H
    a. This section is best taught by a jump pilot or instructor.
    b. A license holders are qualified to jump at locations other than a regular drop zone and should know—
        (1) where to find the information for notifying ATC of the jump.
        (2) equipment and approval requirements for jump aircraft
    c. In general, USPA A-license holders should know what to expect of the aircraft operator at the drop zone in terms of paperwork for modifications and maintenance.

2-6: VERIFYING USPA LICENSES

1. A license
    a. Review SIM Section 3-2 for conducting the USPA A-license check dive and completing the USPA A license application.
    b. Compare and contrast the two A license applications.
        (1) four-page A License Progression Card, designed for use with the ISP
        (2) two-page A License Proficiency Card for use with equivalent programs or for unlicensed jumpers who began training prior to the Basic Safety Requirement for a USPA A license (January, 2001).
2. B and C license
    a. Review SIM Section 3-2 for instructions and procedures regarding the USPA B and C license, with particular attention to the license application checklist.
        (1) exam administration
        (2) verification of qualifications
    b. Review the USPA B-D License Application, available online at uspa.org/downloads.
    c. Only a USPA S&TA, Examiner or member of the USPA Board of Directors may approve D license applications.

A-3 | AFF METHOD

3-1: AFF ROUTINE PROCEDURES

A. INTRODUCTION

1. The nature of AFF provides the instructor with more opportunity for interaction and assistance with the freefall portion of the student's skydive.
2. AFF training and jumping requires special flying and in-air student handling skills.
3. The two-instructor jumps in Categories A through C also require effective teamwork and specific direction for each AFF instructor to handle exit and freefall emergencies.

B. AFF EQUIPMENT

1. Review the BSRs for student and instructor equipment and the instructors' altimeter requirements for harness-hold jumping.
2. Student's main deployment system
   a. BOC activation handle: The main-side instructor should grip low on the leg strap to avoid crowding the student's main deployment handle area.
   b. hand deployment (BOC only) may be equipped with a left-side pouch release
   c. ripcord locations
      (1) BOC makes it virtually impossible to see the handle and promotes arching.
      (2) Main lift web (high or low) allows the student see the ripcord, but requires that the student concentrate on arching while looking at the handle.
      (3) Most ripcord systems can be configured for a redundant left-side activation handle for use by the reserve-side instructor.
3. The following may prove useful for AFF Instructors:
   a. variety of jumpsuits suitable to a range of student fall rates
   b. hard-shelled helmet
   c. audible altimeter
   d. second visual altimeter
   e. suitable footwear
4. AADs, hard-shell helmets, and audible altimeters are strongly recommended for USPA instructional rating holders when making training jumps with students.

C. IN-FLIGHT PROCEDURES

1. Once the seat belts are off, the student should stay relaxed and spend the remainder of the flight mentally rehearsing and self-calming.
2. If possible, just before the approximate deployment altitude, review airport and landing area, opening point, and landing pattern.
3. Continue with a review of the deployment altitude with the student at that point during ascent and review the freefall dive flow and hand signals.
4. After the verbal review, give the student "quiet time" to mentally review the dive flow.
5. Approximately 4,000 feet below exit altitude, instructors perform the pre-exit equipment check, including radio.

D. CLIMB-OUT AND SET-UP PROCEDURES

GENERAL

1. Use a procedure that enables the student to get into position with minimal effort.
   a. The student should be trained to avoid presenting his or her full torso broad to the wind during the transition from the door to the set-up (should "knife" into the wind).
   b. To avoid muscle strain and injury, the student should limit arm and shoulder extension to 90 degrees and avoid reaching to full arm extension while climbing out.
2. The inboard instructor checks and controls hand and foot placement in the door.
3. Single-instructor exit
   a. may be from either side
   b. may result in a different dynamic upon launch
   c. less hands-on supervision during the climb-out required as the student progresses

STRUT EXIT (CESSNA)

1. Student may sit back-to-the-instrument-panel or kneel facing forward by the door.
2. Main-side instructor climbs out first.
   a. Main-side instructor: "Ready to skydive?"
   b. Student: "Yes!"
   c. Main-side instructor: "Put your feet out after me and stop. Take your instructions from the reserve-side instructor."
      (1) Main-side instructor climbs to the end of the strut, left foot on the step, and left hand free to take a grip on the student's leg strap.
      (2) The reserve-side instructor: assists the student into the pre-climb-out position, maintaining a firm harness grip throughout.
      (3) The student moves into the pre-climb-out position, protecting handles, and waits for the climb-out command from the reserve-side instructor.
   d. Reserve-side instructor (after getting the "ready" signal from the outboard instructor): "Climb out!"

Helpful hint: Handle the gear for the student during climb-out, actually lifting the equipment into position and relieving the student of the weight through the transition from the door to the step.

   (1) The student moves into pre-exit position, balanced on one foot, chest forward over the wing strut, and the other leg extended and flying.
   (2) The main-side instructor receives the student's right (outboard) leg strap.
   (3) The reserve-side instructor establishes a second positive grip, moves one foot to the inside of the step, and prepares for exit.
   e. Student (looks at reserve side instructor): "Check in!"
   f. Reserve-side instructor (positive head shake): "OK!" and moves torso-to-torso to prepare to launch the student.
   g. Student (looks at main-side instructor): "Check out!"
   h. Main-side instructor (positive head shake): "OK!"
   i. Student takes a relaxing breath and initiates the exit count.

SIDE DOOR

1. Several methods are used, depending on school preference; choose an exit according to the following criteria (in descending order):
   a. ability for instructors to establish and maintain the maximum number of grips for positive control and launch
   b. ability for instructors to get a clean launch

c. ability for student to present hips to wind during the set-up and count

d. ability for both instructors to follow the student's count

e. ability to set up quickly for spotting and multiple-group exit purposes

2. Examples

   a. student's hands sandwich the forward edge of the door frame ("praying" exit), one instructor floating, one inside

   b. three diving

      (1) requires a wide door, e.g., Twin Otter

      (2) The exit trio dives forward into the relative wind for best results.

   c. three floating

   d. other

3. The student checks in with the inboard instructor first, or front instructor if all three are floating.

TAILGATE

1. All three face forward toward the front of the plane and walk backward into position.

2. Student checks in with reserve-side instructor first.

3. Student counts with physical cadence of up-down-launch ("Arch!").

E. EXIT

1. Outboard instructor

   a. The point of no return is reached once the student's hips break the plane of the door (side-door or tailgate aircraft) and the outboard instructor—

      (1) must leave with the student

      (2) may lead the student once the launch is certain

   b. Under no circumstances should the instructor pull the student out of the door or off the aircraft.

2. The inboard instructor must also ensure that launch is complete once it has begun, which may involve carrying the student over the step (Cessna) or door sill.

3. Reduce unwanted momentum.

   a. The least movement necessary to clear the aircraft will reduce momentum and help make the exit smooth.

   b. Both instructors should exit as close as possible, shoulder-to-shoulder with the student to reduce post-launch dynamics.

4. Both instructors should establish arm grips before or during the exit.

5. Regardless of the count, as the student's hips go, so goes the student.

F. EXIT PROBLEMS

1. The instructors must work together to maintain stability until the student establishes the correct body position.

2. In the initial phase of the freefall, the student may respond to verbal commands (main-side instructor).

3. The reserve-side instructor presents the initial corrective signals during the first CoA, while main side maintains grips as necessary to assist with stability.

G. FREEFALL SEQUENCE (NON-RELEASE)

1. Initial scan priorities

   a. right-side instructor: waist up, with occasional full body scan

   b. left-side instructor: waist down, with occasional full body scan

2. Free arm at the first opportunity and whenever possible.

3. Both instructors respond with signals as necessary, followed by a vigorous "thumbs up!" during the CoAs.

4. Practice deployment assistance (only as needed).

   a. The main-side instructor prompts the student for practice deployments, with the reserve-side instructor as a back-up.

   b. The main-side instructor guides the student's hand to the deployment handle.

      (1) Students may mistakenly grab the instructors left-hand mounted altimeter during practice deployments or on the actual deployment

      (2) Main side instructors should consider moving the altimeter to the right hand or using a chest-mounted altimeter

      (3) Sliding the left hand as far as possible down the student's leg strap will usually provide enough distance from the student's BOC handle to allow the student to reach the BOC handle with no interference from a left-hand mounted altimeter.

   c. The reserve-side instructor prompts the student for correct left-arm placement.

5. Deployment

   a. The main-side instructor prompts as necessary for altitude checks and main canopy deployment (reserve-side as back-up for signaling if main-side can't get the student's attention).

   b. The main-side instructor assists as necessary with main canopy deployment or initiates deployment if below 4,000 feet.

AFF METHOD | A-3

c. The reserve-side instructor ensures student main canopy deployment by 3,500 feet.

d. To reduce the burble, the main-side instructor departs upon initiation of deployment.

e. If hand-deploy pilot chutes are used, the main side instructor must ensure the pilot chute has been thrown by the student before departing.

f. The reserve-side instructor maintains grips through deployment (until inflation begins).

   (1) may be able to assist with a variety of deployment problems and high-speed malfunctions

   (2) must be careful not to pull the student down on one side (roll axis), which may induce a line twist

   (3) must avoid the student's legs to prevent being kicked during deployment and inflation (possibly fatal error)

g. Both instructors must get clear and deploy by 2,500 feet.

H. FREEFALL SEQUENCE (DUAL-INSTRUCTOR RELEASE)

1. Levels of instructor response

   a. Initial student full release by no lower than 6,000 feet.

   b. Fly the slot.

      (1) It is not necessary to touch a student to give hand signals.

      (2) An AFF Instructor needs to be able to stay with a student who is moving around.

   c. Block excessive movement.

      (1) Excessive movement for Category C is a student rotating more than 45 degrees from his heading after the release.

      (2) A block is not a gripped re-dock, but there should still be an appropriate hand signal provided by the candidate following any blocking maneuvers.

   d. Re-dock, correct, re-release.

      (1) Re-dock when learning has ceased or control is in question, such as a rotation of more than 360 degrees during a Category C jump.

      (2) Fix the problem with the correct hand signals, then release immediately.

A-3 | AFF METHOD

(i) Only the initial release must occur above 6,000 feet.

(ii) A common mistake is to re-dock, give a "relax" signal, and re-release.

(iii) A relax signal is not a fix-all; give the appropriate signal specific to the instruction needed.

e. The situation requires a re-dock with no further release if the student's body position or awareness fail to improve even with appropriate signals.

f. No initial release when a student's body position and awareness are inappropriate to earn a release.

2. Once the student has demonstrated relaxed stability, the main-side instructor signals for the reserve-side instructor to release and fly within one arm's length of the student.

3. The main-side instructor releases and flies within one arm's length of the student.

4. Heading drift is acceptable, and instructors should follow.

   a. The instructors correct small movements or body position problems using no-contact hand signals or blocking techniques.

   b. The instructors should provide the student enough room to recognize and correct problems without prompting or assistance.

   c. If the student rotates more than 90 degrees relative to the instructors, the instructors should switch roles rather than struggle to chase the turn to maintain their original positions.

5. On the first jump in Category C (two instructors), the reserve-side instructor may lightly re-grip at 6,000 feet through deployment; however, the student must demonstrate a stable, ungripped deployment before advancing to freefall maneuvers (Category D), according to the BSRs.

6. Re-gripping on evaluations jumps

   a. Re-gripping a stable student is not acceptable for in-air evaluations of the AFF Instructor Rating Course.

   b. AFF Instructor candidates should re-grip only as prescribed in the evaluation procedures.

I. SINGLE-INSTRUCTOR RELEASE

1. The instructor releases the student once he or she demonstrates awareness and control.

2. The instructor flies into the best position to communicate with and assist the student as necessary through the freefall exercises and deployment.

J. UNDER CANOPY

1. Once achieving sufficient separation, the main-side instructor opens as high as possible after the student to provide visual guidance.

2. The reserve-side instructor backs up as necessary.

3. The instructors demonstrate the preferred canopy pattern.

K. DEBRIEF

Both instructors assist with the debrief, corrective training, and record keeping.

3-2: AFF PROBLEM SOLVING

A. INTRODUCTION

1. On any AFF dive, particularly a release dive, the instructor(s) must choose the best course of action, based on the student's performance.

2. The following responses are to be applied as the situation dictates.

B. CLIMB-OUT AND SET-UP

Note: Wherever there is no distinction in the exit between inboard and outboard instructors, such as on a tailgate aircraft, replace "inboard instructor" with "reserve-side instructor."

1. If the student refuses to jump or takes too long to climb out—

   a. If possible, the inboard instructor should retrieve the student's equipment, and the student will follow.

   b. If it's not possible to retrieve the student, jump as planned and make sure the student and instructors deploy high enough to return to the drop zone.

   c. The safety of the student and others in the aircraft must be the first consideration.

2. If the student has difficulty getting foot placement or performing the climb-out procedure correctly—

   a. The inboard instructor physically assists the student into position.

   b. The outboard instructor assists as necessary and if able.

3. If the student climbs out before the instructor's command—

   a. The inboard instructor prevents the student from making further movement.

   b. The outboard instructor grips the student if the student makes it to the set-up position before the inboard instructor gets control of the situation.

C. COUNT

1. If the student won't look at the inboard instructor after climbing outside—

   a. The inboard instructor shakes the student's shoulder or shouts to get the student's attention.

   b. The outboard instructor prompts the student to check in.

2. If the student doesn't start the hotel check or exit count:

   a. The inboard instructor shakes the student for attention and encourages initiation of the count, for example, shouting, "OK!"

   b. The outboard instructor backs up the inboard instructor as necessary.

3. If the student begins or performs the count incorrectly, the instructors follow the student's body movement.

D. LAUNCH

1. If the student initiates a back loop—

   a. The inboard instructor forces the student's upper body down.

   b. The outboard instructor yells, "Arch!" and assists with bringing the formation under control.

2. If the student reverses arch—

   a. The inboard instructor forces the student into an arch.

   b. The outboard instructor maintains stability and yells, "Arch!"

3. If the student goes head down on exit—

   a. The inboard instructor forces the student's upper body up.

   b. The outboard instructor yells, "Arch!" and assists with bringing the formation under control.

4. If the student slides towards the outboard instructor off the strut—

   a. The inboard instructor goes with the student and maintains control of the formation.

   b. The outboard instructor moves to make room for the student and assists with control of the exit.

E. EXIT

1. Above all else, do not deviate from a planned decision when confronted with an unstable student.

2. Tumbling exit

   a. The instructors should attempt to roll with the tumble and get the student facing into the relative wind.

   b. The main-side instructor shakes the student and yells, "Arch!"

c. If the piece does not recover stability (two or three tumbles or more than five seconds), the instructor who is not contributing to stability releases (a very serious decision), and the remaining instructor regains stability.

   (1) If one instructor and the student are stable, the unstable instructor should release, recover, and re-dock.

   (2) If the piece is tumbling with neither instructor able to gain control, only the reserve-side instructor should release to allow the main-side instructor to fly the piece. Follow the plan for a tumbling exit.

3. If the student and remaining instructor are on their backs spinning (roll-over technique)—

   a. The instructor on grips—

      (1) releases the arm grip and flips face-to earth, while maintaining a firm harness grip

      (2) stops any turning or rotation before initiating the roll-over maneuver.

      (3) reaches across the student to a grip on the opposite main lift web or leg strap, clear of any operation handles.

      (4) pushes down on the near grip while pulling on the farther grip to roll the student over, yelling, "Arch!"

   b. The released instructor should remain alongside and no higher than level to assist as soon as the formation re-stabilizes or in case the other instructor loses both grips.

   c. The remaining instructor rejoins the group.

   d. Both instructors continue to work with the student to restore a good body position.

4. AFF jumps should be made from a minimum of 9,500 feet AGL.

F. CATEGORY A AND B PROBLEMS

Throughout the flow of the dive, the instructors should make a mental note of incorrect student performance both for the debrief and as a possible indicator of events to come.

1. No Circle of Awareness after the first five seconds: Main- or reserve-side instructor shakes the student's arm as necessary and signals for the CoA.

2. Problems with the CoA (the student looks at the wrong instructor first; looks away before the instructor acknowledges): The instructors keep the flow of the dive moving.

3. Ripcord handle out of pocket and floating or pilot chute dislodged (possible responses)

   a. Main-side instructor replaces the handle.

   b. Main-side instructor signals for deployment higher than planned.

   c. Main-side instructor deploys for the student as appropriate.

4. If the student establishes an incorrect body position (hard arch, hands too far forward, reverse arch, etc.)—

   a. Instructors note the problem during the initial scan and correct during the CoA.

   b. If correction is needed before the CoA, the reserve-side instructor provides the primary instruction, using hand signals.

5. If the student doesn't start the practice deployments—

   a. Main-side instructor guides the student's hand to the handle.

   b. The reserve-side instructor signals for practice deployments.

6. Incorrect hand placement during practice deployments

   a. The instructors should correct as follows:

      (1) The main-side instructor guides the student's right hand to the deployment handle.

      (2) The reserve-side instructor guides the student's left hand.

   b. If the student's hand placement during the practice deployments is unsafe (for example on the cutaway handle), the instructor should be prepared to stop unsafe movement during the actual deployment.

   c. If the main-side instructor is struggling with the student, the reserve-side instructor should assist with main deployment.

7. If the student's body position deteriorates during or after the practice deployments, the instructor should re-grip if necessary, signal corrections, and note for the debrief.

8. If the practice deployments come too slowly and begin to overlap tasks to be performed at a lower altitude, the instructors should re-grip and signal or otherwise ensure deployment at the correct altitude.

9. If the student panics, the instructors gain the student's attention or otherwise control the situation and initiate a higher-than-normal deployment.

10. Late wave-off (below 5,500 feet)

    a. It is a common procedure for the student to be told to "lock on" to the altimeter 500 feet prior to initiation of the deployment sequence, which generally begins with a wave-off.

    b. The lock-on and wave-off signal the instructors that the student is aware of altitude and ready to act accordingly.

    c. Missing either is an early cue of confusion; procedure—

       (1) Instructors signal for altitude check if above 5,000 feet.

       (2) Instructors signal for deployment if below 5,000 feet.

11. If the student fixates on the video or otherwise loses track of altitude—

    a. The instructors redirect the student's attention back to the skydive.

    b. In the event of video fixation with a videographer who holds an AFF rating, the videographer may signal the student to deploy (included in the student's briefing).

    c. Instructors signal the student to pull or otherwise initiate deployment themselves (according to procedure) by 3,500 feet.

G. CATEGORY C (RELEASE DIVE) PROBLEMS

1. If the student establishes an incorrect body position—

   a. The instructors correct the student prior to release if it appears that the problem will affect stability.

   b. The instructors begin the release procedure (reserve-side first on main-side's signal) tentatively to make sure that the student is controlling the freefall.

2. Heading drift following release: The instructors maintain their position relative to the student without contact and try not to become a distraction.

3. In the event of a spin (heading change greater than 360 degrees at a rate that instructors can't follow), pronounced backslide, or extreme buffeting, the instructors should re-dock.

   a. Main-side instructor presents the corrective signal, with reserve-side instructor as a back-up.

   b. Re-release if the student responds.

4. Stopping a spin

   a. Stop the spin before it becomes hazardous.

   b. Get level with the student and close.

      (1) Don't rush.

      (2) Aim for the rotation point (center) of the spin.

A-3 | AFF METHOD

(3) Drive forward with legs and maintain positive pressure.

(4) When faced with a fast spin, protect your head by raising the forearm that's into the spin.

(5) Take the first grip that presents itself between the elbows and the knees.

(6) Grabbing a student's forearm, wrist, hand, or foot to assist with stability, particularly a spin, usually results in inverting the student.

5. Regaining lost stability following release
   a. React quickly and aggressively in re-docking on a student who requires stability assistance and corrections.
   b. Re-dock at the hips or near the center of mass.
   c. Use the roll-over technique if the student loses stability before the instructors can re-grip.

6. Role reversal
   a. If both instructors are chasing a student following a large separation, the closer instructor should go to closer side of the student.
   b. Instructors should know both roles and not struggle to regain an original position.

H. CATEGORY D (SINGLE INSTRUCTOR) PROBLEMS

1. No circle of awareness after exit:
   a. The instructor assesses the student's body position and (if no major problems exist) moves to the front.
   b. If the student appears attentive and simply missed the CoA, the instructor signals for the practice deployment (optional), if not already completed.
   c. As soon as the student appears in control, the instructor releases and moves into the facing position.

2. If the student does not indicate readiness for release, the instructor encourages the student and releases when safe.

3. If the 2-way piece spins during the transition (grip switch), minor tension (gripped), or minor backsliding (ungripped) on facing 2-way, the instructor signals for "legs out."

4. Turn not initiated following release: The instructor signals that the student should turn (stirring motion).

5. No altitude check (Circle of Awareness following turn): The instructor presents the "CoA" signal.

6. If the student slides during the turn, the instructor remains within arm's reach.

7. If the turn stalls or the student begins to spin—
   a. The instructor becomes more conservative and re-docks to correct the student with the appropriate hand signals, attempting to salvage as much student learning as possible.
   b. The problem is most often solved by having the student extend both legs slightly and relax.

8. If the turn overshoots—
   a. If the student is in control (turn rate constant or decreasing), allow one revolution to correct (stop turn if it exceeds 720 degrees).
   b. If the turn is accelerating (happens rapidly as student tenses), re-dock immediately and correct as required with the appropriate hand signals.

9. If the student is back to earth and not recovering by arching, the instructor re-docks and performs the roll-over technique, carefully watching altitude.

10. If the student tumbles—
    a. The instructor re-docks, restores control, and tries to salvage as much learning as possible.
    b. It may be inappropriate to re-release the student for a solo deployment.

11. If the student is still turning or appears ready to continue turns below 6,000 feet, the instructor re-docks and signals "no more turns," and re-releases only after the student acknowledges.

12. If the student is attempting turns at wave-off altitude, the instructor signals for wave-off or deployment (depending on altitude) and approaches the student in preparation for a re-dock, if required.

13. If the student has difficulty with initiating deployment, signal or assist as appropriate.

I. DEPLOYMENT (BOTTOM-END SEQUENCE)

1. Standard sequence of deployment problem solving
   a. Present "altimeter check" signal.
   b. Signal for deployment.
   c. Re-dock (if released), in case assistance is necessary.
   d. Assist the student with deployment.
   e. Deploy for the student.

2. Category A and B deployment problems
   a. Missed main handle: The main-side instructor guides student's hand to the handle.
   b. The student performs another practice deployment.
      (1) The main-side instructor signals for pull (if above 4,500 feet) and deploys the student's parachute at or below 4,500 feet.
      (2) The reserve-side instructor signals for deployment until 4,500 feet and then deploys the student's main between 4,500 to 4,000 feet
         (i) if the student is equipped with a reserve-side main-activation handle
         (ii) if the primary main activation handle is available to the reserve-side instructor

DEPLOYMENT PROBLEM SEQUENCE FOR CATEGORY C

AFF Main Instructor | AFF Student | AFF Reserve Instructor

	AFF Main Actions	AFF Student Actions	AFF Reserve Actions
Flying Slot	Between Hip & Elbow	Between Instructors	At Hip
6,000 ft.	Present altitude signal	Lock On ←No Response→	Present altitude signal
5,500 ft.	Present pull signal	Wave Off ←No Response→	Present pull signal
5,000 ft.	Re-dock and assist student with pull	Pull ←No Response→	Re-dock and assist student with pull
4,500 ft.	Pull for student (if alone, ride through deployment)	Minimum Pull Altitude ←No Response→	Pull for student and ride through deployment
4,000 ft.			

(3) If the student's main can't be deployed, the reserve-side instructor deploys the student's reserve by 3,000 feet.

3. Deployment problem sequence for Category C skydive (two instructors)

   a. No wave-off at 6,000 feet: The instructors present "altitude check" signals from 6,000 feet to 5,500 feet.

   b. No initiation of deployment at 5,500 feet: The instructors give the student the "pull" signal from 5,500 feet to 5,000 feet.

   c. No response, slow response, or incorrect response to deployment signal

      (1) The main-side instructor re-docks to assist deployment from 5,000 feet to 4,500 feet.

      (2) The reserve-side instructor re-docks to assist stability and continues to give the pull signal.

   d. If the student fights the assist, the main-side instructor deploys for the student between 4,500 feet and no lower than 4,000 feet.

   e. The reserve-side instructor initiates main deployment for the student below 4,500 feet but before 4,000 feet.

   f. If the main can't be deployed, the reserve-side instructor deploys the student's reserve by 3,000 feet.

4. Deployment problem sequence for Category D

Note: The recommended ISP deployment altitude is 500 feet lower in Category D than Category C. Use the following sequence for deployment problem solving on Category C single-instructor jumps, but begin everything 500 feet higher.

   a. No wave-off: The instructor gives a wave-off prompt at 5,500 feet to 5,000 feet.

   b. No response, slow response, or incorrect response to wave-off signal: The instructor gives the pull signal at 5,000 feet.

   c. No response, slow response, or incorrect response to deployment signal: The instructor re-docks to assist at 4,500 feet.

   d. If the student fights the assist: The instructor deploys for the student between 4,500 feet and no lower than 4,000 feet.

   e. If the main can't be deployed, the instructor deploys the student's reserve by 3,500 feet.

5. General

   a. The instructors must ensure student main deployment by 3,500 feet to allow both instructors time to get clear and open by 2,500 feet.

   b. No instructor should ever get above a student.

      (1) A student can deploy without warning.

      (2) AADs sometimes activate higher than the preset altitude.

   c. The instructor(s) must ensure student's reserve deployment by 3,000 feet to get clear and open by 2,500 feet.

   d. Under no circumstances should an instructor attempt to catch a student or remain with a student below the instructor's minimum deployment (2,500 feet).

   e. The instructors must take care that one does not deploy the student's main while the other deploys the reserve.

      (1) Only if the main deployment handle is inaccessible should the reserve-side instructor deploy the student's reserve parachute.

      (2) Many systems have reserve-side instructor deployment handles to make deploying the main parachute easier for the reserve-side instructor.

3-3: AFF EMERGENCIES

A. AIRCRAFT MALFUNCTION

1. The correct response to a low-altitude emergency will always depend on circumstances, including the severity of the problem, the capabilities of the aircraft, the available terrain for landing the plane or parachute, and the abilities of the jumpers aboard.

2. Landing with the aircraft is usually required for most aircraft emergencies that occur below 1,500 feet.

   a. The student takes all direction from the instructor(s).

   b. Fasten seat belts and buckle helmets, as necessary.

   c. For any aircraft descent, disarm the AAD as required (see owner's manual).

   d. Prepare for a hard landing.

3. Bailout: Exit and pull reserve.

   a. The instructor guides the student to the door.

   b. The student places his or her left hand on the reserve ripcord and pulls two seconds after exit.

   c. With sufficient altitude, the student may use a similar procedure with the main parachute.

4. A poised exit and pull with either one or both instructors may be made whenever altitude allows.

   a. Poised exits should be eliminated whenever the exit altitude is below 4,500 feet.

   b. Make a normal climb-out and exit.

   c. The main-side instructor may need to deploy the student's main parachute, depending on the amount of time available and the student's experience and performance.

DEPLOYMENT PROBLEM SEQUENCE FOR CATEGORY D

AFF Student   AFF Main or Reserve Instructor

	AFF Student Actions		AFF Instructor Actions
6,000 ft.	No more maneuvers (shake their head)		Flying out in front
	Student attempts to keep turning →		Just below 6,000 ft., AFFI gives wave-off signal, head shake "no," flies toward closest hip, and blocks turn (no dock)
5,000 ft.	Wave off	No Response →	Present pull signal, dock and assist student hand with pull
4,500 ft.	Pull		
4,000 ft.	Min. pull altitude	No Response →	Pull for student and ride through deployment

A-3 | AFF METHOD

B. PARACHUTE OPEN IN THE AIRCRAFT

1. If the parachute stays inside, first close the door, then notify the pilot.
   a. Main—disconnect the canopy release system and reserve static line, turn off the AAD, and all ride down with the aircraft.
   b. Reserve—
      (1) There are different considerations for an open reserve container depending on the airplane and the location of the jumper in the airplane.
      (2) One response might be to have the jumper completely remove the rig and land with the airplane, although this may not be practical depending on the airplane.
      (3) Another option is to have the jumper contain the reserve pilot chute and press the container against the inside of the fuselage to prevent the reserve freebag from escaping, and land with the airplane.
2. If the parachute goes out the door, the student must exit quickly without waiting for a command from either instructor.

C. PREMATURE DEPLOYMENT DURING THE EXIT SET-UP

1. If possible, the pilot should quickly skid the aircraft to get the horizontal stabilizer out of the path of the deploying parachute.
2. The instructor(s) must get the student off the aircraft immediately.

D. SKYDIVER IN TOW

1. If the student is conscious and recognizes the problem and the parachute is the main parachute, the student should attempt to cut away and deploy the reserve.
2. If the student is unconscious or the parachute is a reserve parachute, the response will depend on the circumstances, including—
   a. controllability of the aircraft
   b. landing terrain or facilities available to the aircraft
3. If the student is in tow due to an entanglement with a seat belt or jump suit, cut the offending attachment.

E. DEPLOYMENT PROBLEMS

1. Student experiences a hard pull.
   a. The instructor(s) re-docks, if necessary.
   b. The main-side instructor assists with the pull until 4,000 feet.
   c. The reserve-side instructor (if available) attempts to deploy the main from 4,000 to 3,500 feet.
   d. If the student has not initiated reserve deployment by 3,500 feet, the instructor (reserve-side, if available) deploys the student's reserve by 3,000 feet.
2. High-speed malfunction (container lock, pilot chute hesitation, pilot chute in tow, bag lock): The reserve-side instructor remains to assist the student to no lower than 3,000 feet and leaves in time to get clear and open by 2,500 feet.

F. INCORRECT SPOT

1. The instructor(s) should check the spot before beginning to exit and re-evaluate once in freefall.
2. If the spot is wrong, the instructor(s) should give the deployment signal high enough for the student and instructors to return to the landing area.
3. If the student opens too low to return to the landing area, the main-side instructor should lead the student into an acceptable alternate landing area, with the reserve-side instructor as a back-up.

4. Instructor's Duties

4-1: CONDUCTING THE JUMP

A. STUDENT PREPARATION (ASSESS, REVIEW, TRAIN)

1. Introduction of student and instructor(s)
   a. on the instructor's initiative
   b. familiarizes the two with each other
   c. sets the tone for the conduct of the training and jump
2. Administrative
   a. paperwork (registration, waiver)
   b. payment
   c. documentation available (logbook, A license application card)
   d. training and review complete
3. Personal
   a. water, food, restroom
   b. pockets cleared, jewelry off, gum disposed
   c. special considerations (medical)
4. Disposition
   a. behavior consistent and positive
   b. perspiration
   c. breath
   d. breathing rate
   e. rate of movement (nervous or jumpy?)
   f. voice

B. TRAINING

1. Each instructor is responsible for all previous training.
   a. thorough review of the student's performance records
      (1) logbook
      (2) A license application card
      (3) DZ master log
      (4) discussion with previous instructors
   b. student's subjective evaluation of the previous jump (What did the student think?)
   c. questions specific to the last skydive
   d. thorough review of the required areas in the Integrated Student Program for that particular category of jump based on student's logbook.
   e. The following training aids may be used during review training:
      (1) aircraft mock-up
      (2) training harness
      (3) landing trainer
      (4) other
   f. The longer the interval between jumps, the more the student will have forgotten.
2. Introduce the performance objectives of the next lesson and advancement criteria for the next jump.
   a. Use the AFF team-teaching concept if possible, otherwise be prepared to teach a solo session.
      (1) If team teaching, split 60/40, main-side/reserve-side instructor.
      (2) The reserve-side instructor facilitates the training and provides quality control.
   b. Use appropriate descriptions and demonstrations.
   c. Conduct informal rehearsals using the appropriate training aids to enhance realism.
3. Be sure the student is equipped correctly for the skydive (equipment check before rigging up).
4. Prepare the canopy flight plan.
5. Conduct a full-dress rehearsal or dirt dive until the student performs everything smoothly and correctly.
   a. without coaching or prompting
   b. real time
6. Perform the pre-boarding equipment check.
   a. Instructors check the student, including all personal items and the radio.
   b. Instructors check each other's equipment in front of the student.

C. ABOARD THE AIRCRAFT

1. Monitor the student's equipment.
2. Coordinate exit position and planned interaction with other jumpers or groups during exit.
3. Encourage self-reliance.
4. Conduct the pre-exit equipment check.
5. Supervise spotting, according to the student's level.

D. JUMP SUPERVISION

According to AFF method

E. POST JUMP

1. Verify that the student has landed safely and returned to the operations center.
   a. All equipment accounted for and put away.
   b. The student knows the debrief plan.
2. Debriefing
   a. The debrief provides instructors with an opportunity to facilitate the learning process by encouraging the student to recognize their achievements and what they did correctly, as well as help them realize what is needed to move forward in their skill development.
   b. The student must become more aware of their strengths and weaknesses and take responsibility for their training.
   c. The debrief process contains the following steps:
      (1) restate the goals
      (2) things that worked
      (3) things that need improvement
      (4) how to improve
      (5) make new goals
   d. Restate the goals
      (1) the student will most likely focus on the negative parts of the jump
      (2) restating the goals helps them open up their mind to the rest of the tasks whether it be the exit, break-off or canopy control tasks
   e. Things that worked
      (1) ask the student what went well on the jump, what he did well
      (2) the student will naturally want to focus on the negative; by having him state what he did well on the jump, it starts the debrief on a positive note
      (3) this process will need to be repeated on several jumps before the student typically starts to enter the debrief on a positive note stating what they liked about their performance then noting what they need to improve on
   f. Things that need improvement
      (1) ask the student what needs improvement

A-4 INSTRUCTOR'S DUTIES

   (2) this lets you know if the student is aware of his errors

   (3) if the student overlooks a part of the skydive that should have been recalled, play through the video again and ask him how he felt about performing the skill to see if it jogs his memory

   (4) if it does not, this is the instructor's opportunity to restate the goals of the jump and provide guidance on how to improve

g. How to improve

   (1) ask this question to the student

   (2) the student should have a good idea of what he needs to work on

   (3) if the student cannot see the answer, this is the opportunity for the instructor to review the correct techniques and assist him to see what is needed

   (4) patience and good listening skills of the instructor will help the student take charge of his learning and become further committed to his goals

h. Make new goals

   (1) ask the student what he would like to do on the next jump

   (2) if the goals and expectations of each jump are clear, the student should be quite realistic about his performance

   (3) if the environment has been set that "mistakes are OK" the student should have a realistic assessment of what he needs to do on the next jump, even if it means repeating the same jump

   (4) the Instructor's role during the debrief should be one of a facilitator

   (5) asking questions and directing the student to the right information through self-realization will be of greater benefit to the student

F. ADDITIONAL TRAINING

The instructor conducts or supervises the required training in equipment, rules and recommendations, and spotting and aircraft appropriate for the student's level of advancement (category).

4-2: VIDEO AND CAMERA

1. Video has proven to be an effective training and marketing aid, but the USPA Instructor must approve and brief the videographer prior to the jump.
2. Refer to the Skydiver's Information Manual, Section 6, for camera flyer recommendations, particularly those pertaining to student jumps.
3. Minimum experience qualifications
   a. 300 group freefall skydives
   b. 50 jumps flying camera with experienced jumpers
   c. hold a USPA Coach rating
4. Considerations for jumpers photographing AFF jumps
   a. The camera flyer needs to remain clear of the student and instructor(s) during exit.
   b. interaction with students
      (1) Only AFF-rated Instructors may interact with students during AFF jumps.
      (2) Camera flyers who hold an AFF rating may interact with students at the discretion of the supervising AFF Instructor(s) on the jump.
      (3) A camera flyer with an AFF rating is not to be considered as one of the required AFF Instructors for the jump; however, the value of wearing a camera while acting as AFF Instructor is recognized.
5. The USPA Instructor(s) should correct any camera flyer actions that cause concern.

4-3: PRE-JUMP CHECKS

A. INTRODUCTION

1. One of the instructor's greatest responsibilities is equipment management.
2. Preparation before boarding prevents accidents.
3. Having an organized routine will make the operation run more smoothly.
4. Conduct three complete equipment checks.
   a. before rigging up
   b. before boarding
   c. before exit

B. EQUIPMENT PREPARATION

1. Always check the rig in a logical order, such as top to bottom, back to front.
2. A typical sequence (varies according to equipment configuration)
   a. automatic activation device
      (1) switched on
      (2) calibrated
   b. reserve ripcord
      (1) movement of the cable in the housing
      (2) pin in place at least halfway, but not shouldered onto the grommet
      (3) closing loop must have no visible wear
      (4) closing loop tight for properly closed container
      (5) reserve in date, seal intact
   c. main closing (hand deployment)
      (1) flap closing order and bridle routing correct
      (2) slack above the curved pin
      (3) pin fully seated
      (4) tight closing loop, with no more than ten percent visible fraying
      (5) pin secured to bridle with no more than ten percent fraying
      (6) collapsible pilot chute cocked
      (7) pilot chute and bridle with no more than ten percent damage at any wear point
   d. main closing (ripcord)
      (1) free movement of the cable in the housing
      (2) secure cable housing ends
      (3) ripcord end not kinked or nicked
      (4) closing loop with no more than ten percent fraying
   e. main deployment handle in place
   f. canopy release system and RSL
      (1) correct canopy release assembly
      (2) RSL connected and routed correctly
   g. chest strap and hardware
      (1) snap type connected and adjusted
      (2) friction adapter type: threaded correctly, adjusted, and running end secured to prevent slippage
   h. reserve ripcord handle
   i. canopy release handle
   j. harness adjustments
   k. leg straps and hardware
      (1) threaded properly
      (2) hardware function (snap operation)
   l. outer clothing (or jumpsuit)
      (1) free movement
      (2) adequate protection on landing
      (3) secure; can't impede handle access

      (4) pockets empty, jewelry removed

      (5) fall rate (if applicable)

3. Using the same sequence, check the equipment after the student is completely rigged everything is adjusted, paying particular attention to the following:

   a. risers over the shoulder, not under the arm
   b. release handle not under the main lift web
   c. proper threading of harness hardware
   d. chest strap routed clear of the reserve ripcord
   e. twisted harness straps
   f. comfort pads in position
   g. overall adjustment and fit: A loose harness may allow the container to shift in freefall, causing stability problems.

4. Student's personal equipment (SHAGGAR, explained below):

   a. **S**hoes
      (1) appropriate for the student jumping; sandals, heels, and leather (or synthetic leather) soles not recommended
      (2) hooks taped
      (3) laces double knotted
   b. **H**elmet
      (1) adequate protection
      (2) fit and adjustment
   c. **A**ltimeter
      (1) readable by student (farsightedness?)
      (2) zeroed
   d. **G**oggles
      (1) correct type for contacts or glasses
      (2) clear and clean
      (3) tight
   e. **G**loves
      (1) worn for jumps into 40 degrees or cooler
      (2) light and flexible
   f. **A**erial photograph for pattern planning (USPA Flight Planner)
   g. **R**adio or other means of communication
      (1) all required equipment in place and ready
      (2) all required personnel coordinated
      (3) entire team informed of the canopy flight plan
      (4) "no-jump" signal prepared
      (5) student's radio on

5. Perform another pre-jump inspection in the aircraft prior to exit.

C. AIRCRAFT PREPARATION

1. Inspect and prepare the aircraft.
   a. familiar with door operation
   b. protrusions removed
   c. smooth edges
   d. seat belts clear
   e. knife aboard
   f. paperwork for jump modifications
   g. pilot rig in date
2. Brief the pilot.
   a. spot
   b. routine procedures
   c. flap settings and airspeeds
   d. emergency procedures
      (1) aircraft malfunctions
      (2) premature openings
   e. flight plan and altitudes for the load

D. JUMP CONDITIONS

1. Up-to-date weather forecast
2. Surface winds and winds aloft
3. Daylight remaining

E. REFER TO SIM 5-4, PRE-JUMP SAFETY CHECKS AND BRIEFINGS

4-4: CURRENCY TRAINING

1. The Examiner and USPA Instructor rating candidates review USPA currency recommendations for students and experienced jumpers found in SIM Section 5-2.
2. Recommended currency training and jumps for most licensed skydivers may be conducted by a USPA Coach under a USPA Instructor's supervision.

A-5 DEMONSTRATION AND GROUND PRACTICE FOR EVALUATIONS

5. Demonstration and Ground Practice for Evaluations

A. PURPOSE

1. After the classroom portion and prior to evaluations, the Examiner and staff demonstrate how to conduct the student training and jump activities for which the candidates are being rated and evaluated.
2. Candidates may practice the skills, supervised by the course staff, keeping in mind that course time is limited and evaluations must soon begin.
3. In the AFF Instructor Rating Course, practice and evaluation training and dives are conducted identically.

B. AFF SESSIONS

1. How to conduct training for the AFF flow of the dive in Categories A-E
   a. freefall and exit
   b. canopy
2. How to conduct practice and evaluation jumps: review and training of a student for Categories C and D
3. Prior-to-boarding sequence
   a. equipment preparation
   b. jump preparation
   c. pre-boarding equipment check
4. Pre-boarding, boarding, climb-to-altitude, and pre-jump sequence
   a. control of the student in the loading area and in the aircraft for boarding and the climb to altitude
   b. view of the airport, landing area, and landing pattern review
   c. dive flow review
   d. pre-exit equipment check procedures
   e. control of the student's movement in the aircraft during climb-out
   f. spotting and pilot communications
5. Exit recovery and rollover techniques
6. Student in-air observation and instruction, including hand signals
7. Pull-time sequence
8. Post-jump critique

C. DIVE FLOWS

With the evaluator acting as student—

EVALUATION JUMP 1

Follow the dive flow from Category C, Dive Plan #1 (two instructors) of the Integrated Student Program.

EVALUATION JUMP 2

Follow the dive flow from Category D, Dive Plan #2 of the Integrated Student Program, but with a gripped exit and 360-degree turns.

6. Candidate Practice and Evaluation

6-1: STANDARD EVALUATION PROCEDURES

A. INTRODUCTION

1. This section of the course is to be presented to the candidates with all evaluators for that course present.
   a. serves as the evaluator's briefing
   b. reassures the candidates that they are fully informed of all evaluation criteria and instructions
   c. provides a dialog and rapport between candidates and evaluators before testing begins
2. The AFF Instructor Rating Course includes two practical evaluation sections
   a. ground preparation, student supervision, and debriefing evaluation
   b. in-air skills and instruction evaluation
3. The course also includes a written exam.
4. There are two formats of evaluation dives:
   a. Category C, two instructors: Each candidate is evaluated on the main and reserve side for—
      (1) ground instruction skills
         (i) At least one Category C ground prep as a team with another candidate
         (ii) At least one Category C ground prep as a solo candidate
      (2) student preparation and supervision prior to the jump and during canopy descent
      (3) ability to deal with climb-out and exit problems
      (4) in-air flying and instructional and skills
      (5) observation and supervision of the student under canopy
      (6) debriefing skills
   b. Category D, single instructor: Each candidate is evaluated as in Category C above, plus—
      (1) solo ground instruction
      (2) in-air solo instruction
      (3) overall control of the skydive
5. Practice training and jump evaluations
   a. Candidates may make complete practice evaluation dives or begin testing without practice.
   b. All evaluations skydives are conducted to an identical standard, whether they are the practice evaluations or actual evaluation jumps.
   c. At the discretion of the AFF Examiner, some ground performance preparations conducted during weather delays may be counted towards the final score for the course.
   d. Course evaluators must wear hard helmets and must be equipped with an automatic activation device for both practice jumps and actual evaluation jumps.

B. GENERAL

1. To ensure standardized procedures, each evaluation should be conducted in generally the same manner and to the same standards of performance.
   a. Scenarios will be drawn from an ordinary skydiving school environment.
   b. Evaluators should make the evaluation scenarios both challenging and a learning experience for the candidates.
      (1) Evaluator challenges will provide opportunities for the candidates to instruct as well as supervise in freefall.
      (2) The evaluator may not correct or assist the candidates during the evaluations with the exception of discrepancies that might compromise safety on that jump.
2. The evaluators comments, including start and stop times, will be recorded on the candidate's evaluation form for discussion and correction during the evaluator's debrief.

C. AREAS TO BE EVALUATED

1. Ground training, supervision, and debriefing ("ground") evaluation: Each AFF Instructor candidate is evaluated in all subject areas and sub-areas shown on the AFF Ground Training, Supervision, and Debriefing Evaluation Form.
   a. preparation
   b. explanation and demonstration
   c. student trial and practice
   d. review and evaluation
   e. Category C
      (1) wing loading
      (2) effective flare
      (3) turbulence
      (4) accidental opening review
      (5) landing off
      (6) downwind landings
      (7) review landing priorities
      (8) pre-flight equipment check
      (9) BSR SIM 2-1.M.2 FAR 65 riggers
      (10) landing in high winds
   f. Category D
      (1) Calculating Freefall time
      (2) Rear riser control
      (3) Emergency procedure review
         (i) Totals malfunctions
         (ii) Partial malfunctions
         (iii) Procedures for questionable canopy
         (iv) Building landing review
      (4) Introduction to AAD
      (5) Pre-equipment check
         (i) introduction 3 ring assembly
         (ii) Checks of threes
         (iii) SHAGG
      (6) Cloud clearance and visibility
      (7) Introduction to spotting
   g. supervision (equipment—three checks, pre-boarding, and boarding)
   h. climb to altitude
      (1) helmet and seat belt
      (2) view of airport
      (3) deployment altitude review
      (4) mental review
      (5) verbal review
      (6) hand signal review
   i. opening to landing
      (1) observe student canopy control
      (2) set good example
   j. debriefing
      (1) walk and talk
      (2) video reviewed
      (3) corrective training
      (4) decision to advance

A-6 CANDIDATE PRACTICE AND EVALUATION

   (5) preview next dive

   (6) paperwork

2. In-air skills and instruction ("air") evaluation: Each candidate is evaluated in all the subject areas and sub-areas shown on the AFF In-Air Skills and Instruction Evaluation Form.

   a. exit

      (1) exit control

      (2) exit funnel actions

   b. circle of awareness

      (1) signal presentation

      (2) correct signals given

      (3) transition (single instructor)

   c. freefall

      (1) release sequence

      (2) remaining in position

      (3) freefall instruction

      (4) slot flying

      (5) maneuver flying

      (6) major separation flying

      (7) re-dock, signal, re-release

      (8) altitude reminders

   d. rollover

      (1) response time

      (2) effective rollover

      (3) instruction and re-release

      (4) altitude reminders

   e. stop spin

      (1) response time

      (2) effective spin stop

      (3) instruction and re-release

      (4) altitude reminders

   f. pull sequence

      (1) altitude reminder

      (2) pull signal

      (3) re-dock

      (4) assist

      (5) pull (or slap) by 3,500 feet

D. EVALUATION SCHEDULE

GROUND EVALUATION

1. The ground evaluation is scored on the AFF Training, Supervision, and Debriefing Evaluation Form.

2. Evaluation for preparation, explanation and demonstration, student trial and practice, and review (ground training)—

   a. begins when the evaluator calls "time in," and the candidate(s) begin training the stand-in student

   b. ends when the candidate(s) declare the ground training portion of the evaluation complete

3. Once the ground training portion of the evaluation is complete, the air evaluations will be conducted in conjunction with the 20-minute call and debrief

   a. The candidate(s) manifest the load.

   b. The candidate(s) inform the evaluator where to meet on the 20-minute call for the load.

   c. The candidate(s) are released until the 20-minute call for the load.

4. The evaluation for supervision and climb to altitude—

   a. begins at the 20-minute call for the load

   b. continues through pre-boarding, aircraft climb, climb-out, and pre-exit procedures

   c. ends when the evaluator's torso clears the threshold of the door or step for the actual release from the aircraft

5. As the exit commences, ground evaluation pauses for the air evaluation and resumes when the air evaluation ends.

6. The evaluation for opening to landing and debriefing—

   a. begins once the group's parachutes are open

   b. continues through canopy descent and the return of the jumpers to the packing area

   c. ends when the candidate(s) complete the debrief of the evaluator, acting as the student

AIR EVALUATION

1. The air evaluation is scored on the AFF In-Air Skills and Instruction Evaluation Form.

2. A score of at least 75% on all applicable sections, with no automatic unsats, is required to pass each air evaluation.

3. The minimum exit altitude for all evaluation jumps is 9,500 feet AGL

4. Evaluation begins when the evaluator is directed to begin their setup at the door or step and ends—

   a. for the main-side instructor candidate when the simulated deployment handle is activated

   b. for the reserve-side instructor candidate after riding through the simulated deployment (evaluator's very vigorous wave-off)

   c. for all at 4,000 feet or with evaluator's end-of-dive wave-off (very vigorous wave-off, or with evaluator, actual deployment and actual ride through by the candidate)

   d. Candidates should not confuse the "student" waving at the video camera flyer with the evaluator's signal that deployment has been accomplished.

E. GROUND RULES FOR EVALUATIONS

1. All ground preparation evaluations will be for Category C and D evaluation jumps.

2. Teaching of aircraft spotting will be conducted during the ground training for Category D jumps only but will be eliminated from the practical (in-aircraft) evaluation of those single-instructor evaluation jumps.

3. Each ground training evaluation will be followed by a practice or actual evaluation jump with the following exceptions at the Examiner's discretion:

   a. The candidate has satisfactorily completed the in-air instruction evaluation sufficiently to pass that part of the course.

   b. For aircraft or weather delays or other special considerations, the Examiner may allow multiple ground training evaluations prior to jumping.

4. Prior to each evaluation session, the evaluator will conduct a briefing with the candidate(s) for all subjects of the evaluation process, to include—

   a. brief review of the evaluation procedures

   b. comprehensive and detailed explanation of the scoring criteria

   c. the level of performance expected

   d. specific safety and scoring reminders

   e. evaluator's equipment

      (1) Evaluators will wear standard student accessory equipment, including clear goggles or visor, shoes, and hard helmet.

      (2) The evaluator will declare equipment to be used on the actual jump and instruct candidates to ignore specific equipment preferences of the evaluator not ordinarily found on students (hook knife, etc.).

CANDIDATE PRACTICE AND EVALUATION — A-6

   (3) All rigging problems must be determined during the pre-boarding equipment check.

   (4) Under no circumstances will an evaluator attempt to board an aircraft with mis-rigged equipment or exit an aircraft with contrived equipment problems.

   (5) The evaluator may present non-safety equipment problems to be caught during the pre-exit check aboard the aircraft.

  f. mock written training record, background, and scenario on the simulated student to be trained, which will include the simulated student's prior performance deficiencies

  g. an opportunity for the candidates to ask questions about the skydive and the evaluation procedure

5. Each candidate is expected to follow the ISP outline for the jump to be trained and include all the points listed on the AFF Instructor Rating Course Ground Preparation Checklist.

6. The candidate(s) arrange for a stand-in, preferably a candidate in the course, to be trained while the evaluator takes notes.

  a. The evaluator briefs the stand-in privately regarding any tendencies or deficiencies of the student the stand-in is portraying.

  b. The stand-in will present an imperfect performance during the training, as briefed by the evaluator, to test the candidates' ability for recognition and corrective training.

  c. Evaluators will base their simulated student performance on the next practice evaluation or actual evaluation jump upon the training given during the ground evaluation.

  d. In the event of a perfect ground evaluation, the evaluator will create challenges that adequately test the candidate's in-air skills.

7. The evaluator may call a "time out" during any part of the evaluation, but the candidates may not, except for safety reasons.

  a. The evaluator should call time-outs only when necessary.

  b. The evaluator will allow time for the candidate(s) to regroup following a time-out.

8. The evaluation and scoring begins at the 20 Minute Call. The evaluator and candidates arrive fully rigged and ready to jump. The evaluation includes testing for the ground and air portions; supervision, pre-boarding, climb to altitude, in-flight procedures, pre-exit procedures, canopy and debrief will all be part of the 20-minute call. The air evaluation will also be part of the 20-min call evaluation, but the ground and air portions will be evaluated and scored separately.

9. Role playing: To aid the candidates to view the evaluator as a student, during the remainder of evaluation the evaluator will play the role of the student just trained in the ground evaluation.

10. During the evaluation for the course, each candidate should be presented with a problem that requires the candidate to simulate a student deployment or pull the simulated reserve side activation handle (when used), indicating deployment of the main canopy.

Note: In case the reserve-side instructor is uncertain whether the simulated deployment has occurred, he or she is encouraged to make a secondary slap, indicating deployment of the main canopy.

11. Fall rate

  a. On Category D evaluation jumps, candidates may be presented with significant vertical and horizontal separation that must be negotiated to continue adequate observation.

  b. Evaluators will not present impossible fall-rate or separation scenarios using experienced skydiver skills.

  c. Evaluators should present fall-rate challenges to the candidates that allow them to demonstrate fall-rate range.

12. Video

  a. It is recommended that a video camera flyer be hired at the candidates' expense to record all evaluation jumps.

  b. The video of the jump may be used to improve the score of a candidate's performance, but never to downgrade it.

  c. Video camera flyers are to deploy at the evaluator's full-body wave-off signaling the end of freefall engagement or 3,500 feet, whichever comes first.

  d. Candidates should not wear helmet-mounted cameras due to a risk of entanglement and injury to the evaluator (and other candidate during Category C1 evaluations) on the evaluation jump.

13. At the end of each evaluation session, the evaluator will debrief the candidate on the performance.

  a. reinforcement of areas where the candidate was successful

  b. where possible, instruction, including demonstration and practice, to correct deficiencies

  c. assignment and necessary explanation of the scoring for that evaluation

F. SCORING

1. Ground evaluation: Each candidate is allowed up to three ground evaluations (not counting practice) to obtain a score of Satisfactory for a minimum of one Category C and one Category D ground evaluation.

2. Air evaluation: Each candidate is allowed up to four jumps to obtain the required 75% score in all three evaluation positions simulating jumps from the USPA Integrated Student Program.

  a. main-side instructor on a two-instructor Category C jump

  b. reserve-side instructor on a two-instructor Category C jump

  c. solo instructor on a Category D jump

3. Unsafe performance

  a. The evaluator must advise the Examiner of any performance that, in the evaluator's opinion, creates a safety hazard during an evaluation jump.

  b. The Examiner may recommend additional training for the candidate or that the candidate not continue with the in-air practical evaluation of the course at this time.

4. Mandatory scores of Unsatisfactory

  a. ground evaluation

   (1) failure to conduct review training based on the outline topics required for the ISP category

   (2) failure to perform training for the performance objectives using the preparation, explanation and demonstration, trial and practice, and evaluation and review method

   (3) insufficient repetition during practice or insufficient correction and positive feedback for the student to acquire the skills

   (4) bad spot where the simulated student would not be able to return to a safe landing area

A-6 CANDIDATE PRACTICE AND EVALUATION

(5) jump in violation of FAA cloud clearance minimums

(6) missed major rigging errors during the pre-jump equipment inspections (three required), including but not necessarily limited to:

   (i) missing altimeter or goggles

   (ii) misrouted three-ring release system or improperly routed RSL (depending on the severity)

   (iii) improperly routed or threaded chest strap

   (iv) unsuitable parachute assembly

   (v) altimeter not zeroed

b. air evaluation

   (1) candidate deployment below 2,500 feet

   (2) failure to simulate student deployment by 4,000 feet

   (3) continuing in the evaluation below 4,000 feet (hard deck)

   (4) failure for reserve-side or remaining instructor to ride through deployment (until evaluator's "student deployment" wave-off or 4,000 feet or the main canopy deployment if the evaluator uses the actual main deployment as part of the evaluation.)

Note: No malfunctions will be simulated, except floating deployment handle or hard pull.

   (5) candidate's failure to obtain sufficient horizontal separation after break-off

   (6) creating instability for the evaluator at the simulated deployment time

   (7) collision with the evaluator or another candidate

   (8) deployment of the "student" above 4,500 feet

   (9) hindering student learning

   (10) inability to assist simulated unstable student

   (11) other

Note: "Other" is not meant as an open or broad interpretation of the reasons for a score of Unsatisfactory; rather, it is reserved for unforeseeable situations that in the judgment of the evaluator and the Examiner would compromise the safety of an evaluator or a real student.

G. RETESTING

1. Ground evaluation retesting

   a. Failure to obtain a score of Satisfactory in all areas of the AFF Training, Supervision, and Debriefing Evaluation Form after three sessions will require retesting for the entire ground evaluation section at another AFF Instructor Rating Course.

   b. After failure to achieve a score of Satisfactory on the review and evaluation area of the AFF Training, Supervision, and Debriefing Evaluation Form after three training sessions and if that candidate has passed all other sections of the course, the candidate may repeat the evaluation for only that subsection when retesting is performed within 12 months of the original course.

   c. If the candidate is unsuccessful in the repeat evaluation, he must retake the complete AFFIRC.

2. Air evaluation retesting: A candidate must repeat the air evaluation section who has:

   a. completed three two-instructor evaluation jumps in Category C without obtaining all the required scores of 75 percent on the In-Air Skills and Instruction Evaluation Form acting as both main-side and reserve-side instructor

   b. completed four evaluation jumps and has not obtained all the required scores of 75 percent on the In-Air Skills and Instruction Evaluation Form on a single-instructor evaluation jump in Category D

   c. The candidate may repeat the air evaluation process at another AFF Instructor Rating Course or by appointment with a USPA AFF Examiner when retesting is performed within 12 months of the original course.

   d. If the candidate is unsuccessful in the repeat evaluation, he must retake the complete AFFIRC.

3. Written exam retesting

   a. Each candidate will be provided a second opportunity to pass the test during the course.

   b. Failure to answer 100 percent of the questions correctly on the second attempt will require the candidate to study, retake the classroom portion of a future AFF Instructor Rating Course, and pass the written exam at that course.

4. A candidate who fails to obtain a score of Satisfactory in one or all areas of the AFF Instructor Rating Course will be required to wait fourteen (14) days before attending another AFFIRC, unless a detailed training plan is developed for the candidate by the Examiner, which is executed within the time frame decided upon by both parties before the candidate may attend another USPA AFF Instructor Rating Course. The disqualified candidate may act as a stand-in student for ground evaluations as approved by the attending Examiner.

5. Retesting fees: All retesting and re-evaluation fees are at the discretion of the Examiner.

6. All portional retesting must be accomplished within 12 months of the failed or incomplete course, or the candidate must retake the complete course.

AFF INSTRUCTOR RATING COURSE
GROUND EVALUATION CHECKLIST

1. **Introduction (15-20 minutes)**
   a. **Instructor(s)**
      - [ ] names
      - [ ] backgrounds
   b. **student**
      - [ ] motivations
      - [ ] physical condition: medical, vision, hearing, age, weight, dental, scuba, injuries, blood donations, prescription and non-prescription drugs, alcohol
      - [ ] USPA membership, waiver, etc.
      - [ ] appropriate clothing (pockets, jewelry)
      - [ ] non-jump background
      - [ ] logbook
      - [ ] video (previous, this jump?)
      - [ ] student's subjective evaluation
      - [ ] procedure to prepare for jump (time frame, etc.)
   c. **skydive**
      - [ ] tie-in to previous experience
      - [ ] introduce objectives (emphasis on pull altitude)
      - [ ] brief description (concept, flow)
      - [ ] demonstration and video, if available
   d. **major changes**
      - [ ] intentional release (Category C)
      - [ ] one instructor (Category C and higher)
      - [ ] potentially steeper exit
      - [ ] not following instructor to side, head toward instructor, help with transition to instructor in front

2. **Review (20-25 minutes)**
   a. **equipment**
      - [ ] use of checklist or flight planner
      - [ ] equipment (student checks rig in Category D)
   b. **aircraft**
      - [ ] use of mock-up or aircraft
      - [ ] low altitude (landing with aircraft)
      - [ ] bail out
      - [ ] poised exit
   c. **freefall**
      - [ ] loss of one instructor
      - [ ] alone in freefall (new for Category C)
      - [ ] unstable at pull time
      - [ ] loss of altitude awareness
      - [ ] unable to regain stability and over on back
      - [ ] five-second rule
      - [ ] pull priorities
      - [ ] instructor pull
   d. **equipment emergencies**
      - [ ] use of training aids (harness, photographs, pilot chute or ripcord mock-up)
      - [ ] premature container opening
      - [ ] floating ripcord, lost handle
      - [ ] hard pull
      - [ ] total malfunction
      - [ ] pilot chute in tow
      - [ ] horseshoe
      - [ ] two canopies out
      - [ ] inflation malfunctions (bag lock, streamer, line-over, major damage, etc.)
      - [ ] minor problems (pilot chute hesitation, line twists, end cells, stuck slider, minor damage, control line malfunction, etc.)
      - [ ] identification and controllability check (acronym, e.g., "there, square, steerable," etc.)
      - [ ] decision and execution altitudes
      - [ ] do-not-cut-away-below altitude
      - [ ] collisions and avoidance
      - [ ] open container
   e. **landing**
      - [ ] use of landing trainer mock-up
      - [ ] water
      - [ ] trees
      - [ ] wires
      - [ ] other obstacles, prevention, drag recovery
      - [ ] avoidance
      - [ ] PLF demonstrated by student

3. **Hand Signals (5 minutes)**
   (best done during dirt dives)
   - [ ] pull signal
   - [ ] close knees signal (Category C)
   - [ ] wave off and "tongue out" signal (single instructor)
   - [ ] other signals

4. **Aircraft Procedures (10 minutes)**
   - [ ] climb out and exit
   - [ ] all aircraft covered
   - [ ] spotting

5. **Canopy Control (10 minutes)**
   - [ ] use of DZ photo or flight planner; walk in field
   - [ ] main
   - [ ] reserve
   - [ ] exit point
   - [ ] holding area
   - [ ] landing pattern from different directions
   - [ ] ground guidance
   - [ ] alternate guidance (instructor, etc.)
   - [ ] landing procedure: flare height, stall recovery
   - [ ] effect of low turn

6. **New Training (30 minutes)**
   a. **instructional strategy**
      - [ ] lesson and training environment prepared
      - [ ] explanations and demonstrations correct
      - [ ] effective mix of explanation and demonstration with trial and practice
      - [ ] on-the-spot correction, using hand signals when possible
      - [ ] performance objectives explained thoroughly and properly
      - [ ] each objective explained and demonstrated individually, with student trial and practice for each
      - [ ] skills mastered individually, then combined
      - [ ] effective mix of vertical and horizontal training
      - [ ] real-time dirt dives without coaching
      - [ ] realism
   b. **training aid use**
      - [ ] vertical trainer
      - [ ] horizontal trainer (body position and techniques must be correct at all times; simulate overshoot of turns for realism)
      - [ ] real time use (e.g., clock altimeter)

7. **Meeting Student (20-Minute Call)**
   - [ ] pre-jump equipment check (student and instructors)
   - [ ] pre-boarding supervision
   - [ ] full-dress rehearsal at mock-up or aircraft
   - [ ] boarding

8. **Climb to Altitude**
   - [ ] helmet and seat belt
   - [ ] view of airport from aircraft
   - [ ] deployment altitude review (at correct altitude)
   - [ ] student mental rehearsal
   - [ ] student verbal rehearsal with instructor(s)
   - [ ] spotting
   - [ ] supervision during pre-exit and climb-out

9. **Opening to Landing**
   - [ ] observe canopy control
   - [ ] set good example

10. **Debriefing (10-15 minutes)**
    - [ ] use of appropriate area (aircraft, mock up, etc.)
    - [ ] walk and talk
    - [ ] student's view first
    - [ ] student's perceptions correct
    - [ ] instructor's perceptions thorough and accurate
    - [ ] proper review of video, if used
    - [ ] emphasis on positive
    - [ ] advancement/non-advancement decision
    - [ ] corrective training
    - [ ] introduction of objectives for next level (if advanced) and flow of dive
    - [ ] paperwork, log entry

SAMPLE EVALUATION FORM

Preparation ☐ Unsatisfactory ☐ Satisfactory

Individual knowledge. Organization, teamwork, instructional flow, preparation and control of training area, and use of training aids.

Explanation and Demonstration (Presentation) ☐ Unsatisfactory ☐ Satisfactory

Includes introduction. Objectives and flow of the dive, followed by a more detailed explanation of each point. It should be clear and understandable. Horizontal and vertical demonstrations.

Student Trial and Practice (Application) ☐ Unsatisfactory ☐ Satisfactory

Efficient and effective. Develops student performance to the degree that the student (after mastering each individual skill) can perform the dirt dives in real time without coaching. Emphasis on horizontal. Step by step.

Review (Evaluation) ☐ Unsatisfactory ☐ Satisfactory

Emphasis on requiring student demonstrations of skills with continual evaluation of progress. Effective written checklist with key questions. Complete (especially four emergency areas: aircraft, freefall, equipment, landing).

Supervision (equipment, pre-boarding, boarding, canopy descent) ☐ Unsatisfactory ☐ Satisfactory

Control during full-dress rehearsal, pre-boarding, and boarding. Canopy descent and landing pattern review. Equipment check—three required.

- ❑ observe student canopy control
- ❑ set good example
- ❑ demonstration of correct heading
- ❑ demonstration of landing pattern

Climb to Altitude ☐ Unsatisfactory ☐ Satisfactory

Orienting the student to the DZ and ground winds, reviewing significant altitudes (no-more turns, lock-on, deployment), student's mental preparation, required description of the dive from the student, hand-signal review, pre-exit equipment check, spotting (involving the student in the process and effectiveness), supervision while moving to the door and getting into position for exit.

- ❑ helmet and seat belt
- ❑ view of airport
- ❑ deployment altitude review
- ❑ mental review
- ❑ verbal review
- ❑ spotting
- ❑ climb-out

Debriefing ☐ Unsatisfactory ☐ Satisfactory

Use of walk and talk technique (post dive with the student's story first). Thorough and accurate. Beneficial to the student. Positive and upbeat approach. Advancement decision. Corrective training. Paperwork (logbook, DZ records).

- ❑ walk and talk
- ❑ video reviewed
- ❑ corrective training
- ❑ advance decision
- ❑ lesson preview
- ❑ paperwork

SCORING AND CRITERIA EXAMPLES

Exit	Exit Control	If it applies; ensuring student stability (shakes) does not roll, tumble, or controls/corrects immediately
	Exit Funnel Actions	If it applies; how long to correct (less than 2,000 ft or 15-seconds), does 1-instructor release then fly close for additional control, does the other instructor correct and control
COA	*during the COA a thumbs-up or head nod is standard practice, and proper placement.*	
	Signal Presentation	If required; stability issue or does not initiate coa within 5-seconds
	Correct Signal Given	If required; based on lack of student performance
	Transition	Category D for movement to the front (can be a grip switch or free flown to the facing 2-way)
Freefall	Release Sequence/Position	Category C reserve side releases first, main side second after body scan
	Freefall Instruction	Appropriate signal(s), based on student's demonstrated performance, and in students view
	Altitude Reminders	If required; student doesn't check
	Slot Flying	For Category C approximately 90 degrees to the students head (main or reserve side), at least level and close enough to give signals (within 1-arms length), even when the student is sliding, drifting, or turning less than 45 degrees
	Maneuver Flying	Moving back into a slot or close proximity (arms length) from the student to fly a slot, give signals, block excessive movement, role reversal, etc
	Major Separation Flying	Moving 20 ft (horizontal and or vertical) or more from the candidate(s) and how long it takes for recovery (not more than 5 seconds)
	Re-Dock, Signal, Re-Release	Must have a reason; category c turns greater than 360 degrees, severe buffeting, backsliding, etc.; category d turns greater than 720 degrees, accelerating (potential spin)
Rollover	Response Time	Based on distance; within 5 ft 2-3 seconds, 10-15 ft 5-7 seconds, 20 ft up to 10 seconds
	Effective Rollover	Must use control, must stay docked, and lend stability, not a tackle
	Instruction Re-Release	Correct body position and continue
Stop Spin	Response Time	Based on distance; within 5 ft 2-3 seconds, 10-15 ft 5-7 seconds, 20 ft up to 10 seconds
	Spin Stopped Effectively	Must use control, lend stability, must stay docked
	Instruction Re-Release	Correct body position and continue
Pull Sequence	Altitude Signal	Undocked, free flying (if student is stable)
	Pull Signal	Undocked, free flying (if student is stable)
	Re-Dock	If no attempt to pull is made by the student, main side re-docks to assist reserve side re-docks to lend stability
	Assist	Main side only if required
	Pull (Or Slap) And Altitude	The student handle is pulled between 4,500 ft and 4,000 ft
Automatic Unsats	Hard Deck	Failure to pull a student handle by 4,000 ft AGL
	Create Instability At Pull time	Re-docking and creating a stability issue for the student
	Low Pull	As the candidate tracks away they deploy their main canopy below 2,500 ft AGL
	Hard Hit	The student is stable and the candidate collides with the student creating instability. could also mean 1-candidate collides with another making them ineffective
	Horizontal Separation	The candidate must gain at least 200 ft of horizontal separation from the student not vertical
	High Deployment	Pulling the student handle above 4,500 ft AGL
	Failure To Ride Through	The candidate does not hold onto the student through deployment (actual or experienced, full body wave off)
	Unable To Assist An Unstable Student	If student is unstable (spinning, on back, etc.) the candidate must assist within 20 seconds
	Hindering Student Learning	Re-docking or holding onto the student without a reason
	Other	Safety; actually deploying the students main or reserve canopy, pulling the students cutaway handle, candidate deploys within 50 ft of the student etc.

IAD AND STATIC-LINE INSTRUCTOR RATING

IAD SLI -1: INTRODUCTION AND ORIENTATION

1. Introduction and Orientation

A. WHAT IS A USPA IAD OR STATIC-LINE INSTRUCTOR?

1. The USPA Instructor is one of three instructional ratings USPA administers, preceded by USPA Coach and followed by Examiner.
2. A USPA IAD or Static-Line Instructor may—
   a. exercise all privileges of the USPA Coach rating
   b. conduct student training and jumps according to his or her rating
      (1) using instructor-assisted deployment with a throw-out, hand deployed pilot chute (IAD) or static-line
      (2) teach the IAD or static-line first-jump course
      (3) conduct method-specific training
   c. conduct training in the general portions of any first-jump course
   d. train and supervise jumps with non-method-specific students
   e. conduct the A license quiz and check dive
   f. verify certain USPA license applications, according to the requirements in SIM Section 3
   g. supervise a USPA Coach in training students and making currency jumps with licensed skydivers
3. Supervision (BSRs)
   a. All student training is conducted under the supervision as required by an appropriately rated USPA Instructor (refer to the BSRs).
   b. All general, non-method-specific student training and jump supervision may be conducted by any USPA Instructor, but method-specific training and jumps (AFF, IAD, static-line, and tandem) require the instructor to hold that method-specific rating.
4. Candidates who have met all the following requirements may attend the USPA IAD or Static-Line Instructor Rating course:
   a. reached the age of 18 years
   b. holds or has held any USPA instructional rating
   c. issued a USPA C license
5. Candidates who have completed the following may earn the USPA IAD or Static-Line Rating:
   a. completed the USPA IAD and Static-Line Instructor Proficiency Card (applicable portions)
   b. satisfactorily completed a USPA IAD or Static-Line Instructor Rating Course

B. IAD AND STATIC-LINE TRAINING BACKGROUND

1. Both training methods employ a means of deploying the parachute on exit during the initial training jumps, followed by independent solo freefall training.
   a. Instructor-assisted deployment
      (1) operated under waiver to the BSRs at several USPA drop zones prior to approval
      (2) was accepted by USPA in 1995
      (3) allows a center to use one type of main-deployment system for all solo student training
   b. Static line is the oldest means and was once the only means of introducing students to the sport.
2. IAD and static-line training follow the same progression in the USPA Integrated Student Program syllabus.

C. THE NATURE OF THE COURSE

1. This course may be conducted—
   a. as an initial USPA Instructor rating course for USPA Coaches
   b. as a shorter transition course for current USPA Instructors rated in another method
2. Each candidate is required to arrive at this course with all prerequisites completed, as specified on the IAD and Static-Line Instructor Proficiency Card.
3. The course will cover the USPA Integrated Student Training Program—
   a. as it applies to IAD or static-line training
   b. subsequent training and jumps to the A license
   c. transition from another training discipline
4. The classroom, training, and evaluation for this course should be conducted over a minimum of three full days.
5. This course may requalify USPA Instructors who have let their IAD or static-line rating lapse.

D. WHO MAY CONDUCT THIS COURSE?

1. A Static-Line or IAD Examiner who has maintained currency as follows: conducted at least one USPA Static-Line or IAD Instructor Rating Course within the past 24 months
2. Continues to meet all of the requirements to qualify as a course evaluator (listed in Section E, "How to become a USPA Static-Line or IAD Examiner."

E. WHAT IS REQUIRED TO PASS THIS COURSE?

1. Candidates for the USPA IAD and Static-Line Instructor rating will be evaluated during the course for their ability to conduct training and jumps for students making jumps in their discipline and through the USPA A license.
   a. Candidates for the USPA IAD Instructor rating will be evaluated during the course for their ability to understand, safely prepare, and handle instructor-assisted deployment jumps with hand-deployed pilot chutes during actual IAD jumps using as simulated students either evaluators or jumpers with at least 100 jumps who hold a USPA B or higher license.
   b. Candidates for the USPA Static-Line Instructor rating will be evaluated during the course for their ability to understand, safely prepare, and handle commonly used static-line equipment during actual static-line jumps using as simulated students either evaluators or jumpers with at least 100 jumps who hold a USPA B or higher license.
   c. All candidates will successfully train, observe, and critique at least one freefall jump taken from the static-line and instructor-assisted deployment dive flows in Categories D and performed by the Examiner or evaluators supervised by the Examiner during the course (waived for instructors who hold a USPA Instructor rating in another discipline).
2. Written: Prior to attending the course, each candidate must correctly answer at least 80 percent of the questions on an open-book written examination covering the following:
   a. this syllabus
   b. the complete ISP syllabus

c. the USPA Basic Safety Requirements
d. SIM Section 5
e. FARs

3. Commencement of privileges
   a. The privileges of any instructional rating will commence upon successful completion of the rating course and will be valid for 15 days with a candidate logbook endorsement by the Examiner.
   b. The rating must be processed at USPA headquarters to be considered valid after the 15-day grace period expires

4. Currently rated instructors attending this course do not need to meet the first-jump course requirements. The method-specific first-jump course topics will be covered in detail during the course by the examiner.

F. PROCEDURES FOR RENEWING AN EXPIRED IAD OR STATIC-LINE INSTRUCTOR RATING

1. Ratings expire with USPA memberships. Persons with an expired USPA IAD or Static-Line Instructor rating (up to two years) must:
   a. satisfactorily conduct at least one complete student evaluation jump with a method-specific Designated Evaluator or Examiner acting as a simulated student using the deployment method for which the candidate was rated, to include all jump preparation, supervision during the jump and debriefing
   b. pass the IAD or Static-Line Instructor Course written exam with a score of at least 80 percent

2. Persons with an expired USPA IAD or Static-Line Instructor rating of more than two years must requalify by successfully passing the USPA IAD or Static-Line Instructor Rating Course (method specific).

G. KEEPING A USPA IAD OR STATIC-LINE INSTRUCTOR RATING CURRENT

1. USPA IAD and Static-Line Instructors may annually renew their ratings with their USPA membership by paying the annual rating renewal fee and providing documentation of any of the following:
   a. that the rating was initially earned within the current membership cycle (renewal fee and signature required), in which case the annual minimum static-line or IAD jump numbers do not apply
   b. that the applicant has met the annual rating renewal requirements by performing all of the following within the previous 12 months
      (1) acted as instructor for ten IAD or static-line students (per rating) or ten licensed skydivers acting as simulated students (per rating) who have been fully briefed on the procedures related to that particular exit and deployment method and acted as an instructor for five freefall students who have not yet been cleared to freefall self-supervision
      (2) attended a USPA Instructor seminar
      (3) has conducted training or complete review training in Category A, having taught or assisted with at least one entire first-jump course for the method in which the instructor is rated
      (4) acquire the signature of a current S&TA, Examiner, or member of the USPA Board of Directors on the renewal application to verify that the renewal requirements were met
   c. or, having met the renewal requirements for an expired rating

2. A skydiver may not verify his or her own rating renewal requirements.

3. Renewing an instructor rating automatically renews a coach rating.

H. CONVERTING A NON-USPA IAD OR SL RATING TO A USPA IAD OR SL RATING

1. A jumper with a current IAD Instructor rating from a non-U.S. skydiving federation may convert that rating to a USPA IAD Instructor Rating by completing a USPA IAD course, excluding the first-jump-course training on the IAD and Static-Line Instructor Rating Course Proficiency Card

2. A jumper with a current Static-Line Instructor rating from a non-U.S. skydiving federation may convert that rating to a USPA Static-Line Instructor Rating by completing a USPA Static-Line course, excluding the first-jump-course training on the IAD and Static-Line Instructor Rating Course Proficiency Card

I. COURSE OVERVIEW

1. USPA's Integrated Student Program for IAD and static-line students
   a. the first-jump course
   b. first-jump course performance standards
   c. Categories B-E, basic skydiving skills

INTRODUCTION AND ORIENTATION | IAD SLI -1

   d. group skydiving skills
2. IAD and static-line methods
3. Problem solving
4. General instructor's duties
5. Jump preparation and equipment checks
6. Demonstration and practice sessions
7. Evaluation

IAD SLI -2 | THE INTEGRATED STUDENT PROGRAM

2. The Integrated Student Program

2-1: ISP OVERVIEW

1. The USPA Integrated Student Program is a complete and detailed outline recommended by USPA to train students from the first jump through the A license.

2. The ISP integrates all USPA-recognized methods for teaching skydiving, particularly in the early portion of the training: harness hold (USPA Accelerated Freefall), instructor-assisted deployment, static line, and tandem.

3. Schools using the ISP outline or its equivalent can easily track a student's performance and interchange the various training methods to make the most effective use of their training resources.

   a. There are eight categories of advancement, A-H.
      (1) Categories A-D focus on basic skydiving survival skills and are very closely supervised.
      (2) During Categories E through H, students become more independent and supervision requirements are relaxed.
      (3) Categories G and H concentrate on group freefall skills and help to prepare a student to jump without supervision and the USPA A license.

   b. Each category following Category A, the first-jump course, is divided into six skills and knowledge sets:
      (1) exit and freefall
      (2) canopy
      (3) emergency procedure review
      (4) equipment
      (5) rules and recommendations
      (6) spotting and aircraft

   c. Each student, except those making tandem jumps, should complete training in the freefall, canopy, and emergency review sections prior to making a jump in any category.
      (1) Some freefall dive flows require the freefall and emergency procedure training and review for the student to safely perform them.
      (2) The canopy dive flows require canopy training first so the student can understand what to practice.
      (3) The student becomes more independent and less supervised as he or she progresses and may require the information in these three areas when encountering new experiences during jumps in that category.

4. An oral quiz follows each category.

   a. It may be given after the student completes the last jump in the category or serve as a review preceding training in the next category.

   b. The USPA Instructor conducting the A license check dive draws from the quiz questions for the oral testing portion of the license review.

2-2: THE ISP FIRST-JUMP COURSE FOR IAD AND STATIC LINE

1. Using the following outline, the Examiner expands on the topics detailed in the IAD/static-line first-jump course from the ISP.

2. The number of students in the first-jump course should be appropriate for the number of staff available to facilitate the course.

A. EQUIPMENT

1. The student should know the location of all operation handles he or she may be expected to use.

2. Limiting the equipment discussion for first-jump students

   a. The instructor describes the parachute opening in the three significant stages that determine the response from the jumper: activation (container opening), deployment, and inflation.

   b. Describe only a correct opening when first introducing the concept, but in terms the student will hear throughout the course and the actual jump.

3. Equipment responsibilities

   a. The USPA Instructor is primarily responsible for—
      (1) choosing the correct system and preflighting it
      (2) putting the equipment on the student, adjusting it properly, and performing a complete pre-boarding equipment check
      (3) checking that the equipment is ready to jump before the student exits the aircraft
      (4) proper handling of the deployment device (hand-deployed pilot chute or static line)

   b. Students are responsible for—
      (1) making sure the instructor checks the equipment at these three points (pre-flight, pre-boarding, and prior to exit) and prepares the deployment device
      (2) checking the deployment device (IAD or static line) prior to exiting the aircraft

4. Students are taught to protect the parachute system operation handles, but monitoring the equipment throughout the jump operation is a primary duty of the instructor.

5. The student should know that the responsibility for the equipment shifts from the instructor to the student later as the student progresses.

6. The student should be familiar with any other equipment operation he or she is expected to perform independently (personal items, equipment recovery and return, etc.).

7. Discussion

B. EXIT

1. Two IAD or static-line jumps minimum are recommended in Category A.

2. Prior to exit, the student should be responsible to check:

   a. that the instructor has performed the final in-aircraft equipment check, including radio when used

   b. that the deployment device is prepared
      (1) IAD: that the instructor has a satisfactory grip on the pilot chute
      (2) static-line: attachment to the aircraft

3. Students should count aloud on exit to maintain awareness of time.

4. The student should exhibit at least reasonable control during climb-out and exit before advancing.

C. HAND SIGNALS

1. Presenting hand signals

   a. All hand signals are performed with one hand and must be placed in plain view of the student, generally no closer than 12 inches from the student's face and held for a minimum of three seconds.

 b. The instructor may need to get the attention of the student first.

2. Suggested signals are shown in the Skydiver's Information Manual, Appendix A.
3. Limit hand signals to those that may be required based on observation during the student's training.

 a. Arch and leg position signals may be effective signals for students preparing for an IAD or static-line exit.

 b. Additional hand signals can be introduced during subsequent training.

D. CANOPY

1. Exit and deployment altitude is recommended at 3,500 feet to increase canopy learning time.
2. Introduce the student to the canopy in terms that will be used throughout the course and during radio instruction.
3. Canopy training should be based on flying a specific, pre-planned pattern into a clear landing area.

 a. This portion of the training is best taught in the landing area with an aerial photograph.

 b. Refer to the canopy training outline and illustrations in Category A of the ISP syllabus for this portion of the lesson.

4. Students should be taught to look for traffic before turning.
5. The student should remain upwind in a pre-planned holding area until ready to enter the landing pattern at 1,000 feet.
6. If unable to make the planned landing area, decide on a clear alternate landing area by 2,000 feet and apply the planned pattern to the new area.
7. Final approach

 a. The student should fly a straight final approach to avoid collisions.

 b. S-turns should be avoided, except when clear of all traffic, but may be valuable in an off-field landing.

8. Discussion

E. LANDINGS

1. This section is best taught using a practical landing trainer, where the student simulates parachute landings.
2. Teach the student a prepare-to-land position that will enable an easy transition into a proper PLF.
3. The student should learn all types of obstacle landings with emphasis on obstacles the student might encounter at that DZ.
4. Round reserve training and backward PLFs may be omitted from the course if all the school's student equipment is equipped with a ram-air reserve, but a note on the type of reserve should be entered in the log of each student's jump ("RAM").
5. Students with prior tandem experience using special tandem landing techniques need to know that those techniques are not correct for a hard landing when jumping solo; introduce and demonstrate the PLF.
6. Discussion

F. EQUIPMENT EMERGENCIES

1. A USPA Coach or higher rating holder should assist and critique the jumper throughout all ground training.
2. A watch or training altimeter may be used during parachute emergency drills to help the student develop time awareness.
3. The harness trainer should be equipped with a cutaway handle and a reserve ripcord handle or a single operating system (SOS) handle, each of which can actually be pulled.
4. Teach the school procedures for all parachute situations the student may encounter (follow the Category A emergency procedure outline).
5. Prior to any jump in Category A, solo students should review all emergency procedures on that day.

 a. A second complete emergency procedure review performed during Category A on another day can count toward one of the two complete reviews (one scheduled in Category B) required for the USPA A license.

 b. In the ISP program, the same review can be applied towards the emergency procedure review session in Category B.

G. AIRCRAFT EMERGENCIES

The appropriately rated USPA Instructor must train first-jump or crossover students for aircraft emergency procedures specific to IAD or static-line.

H. ADDITIONAL STUDY

1. First-jump students who wish to return should be introduced to the SIM and encouraged to study all aspects of the sport that will eventually fall under their responsibility.
2. The "Book Stuff" recommended reading in ISP Category A introduces the students to the FARs and other recommendations in preparation for the oral quiz.

 a. Instructors can inform students of the seat belt requirements while boarding, and the student can study the rule from the SIM.

 b. Jumpers who make a solo canopy descent assume the responsibility to land in an open area clear of persons and property on the ground even on the first jump.

3. Introduction of the oral quiz (which can also serve as a review prior to the next jump)—

 a. establishes the student's responsibility to acquire the supporting knowledge of the sport

 b. helps generate discussion about aspects of skydiving that the student will need to understand as an A-license holder

I. REVIEW CATEGORY A QUIZ

2-3: FJC TRAINING PERFORMANCE STANDARDS FOR IAD AND STATIC-LINE STUDENTS

A. ASSESSING BY SPECIFIC OBJECTIVES

1. All first-jump ground training should be specific and oriented to measurable goals.
2. Students should be correct and consistent in demonstrating their ability to perform the tasks of the ground training in preparation for their parachute jump.
3. This section provides sample performance criteria for use in the first-jump course to help determine a student's aptitude for a solo (AFF, IAD, or static-line) jump.

B. EQUIPMENT KNOWLEDGE FOR IAD AND STATIC-LINE STUDENTS

1. Can find and operate all handles
2. Understands the use of the altimeter under canopy
3. Knows to expect three complete equipment checks

C. CLIMB-OUT AND EXIT (AT THE MOCK-UP)

1. Understands and can perform the climb-out, set-up, and launch following the instructor's commands
2. Demonstrates sufficient strength, agility, and mental faculties during practice to perform the tasks

IAD SLI -2 | THE INTEGRATED STUDENT PROGRAM

D. APTITUDE FOR THE FREEFALL POSITION

1. Able to arch sufficiently to lift both shoulders and knees off a flat surface and hold for ten-second intervals without straining
2. During arch practice, controls both legs and arms with symmetry and extends both legs slightly

E. UNDERSTANDING OF CANOPY DESCENT

1. Understands canopy descent strategies well enough to solve contrived descent problems from opening to 1,000 feet:
   a. too close to the planned pattern entry point at too high an altitude—face upwind
   b. more than halfway down, but not yet halfway back—plan an alternate landing area
2. Can solve contrived landing approach problems (e.g., ISP model):
   a. too high at the planned 600-foot point—arc the base leg
   b. too low at the planned 600-foot point—cut the corner for the planned 300-foot point

F. LANDING AND LANDING EMERGENCY DRILLS

1. Prior to jumping, demonstrates a proper PLF
2. Demonstrates the correct procedure for each landing hazard at or near the planned drop zone:
   a. power lines
   b. water
   c. trees
   d. buildings
   e. other hazards specific to the drop zone

G. EQUIPMENT PROBLEMS AND EMERGENCY DRILLS

1. Responds correctly to questions about how to handle an open parachute in the aircraft
2. Demonstrates in the training harness—
   a. response to lost deployment handle, hard extraction
   b. how to clear a pilot chute hesitation (main or reserve)
   c. within five seconds, the correct response to contrived partial and total malfunction situations, including looking at the emergency handle(s)
   d. correct response to line twists, slider up, and end-cell closures and addresses them in that order (in case they are experienced simultaneously)
   e. the correct response to all three two-canopy-out scenarios discussed in Category A

H. REMEDIES

Students who do not meet these standards may—

a. review the deficient sections of the first-jump course until demonstrating a satisfactory performance
   (1) Review on the same day if the student shows improvement during the review.
   (2) Because of the taxing nature of a solo first-jump course, some students may perform better after reviewing deficiencies another day.
b. transfer to another discipline that doesn't require the deficient skill
c. be discouraged from engaging in skydiving

2-4: CATEGORIES B-E BASIC SKYDIVING SKILLS

The course staff and candidates discuss the Category B-E outline in the ISP.

CATEGORY B

A. EXIT AND FREEFALL

1. Category B prepares the student for solo freefall.
   a. increased body awareness
   b. relaxed performance from exit through deployment
   c. familiarization and practice with initiating main deployment (in-air practice deployments)
   d. It is recommended that the last PPCT or PRCP should be done on the same day of the student's first clear and pull.
2. The student should demonstrate increasing comfort with the climb-out, set-up, and exit.
3. Advancement criteria (Examiner reviews with candidates)
   a. With the Examiner, candidates review the Category B advancement criteria and the freefall dive flow from the ISP.
   b. BSR advancement criteria for IAD and static-line students

B. CANOPY

1. Recommended minimum exit altitude remains at 3,500 feet to increase canopy learning time.
2. With the Examiner, candidates review Category B advancement criteria and the canopy dive flow from the ISP.
3. AFF students deficient in canopy skills may consider IAD or static-line training, which places fewer demands on the student during each jump.
4. Students who can't meet the canopy advancement criteria in IAD or static-line may consider canopy training in tandem, which offers the benefit of an instructor present throughout the descent.

C. EMERGENCY PROCEDURE REVIEW

1. Because so much information is presented during the first-jump course, many students soon forget a great deal of their emergency procedure training.
2. The emergency procedure section of Category B serves several functions:
   a. review of first-jump course emergency procedures
   b. review for all returning first-jump solo students who did not get to jump on the day of their course (log as the first or Category B emergency procedure review on the USPA A license application)
   c. review for students and experienced jumpers making currency skydives (adjust the cutaway decide-and-act altitude according to that jumper's license level)
3. Tandem students already trained in emergency procedures on another day should review them on the same day prior to making any jump in Category C.

D. EQUIPMENT

1. How a parachute opens
   a. to differentiate between malfunctions requiring only a reserve deployment and those requiring a cutaway and reserve deployment
   b. easily taught while packing or unpacking a parachute
2. Reviewing equipment retrieval at this point facilitates packing operations later for the staff.

E. RULES AND RECOMMENDATIONS

1. To make informed decisions about the safety of his or her own jumps, each student should be made aware of the pertinent BSRs.
2. Knowing the rules helps the student understand why the DZ won't allow jumps when conditions exceed the BSR limits for student operations.

THE INTEGRATED STUDENT PROGRAM | IAD SLI -2

F. SPOTTING AND AIRCRAFT

1. Review handle protection as a responsibility of the student.
2. Familiarize the student with the compass orientation and length of the runway in preparation for upcoming training in spotting.
3. Teaching aircraft traffic patterns early will help prevent student-aircraft conflicts on final approach and on the runway.

G. METHOD TRANSITION STUDENTS (TO IAD OR STATIC LINE)

1. Review "Transitions" in the Introduction to Category B.
2. Who may teach the transition course
    a. A USPA IAD or Static-Line Instructor may teach the aircraft procedures, climb-out, exit, and aircraft emergencies.
    b. A USPA Coach or a USPA Instructor rated in another discipline may teach the remaining, general portions of the transition course for former tandem students.

H. REVIEW CATEGORY B QUIZ

CATEGORY C

A. EXIT AND FREEFALL

1. Three jumps minimum are recommended, including a qualifying IAD or static-line jump the same day as the first freefall.
    a. stable clear and pull not to exceed five seconds
    b. two ten-second freefalls
2. Relaxed freefall position ("altitude, arch, legs, relax")
    a. "Altitude" means the student must read the altimeter and understand the altitude; or students on freefall in the IAD or static-line progression performing short delays need to know their altitude by the count in seconds from exiting the aircraft.
    b. "Arch" means to push the hips forward slightly and smoothly and to keep them there.
    c. "Legs" means to pay attention to the leg position and place both legs in the correct position, probably extending them slightly.
    d. "Relax" means to take a breath and relax the muscles that aren't needed for the correct body position.
3. Heading control
    a. Heading control may be passive ("altitude, arch, legs, relax").
    b. The instructor should introduce active heading control (turn method), but the student must understand that a correct body position is necessary for effective active heading control.
    c. The student's objectives are hover control using a coordinated and trimmed body position to maintain balance in freefall.
4. Introduction to wave-off (ten-second freefalls)
    a. teaches the student the wave-off signal early
    b. helps protect instructors who may follow the student on future jumps
    c. trains for safety on future group freefall jumps
5. Introduce the altimeter as a back-up to counting and looking at the ground.
6. At least two successful ten-second freefalls are recommended before advancing.
    a. control within five seconds of exit
    b. reasonable heading control
7. Recommended minimum deployment is 4,000 feet, particularly for students making ten-second freefalls and reaching deployment altitude at near-terminal velocity.
8. Pull priorities
    a. Pull.
    b. Pull at the correct altitude.
    c. Pull while stable.
9. Review the Category C advancement criteria and the freefall dive flow recommendations from the ISP.

B. CANOPY

1. Introduction to wing loading (ISP syllabus)
    a. The wing-loading exercise is especially important for drop zones with higher performance student canopies.
    b. Each student should be referred to the canopy manufacturers' websites to study recommended loading.
2. Flaring
    a. Review of the concept that flaring momentarily converts forward speed to lift (from Category A).
    b. The discussion continues with the concept of the jumper swinging forward and momentarily increasing the canopy's angle of attack.
    c. The student should understand that flaring the canopy produces three results.
        (1) Pulling on the tail increases the amount of air the tail deflects to produce additional lift.
        (2) The additional drag abruptly slows the forward speed.
        (3) As the jumper swings forward, the nose raises and the momentary increased angle of attack causes the canopy to attempt to climb.
    d. A canopy enters a dynamic stall when the jumper swings back under the canopy, the nose lowers, and the canopy begins a slight dive.
    e. The canopy enters a full stall when the tail is held below the nose and the canopy begins to fly backward.
    f. Maintaining maximum lift (prior to stall or sink) provides a softer landing, even when significant forward speed remains.
    g. Review of early flare and stall recovery actions are critical canopy survival skills and must not be overlooked.
3. Effects of higher winds
    a. Students who have exhibited good pattern flying skills in Categories A and B are introduced to—
        (1) turbulence
        (2) off-field landings
        (3) collapsing the canopy in winds (introduction for most students)
    b. The effects of a downwind landing are potentially greater, so downwind landing technique is discussed.
        (1) Flare according to height, not ground speed.
        (2) Flare normally to maximize lift and minimize final ground speed.
        (3) PLF
4. The student should by this time be able to fly a proper landing pattern with minimal assistance.
5. IAD and static-line instructors should assign someone reliable to observe a student's pattern work and landings.
6. Landings: Students should understand when it is safe and unsafe to attempt a stand-up landing.
7. Candidates review the Category C canopy dive plan with the Examiner.

IAD SLI-2 THE INTEGRATED STUDENT PROGRAM

C. EMERGENCY PROCEDURE REVIEW

1. Training for main deployment problems (ripcord or hand deployment) must be included prior to freefall.
2. Emphasize that the student must deploy at the correct altitude, regardless of stability.
3. Review in detail all aspects of preventing an open container in the aircraft and the associated emergency procedures.
4. Stability recovery (planned ten second freefall or longer)
   a. altitude, arch, legs, relax
   b. if caught on back, roll-out-of-bed technique
   c. if still out of control, think "AIR: Altitude aware, In control, and Relaxed."
      (1) The student must know his altitude at all times.
      (2) The student can use up to five seconds to regain control if altitude permits.
      (3) The student should be relaxed to help ensure a smooth freefall.
      (4) If still not in control, the student should deploy the main canopy.
5. Discuss in detail all aspects of landing off the intended DZ.
   a. selecting a suitable landing area
   b. anticipating and avoiding turbulence in the area
   c. other jumpers in the pattern
   d. procedures for returning without damaging property and equipment
6. Review landing priorities.

D. EQUIPMENT

1. The instructor introduces the student to equipment in more detail, including the AAD, RSL, and the strategy for the equipment check before rigging up.
   a. The introduction can be performed as the student is preparing to gear up for the jump.
   b. The student will check his or her equipment, supervised by a USPA Instructor.
2. Details about the three-ring system, AAD, and RSL are included in future categories; this is merely an introduction.
3. Because of the introduction to the AAD and RSL in Category C, discussions on them can be postponed from the first-jump course.

E. RULES AND RECOMMENDATIONS

1. BSRs for student equipment
2. FARs for parachute packing (FAR 105.43)
3. state and local regulations
4. drop zone neighbor relations (with DZ manager)

F. SPOTTING AND AIRCRAFT

Planning a landing pattern for a day with moderate winds

G. METHOD TRANSITION STUDENTS

Review "Transitions" in the introduction to Category C.

H. REVIEW CATEGORY C QUIZ

CATEGORY D

A. EXIT AND FREEFALL

1. The lesson on turning should emphasize the importance of a neutral body position prior to initiating a turn.
2. A simple technique for changing heading, such as upper body turns only, will increase confidence and improve chances for success; after the student has completed the A-license program, techniques for center-point turns can be easily added.
   a. multiple 90-degree turns only on the first jump where turns are attempted
      (1) reduces student stress and workload
      (2) increases confidence in heading control prior to initiating bigger turns, leading to greater success
      (3) reduces the likelihood of uncontrolled spins
   b. 180- and 360-degree turns, once 90-degree turns have been mastered
   c. In the event of lost heading control (spin), the student should recover lost control with "altitude, arch, legs, relax," before initiating opposite turn input.
   d. If the turn is sluggish or seems to go opposite the direction intended, the student should, provided altitude allows—
      (1) return to neutral arch
      (2) relax
      (3) extend legs
      (4) attempt the turn again
3. Maneuvers should be finished by 5,000 feet.
4. The instructor may accompany the student to observe heading control whenever practical.
   a. A USPA IAD, Static-Line or Tandem instructor seeing a student in danger of a low pull should immediately get clear and deploy his or her own parachute by 3,500 feet.
   b. Any student who is being accompanied by a USPA IAD, Static-Line, or Tandem Instructor should be told to deploy immediately upon seeing the instructor's parachute begin to open.
   c. A USPA IAD, Static-Line, or Tandem Instructor may not assist with the deployment of a student in freefall.
5. Review the importance of deployment at the correct altitude, regardless of stability.
6. Introduce alternate altitude references, e.g., looking at the ground, cloud bases, mountain tops, etc.
7. Increase exit altitude gradually as the jumper exhibits comfort with longer freefalls.
8. The student should begin this category with a 15-second freefall.
9. Four jumps are recommended.
10. Recommended minimum deployment altitude is 4,000 feet.
11. The candidates review the Category D freefall dive flows with the Examiner.

B. CANOPY

1. Introduction of rear riser steering and flaring
   a. back-riser steering with brakes on for evasive maneuvers immediately after opening
   b. steering with brakes off to evaluate controllability with a disabled toggle
   c. flaring to be able to decide whether a canopy can be landed safely with disabled controls
2. It is not recommended that a student practice an actual landing using rear risers to flare.
3. Students should practice all maneuvers above 1,000 feet with frequent traffic and position checks.
4. Landing within 50 meters with minimal assistance is recommended before advancing.

5. The candidates review the Category D canopy dive flow with the Examiner.

C. EMERGENCY PROCEDURE REVIEW

1. Because of the lower planned deployment altitude, students should by now demonstrate the ability to rapidly recognize and respond to equipment malfunctions.
    a. Category D includes the last formal training harness review of parachute malfunctions with an instructor as required for the A license, although the student should continue to self-review each new day of jumping (at least every 30 days).
    b. Review the cutaway decide-and-act altitude (2,500 feet).
2. Various categories of the ISP provide the instructor the opportunity to review emergency procedures taught in the first-jump course and discuss them in greater detail.
3. Whenever possible, emergency procedure review topics coincide with other related concepts from that category.
4. Conduct a detailed building or structure landing review, including disconnecting the RSL.

D. EQUIPMENT

1. The student should be calculating wing loading on both canopies (USPA Flight Planner) prior to each jump.
2. Introduce the AAD in detail.
    a. The student should operate the AAD.
    b. Ask the student to study the AAD owner's manual.
    c. Explain three-ring assembly and operation in detail.
    d. The student will disconnect and service the three-ring assembly in Category H.
3. Demonstrate a jumper equipment self-check and ask the student to perform it in the aircraft, followed by a check of the back of the rig by the instructor.
4. Discuss outerwear.

E. RULES AND RECOMMENDATIONS

The student should memorize the cloud clearance requirements from FAR 105.17 sufficiently to pass the Category D quiz and, later, the oral quiz as part of the USPA A-license check dive.

F. SPOTTING AND AIRCRAFT

1. The student should lead the pattern planning.
2. Introduction to spotting
    a. basic procedure overview
    b. looking straight down is the proper technique for observing the ground track of the aircraft
3. Technique for determining straight down
4. Coordinating spotting training with other jumpers
    a. In most aircraft, it is easy for the student to spot from the door and then move into position for a later exit.
    b. Experienced jumpers may need encouragement when introducing the modified pre-exit procedures.
    c. Coordinate and practice the procedures prior to takeoff.

G. METHOD TRANSITION STUDENTS

Review "Transitions" in the introduction to Category D.

H. REVIEW CATEGORY D QUIZ

CATEGORY E

A. EXIT AND FREEFALL

1. The student should attempt a stable unpoised exit.
2. Students begin this category directly supervised by a USPA Instructor until they can demonstrate reliable recovery from instability.
    a. Each student shows the ability twice to recover stability and altitude awareness within five seconds following an intentional disorienting maneuver.
    b. The first maneuver attempted should be a barrel roll, which has a natural recovery mode from back-to-earth fall.
    c. Recovery within five seconds (twice) is required to clear the student to freefall self-supervision.
3. Once any student has demonstrated stability recovery, he or she may self-supervise in freefall (requires the sign-off of a USPA Instructor).
4. Once signed off, the student should be supervised by a USPA instructional rating holder aboard the aircraft, who—
    a. is responsible and available for all training, spotting supervision, equipment choice, exit order, group separation on exit, and pre-jump equipment checks
    b. is encouraged to jump with and observe the student
    c. may make gripped exits
5. Once a student has qualified for freefall self-supervision, that student's previous training discipline is recognized only for the purpose of currency training (see SIM Section 5 on currency training).
6. Students may self-assess for the heading control required for the A license check dive (backloop within 60 degrees of the initial heading).
7. Three jumps are recommended in Category E for all students.
8. Hazards of aerobatics
    a. erratic fall rate and altimeter readings (chest mount, etc.)
    b. disorientation (altitude, arch, legs, relax)
    c. equipment considerations
9. The candidates review the Category E freefall dive flow with the Examiner.

B. CANOPY

1. Instructor's level of understanding
    a. Candidates for the USPA Instructor rating should have a working knowledge of the aerodynamic principles of a ram-air canopy.
    b. During the course, discussion on these topics led by knowledgeable individuals is encouraged.
2. By Category E, the student should now have sufficient canopy experience to recognize the results of different flare entries (review the "nine flares" discussion in the Canopy outline in Category E).
3. The goal is for the student to learn how to assess the flare on any new or unfamiliar canopy before landing.
4. The student learns to evaluate the result of the flare by recognizing a dynamic stall following a flare on landing and to adjust flare height, flare rate, and flare depth for the next landing.
5. The candidates review the Category E canopy dive flow with the Examiner.

C. EMERGENCY PROCEDURE REVIEW

Two canopies out: Review the "Two Canopies Out" discussion in SIM Section 5-1.

D. EQUIPMENT

1. The student should be performing a pre-flight inspection on the equipment

IAD SLI-2 — THE INTEGRATED STUDENT PROGRAM

(USPA Flight Planner checklist) prior to each jump.

2. Characteristics of different canopy designs (overview)
3. A person with appropriate knowledge should introduce the student to the open parachute canopy, identifying and naming all the significant parts in preparation for packing.

E. RULES AND RECOMMENDATIONS

1. Detailed discussion on winds pertinent to the student's increased level of experience and to prepare the student to make informed decisions as a USPA A license holder
2. Discussion with pilot on portions of FAR 91 applicable to jump operations (Section 9 of the SIM)

F. SPOTTING AND AIRCRAFT

1. Category E aircraft briefing
   a. interaction between jumpers and aircraft control
   b. reading a winds-aloft report
   c. spotting procedures
2. The USPA Instructor should be sure the student has been trained for independent action in all aircraft emergency procedures (Category E aircraft briefing) before clearing the student to freefall self-supervision.
3. Technique for determining opening point by averaging the speed and direction of winds forecast at opening altitude and read at the surface on the drop zone

G. REVIEW CATEGORY E QUIZ

2-5: GROUP SKYDIVING SKILLS

1. The last three categories of the Integrated Student Program prepare the student to jump safely and effectively in groups:
   a. tracking
   b. group exits
   c. group flying skills
   d. breakoff procedures
   e. flying the canopy in groups
2. Students who complete Category H should be ready for
   a. the USPA A-license checkout with an appropriately rated USPA Instructor
   b. independent skydiving at most skydiving centers
   c. jumping at off-site DZs that meet the A-license landing area criteria (non-demos)
3. The exit and freefall sections of Categories F through H are included in the USPA Coach Rating Course syllabus.

CATEGORY F

A. EXIT AND FREEFALL

1. Tracking
   a. Emphasize legs fully extended as the primary means of movement.
   b. Demonstrate shoulder steering using a creeper or similar training aid.
   c. Make heading control the primary objective (over speed).
   d. This training will lead toward developing a better flat track during Categories G and H.
2. Two tracking dives minimum are recommended in Category F.
3. Clear and pull: Students trained in the AFF method should gain confidence with a stable exit and pull at a higher altitude (5,500 feet) before attempting the actual clear and pull at 3,500 feet.
4. The candidates review the Category F freefall dive flow with the Examiner.

B. CANOPY

1. Encourage students to become familiar with braked flight and braked landings to prevent the mistake of making a low single-toggle turn when presented with the need for a low heading change.
   a. sudden recognition of an obstacle
   b. returning from a long spot and misjudging the final turn (frequently committed error)
   c. being cut off by another jumper in the landing area
2. Use of brakes or rear risers to increase glide
   a. Anticipate loss of the tailwind nearer the ground and keep an alternate landing area in mind between the jumper's position and the target.
   b. Different canopies exhibit different flight characteristics with brake or rear riser input.
3. Anticipate a much broader landing pattern and longer final approach when flying in brakes with some canopies.
4. It is important for the USPA Instructor to understand and experience these aspects of canopy flight, particularly how they apply to the canopy the student is jumping.
5. The candidates review the Category F canopy dive flow with the Examiner.

C. EMERGENCY PROCEDURE REVIEW

Detailed power-line avoidance and landing review

D. EQUIPMENT

1. Focus on packing
2. Equipment check on another jumper (with that jumper's permission)

E. RULES AND RECOMMENDATIONS

The USPA Instructor should familiarize students with USPA currency recommendations in SIM Section 5.

F. SPOTTING AND AIRCRAFT

1. The student should be calculating the opening point on each jump (USPA Flight Planner).
2. Averaging the winds aloft to determine the jump run and exit point (effective only in routine conditions)
3. Separating groups according to distance across the ground
4. A dedicated spotting training and practice flight has shown to be an effective method of familiarizing students with spotting.

CATEGORIES G AND H

The course staff and candidates discuss the Category G and H outline in the ISP.

A. CANOPY

1. Category G
   a. Performance turns teach the student necessary information about his or her canopy.
      (1) how to keep the center of lift and pressure in the center of the canopy during turn entry and exit and avoid a collapse or line twist
      (2) the limits of control on that canopy with that student's weight before it develops line twists or collapses from over control
      (3) how to test the limits of any new or unfamiliar canopy
      (4) potential consequences of high-performance maneuvers near the ground
   b. Review collision avoidance, focusing on the group skydiving environment, including rights of way and the importance of avoiding a collision, regardless of the rules and courtesies.
2. Category H

a. Front risers provide a potential third set of controls.
   b. Some jumpers will not be able to take advantage of front riser control, but should realize their limits compared to other jumpers.
   c. Emphasize front riser safety: The canopy must be returned to straight and level flight in time for landing.

B. EMERGENCY PROCEDURE REVIEW

1. Category G
   a. A USPA Instructor reviews in detail the procedures for responding to an imminent canopy collision and what to do in the event of an entanglement.
   b. A canopy formation specialist makes a good resource for teaching this topic.
2. Category H (USPA Instructor or Examiner)
   a. training for an unintentional water landing
   b. training for an unplanned low turn under canopy

C. EQUIPMENT

1. Category G
   a. The student continues to focus on packing and should pack one parachute without assistance prior to advancing to Category H.
   b. An FAA rigger or an instructor should conduct the wear and maintenance seminar outlined in this Section of the ISP syllabus, including a review of the FARs concerning maintenance personnel.
2. Category H
   a. three ring disassembly, maintenance, and reassembly
   b. discussion of stow band choice (review)
   c. replacement and adjustment of a main closing loop

D. RULES AND RECOMMENDATIONS

1. Category G: repack cycle (review) and rigger maintenance
2. Category H: general review of the oral quizzes for the A-license check dive

E. SPOTTING AND AIRCRAFT

1. Category G
   a. The student should be calculating the spot, including the exit point, for each jump in routine winds (USPA Flight Planner).
   b. Jumpers need to be responsible for knowing the kinds of weather that can get them into trouble.
   c. The instructor or pilot should review the various means of finding weather forecasts.
2. Category H
   a. This section is best taught by a jump pilot or instructor.
   b. A license holders are qualified to jump at locations other than a regular drop zone and should know—
      (1) where to find the information for notifying ATC of the jump.
      (2) equipment and approval requirements for jump aircraft
   c. In general, USPA A-license holders should know what to expect of the aircraft operator at the drop zone in terms of paperwork for modifications and maintenance.

2-6: VERIFYING USPA LICENSES

1. A license
   a. Review SIM Section 3-2 for conducting the USPA A-license check dive and completing the USPA A license application.
   b. Compare and contrast the two A license applications.
      (1) four-page A License Progression Card, designed for use with the ISP
      (2) two-page A License Proficiency Card for use with equivalent programs or for unlicensed jumpers who began training prior to the Basic Safety Requirement for a USPA A license (January, 2001).
2. B and C license
   a. Review SIM Section 3-2 for instructions and procedures regarding the USPA B and C license, with particular attention to the license application checklist.
      (1) exam administration
      (2) verification of qualifications
   b. Review the USPA B-D License Application included in the back of the SIM.
   c. Only a USPA S&TA, Examiner, or member of the USPA Board of Directors may approve D license applications.

3. IAD and Static-Line Methods

3-1: ROUTINE PROCEDURES

A. INTRODUCTION

1. The IAD and static-line methods require special equipment knowledge both for preparation and use.
2. The two methods share common techniques and procedures, as well as being subject to unique operations and malfunctions.
3. Special FAA rules apply to the use of static-line equipment.

B. STATIC-LINE RIGGING

1. The static-line assembly
   a. A static line assembly should be at least 3,500 pounds tensile strength with a MS70120 static-line snap for attachment to the aircraft.
   b. After deployment, the static line or deployment bag must not contact aircraft control surfaces.
   c. The static line must be secured to the container in such a manner that the student may climb to the farthest point from the attachment without loading the static line and opening the container.
   d. The static line needs to be secured to the container (elastic bands, etc.) so the wind cannot shake and extract the closing pin or device from the closing loop and open the main container during climb-out.
2. Static-line deployment types
   a. When correctly used, direct-bag static-line deployment is the most reliable means of deploying a ram-air main parachute.
      (1) Deployment does not guarantee a canopy suitable for landing.
      (2) Direct-bag deployment often leads to line twist, the significance of which depends on the performance characteristics of the canopy.
      (3) If mishandled, direct-bag deployment can lead to injury for the student or the instructor.
   b. The pilot-chute assist method presents an acceptable alternative for static-line deployment.
      (1) A static-line-rigged main parachute using a pilot chute requires a separable assist device (FAR 105.47).
      (2) The student may be able to grab and hold the pilot chute during an unstable exit.
      (3) If the instructor holds the static line too low, the pilot chute can deploy under the student's inboard arm, presenting an invitation for the student to grab the deploying parachute.
      (4) The less-positive deployment results in slower deployments than with direct bag.
      (5) Pilot-chute assist often results in a slower and more on-heading inflation than direct bag.
3. A rig static-lined for a right hand door may sustain damage if used in an aircraft with a left-hand door.
4. The aircraft plays an integral role in the rigging.
   a. The static line attachment point needs to be anchored securely to the airframe (FAA Form 337 or STC approval).
   b. Attaching the static line to a seat belt assembly may result in the failure of the seat belt hardware or mountings.
   c. Attachment to the pilot's seat may result in its sudden removal from the aircraft as a result of a mis-rigged static-line system.
   d. The static-line attachment point must be secure and in good condition.

C. STATIC-LINE HANDLING

1. All static lines require careful handling on the part of the instructor to facilitate a good deployment and prevent instructor and student injuries that occur from fouling with the static line.
   a. The instructor must hold the static line high enough to prevent student interference with deployment, which could lead to a malfunction or injury.
   b. The instructor must not allow any part of his or her body to get between the load path of the static line and any part of the aircraft.
   c. The practice of the instructor putting one leg on the step of a Cessna to be closer to the student is not recommended.
2. Before actual student operations using any new aircraft, the static-line instructor should practice many times with connecting and disconnecting a static line while wearing protective gloves (strongly recommended for conducting static-line jumps).
3. The instructor should disconnect and securely stow each static line assembly prior to any subsequent jump operation from that aircraft.

D. SPECIAL CONSIDERATIONS FOR IAD

1. The main container must be rigged correctly, including a tight, well-maintained closing loop to prevent premature container opening during climb-out or on the step.
2. The throw-out pilot chute
   a. collapsible pilot chutes
      (1) Kill-line pilot chutes must be cocked during packing and checked during the equipment pre-flight.
      (2) A Kill-line pilot chute must be folded and handled in such a way that it remains cocked after it is folded and during the deployment.
      (3) Bungee-type, elastic shock cord centerline types are not recommended.
   b. folding the pilot chute
      (1) The pilot chute should be extracted and refolded in the aircraft so it can be handled easily and not be prone to an accidental premature deployment (dropping it in the windstream).
      (2) The bridle should be folded in a manner that allows it to extend in an orderly fashion when the pilot chute is thrown.
   c. The pouch needs to be tight, in good working order, and mounted in a location accessible for IAD operations.
      (1) bottom of container
      (2) leg strap (not suitable for student freefall)
3. Student climb-out
   a. The IAD student must verify that the IAD Instructor has control of the pilot chute before climbing out.
   b. For wing-strut type aircraft, having the student kneel next to the door and face forward provides the instructor good control.
   c. pilot chute position

(1) The instructor should hold the folded pilot chute under the bottom of the student's main container during climb-out and launch.

(2) Throwing the pilot chute from the yoke of the container may increase the chance of a pilot-chute hesitation.

d. For wing-strut type aircraft, a hanging exit is recommended.

4. The IAD Instructor must get into a position on the step close enough to the student to prevent tension on the pilot-chute bridle from opening the main container.

a. Some instructors climb out with the student, keeping the pilot chute on the student's backpack and out of the airstream.

b. The student should be taught to climb out slowly so the instructor can stay close with the pilot chute in hand.

c. A bridle artificially secured to the container (to prevent a premature opening) may fail to release after the pilot chute is deployed, resulting in a pilot-chute-in-tow malfunction.

5. The IAD Instructor must deploy the pilot chute out and down in a manner that ensures clearance from all parts of the aircraft.

a. as the student commits to the launch and releases from the aircraft

b. immediately, in the case of a premature container opening on the step

6. Airflow

a. The pilot should apply sufficient flaps during IAD operations to ensure the deploying pilot chute blows under the horizontal stabilizer of the aircraft.

b. To test for a safe airflow and pilot chute dispatch, use newspaper to simulate parachute fabric during an actual flight before conducting actual IAD operations.

E. STUDENT'S MAIN DEPLOYMENT SYSTEM

1. Hand deployment
   a. BOC only
   b. practice handles must be mounted so that IAD or static-line deployment doesn't cause them to move (a consideration with a BOC mounting).

2. Ripcord locations
   a. BOC makes it impossible to see the handle and promotes arching.

b. Main lift web (high or low) allows the student see the ripcord, but requires that the student concentrate on arching while looking at the handle.

F. IN-FLIGHT PROCEDURES

1. At 1,500 feet, unfasten all seat belts prior to hooking up any static lines or preparing any hand deployed pilot chutes for IAD operations.

2. Once the seat belts are off and the static line of the first jumper is connected and checked or the pilot chute of the first IAD jumper is prepared and verified by the student, the student should spend the remainder of the flight mentally rehearsing and self-calming.

3. At approximately 3,000 feet AGL, review airport and landing area, opening point, and landing pattern.

4. On freefall jumps, review the deployment altitude with the student at that point during ascent, then have the student verbally review the freefall and canopy dive flows

5. After the verbal review, give the student "quiet time" to mentally rehearse the dive.

6. Following the "quiet time" and prior to the exit, the instructor performs the pre-exit equipment check, including the hand-deployed pilot chute or static line and radio.

G. CLIMB-OUT PROCEDURES

1. Use a procedure that enables the student to get into position with minimal effort.

a. The student should avoid presenting the full torso broad to the wind during the transition from the door to the step ("knife" into the wind).

b. The student should limit arm and shoulder extension to 90 degrees to avoid muscle strain and injury and avoid reaching to full arm extension while climbing out.

STRUT EXIT (CESSNA)

1. Improves the student's chance for a stable exit and deployment

2. Hanging exit considerations
   a. requires the student to move to a launch position far enough out on the wing strut to clear the wheel and the step on release
   b. possible problems if the student hangs prior to reaching the end of the step
   c. requires more strength from the student to hang prior to exit
   d. requires the static line be very tightly secured against the wind blast

IAD AND STATIC-LINE METHODS | IAD SLI – 3

e. allows the instructor to coach the student for a better body position prior to release

f. less likelihood of a backflip on exit

g. If it is obvious the student lacks the strength for a hanging exit, it may be better to train for a step exit.

3. Step exit considerations
   a. easier for the student to maintain a grip on the strut prior to launch
   b. less static line exposed to the wind blast
   c. less likelihood of the student launching or falling ahead of the step, but more likelihood of a poor legs-first launch resulting in the student striking the step
   d. more likelihood of a hands-first release, resulting in a possible backflip
   e. difficult to pre-arch or respond to corrective hand signals from the instructor prior to release

4. Allow as much as a minute from climb-out to release for beginners.
   (1) Advance the first command accordingly.
   (2) For smaller students, ask the pilot for a slower airspeed during the transition from the door to the step.

Helpful hint: Handle the gear for the student during climb-out, actually lifting the equipment into position and relieving the student of the weight through the transition from the door to the step.

5. Use three commands, for example—
   a. At "In the door!" the student—
      (1) places both feet outside and one hand on the wing strut near the base
      (2) continues to protect the deployment handles
      (3) looks at the instructor for the next command
   b. (hanging exit) At "Hang from the strut!" the student—
      (1) shifts all his or her weight to both feet and places both hands on the wing strut
      (2) moves completely to the end of the wing strut
      (3) removes both feet from the step and gets into the arch position with legs extended

IAD SLI-3 | IAD AND STATIC-LINE METHODS

(4) looks at the instructor for the next command

c. (step exit): At "On the step!" the student—

(1) shifts all his or her weight to both feet and places both hands on the wing strut

(2) places the inboard foot on the end of the step

(3) trails the outboard foot, pre-arches (chest over the strut and head up)

(4) looks at the instructor for the next command

d. On "Go!" the student looks up, takes a breath, and releases from the aircraft.

SEATED SIDE-DOOR EXIT

1. On "Sit in the door!" the student faces the wind blast.
   a. seated on the edge of the door (inboard thigh and buttock only on the floor, outboard hanging over the edge)
   b. both knees facing the front of the aircraft
   c. the inboard hand ready to push off
2. The instructor faces the door and controls the deployment device and the student.
3. The instructor maintains control of the student until the student clears the aircraft on "Go!" (instructor assists as necessary).

H. EQUIPMENT

1. Review BSRs on student equipment.
2. AADs and audible altimeters are recommended for USPA instructional rating holders when making training jumps with students.

I. FARS CONCERNING STATIC LINES

1. Assist devices
   a. Ram-air parachutes rigged with a direct bag do not require a positive assist device, and the use of one could damage the canopy.
   b. When using a static line to initiate the deployment of a main parachute equipped with a pilot chute, the FAA requires an assist device attached to the pilot chute with a static load strength of at least 28 and no more than 160 pounds.
2. Only an FAA rigger or the person making the jump may attach an assist device to a parachute to be deployed with a static line.

3-2: IAD AND STATIC-LINE PROBLEM SOLVING

A. INTRODUCTION

1. On any IAD or static-line jump dive, particularly a first jump, the instructor must choose the best course of action, based on the student's performance.
2. The following responses are to be applied as the situation dictates.

B. CLIMB-OUT AND EXIT

1. If the student refuses to climb out, close the door and go around.
   a. Encourage the student using positive mental images.
   b. Review the climb-out and launch, getting the student to visualize.
   c. Repeat the pre-jump equipment check.
   d. Involve the student in all procedures as much as possible on the second jump run.
      (1) door open
      (2) spot observation
      (3) pilot communication
   e. Start the second climb-out early.
2. Refusal: In the case of multiple students aboard, extra caution is required to reposition students in the aircraft should one decide not to jump.
3. If the student takes too long to climb out for a good spot—
   a. Using the student's harness, assist the student in returning to the "in the door" position, then back into the aircraft.
   b. If it's not possible to retrieve the student, work with the pilot to release the student over a safe landing area.
      (1) Add power and airspeed.
      (2) Shake the wing (Cessna).
   c. The safety of the student and others in the aircraft must be the first consideration.
4. If the student climbs only partway into position, encourage the student into a safe launch position using verbal and hand signals.
5. If the student presents a poor arch—
   a. Yell, "Arch!" prior to, "Go!"
   b. Present the student with a pre-arranged "arch" signal.

3-3: IAD AND STATIC-LINE EMERGENCIES

A. AIRCRAFT MALFUNCTION

1. The correct response to a low-altitude emergency will always depend on circumstances, including the severity of the problem, the capabilities of the aircraft, the available terrain for landing the plane or parachute, and the abilities of the jumpers aboard.
2. Landing with the aircraft is usually required up to 1,500 feet.
   a. The student takes all direction from the instructor.
   b. Fasten seat belts and buckle helmets.
   c. Disconnect the static line, if attached.
   d. For any aircraft descent, disarm the AAD as required (see owner's manual).
   e. Prepare for a hard landing.
3. Bailout: Exit and pull reserve.
   a. The instructor guides the student to the door.
   b. The student places the left hand on the reserve ripcord and pulls two seconds after exit or with sufficient altitude.
      (1) The instructor and student may use the bail-out procedure with the static-lined main parachute.
      (2) Freefall students may use a similar procedure with the main parachute.
4. A poised exit with the static-line hooked up whenever altitude allows.

B. PARACHUTE OPEN IN THE AIRCRAFT

1. If the parachute stays inside, first close the door.
   a. Main—disconnect the canopy release system and reserve static line, and all ride down with the aircraft.
   b. Reserve—remove the rig, if practical, and all ride down with the aircraft.
2. If the parachute goes out, the student must exit quickly without waiting for a command from the instructor.

C. PREMATURE DEPLOYMENT DURING THE EXIT SET-UP

1. If possible, the pilot should quickly skid the aircraft to get the horizontal stabilizer out of the path of the deploying parachute.

2. The instructor must get the student off the aircraft immediately.

D. STUDENT IN TOW (STATIC-LINE)

1. Static line fails to release (conscious student).
   a. If the student signals readiness via a pre-arranged signal, ask the pilot to continue to climb, if possible, and fly to an area that will allow the student to land in a clear field or the drop zone.
   b. Cut the static line as close to the student's container as possible (always carry a knife aboard the aircraft).
   c. If no other students are aboard the aircraft, follow the student to his or her landing area.
2. Static line fails to release (student unconscious).
   a. Have the pilot climb and fly over a clear, unobstructed area.
   b. The instructor cuts the static line and trusts the AAD to open the student's reserve.

E. SKYDIVER IN TOW

1. If the student is conscious and recognizes the problem and the parachute is the main parachute, he or she should attempt to cut away and deploy the reserve.
2. If the student is unconscious or the parachute is a reserve parachute, the response will depend on the circumstances, including—
   a. controllability of the aircraft
   b. landing terrain or facilities available to the aircraft
3. If the student is in tow due to an entanglement with a seat belt or jump suit, the offending attachment should be cut.

IAD SLI-4: INSTRUCTOR'S DUTIES

4-1: CONDUCTING THE JUMP

A. STUDENT PREPARATION

1. Introduction of student and instructor
   a. on the instructor's initiative
   b. familiarizes the two with each other
   c. sets the tone for the conduct of the training and jump
2. Administrative
   a. paperwork (registration, waiver)
   b. payment
   c. documentation available (logbook, A license application card)
   d. training and review complete
3. Personal
   a. water, food, restroom
   b. pockets cleared, jewelry off, gum disposed
   c. special considerations (medical)
4. Disposition
   a. behavior consistent and positive
   b. perspiration
   c. breath
   d. breathing rate
   e. rate of movement (nervous or jumpy?)
   f. voice

B. TRAINING

1. Each instructor is responsible for all previous training.
   a. thorough review of the student's performance records
      (1) logbook
      (2) A license application card
      (3) DZ master log
      (4) discussion with previous instructors
   b. student's subjective evaluation of the previous jump (What did the student think?)
   c. questions specific to the last skydive
   d. thorough review of the four emergency areas—aircraft, freefall, equipment, landing—using the appropriate training aids
      (1) aircraft mock-up
      (2) training harness
      (3) landing trainer
      (4) other
   e. the longer the interval between jumps, the more the student will have forgotten
2. Introduce the performance objectives of the next lesson and advancement criteria for the next jump.
   a. Use appropriate descriptions and demonstrations.
   b. Conduct informal rehearsals using the appropriate training aids to enhance realism.
3. Be sure the student is equipped correctly for the skydive (equipment check before rigging up).
4. Prepare the canopy flight plan.
5. Conduct a full-dress rehearsal or dirt dive until the student performs everything smoothly and correctly.
   a. without coaching or prompting
   b. real time
6. Assemble and brief a ground crew.
   a. canopy instruction (radio)
   b. student assistance and retrieval
7. Perform the pre-boarding equipment check, including all personal items and the radio.

C. ABOARD THE AIRCRAFT

1. Monitor the student's equipment.
2. Coordinate exit position and planned interaction with other jumpers or groups during exit.
3. Encourage self-reliance.
4. Conduct the pre-exit equipment check.
5. Supervise spotting, according to the student's level.

D. JUMP SUPERVISION AND OBSERVATION

1. An instructor should be able to effectively observe a student making short freefalls (up to ten seconds) from the aircraft.
2. The instructor may jump with students making longer freefalls to observe and critique for retraining during the debrief.

E. POST JUMP

1. Verify that the student has landed safely and returned to the operations center.
   a. All equipment accounted for and put away.
   b. The student knows the debrief plan.
2. Debriefing
   a. The debrief provides instructors with an opportunity to facilitate the learning process by encouraging the student to recognize their achievements and what they did correctly, as well as help them realize what is needed to move forward in their skill development.
   b. The student must become more aware of their strengths and weaknesses and take responsibility for their training.
   c. The debrief process contains the following steps:
      (1) restate the goals
      (2) things that worked
      (3) things that need improvement
      (4) how to improve
      (5) make new goals
   d. Restate the goals
      (1) the student will most likely focus on the negative parts of the jump
      (2) restating the goals helps them open up their mind to the rest of the tasks whether it be the exit, break-off or canopy control tasks
   e. Things that worked
      (1) ask the student what went well on the jump, what he did well
      (2) the student will naturally want to focus on the negative; by having him state what he did well on the jump, it starts the debrief on a positive note
      (3) this process will need to be repeated on several jumps before the student typically starts to enter the debrief on a positive note stating what they liked about their performance then noting what they need to improve on
   f. Things that need improvement
      (1) ask the student what needs improvement
      (2) this lets you know if the student is aware of his errors
      (3) if the student overlooks a part of the skydive that should have been recalled, play through the video again and ask him how he

felt about performing the skill to see if it jogs his memory

(4) if it does not, this is the instructor's opportunity to restate the goals of the jump and provide guidance on how to improve

g. How to improve

(1) ask this question to the student

(2) the student should have a good idea of what he needs to work on

(3) if the student cannot see the answer, this is the opportunity for the instructor to review the correct techniques and assist him to see what is needed

(4) patience and good listening skills of the instructor will help the student take charge of his learning and become further committed to his goals

h. Make new goals

(1) ask the student what he would like to do on the next jump

(2) if the goals and expectations of each jump are clear, the student should be quite realistic about his performance

(3) if the environment has been set that "mistakes are OK" the student should have a realistic assessment of what he needs to do on the next jump, even if it means repeating the same jump

(4) the Instructor's role during the debrief should be one of a facilitator

(5) asking questions and directing the student to the right information through self-realization will be of greater benefit to the student

F. ADDITIONAL TRAINING

The instructor conducts or supervises the required training in equipment, rules and recommendations, and spotting and aircraft appropriate for the student's level of advancement (category).

4-2: VIDEO AND CAMERA

1. Video has proven to be an effective training and marketing aid, but the USPA Instructor must approve and brief the videographer prior to the jump.
2. Refer to the Skydiver's Information Manual, Section 6, for camera flyer recommendations, particularly those pertaining to student jumps.
3. Minimum experience qualifications
   a. 300 group freefall skydives
   b. 50 jumps flying camera with experienced jumpers

4. Considerations for photographers on IAD and static-line jumps
   a. The camera flyer needs to remain clear of the student during and following exit.
   b. Only USPA-rated Instructors may interact with students during exit and freefall until the student is cleared to freefall self-supervision.
5. The USPA Instructor should correct any camera flyer actions that cause concern.

4-3: PRE-JUMP CHECKS

A. INTRODUCTION

1. One of the instructor's greatest responsibilities is equipment management.
2. Preparation before boarding prevents accidents.
3. Having an organized routine will make the operation run more smoothly.
4. Conduct three complete equipment checks.
   a. before rigging up
   b. before boarding
   c. before exit

B. EQUIPMENT PREPARATION

1. Always check the rig in a logical order, such as top to bottom, back to front.
2. A typical sequence (varies according to equipment configuration)
   a. automatic activation device
      (1) switched on
      (2) calibrated
   b. reserve ripcord
      (1) movement of the cable in the housing
      (2) pin in place at least halfway, but not shouldered onto the grommet
      (3) closing loop must have no visible wear
      (4) closing loop tight for properly closed container
      (5) reserve in date, seal intact
   c. main closing (hand deployment)
      (1) flap closing order and bridle routing correct
      (2) slack above the curved pin
      (3) pin fully seated
      (4) tight closing loop, with no more than ten percent visible fraying
      (5) pin secured to bridle with no more than ten percent fraying
      (6) collapsible pilot chute cocked

(7) pilot chute and bridle with no more than ten percent damage at any wear point

d. main closing (ripcord)
   (1) free movement of the cable in the housing
   (2) secure cable housing ends
   (3) ripcord end not kinked or nicked
   (4) closing loop with no more than ten percent fraying
e. main deployment handle in place
f. canopy release system and RSL
   (1) correct canopy release assembly
   (2) RSL connected and routed correctly
g. chest strap and hardware
   (1) snap type connected and adjusted
   (2) friction adapter type: threaded correctly, adjusted, and running end secured to prevent slippage
h. reserve ripcord handle
i. canopy release handle
j. harness adjustments
k. leg straps and hardware
   (1) threaded properly
   (2) hardware function (snap operation)
l. outer clothing (or jumpsuit)
   (1) free movement
   (2) adequate protection on landing
   (3) secure; can't impede handle access
   (4) pockets empty, jewelry removed
   (5) fall rate (if applicable)

3. Using the same sequence, check the equipment after the student is completely rigged and with everything adjusted, paying particular attention to the following;
   a. risers over the shoulder, not under the arm
   b. release handle not under the main lift web
   c. proper threading of harness hardware
   d. chest strap routed clear of the reserve ripcord

IAD SLI – 4 | INSTRUCTOR'S DUTIES

   e. twisted harness straps
   f. comfort pads in position
   g. overall adjustment and fit: A loose harness may allow the container to shift in freefall, causing stability problems.
4. Student's personal equipment (SHAGGAR, explained below)
   a. **S**hoes
      (1) appropriate for the student jumping; sandals, heels, and leather (or synthetic leather) soles not recommended
      (2) hooks taped
      (3) laces double knotted
   b. **H**elmet
      (1) adequate protection
      (2) fit and adjustment
   c. **A**ltimeter
      (1) readable by student (farsightedness?)
      (2) zeroed
   d. **G**oggles
      (1) correct type for contacts or glasses
      (2) clear and clean
      (3) tight
   e. **G**loves
      (1) worn for jumps into 40 degrees or cooler
      (2) light and flexible
   f. **A**erial photograph for pattern planning (USPA Flight Planner)
   g. **R**adio or other means of communication
      (1) all required equipment in place and ready
      (2) all required personnel coordinated
      (3) entire team informed of the canopy flight plan
      (4) "no-jump" signal prepared
      (5) student's radio on
5. Perform another pre-jump inspection in the aircraft prior to exit.

C. AIRCRAFT PREPARATION

1. Inspect and prepare the aircraft.
   a. familiar with door operation
   b. protrusions removed
   c. smooth edges
   d. seat belts clear
   e. knife aboard
   f. pilot rig in date
2. Brief the pilot.
   a. spot
   b. routine procedures
   c. flap settings and airspeeds
   d. emergency procedures
      (1) aircraft malfunctions
      (2) premature openings
      (3) ensuring a knife is available for the pilot to use in an emergency
   e. flight plan and altitudes for the load

D. JUMP CONDITIONS

1. Up-to-date weather forecast
2. Surface winds and winds aloft
3. Daylight remaining

E. REFER TO SIM 5-4, PRE-JUMP SAFETY CHECKS AND BRIEFINGS

4-4: PRE-JUMP CHECKS (STATIC-LINE SUPPLEMENT)

A. STATIC-LINE PREPARATION

1. Correct length for that aircraft
2. Routing correct for pack opening and orientation to aircraft door
3. Static line secured against the windblast (extra stow bands, etc.)
4. Closing pin(s) or cables
   a. in place in a manner to prevent release during climb-out
   b. no more than ten percent visible damage at attachment to static line
   c. not bent or cracked
5. Main closing loop(s) tight and no more than ten percent visible damage
6. Static-line abrasion
   a. No more than ten percent damage anywhere on static line assembly
   b. If damage is visible on the static line, connect it to the aircraft to see if the damaged area is abrading on the aircraft.
7. Assist device attached (pilot chute assist type)
8. Perform another pre-jump inspection in the aircraft just after hook-up.

B. AIRCRAFT PREPARATION

1. Special aircraft configuration
   a. static-line attachment sturdy and recently inspected by an aircraft mechanic
   b. knife aboard
2. Brief the pilot for special static-line procedures and emergencies
   a. go-arounds
   b. student refusal; retrieval impossible
   c. premature opening on step
   d. student in tow

C. AT 1,500 FEET (OR DZ POLICY)

1. Seat belts off (all jumpers)
2. Static line hooked up and checked by the student(s) on the first pass only
3. Pre-exit equipment check, including static-line routing from backpack to attachment and radio

4-5: CURRENCY TRAINING

1. The Examiner and USPA Instructor rating candidates review USPA currency recommendations for students and experienced jumpers found in SIM Section 5-2.
2. Recommended currency training and jumps for most licensed skydivers may be conducted by a USPA Coach under a USPA Instructor's supervision.

5. Demonstration and Ground Practice for Evaluations

A. PURPOSE

1. After the classroom portion and prior to evaluations, the instructor examiner and staff demonstrate how to conduct the student training and jump activities for which the candidates are being rated and evaluated.
2. Candidates may practice the skills, supervised by the course staff, keeping in mind that course time is limited and evaluations must soon begin.

B. IAD AND STATIC-LINE SESSIONS

1. Prior-to-boarding sequence
   a. pre-jump training of students in Category B (includes practice deployments)
   b. static-line rigging and other equipment preparation
   c. jump preparation
   d. pre-boarding equipment check
2. Pre-boarding, boarding, climb-to-altitude, and pre-jump sequence:
   a. control of the student in the loading area and in the aircraft for boarding and the climb to altitude
   b. deployment system preparation and pre-exit equipment check procedures
   c. control of the student's movement in the aircraft during climb-out
   d. spotting and pilot communications
3. Student observation
4. Post-jump critique

C. FREEFALL SESSION

1. Conduct Category D training using the ISP outline
2. Using the mock-up, the correct procedures for pre-boarding, boarding, climb to altitude, climb-out, and exit
3. Using a simulated student performance scenario, a proper debrief

D. DIVE FLOWS

EVALUATOR ACTING AS STUDENT

JUMP 1

Use the dive flow for Category B in the Integrated Student Program.

JUMP 2 (SOLO FREEFALL)

Use the dive flow for Category D, Dive Plan 2 in the Integrated Student Program

IAD SLI-6 | CANDIDATE EVALUATION

A. INTRODUCTION

1. This section of the course is to be presented to the candidates with all evaluators for that course present.
   a. serves as the evaluator's briefing
   b. reassures the candidates that they are fully informed of all evaluation criteria and instructions
   c. provides a dialog and rapport between candidates and evaluators before testing begins
2. The IAD and Static-Line Instructor Rating Course includes two practical evaluation sections.
   a. IAD or static-line jumps
      (1) ground training
      (2) in the air (actual jumping)
   b. solo jump training, observation, and debrief
3. The course also includes a written exam.
4. There are two formats of evaluation dives.
   a. satisfactorily plan and execute two IAD or static-line jumps taken from Category B of the ISP (with practice deployments)
   b. satisfactory non-method-specific freefall training and observation jump

B. GENERAL

1. To ensure standardized procedures, each evaluation should be conducted in generally the same manner and to the same standards of performance.
2. For the IAD and static-line jump evaluations, the Examiner may divide the candidates into teams of two, supervised by an evaluator; may switch team members; or the evaluator may act as student.
3. The evaluator explains in detail what will be considered a satisfactory performance during the training and jump operations.
4. For the freefall student evaluation(s), only evaluators will portray students participating in a training jump.

C. AREAS TO BE EVALUATED

IAD OR STATIC-LINE JUMP EVALUATION

Each candidate is evaluated in all the subject areas and sub-areas shown on the IAD and Static-Line In-Air Skills Evaluation Form.

1. Preparation
2. Explanation and demonstration
3. Student trial and practice
4. Review and evaluation
5. Jump preparation
   a. student's flight plan
   b. ground support personnel (radio, student retrieval)
   c. aircraft preparation
   d. pilot briefing
6. Equipment check—three required
7. Supervision (equipment, pre-boarding, and boarding)
8. Climb to altitude
   a. helmet and seat belt
   b. view of airport
   c. verbal review
   d. mental review
   e. spotting
9. Deployment system preparation and pre-exit equipment check
10. Climb-out control
    a. student
    b. deployment device

FREEFALL JUMP EVALUATION

Each candidate is evaluated in all the subject areas and sub-areas shown on the Freefall Ground Training, Supervision, and Debriefing Evaluation Form.

1. Preparation
2. Explanation and demonstration
3. Student trial and practice
4. Review
5. Supervision (equipment—three checks, pre-boarding, and boarding)
6. Climb to altitude
   a. helmet and seat belt
   b. view of airport
   c. deployment altitude review
   d. mental review
   e. verbal review
   f. equipment check prior to exit
   g. spotting
7. Exit and freefall observation and altitude monitoring
8. Opening to landing
   a. observe student canopy control
   b. set good example
9. debriefing
   a. walk and talk
   b. corrective training
   c. decision to advance
   d. preview next dive
   e. paperwork
10. The freefall ground training, air evaluation, and post-jump debrief is required for all candidates, regardless of whether the candidate holds any USPA instructor ratings in other disciplines

D. SCHEDULE

IAD AND STATIC-LINE EVALUATIONS

1. The IAD and static-line evaluations are scored on the IAD and Static-Line Training and Supervision Evaluation Form.
2. Evaluation for preparation, explanation and demonstration, student trial and practice, and review (ground training)—
   a. begins when the evaluator calls "time in," and the candidate begins training the stand-in student
   b. ends when the candidate declares the ground training portion of the evaluation complete
3. Once the ground training portion of the evaluation is complete—
   a. The candidate manifests the load.
   b. The candidate informs the evaluator where to meet on the 20-minute call for the load.
   c. The candidate is released until the 20-minute call for the load.
4. The remainder of the evaluation
   a. begins at the 20-minute call for the load and continues through pre-boarding, climb-out, and the jump
   b. breaks for aircraft and canopy descent and the return of the jumpers to the packing area
   c. resumes after the candidate receives the mock ground crew report from the evaluator on the student's canopy descent
   d. continues as the candidate begins the debrief of the evaluator or person acting as the student (with the evaluator present)
   e. ends when the candidate completes the debrief

CANDIDATE EVALUATION | IAD SLI – 6

FREEFALL JUMP EVALUATION

1. The freefall evaluations are scored on the IAD, Static-Line, and Tandem Training, Supervision, and Debriefing Evaluation Form.
2. Evaluation for preparation, explanation and demonstration, student trial and practice, and review (ground training)—
   a. begins when the evaluator calls "time in," and the candidate begins training the stand-in student
   b. ends when the candidate declares the ground training portion of the evaluation complete
3. Once the ground training portion of the evaluation is complete:
   a. The candidate manifests the load.
   b. The candidate informs the evaluator where to meet on the 20-minute call for the load.
   c. The candidate is released until the 20-minute call for the load.
4. The remainder of the evaluation begins at the 20-minute call for the load and ends when the candidate completes the debrief of the evaluator, acting as the student.

E. GROUND RULES

1. General
   a. Prior to each evaluation session, the evaluator will conduct a briefing with the candidate for all subjects of the evaluation process, to include—
      (1) a brief review of the evaluation procedures
      (2) comprehensive and detailed explanation of the scoring criteria
      (3) the level of performance expected
      (4) specific safety and scoring reminders
      (5) mock written training record, background, and scenario on the simulated student to be trained, which will include the simulated student's prior performance deficiencies
      (6) an opportunity for the candidates to ask questions about the skydive and the evaluation procedure
   b. Each candidate is expected to follow the ISP outline for the jump to be trained and include all the points listed on the IAD and Static Line Instructor Rating Course Ground Preparation Checklist.
   c. The candidate arranges for a stand-in, preferably a candidate in the course, to be trained while the evaluator takes notes.
      (1) The evaluator briefs the stand-in privately regarding any tendencies or deficiencies of the student the stand-in is portraying.
      (2) The stand-in will present an imperfect performance during the training, as briefed by the evaluator, to test the candidates' ability for recognition and corrective training.
   d. The evaluator may call a "time out" during any part of the evaluation, but the candidates may not, except for safety reasons.
      (1) The evaluator should call time-outs only when necessary.
      (2) The evaluator will allow time for the candidate to regroup following a time-out.
   e. evaluator's equipment
      (1) Evaluators will wear standard student accessory equipment, including clear goggles or visor, shoes, and hard helmet.
      (2) The evaluator will declare equipment to be used on the actual jump and instruct candidates to ignore specific equipment preferences of the evaluator not ordinarily found on students (hook knife, etc.).
      (3) All rigging problems must be determined during the pre-boarding equipment check.
      (4) Under no circumstances will an evaluator attempt to board an aircraft with mis-rigged equipment or exit an aircraft with contrived equipment problems.
      (5) The evaluator may present non-safety equipment problems to be caught during the pre-exit check aboard the aircraft.
   f. Under ordinary circumstances, each training session will be followed by a practice or actual evaluation jump; however, the Examiner may allow multiple ground training evaluations prior to jumping.
2. IAD and static-line evaluation jumps
   a. The candidate conducts actual IAD or static jumps with the evaluator observing or acting as student (another candidate or a jumper with a minimum USPA B license and 100 jumps may also act as student).
   b. Each candidate must make at least one IAD or static-line jump during the course, according to the rating the candidate seeks.
   c. During IAD or static-line jumping evaluations, the jumper acting as the student will cooperate and communicate as an experienced jumper during all phases of the jump.
      (1) The evaluator may present or direct the candidate acting as the student to present certain scenarios to challenge and enhance the experience of the candidate acting as instructor.
      (2) In each case, the candidate acting as instructor must be fully informed of the scenario and reviewed on the expected response.
      (3) The person acting as student will exit in a stable position.
   d. The evaluator determines who will be in charge during aircraft and jump operations; everyone must know who's in charge at any given time.
   e. Aircraft emergencies will not be simulated during actual jumps, although in coordination with all aboard the aircraft, the evaluator may call out certain emergency style scenarios during the ride to altitude to evaluate the candidate's response.
   f. After the jump, the evaluator provides the candidate a mock ground crew evaluation of the student's canopy descent to be included as part of the debrief.
3. Freefall evaluation jumps
   a. Scenarios will be drawn from an ordinary skydiving school environment.
   b. Evaluators should make the evaluation scenarios both challenging and a learning experience for the candidates.
      (1) Evaluator challenges will provide opportunities for the candidates to observe problems in freefall for subsequent review and correction.
      (2) The evaluator may not correct or assist the candidates during the evaluations with the exception of discrepancies that might compromise safety on that jump.
   c. Teaching of aircraft spotting will be conducted during the ground training for Category D jumps and will be included in the practical (in-aircraft) evaluation of freefall evaluation jumps.

IAD SLI-6 CANDIDATE EVALUATION

d. Role playing: To aid the candidates to view the evaluator as a student, during the remainder of evaluation the evaluator may play the role of the student just trained.

e. fall rate
   (1) On Category D evaluation jumps, candidates may be presented with significant vertical and horizontal separation that must be negotiated to continue adequate observation.
   (2) Evaluators will not present impossible fall-rate or separation scenarios using experienced skydiver skills.
   (3) Evaluators should present fall-rate challenges to the candidate(s) that allow them to demonstrate fall rate range.

f. During the evaluation, the candidate should be presented with a loss-of-altitude awareness scenario, requiring the candidate to get clear and deploy by 3,500 feet.

g. At the end of each evaluation session, the evaluator will debrief the candidate on the performance.
   (1) reinforcement of areas where the candidate was successful
   (2) where possible, instruction, including demonstration and practice, to correct deficiencies
   (3) assignment and and necessary explanation of the scoring for that evaluation

F. SCORING

IAD AND STATIC LINE EVALUATIONS

1. Each candidate is allowed up to four evaluation sessions and jumps to conduct the following in his or her specific method:
   a. one satisfactory complete training session in Category B
   b. two satisfactory Category B jumps

2. The candidate completes a satisfactory pre-jump check of all associated systems, meaning that everything is inspected and prepared necessary for a safe jump under ordinary circumstances.
   a. student's parachute equipment and personal items
   b. ground support personnel
   c. aircraft and pilot

3. Each candidate must earn a score of Satisfactory on all sections and subsections of the IAD and Static-Line In-Air Skills and Instruction Evaluation Form and the Training, Supervision, and Debriefing Evaluation Form.
   a. correct preparation of the deployment device, including actively engaging the simulated student in checking it
   b. radio check
   c. spots the aircraft correctly
   d. control of the climb-out (student and deployment device)

4. Unsafe performance
   a. The evaluator must advise the Examiner of any performance that, in the evaluator's opinion, creates a safety hazard during an evaluation jump.
   b. The Examiner may recommend additional training for the candidate or that the candidate not continue with the in-air practical evaluation of the course at this time.
   c. This also applies to freefall evaluation jumps.

5. Mandatory scores of Unsatisfactory:
   a. failure to review previous information, including the four emergency areas
   b. failure to perform training for the performance objectives using the preparation, explanation and demonstration, trial and practice, and evaluation and review method
   c. insufficient repetition during practice or insufficient correction and positive feedback for the student to acquire the skills
   d. neglects to conduct any of the three pre-jump equipment checks
   e. missed major rigging errors during the pre-jump equipment inspections, including but not necessarily limited to—
      (1) missing altimeter
      (2) misrouted three-ring release system or improperly routed RSL (depending on the severity)
      (3) improperly routed or threaded chest strap
      (4) unsuitable parachute assembly
      (5) altimeter not zeroed
   f. failure to fasten all seat belts for taxi and take off
   g. failure to recognize a misrouted deployment device
   h. allowing a premature container opening at any time during climb to altitude or student climb-out
   i. static line
      (1) failure to properly route or hook up the static line
      (2) during a stable exit, allowing the static line to get under or around the arm of the jumper acting as student
      (3) failure to unhook all static lines prior to candidate jumping
   j. IAD
      (1) failure to withdraw the pilot chute
      (2) allowing a premature container opening
      (3) dropping the pilot chute prior to student launch
      (4) during exit, allowing the pilot chute bridle to contact the jumper's arm or any part of the aircraft
   k. jump in violation of FAA cloud clearance minimums
   l. bad spot where the simulated student would not be able to return to a safe landing area
   m. other

Note: "Other" is not meant as an open or broad interpretation of the reasons for a score of Unsatisfactory; rather, it is reserved for unforeseeable situations that in the judgment of the evaluator and the Examiner would compromise the safety of an evaluator or a real student.

NON-METHOD-SPECIFIC EVALUATION SCORING

Note: This Section is waived for current USPA Instructors in other disciplines.

1. The candidate is allowed two teaching sessions before an evaluator to earn a score of Satisfactory conducting the freefall and canopy training in Category D (refer to the ISP syllabus).

2. The candidate is allowed two opportunities to earn a score of Satisfactory on at least one jump where the instructor examiner, or his designated evaluator acting as a student, performs a jump from Category D, Dive Plan #2.

3. The candidate observes and critiques common deficiencies as presented by the evaluator.

4. Mandatory scores of Unsatisfactory (in addition to those listed for IAD and static-line evaluations):
   a. candidate failure to recognize evaluator's (acting as student) loss of altitude awareness and to get clear and deploy by 3,500 feet
   b. collision with the evaluator

G. RETESTING

1. IAD or static-line jump retesting: A candidate who fails to obtain a score of Satisfactory in all areas of the IAD and Static-Line In-Air Skills Evaluation Form must retake that portion of the USPA IAD or Static-Line Instructor Rating Course at another time.

2. Non-method-specific retesting: A candidate who fails to obtain a score of Satisfactory in all areas of the Ground Training, Supervision, and Debriefing Evaluation Form will require retesting at another USPA IAD, Static-Line, or Tandem Instructor Rating Course.

3. A candidate who fails to obtain a score of Satisfactory in one or all areas of the IAD and Static-Line Instructor Rating Course will be required to wait fourteen (14) days before attending another IAD and Static-Line Instructor Rating Course, unless a detailed training plan is developed for the candidate by the Examiner, which is executed within the timeframe decided upon by both parties before the candidate may attend another USPA IAD and Static-Line Instructor Rating Course. The disqualified candidate may act as a stand-in student for ground evaluations as approved by the attending Examiner.

4. Written exam retesting

    a. Each candidate will be provided a second opportunity to pass the test during the course.

    b. Failure to answer 100% of the questions correctly on the second attempt will require the candidate to study, retake the classroom portion of a future IAD or Static-Line Instructor Rating Course, and pass the written exam at that course.

5. Retesting fees: All retesting and re-evaluation fees are at the discretion of the Examiner.

6. All portional retesting must be accomplished within 12 months of the failed or incomplete course, or the candidate must retake the complete course.

IAD, Static-Line and Tandem Instructor Rating Course Ground Evaluation Checklist

1. **Introduction (15-20 minutes)**
   a. **Instructor**
      - [ ] name
      - [ ] background
   b. **student**
      - [ ] motivations
      - [ ] physical condition: medical, vision, hearing, age, weight, dental, scuba, injuries, blood donations, prescription and non-prescription drugs, alcohol
      - [ ] USPA membership, waiver, etc.
      - [ ] appropriate clothing (pockets, jewelry)
      - [ ] non-jump background
      - [ ] logbook
      - [ ] video (previous, this jump?)
      - [ ] student's subjective evaluation
      - [ ] procedure to prepare for jump (time frame, etc.)
   c. **skydive**
      - [ ] tie-in to previous experience
      - [ ] introduce objectives (emphasis on pull altitude)
      - [ ] brief description (concept, flow)
      - [ ] demonstration and video, if available
   d. **major changes**
      - [ ] practice deployment (Category B IAD and static line)
      - [ ] intentional turns (Category D)
      - [ ] instructor low deployment (Category D)

2. **Review (20-25 minutes)**
   a. **equipment**
      - [ ] use of checklist or flight planner
      - [ ] equipment (student explains and demonstrates rig in Category D)
   b. **aircraft**
      - [ ] use of mock-up or aircraft
      - [ ] low altitude (landing with aircraft)
      - [ ] bail out
      - [ ] poised exit
      - [ ] open container
   c. **freefall (Category D)**
      - [ ] unstable at pull time
      - [ ] loss of altitude awareness
      - [ ] unable to regain stability and over on back
      - [ ] five-second rule
      - [ ] pull priorities
      - [ ] instructor deploys
   d. **equipment emergencies**
      - [ ] use of training aids (harness, photographs, pilot chute or ripcord mock-up)
      - [ ] premature container opening
      - [ ] floating ripcord, lost handle
      - [ ] hard pull
      - [ ] total malfunction
      - [ ] pilot chute in tow
      - [ ] student in tow
      - [ ] horseshoe
      - [ ] two canopies out
      - [ ] inflation malfunctions (streamer, bag lock, lineover, major damage, etc.)
      - [ ] minor problems (line twists, pilot chute hesitation, end cells, stuck slider, minor damage, control line malfunction, etc.)
      - [ ] identification and controllability check (acronym, e.g., "there, square, steerable," etc.)
      - [ ] decision and execution altitudes
      - [ ] do-not-cut-away-below altitude
      - [ ] collisions and avoidance
   e. **landing**
      - [ ] use of landing trainer mock-up
      - [ ] water
      - [ ] trees
      - [ ] wires
      - [ ] other obstacles, prevention, drag recovery
      - [ ] avoidance
      - [ ] PLF demonstrated by student

3. **Aircraft Procedures (10 minutes)**
   - [ ] climb out and exit
   - [ ] all aircraft covered
   - [ ] spotting

4. **Canopy Control (10 minutes)**
   - [ ] use of DZ photo or flight planner; walk in field
   - [ ] main
   - [ ] reserve
   - [ ] exit point
   - [ ] holding area
   - [ ] landing pattern from different directions
   - [ ] ground guidance
   - [ ] alternate guidance (instructor, etc.)
   - [ ] landing procedure: flare height, stall recovery
   - [ ] effect of low turn

5. **New Training (30 minutes)**
   a. **instructional strategy**
      - [ ] lesson and training environment prepared
      - [ ] explanations and demonstrations correct
      - [ ] effective mix of explanation and demonstration with trial and practice
      - [ ] on-the-spot correction
      - [ ] performance objectives explained thoroughly and properly
      - [ ] each objective explained and demonstrated individually, with student trial and practice for each
      - [ ] skills mastered individually, then combined
      - [ ] effective mix of vertical and horizontal training
      - [ ] real-time dirt dives without coaching
      - [ ] realism
   b. **training aid use**
      - [ ] vertical trainer
      - [ ] horizontal trainer (body position and techniques must be correct at all times; simulate overshoot of turns for realism)
      - [ ] real time use (e.g., clock altimeter)

6. **Meeting Student (20-Minute Call)**
   - [ ] pre-jump equipment check (student and instructors)
   - [ ] pre-boarding supervision
   - [ ] full-dress rehearsal at mock-up or aircraft
   - [ ] boarding

7. **Climb to Altitude**
   - [ ] helmet and seat belt
   - [ ] deployment system prepared and checked
   - [ ] view of airport from aircraft
   - [ ] deployment altitude review (at correct altitude)
   - [ ] student mental rehearsal
   - [ ] student verbal rehearsal with instructor
   - [ ] spotting
   - [ ] supervision during pre-exit and climb-out

8. **Opening to Landing (Category D)**
   - [ ] observe canopy control
   - [ ] set good example

9. **Debriefing (10-15 minutes)**
   - [ ] use of appropriate area (aircraft, mock up, etc.)
   - [ ] walk and talk
   - [ ] student's view first
   - [ ] student's perceptions correct
   - [ ] instructor's perceptions thorough and accurate
   - [ ] proper review of video, if used
   - [ ] emphasis on positive
   - [ ] advancement/non-advancement decision
   - [ ] corrective training
   - [ ] introduction of objectives for next level (if advanced) and flow of dive
   - [ ] paperwork, log entry

SAMPLE EVALUATION FORM

Preparation ☐ Unsatisfactory ☐ Satisfactory

Individual knowledge. Organization, teamwork, instructional flow, preparation and control of training area, and use of training aids.

Explanation and Demonstration (Presentation) ☐ Unsatisfactory ☐ Satisfactory

Includes introduction. Objectives and flow of the dive, followed by a more detailed explanation of each point. It should be clear and understandable. Horizontal and vertical demonstrations.

Student Trial and Practice (Application) ☐ Unsatisfactory ☐ Satisfactory

Efficient and effective. Develops student performance to the degree that the student (after mastering each individual skill) can perform the dirt dives in real time without coaching. Emphasis on horizontal. Step by step.

Review (Evaluation) ☐ Unsatisfactory ☐ Satisfactory

Emphasis on requiring student demonstrations of skills with continual evaluation of progress. Effective written checklist with key questions. Complete (especially four emergency areas: aircraft, freefall, equipment, landing).

Supervision (equipment, pre-boarding, boarding, canopy descent) ☐ Unsatisfactory ☐ Satisfactory

Control during full-dress rehearsal, pre-boarding, and boarding. Canopy descent and landing pattern review. Equipment check—three required.

Climb to Altitude ☐ Unsatisfactory ☐ Satisfactory

Orienting the student to the DZ and ground winds, reviewing significant altitudes (no-more turns, lock-on, deployment), student's mental preparation, required description of the dive from the student, hand-signal review, pre-exit equipment check, spotting (involving the student in the process and effectiveness), supervision while moving to the door and getting into position for exit.

- ☐ helmet and seat belt
- ☐ view of airport
- ☐ deployment altitude review
- ☐ mental review
- ☐ verbal review
- ☐ spotting
- ☐ climb-out

Exit, Freefall Observation, and Altitude Monitoring ☐ Unsatisfactory ☐ Satisfactory

Within range to observe, altitude aware, non-interference

Opening to Landing ☐ Unsatisfactory ☐ Satisfactory

Observe student canopy control and set good example.

Debriefing ☐ Unsatisfactory ☐ Satisfactory

Use of walk and talk technique (post dive with the student's story first). Thorough and accurate. Beneficial to the student. Positive and upbeat approach. Advancement decision. Corrective training. Paperwork (logbook, DZ records).

- ☐ walk and talk
- ☐ video reviewed
- ☐ corrective training
- ☐ advance decision
- ☐ lesson preview
- ☐ paperwork

SCORING AND CRITERIA EXAMPLES

Preparation		
Explain and Demo	Presentation	Accurate and correct
Trial and Practice	Application	Student performance as close to perfect as possible
Review	Evaluation	Feedback from student performance
Jump Preparation	Students Flight Plan	If it applies; Can be USPA format or DZ format. Minimum of a specific and accurate pattern
	Ground Support Personnel	Ground guide (radio, arrow, paddles, etc)
	Aircraft Preparation	Anchor point, hook knife (metal constructed), door operation, step, etc.
	Pilot Briefing	Specifics for effective communication
Equipment Checks	Three Required	Pre-flight (observed), before boarding, before exiting. The evaluator cannot enter an aircraft misrigged
Supervision	Guidance for Boarding and Climb	Loading sequence according to DZ, protecting handles, helmet on, under supervision, etc.
Climb to Altitude	Helmet and Seatbelt	On for taxi/takeoff up to 1,500 ft (or DZ policy)
	Verbal Review	Verbal after altimeter cross check
	Mental Review	Student focus on the "perfect skydive"
	Spotting	Ensure location for exit and, if possible, show to student before exiting (cloud clearance, traffic)
Deployment System	Preparation and Pre-Exit Check	Static-line attached/controlled or pilot chute controlled
Climb-Out Control	Student	Positive and assisting as necessary
	Deployment Device	Control and recovery (static-line pulled back in)
Automatic Unsats	Seat Belts	Not fastened for taxi or takeoff, not unfastened prior to exit (safety issue)
	Deployment Device	Not attached (static-line) not thrown (IAD)
	Premature Container Opening	Created by the candidate
	Static-Line Fouled	Misrouted so it may cause a "hung jumper"
	Dropped Pilot Chute (IAD)	Could create out of sequence deployment
	Pilot Chute Contact with the Aircraft (IAD)	Could create premature opening or "hung jumper"
	Bad Spot or Clouds	Landing off the DZ due to improper exit point or falling through a cloud
	Other	Safety; actually deploying the students main or reserve canopy, pulling the students cutaway handle, forcing the student to exit without consent

TANDEM INSTRUCTOR RATING COURSE

T-1 INTRODUCTION AND ORIENTATION

1. Introduction and Orientation

A. WHAT IS A TANDEM INSTRUCTOR?

1. The USPA Instructor is the one of three instructional ratings USPA administers, preceded by USPA Coach and followed by Examiner.

2. A USPA Tandem Instructor may—
   a. exercise all privileges of the USPA Coach rating
   b. conduct tandem instruction jumps and the tandem first-jump course or transition training to the tandem method
   c. conduct training in the general portions of any first-jump course
   d. train and supervise jumps with non-method-specific students
   e. conduct the A license oral quiz and check dive
   f. verify certain USPA license applications, according to the requirements in SIM Section 3
   g. supervise a USPA Coach in training students and making currency jumps with licensed skydivers

3. Supervision (BSRs)
   a. All student training is conducted under the supervision as required by an appropriately rated USPA Instructor (refer to the BSRs).
   b. All general, non-method-specific student training and jump supervision may be conducted by any USPA Instructor, but method-specific training and jumps (AFF, IAD, static-line, and tandem) require the instructor to hold that method-specific rating.

4. Candidates who have met all the following requirements may attend the USPA Tandem Instructor Rating Course:
   a. reached the age of 18 years
   b. holds or has held any USPA instructional rating
   c. issued a USPA D license
   d. logged 500 jumps on a ram-air canopy
   e. a minimum of three years experience in parachuting (FAR 105.45)
   f. presented a current FAA Class 3 Medical Certificate or the equivalent acceptable to USPA
      (1) USPA will issue a Tandem Instructor rating, even if the medical certificate will expire prior to the expiration date of the rating.
      (2) Each USPA Tandem Instructor is responsible to keep his or her medical certificate current.
      (3) Currently acceptable medical certificates are listed in the Basic Safety Requirements.
      (4) The original medical certificate must be verified by the examiner and a copy must be submitted to USPA Headquarters for the initial rating and at each rating renewal.

5. Candidates who have completed the following may earn the USPA Tandem Instructor rating:
   a. demonstrated five practice tandem cutaways wearing tandem equipment and with a simulated student in the student harness in the presence of a USPA Tandem Instructor or Tandem (Examiner).
   b. completed the USPA Tandem Instructor Proficiency Card
   c. satisfactorily completed a USPA Tandem Instructor Rating Course including training for at least one manufacturer's brand model (type) of tandem jumping equipment

6. Tandem rating types and abbreviations
   a. The distinction of "type" is determined by joint agreement between the manufacturer of the equipment and USPA.
   b. If there is a disagreement, USPA's distinction between or grouping of types is operative.
   c. Current types:
      (1) Parachute Labs Racer (PR)
      (2) United Parachute Technologies Sigma (US)
      (3) United Parachute Technologies Vector (UV)
      (4) Stunts Adventure Equipment Eclipse (SA)
      (5) Strong Enterprises (SE)
      (6) Wings Tandem (WT)
      (7) Firebird Omega (FO)
      (8) Paraavis (PA)
      (9) Fire Tandem (FT)
   d. Upon successful completion of the course and with all requirements satisfied, the Examiner will enter into the candidate's logbook the type of tandem system for which the USPA Tandem Instructor is rated.

B. TANDEM TRAINING BACKGROUND

1. Tandem jumping officially began in the United States when the FAA issued an exemption to two Florida equipment manufacturers, Strong Enterprises and the Relative Workshop, now known as United Parachute Technologies, to conduct tandem jumping as an experimental program.

2. USPA began issuing tandem ratings to factory-trained instructors in 1996.

3. On July 9, 2001, tandem jumping became legal without an exemption as part of a major revision to FAR 105.

4. On June 3, 2002, the FAA approved the USPA Tandem Instructor Rating Course as a stand alone certification course to train tandem instructors, giving USPA the ability to issue tandem ratings independently through qualified USPA tandem rating course directors additionally approved by the various tandem manufacturers.

5. Tandem jumping is recognized as the most popular method for first-time jumpers.

6. Tandem jumping has always been conducted under two philosophies, according to school policy and with varying degrees of application.
   a. an introductory or orientation jump where the USPA Tandem Instructor conducts a minimum safety briefing and controls as many aspects of the jump as possible
   b. complete first-jump course training toward independent solo jumping, with the student participating in as much of the jump as possible

C. THE NATURE OF THE COURSE

1. This course may be conducted—
   a. as an initial USPA Instructor rating course for USPA Coaches
   b. as a shorter transition course for current USPA Instructors rated in another method

2. Each candidate is required to arrive at this course with all prerequisites completed, as specified on the Tandem Instructor Proficiency Card.

3. The course will cover the USPA Integrated Student Training Program
   a. as it applies to tandem training

b. subsequent training and jumps to the A license

c. transition from another training discipline

4. The classroom, training, and evaluation for this course should be conducted over a minimum of three full days.

5. This course may re-qualify those who have let their USPA Tandem Instructor rating lapse.

D. WHO MAY CONDUCT THIS COURSE?

1. A Tandem Examiner who has conducted at least one USPA Tandem Instructor Rating Course within the past 24 months

2. Continues to meet all of the requirements to qualify as a course evaluator (listed in Section E, "How to become a Tandem Examiner").

E. RENEWING AN EXPIRED USPA TANDEM INSTRUCTOR RATING

1. Ratings expire with USPA memberships. Persons with an expired USPA Tandem Instructor rating must:

   a. Meet manufacturer's requirements for the ground training necessary before the tandem recertification jumps are conducted (must include a full review of standard tandem procedures and emergency procedures, including practice of emergency procedures in a training harness).

   b. Meet the manufacturer's requirements for tandem recertification jumps.

      (1) The required jumps vary between different manufacturers.

      (2) Tandem instructors with longer lay-offs or less tandem experience will require more thorough refresher training with an examiner.

      (3) Check with the manufacturer of the tandem system used for the rating for specific refresher training guidelines.

   c. conduct training or complete review training for solo student first jump course and ISP ground training for tandem progression Categories A and B.

   d. Pass the USPA Tandem Instructor rating course written exam with a score of at least 80 percent.

   e. Send a copy of the signed rating renewal form, medical certificate and the rating renewal fee to USPA Headquarters for processing. For ratings expired for two years or more, the examiner must also attach a notice stating that the tandem instructor has completed refresher training.

F. CONVERTING A MANUFACTURER OR FOREIGN COUNTRY TANDEM RATING TO A USPA TANDEM INSTRUCTOR RATING

1. For persons with a USPA Coach rating (current or expired), current tandem manufacturer rating recognized by USPA, to convert a manufacturer's rating to a USPA Tandem Instructor rating:

   a. Must have logged at least 15 tandem jumps in the previous 12 months.

   b. Must have or have had a manufacturer's rating and must meet the manufacturer's currency requirements for the previous 90-day period.

   c. Completed items USPA 1, 2, 3, and the starred sections on the USPA Tandem Instructor rating course proficiency card.

   d. Provide proof of the manufacturer's rating to USPA Headquarters, such as the tandem instructor rating card issued by each manufacturer.

   e. Provide a copy of the USPA Tandem Instructor rating course proficiency card, medical certificate and the rating fee to USPA Headquarters for processing.

2. For persons with another USPA Instructor rating (current or expired), current tandem manufacturer rating recognized by the USPA, to convert a manufacturer's rating to a USPA Tandem Instructor rating:

   a. Must have logged at least 15 tandem jumps in the previous 12 months.

   b. Must meet the manufacturer currency requirements for the previous 90-day period.

   c. Correctly answer at least 80% of the questions on the tandem instructor written exam.

   d. Provide proof of the manufacturers rating to USPA Headquarters, such as the tandem instructor rating card issued by each manufacturer.

   e. Provide a copy of the USPA Tandem Instructor rating course proficiency card, medical certificate and the rating fee to USPA Headquarters for processing.

3. For persons with no USPA rating, but hold a current tandem manufacturer rating recognized by the USPA, to convert a manufacturer's rating to a USPA Tandem Instructor rating:

   a. Must have logged at least 15 tandem jumps in the previous 12 months.

INTRODUCTION AND ORIENTATION — T-1

   b. Must meet the manufacturer currency requirements for the previous 90-day period.

   c. Earn the USPA Coach rating by attending the complete Coach course or testing out of the Coach rating.

   d. Completed items 1, 2, 3, 15, and the starred sections on the USPA Tandem Instructor rating course proficiency card.

   e. Provide proof of the manufacturers rating to USPA Headquarters, such as the tandem instructor rating card issued by each manufacturer.

   f. Provide a copy of the USPA Tandem Instructor rating course proficiency card, medical certificate and the rating fee to USPA Headquarters for processing.

4. For all other persons with no manufacturer rating recognized by USPA but who hold a tandem rating issued by a non-U.S. skydiving federation or aero club:

   a. Must have logged at least 15 tandem jumps in the previous 12 months.

   b. Must meet the manufacturer currency requirements for the previous 90-day period.

   c. Earn the USPA Coach rating by attending the complete Coach course or testing out of the Coach rating.

   d. Completed items 1, 2, 3, 11, and the starred sections on the USPA Tandem Instructor rating course proficiency card.

   e. Provide a copy of the foreign aero club tandem rating, USPA Tandem Instructor rating course proficiency card, medical certificate and the rating fee to USPA Headquarters for processing.

G. WHAT IS REQUIRED TO PASS THIS COURSE?

1. Practical: Candidates for the USPA Tandem Instructor rating will be evaluated during the course for their ability to understand tandem jumping equipment and safely prepare and handle tandem students during actual tandem jumps with simulated students.

2. Tandem evaluation—

   a. initial tandem evaluation phase: The candidate will make five tandem jumps using tandem equipment

T-1 INTRODUCTION AND ORIENTATION

   under the supervision of the USPA Tandem Examiner.
   b. practice tandem phase
      (1) The candidate will make a minimum of five tandem jumps under supervision of the course staff before continuing to make the practice jumps in phase 2.
      (2) The progression through the first five jumps will vary depending on the type of the tandem system.
      (3) The course staff and candidates will follow the manufacturer progression for the type of tandem equipment used in the course for the first five training jumps.
      (4) In phase 2, the candidate must teach ISP ground training for Category A and B twice each during the practice tandem phase to include full debrief of the ride to altitude, jump and landing.
      (5) At the completion of the practice tandem phase, the candidate's USPA Tandem Instructor Proficiency Card is sent to USPA Headquarters.
   c. The candidate must show competence in inspecting and packing the tandem equipment of the type for which he or she is being rated.
3. Written exam
   a. Prior to attending the course, each candidate must correctly answer at least 80% of the questions on an open-book written examination covering the following:
      (1) this syllabus
      (2) the complete ISP syllabus
      (3) the USPA Basic Safety Requirements
      (4) SIM Section 5
      (5) FARs
   b. The tandem equipment manufacturer may also require a written examination.
4. Currently rated instructors attending this course do not need to meet the first-jump course requirements. The method-specific first-jump course topics will be covered in detail during the course by the examiner.
5. Commencement of privileges
   a. The privileges of any instructional rating will commence upon successful completion of the rating course and will be valid for 15 days with a candidate logbook endorsement by the Examiner.
   b. The rating must be processed at USPA headquarters to be considered valid after the 15-day grace period expires.
6. Initial Tandem Skydiving Procedures
   a. After completing the tandem course, the tandem instructor may begin jumping with actual tandem students.
   b. The tandem instructor should make at least 15 tandem jumps with similar sized students and in similar conditions to continue building on the skills learned in the tandem course.
      (1) The students should be of a similar height and weight as the tandem instructor
      (2) The jumps should be conducted in smooth winds, avoiding gusty or turbulent conditions
      (3) The similar wing-loading and wind conditions will help with improving freefall and canopy skills as the tandem instructor gains experience

H. KEEPING A USPA TANDEM INSTRUCTOR RATING CURRENT

1. Meet all manufacturer currency requirements.
2. USPA Tandem Instructors may annually renew their ratings with their USPA membership by paying the annual rating renewal fee and providing documentation of any of the following:
   a. that the applicant has met the annual rating renewal requirements by performing all of the following:
      (1) acted as tandem instructor on a minimum of 15 tandem jumps unless the rating was initially earned within the current membership cycle (renewal fee and signature required), in which case the annual minimum tandem jump number does not apply
      (2) acted as tandem instructor on one tandem jump within the previous 90 days on the specific system to be used for conducting tandem jumps with students
      (3) have a current FAA Class 3 (or higher) Medical Certificate or an equivalent acceptable to USPA on file with USPA Headquarters and submit a rating renewal form to USPA Headquarters
      (4) attended a USPA Instructor seminar within the previous 12 months
      (5) has conducted training or complete review training for solo student transition having taught or assisted with at least one entire first-jump course and ISP ground training for tandem progression in Categories A and B
      (6) within the previous six months, has completed a full review of all tandem emergency procedures including a demonstration of responding properly to each malfunction with the use of a training harness
      (7) acquired the signature of a current S&TA, Examiner or member of the USPA Board of Directors on the renewal application to verify that the renewal requirements were met
   b. or, having met the renewal requirements for an expired rating
3. A skydiver may not verify his or her own rating renewal requirements.
4. Renewing an instructor rating automatically renews a coach rating.

I. COURSE OVERVIEW

1. USPA's Integrated Student Program for tandem students
   a. the first-jump course
      (1) orientation jump
      (2) for ISP Category A objectives
   b. first-jump course performance standards
   c. Categories B-E, basic skydiving skills
   d. group skydiving skills
2. Tandem method
   a. equipment
   b. routine procedures
   c. tandem problem solving
   d. tandem emergencies
   e. freefall student emergencies
3. General instructor's duties
4. Jump preparation and equipment checks
5. Demonstration and practice sessions
6. Evaluation

2. The Integrated Student Program

2-1: ISP OVERVIEW

1. The USPA Integrated Student Program is a complete and detailed outline recommended by USPA to train students from the first jump through the A license.
2. The ISP integrates all USPA-recognized methods for teaching skydiving, particularly in the early portion of the training: harness hold (USPA Accelerated Freefall), instructor-assisted deployment, static line, and tandem.
3. Schools using the ISP outline or its equivalent can easily track a student's performance and interchange the various training methods to make the most effective use of their training resources.
   a. There are eight categories of advancement, A-H.
      (1) Categories A-D focus on basic skydiving survival skills and are very closely supervised.
      (2) During Categories E through H, students become more independent and supervision requirements are relaxed.
      (3) Categories G and H concentrate on group freefall skills and to prepare a student to jump without supervision and the USPA A license.
   b. Each category following Category A, the first-jump course, is divided into six skills and knowledge sets:
      (1) exit and freefall
      (2) canopy
      (3) emergency procedure review
      (4) equipment
      (5) rules and recommendations
      (6) spotting and aircraft
   c. Each student, except those making tandem jumps, should complete training in the freefall, canopy, and emergency review sections prior to making a jump in any category.
      (1) Some freefall dive flows require the freefall and emergency procedure training and review for the student to safely perform them.
      (2) The canopy dive flows require canopy training first so the student can understand what to practice.
      (3) The student becomes more independent and less supervised as he or she progresses and may require the information in these three areas when encountering new experiences during jumps in that category.
4. An oral quiz follows each category.
   a. It may be given after the student completes the last jump in the category or serve as a review preceding training in the next category.
   b. The USPA Instructor conducting the A license check dive draws from the quiz questions for the oral testing portion of the license review.

2-2: THE ISP FIRST-JUMP COURSE FOR TANDEM

1. The ISP recognizes that a tandem first-jump course may be a skydiving familiarization and orientation jump with a minimum of training or one that enables the student to progress to Category B of the ISP.
2. This Section of the Tandem Instructor Rating Course refers only to tandem jumps used to complete Category A advancement criteria in the ISP.
3. For tandem orientation jumps without the immediate goal of progression, refer to the tandem section in Category A of the ISP and the BSRs.
4. The number of students in the first-jump course should be appropriate for the number of staff available to facilitate the course.

A. EQUIPMENT

1. The student should know the location of the drogue release handle.
2. Limiting the equipment discussion for first-jump students
   a. The instructor describes the parachute opening in the three significant stages that determine the response from the jumper: activation (container opening), deployment, and inflation.
   b. Describe only a correct opening when first introducing the concept, but in terms the student will hear throughout the course and the actual jump.
   c. Make all references to solo-jumping equipment.
3. For a tandem jump, the USPA Instructor is primarily responsible for—
   a. choosing the correct system and performing a complete pre-jump equipment check
   b. putting the equipment on the student and himself or herself and adjusting it properly
   c. adjusting the student's harness to securely contain the student and correctly distribute the load on the harness for the student's comfort under canopy (see the manufacturer's equipment manual)
   d. conducting a complete equipment check after putting on the student's gear and before boarding the aircraft
   e. checking that the equipment is ready to jump before the student exits the aircraft
4. Tandem students are responsible for—
   a. making sure the instructor performs complete pre-jump equipment check at the three crucial points
   b. verifying attachment of the student's and instructor's harness.
5. Students training for solo jumps are taught to protect the parachute system operation handles, but monitoring the equipment throughout the jump operation is a primary duty of the instructor.
6. The student should be familiar with any other equipment operation he or she is expected to perform independently (personal items, equipment recovery and return, etc.)
7. The student should know that the responsibility for the equipment shifts from the instructor to the student later as the student progresses.
8. Discussion

B. EXIT

1. A minimum one full-training tandem jump is recommended in Category A.
2. Prior to exit the tandem student should be responsible to verify that the tandem harness is attached in four places to the instructor's harness, two at the shoulders and two at the hips.
3. Exit technique for various types of aircraft (discussed in Section 5, "Tandem Method")
4. First-jump tandem students should exit with both hands in a "safe position" (both hands on the harness main lift web or across the chest) and be told to

T-2 | THE INTEGRATED STUDENT PROGRAM

keep them there at all times unless instructed otherwise during the jump by the tandem instructor.

   a. on the harness away from any operation handles
   b. in a position that promotes a good upper-body arch

5. On the tandem instructor's cue (e.g., two taps on both shoulders), the student may assume a normal solo freefall position.
6. The student should exhibit at least reasonable control during climb-out and exit before advancing.

C. FREEFALL FLOW OF THE DIVE

1. First-jump students should expect a momentary period of sensory overload, after which they can begin the freefall dive plan.
2. Circle of awareness (CoA) for tandem students
   a. The student selects a prominent heading reference towards the horizon.
   b. The student focuses on the altimeter and it reads it out loud.
   c. The student reports the altitude to the instructor verbally, who responds verbally or with a vigorous "thumbs up" signal.
   d. Tandem instructors must take care not to place their hands within reach of a student.
3. Three practice deployments: The instructor may need to guide the student's right hand to the deployment handle and the student's left hand to the overhead position.
4. Second circle of awareness: The instructor may need to coach the student for body position verbally or via hand signals.
5. The student continues to monitor altitude until the wave-off at 6,000 feet, followed by drogue release.
   a. The instructor should watch for signs of distraction, especially with a video camera flyer present.
   b. The instructor ensures drogue release by 5,000 feet minimum, 5,500 feet recommended.

D. HAND SIGNALS

1. Presenting hand signals
   a. All hand signals are performed with one hand and must be placed in plain view of the student, generally no closer than 12 inches from the student's face and held for a minimum of three seconds.
   b. The instructor may need to get the attention of the student first.
   c. Tandem instructors need to take precautions to prevent a student from grabbing their arm when presenting hand signals.
2. Suggested signals are shown in the Skydiver's Information Manual, Appendix A.
3. Limit hand signals to those six or seven that may be required based on observation during the student's training.
   a. For example, perfecting a student's arm position may be of low relative importance during the first jump compared to a poor arch or a tendency toward an incorrect leg position observed in training.
   b. Additional hand signals can be introduced during subsequent training.
4. Verbal instructions
   a. Tandem students can often hear the instructor in freefall and droguefall.
   b. Speak loudly and clearly into the student's ear; preferably have the student turn his or her head to get one ear out of the wind and speak into that ear.
   c. Use cue words the student will recognize from ground training.

E. CANOPY

1. Introduce the student to the canopy in terms that will be used throughout the course and during radio instruction.
2. Canopy training should be based on flying a specific, pre-planned pattern into a clear landing area.
   a. In tandem, this portion of the training is best demonstrated and explained while under canopy.
   b. Refer to the canopy training outline and illustrations in Category A of the ISP syllabus for further explanation of this portion of the lesson.
3. Students should be taught to look for traffic before turning.
4. If unable to make the planned landing area, decide on a clear alternate landing area by 2,000 feet and apply the planned pattern to the new area.
5. The student should remain upwind in a pre-planned holding area until ready to enter the landing pattern at 1,000 feet.
6. Final approach
   a. The student should fly a straight final approach to avoid collisions.
   b. S-turns should be avoided, except when clear of all traffic, but may be valuable in an off-field landing.
7. Discussion

F. LANDINGS

1. This section is best taught using a practical landing trainer, where the student simulates parachute landings.
2. Teach the student a prepare-to-land position that will enable an easy transition into a proper PLF.
3. Tandem students using special tandem landing techniques need to know that they are not the correct techniques for a hard landing when jumping solo.
4. Discussion

G. EMERGENCIES

1. Before boarding the aircraft, prepare the student for any action required in the event of an aircraft, freefall, equipment, or landing emergency (FAR 105.45(2)).
2. Students should be told that the instructor may ask them to return their hands to a "safe position" at any time.
3. The student should always take directions from the instructor.
4. If a significant hazard exists in the airport area (large body of water, forest, etc.), the instructor should prepare each tandem student for that possibility.
5. Any other special consideration or procedure should be trained in advance of the jump.

H. ADDITIONAL STUDY

1. Category A tandem students should possess equivalent skills and knowledge to a student in the solo disciplines, except for those aspects to be covered in the solo-jump transition course (aircraft emergencies, malfunctions, obstacle landings, solo-method climb-out and exit, etc.).
2. First-jump students who wish to return should be introduced to the SIM and encouraged to study all aspects of the sport that will eventually fall under their responsibility.
3. The "Book Stuff" recommended reading in ISP Category A introduces the students to the FARs and other recommendations in preparation for the oral quiz.
   a. Instructors can inform students of the seat belt requirements while boarding, and the student can study the rule from the SIM.
   b. Jumpers who make a solo canopy descent assume the responsibility to land in an open area clear of persons and property on the ground even on the first jump.

4. Introduction of the oral quiz (which can also serve as a review prior to the next jump)—

   a. establishes the student's responsibility to acquire the supporting knowledge of the sport

   b. helps generate discussion about aspects of skydiving that the student will need to understand as an A-license holder

I. REVIEW CATEGORY A QUIZ

2-3: FJC TRAINING PERFORMANCE STANDARDS FOR TANDEM STUDENTS

A. ASSESSING BY SPECIFIC OBJECTIVES

1. All first-jump ground training should be specific and oriented to measurable goals.

2. Students should be correct and consistent in demonstrating their ability to perform the tasks of the ground training in preparation for their parachute jump.

3. This section provides sample performance criteria for use in the tandem first-jump course to help determine a tandem student's aptitude for meeting the Category A advancement criteria.

B. EQUIPMENT KNOWLEDGE FOR TANDEM STUDENTS

1. Knows to verify harness attachment prior to exit

2. If training for Category A objectives—

   a. can find and operate the main deployment handle

   b. understands the use of the altimeter in freefall and under canopy

C. CLIMB-OUT AND EXIT (AT THE MOCK-UP)

1. Understands and can perform the climb-out, set-up, count, and launch following the instructor's commands

2. Demonstrates sufficient strength, agility, and mental faculties during practice to perform the tasks

D. APTITUDE FOR FREEFALL

1. Able to arch sufficiently to lift both shoulders and knees off a flat surface and hold for ten-second intervals without straining

2. During arch practice, controls both legs and arms with symmetry and extends both legs slightly

E. UNDERSTANDING OF CANOPY DESCENT

1. Canopy instruction for tandem students is most effectively taught under canopy and during the debrief of a well-conducted in-air lesson.

2. Each USPA Tandem Instructor should develop and practice an interactive in-air lesson plan to help the student understand canopy flight at the Category A and B levels.

3. The following standards should be applied to each tandem student prior to making a solo jump:

   a. Understands canopy descent strategies well enough to solve contrived descent problems from opening to 1,000 feet:

      (1) too close to the planned pattern entry point at too high an altitude—face upwind

      (2) more than halfway down, but not yet halfway back—plan an alternate landing area

   b. Can solve contrived landing approach problems (e.g., ISP model):

      (1) arriving at the pattern entry point too high or too low

      (2) arriving too high or too low at other pre-planned pattern points (avoid S-turns on final approach)

F. LANDING AND LANDING EMERGENCY DRILLS

Each tandem student should be capable of attaining the necessary leg position to prepare for landing using a harness or other suitable landing simulator prior to jumping.

G. EQUIPMENT PROBLEMS AND EMERGENCY DRILLS

1. Equipment problems and emergency procedures can be discussed effectively while under canopy, especially when a routine canopy problem (line twist, slider up, closed end cells) presents itself.

2. Tandem students can also practice cutaway procedures while under canopy using practice handles attached to the student's tandem harness.

H. REMEDIES

1. Category A tandem students who do not meet these standards may—

   a. make an orientation tandem jump without engaging in Category A activities

   b. review the deficient sections of the first-jump course until demonstrating a satisfactory performance or return for retraining another day

2. Tandem orientation students (no Category A objectives)

   a. For students who can't perform the pre-jump training tasks without assistance (hands in a safe position, arch and foot and leg position for landing), special training or equipment may be required.

   b. Students who can't participate in skydiving safely should be encouraged to try other, less demanding activities.

2-4: TRANSITION TO SOLO JUMPING

A. GENERAL

1. Students may transition from tandem jumping to solo jumping at any time

   a. following the BSRs

   b. following the recommendations of the ISP

2. Transition reminders appear at the end of the introduction to each category in the ISP.

B. EQUIPMENT EMERGENCIES (USPA COACH)

1. A USPA Coach or higher rating holder should assist and critique the jumper throughout all general ground training.

2. Equipment emergency procedures and review

   a. A watch may be used during parachute emergency drills to help the student develop time awareness.

   b. The harness trainer should be equipped with a main deployment handle, a cutaway handle, and a reserve ripcord handle or a single operating system (SOS) handle, all of which can actually be pulled.

   c. Prior to making any jump in Category C (or solo jumps in any prior category), former tandem students should review all emergency procedures on that day (includes open parachute in the aircraft).

   d. A second complete emergency procedure review performed on another day subsequent can count towards one of the two complete emergency reviews required for the USPA A license.

3. The following standards should be applied to students prior to making a solo jump.

   a. Responds correctly to questions about how to handle an open parachute in the aircraft

T-2 | THE INTEGRATED STUDENT PROGRAM

b. Demonstrates in the training harness—
   (1) response to lost deployment handle, hard extraction
   (2) how to clear a pilot chute hesitation (main or reserve)
   (3) within five seconds, the correct response to contrived partial and total malfunction situations, including looking at the emergency handle(s)
   (4) correct response to line twists, slider up, and end-cell closures and addresses them in that order (in case they are experienced simultaneously)
   (5) the correct response to all three two-canopy-out scenarios discussed in Category A
   (6) special method-specific emergencies, e.g., static-line student in tow, loss of instructor in freefall (the five-second rule), loss of altitude awareness, pilot chute in tow problems, etc.)

C. AIRCRAFT EMERGENCIES (USPA METHOD-SPECIFIC INSTRUCTOR)

The appropriately rated USPA Instructor must train first-jump or crossover students for aircraft emergency procedures specific to that method.

1. Loading, seat belt use with the solo harness, helmet, static line or IAD pilot chute procedures (if applicable)
2. Climb to altitude
3. Climb out and exit
4. All aircraft emergencies

D. LANDING AND LANDING EMERGENCIES (USPA COACH)

1. Transition from a tandem landing to a proper PLF
2. Correct procedure for each landing hazard at or near the planned drop zone
   a. power lines
   b. water
   c. trees
   d. buildings
   e. other hazards specific to the drop zone

E. EXIT AND FREEFALL (USPA METHOD-SPECIFIC INSTRUCTOR)

1. routine procedures
2. AFF students: hand signals
3. freefall emergencies according to the method-specific discipline
4. Pull priorities
   a. Pull.
   b. Pull at the correct altitude.
   c. Pull while stable.

2-5: CATEGORIES B-E, BASIC SKYDIVING SKILLS

The course staff and candidates discuss the Category B-E outline in the ISP.

CATEGORY B

A. EXIT AND FREEFALL

1. Category B serves primarily a confidence builder for the returning student.
2. The student should demonstrate increasing comfort with the climb-out, set-up, and exit.
3. Relaxed freefall position ("altitude, arch, legs, relax").
   a. "Altitude" means the student must read the altimeter and understand the altitude.
   b. "Arch" means to push the hips forward slightly and smoothly and to keep them there.
   c. "Legs" means to pay attention to the leg position and place both legs in the correct position, probably extending them slightly.
   d. "Relax" means to take a breath and relax the muscles that aren't needed for the correct body position.
4. Leg extensions and turns help the student to understand freefall control and gain overall body awareness.
5. Reinforce the importance of an altitude check between each maneuver, when having difficulty with a maneuver, or every five seconds, whichever comes first.
6. Two Category B jumps minimum are recommended for tandem students.
7. With the Examiner, candidates review the Category B advancement criteria and the freefall dive flow from the ISP.

B. CANOPY

1. With the Examiner, candidates review the Category B advancement criteria and canopy dive flow from the ISP.
2. AFF, IAD, or static-line students deficient in canopy skills may benefit from tandem training, which places fewer demands on the student during each jump and provides an in-air instructor.
3. Those students should remain in the tandem program until meeting these simple objectives.

C. EMERGENCY PROCEDURE REVIEW

1. Tandem students should complete the emergency procedures section of the first-jump course prior to being cleared to solo freefall in Category C.
2. Because so much information is presented during the solo first-jump course, many students soon forget a great deal of their emergency procedure training.
3. The emergency procedure section of Category B serves several functions.
   a. review of first-jump-course emergency procedures
   b. review for all returning first-jump solo students who did not get to jump on the day of their course (log as the first or Category B emergency procedure review on the USPA A license application)
   c. review for students and experienced jumpers making currency skydives (adjust the cutaway decide-and-act altitude according to that jumper's license level)
4. Tandem students already trained in emergency procedures on another day should review them on the same day prior to making any jump in Category C.

D. EQUIPMENT

1. How a parachute opens
   a. to differentiate between malfunctions requiring only a reserve deployment and those requiring a cutaway and reserve deployment, as appropriate to school policies
   b. easily taught while packing or unpacking a parachute
2. Reviewing equipment retrieval at this point facilitates packing operations later for the staff.

E. RULES AND RECOMMENDATIONS

1. To make informed decisions about the safety of his or her own jumps, each student should be made aware of the pertinent BSRs.
2. Knowing the rules helps the student understand why the DZ won't allow jumps when conditions exceed the BSR limits for student operations.

F. SPOTTING AND AIRCRAFT

1. Review handle protection as a responsibility of the student.
2. Familiarize the student with the compass orientation and length of the runway in preparation for upcoming training in spotting.

3. Teaching aircraft traffic patterns early will help prevent student-aircraft conflicts on final approach and on the runway.

G. METHOD TRANSITION STUDENTS (TO TANDEM)

1. Review "Transitions" in the introduction to Category B.
2. A USPA Tandem Instructor may teach the aircraft procedures, climb-out, exit, equipment and aircraft emergencies, and landings.
3. A USPA Coach or a USPA Instructor rated in another discipline may teach the remaining, general portions of the transition course.

H. REVIEW CATEGORY B QUIZ

CATEGORY C

A. GENERAL

1. USPA Tandem Instructors are not authorized to make harness-hold jumps or conduct IAD or static-line jumps (unless they are otherwise rated to do so), but they may train and supervise students making solo freefalls once the student is cleared for freefall.
2. With the Examiner, review and discuss the BSR advancement criteria for harness hold, IAD, and static-line students.
3. Follow the USPA IAD and Static-Line Instructor Rating Course outline for the ISP progression in Category C-F.
4. The Tandem Instructor Rating Course outline for Categories C-F is identical to the one for IAD and Static-Line Instructor candidates.

B. EXIT AND FREEFALL

1. Three jumps minimum are recommended, including a qualifying IAD or static-line jump the same day prior to the first freefall.
   a. stable clear and pull not to exceed five seconds
   b. two ten-second freefalls
2. Relaxed freefall position ("altitude, arch, legs, relax"); introduction for IAD and static-line students.
   a. "Altitude" means the student must read the altimeter and understand the altitude; or students on freefall in the IAD or static-line progression performing short delays need to know their altitude by the count in seconds from exiting the aircraft or read the altimeter.
   b. "Arch" means to push the hips forward slightly and smoothly and to keep them there.
   c. "Legs" means to pay attention to the leg position and place both legs in the correct position, probably extending them slightly.
   d. "Relax" means to take a breath and relax the muscles that aren't needed for the correct body position.
3. Heading control
   a. Heading control may be passive ("altitude, arch, legs, relax").
   b. The instructor should introduce active heading control (turn method), but the student must understand that a correct body position is necessary for effective active heading control.
   c. The student's objectives are hover control using a coordinated and trimmed body position to maintain balance in freefall.
4. Introduction to wave-off (10-second freefalls)
   a. teaches the student the wave-off signal early
   b. helps protect instructors who may follow the student on future jumps
   c. trains for safety on future group freefall jumps
5. For IAD and static-line students, introduce the altimeter as a back-up to counting and looking at the ground.
6. At least two successful ten-second freefalls are recommended before advancing.
   a. control within five seconds of exit
   b. reasonable heading control
7. Recommended minimum deployment is 4,000 feet, particularly for students making ten-second freefalls and reaching deployment altitude at near-terminal velocity.
8. Pull priorities (introduction for IAD and static-line students)
   a. Pull.
   b. Pull at the correct altitude.
   c. Pull while stable.
9. Review the Category C advancement criteria and the freefall dive flow recommendations from the ISP.

C. CANOPY

1. Introduction to wing loading (ISP syllabus)
   a. The wing-loading exercise is especially important for drop zones with higher performance student canopies.
   b. Each student should be referred to the canopy manufacturers' websites to study recommended loading.
2. Flaring
   a. Review of the concept that flaring momentarily converts forward speed to lift (from Category A).
   b. The discussion continues with the concept of the jumper swinging forward and momentarily increasing the canopy's angle of attack.
   c. The student should understand that flaring the canopy produces three results.
      (1) Pulling on the tail increases the amount of air the tail deflects to produce additional lift.
      (2) The additional drag abruptly slows the forward speed.
      (3) As the jumper swings forward, the nose raises and the momentary increased angle of attack causes the canopy to attempt to climb.
   d. A canopy enters a dynamic stall when the jumper swings back under the canopy, the nose lowers, and the canopy begins a slight dive.
   e. The canopy enters a full stall when the tail is held below the nose and the canopy begins to fly backwards.
   f. Review of early flare and stall recovery actions are critical canopy survival skills and must not be overlooked.
3. Effects of higher winds
   a. Students who have exhibited good pattern flying skills in Categories A and B are introduced to—
      (1) turbulence
      (2) off-field landings
      (3) collapsing the canopy in winds (introduction for most students)
   b. The effects of a downwind landing are potentially greater, so downwind landing technique is discussed.
      (1) Flare according to height, not ground speed.
      (2) Flare normally to maximize lift and minimize final ground speed.
      (3) PLF
4. The student should by this time be able to fly a proper landing pattern with minimal assistance.
5. Landings: Students should understand when it is safe and unsafe to attempt a stand-up landing.
6. Candidates review Category C the canopy dive flow with the Examiner.

T-2 | THE INTEGRATED STUDENT PROGRAM

D. EMERGENCY PROCEDURE REVIEW

1. Remind the student that he or she must deploy at the correct altitude, regardless of stability.
2. Review in detail all aspects of preventing an open container in the aircraft and the associated emergency procedures.
3. Stability recovery (planned ten second freefall or longer)
   a. altitude, arch, legs, relax
   b. if caught on back, roll-out-of-bed technique
   c. if still out of control, think "AIR: Altitude aware, In control, and Relaxed."
      (1) The student must know the altitude at all times.
      (2) The student can use up to five seconds to regain control if altitude permits.
      (3) The student should be relaxed to help ensure a smooth freefall.
      (4) If still not in control, the student should deploy the main canopy.
4. Discuss in detail all aspects of landing off the intended DZ.
   a. selecting a suitable landing area
   b. anticipating and avoiding turbulence in the area
   c. other jumpers in the pattern
   d. procedures for returning without damaging property and equipment
5. Review landing priorities.

E. EQUIPMENT

1. The instructor introduces the student to equipment in more detail, including the AAD, RSL, and the strategy for the equipment check before rigging up.
   a. The introduction can be performed as the student is preparing to gear up for the jump.
   b. The student will check his or her equipment, supervised by a USPA Instructor.
2. Details about the three-ring system, AAD, and RSL are included in future categories; this is merely an introduction.
3. Because of the introduction to the AAD and RSL in Category C, discussions on them can be postponed from the first-jump course.

F. RULES AND RECOMMENDATIONS

1. BSRs for student equipment
2. FARs for parachute packing (FAR 105.43)
3. state and local regulations
4. drop zone neighbor relations (with DZ manager)

G. SPOTTING AND AIRCRAFT

Planning a landing pattern for a day with moderate winds

H. METHOD TRANSITION STUDENTS

Review "Transitions" in the Introduction to Category C.

I. REVIEW CATEGORY C QUIZ

CATEGORY D

A. EXIT AND FREEFALL

1. The lesson on turning should emphasize the importance of a neutral body position prior to initiating a turn.
2. A simple technique for changing heading, such as upper body turns only, will increase confidence and improve chances for success; after the student has completed the A license program, techniques for center-point turns can be easily added.
   a. multiple 90-degree turns only on the first jump where turns are attempted
      (1) reduces student stress and workload
      (2) increases confidence in heading control prior to initiating bigger turns, leading to greater success
      (3) reduces the likelihood of uncontrolled spins
   b. 180- and 360-degree turns, once 90-degree turns have been mastered
   c. In the event of lost heading control (spin), the student should recover lost control with "altitude, arch, legs, relax," before initiating opposite turn input.
   d. If the turn is sluggish or seems to go opposite the direction intended, the student should, provided altitude allows—
      (1) return to neutral arch
      (2) relax
      (3) extend legs
      (4) attempt the turn again
3. Maneuvers should be finished by 5,000 feet.
4. The instructor may accompany the student to observe heading control whenever practical.
   a. A USPA IAD, Static-Line or Tandem instructor seeing a student in danger of a low pull should immediately get clear and deploy his or her own parachute by 3,500 feet.
   b. Any student who is being accompanied by a USPA IAD, Static-Line, or Tandem Instructor should be told to deploy immediately upon seeing the instructor's parachute begin to open.
   c. A USPA IAD, Static-Line, or Tandem Instructor may not assist with the deployment of a student in freefall.
5. Review the importance of deployment at the correct altitude, regardless of stability.
6. Introduce alternate altitude references, e.g., looking at the ground, cloud bases, mountain tops, etc.
7. Increase exit altitude gradually as the jumper exhibits comfort with longer freefalls.
8. The student should begin this category with a 15-second freefall.
9. The student learns to use the altimeter as a primary altitude reference on longer freefalls.
10. Three jumps are recommended.
11. Recommended minimum deployment altitude is 4,000 feet.
12. The candidates review the Category D freefall dive flows with the Examiner.

B. CANOPY

1. Introduction of rear-riser steering and flaring
   a. rear-riser steering with brakes on for evasive maneuvers immediately after opening
   b. steering with brakes off to evaluate controllability with a disabled toggle
   c. flaring to be able to decide whether a canopy can be landed safely with disabled controls
2. It is not recommended that a student practice an actual landing using rear risers to flare.
3. Students should practice all maneuvers above 2,000 feet with frequent traffic and position checks.
4. Landing within 50 meters with minimal assistance is recommended before advancing.
5. The candidates review the Category D canopy dive flow with the Examiner.

C. EMERGENCY PROCEDURE REVIEW

1. Because of the lower planned deployment altitude, students should

by now demonstrate the ability to rapidly recognize and respond to equipment malfunctions.

  a. Category D includes the last formal training harness review of parachute malfunctions with a USPA Coach or higher rating holder as required for the A license, although the student should continue to self-review each new day of jumping (at least every 30 days).

  b. Review the cutaway decide-and-act altitude (2,500 feet).

2. Various categories of the ISP provide the instructor the opportunity to review emergency procedures taught in the first-jump course and discuss them in greater detail.

3. Whenever possible, emergency procedure review topics coincide with other related concepts from that category.

4. Conduct a detailed building or structure landing review, including disconnecting the RSL.

D. EQUIPMENT

1. The student should be calculating wing loading on both canopies (USPA Flight Planner) prior to each jump.

2. Introduce the AAD in detail.

  a. The student should operate the AAD.

  b. Ask the student to study the AAD owner's manual.

  c. Explain three-ring assembly and operation in detail.

  d. The student will disconnect and service the three-ring assembly in Category H.

3. Demonstrate a jumper equipment self-check and ask the student to perform it in the aircraft, followed by a check of the back of the rig by the instructor.

4. Discuss outerwear.

E. RULES AND RECOMMENDATIONS

The student should memorize the cloud clearance requirements from FAR 105.17 sufficiently to pass the Category D quiz and, later, the oral quiz as part of the USPA A-license check dive.

F. SPOTTING AND AIRCRAFT

1. The student should lead the pattern planning.

2. Introduction to spotting

  a. basic procedure overview

  b. looking straight down is the proper technique for observing the ground track of the aircraft

3. Technique for determining straight down

4. Coordinating spotting training with other jumpers.

  a. In most aircraft, it is easy for the student to spot from the door and then move into position for a later exit.

  b. Experienced jumpers may need encouragement when introducing the modified pre-exit procedures.

  c. Coordinate and practice the procedures prior to takeoff.

G. METHOD TRANSITION STUDENTS

Review "Transitions" in the introduction to Category D.

H. REVIEW CATEGORY D QUIZ

CATEGORY E

A. EXIT AND FREEFALL

1. The student should attempt a stable unpoised exit.

2. Students begin this category directly supervised by a USPA Instructor until they can demonstrate reliable recovery from instability.

  a. Each student shows the ability twice to recover stability and altitude awareness within five seconds following an intentional disorienting maneuver.

  b. The first maneuver attempted should be a barrel roll, which has a natural recovery mode from back-to-earth fall.

  c. Recovery within five seconds (twice) is required to clear the student to freefall self-supervision.

3. Once any student has demonstrated stability recovery, he or she may self-supervise in freefall (requires the sign-off of a USPA Instructor).

4. Once signed off, the student should be supervised by a USPA instructional rating holder aboard the aircraft, who—

  a. is responsible and available for all training, spotting supervision, equipment choice, exit order, group separation on exit, and pre-jump equipment checks

  b. is encouraged to jump with and observe the student

  c. may make gripped exits

5. Once a student has qualified for freefall self-supervision, that student's previous training discipline is recognized only for the purpose of currency training (see SIM Section 5 on currency training).

6. Students may self-assess for the heading control required for the A license check dive (back loop within 60 degrees of the initial heading).

7. Three jumps are recommended in Category E for all students.

8. Hazards of aerobatics

  a. erratic fall rate and altimeter readings (chest mount, etc.)

  b. disorientation (altitude, arch, legs, relax)

  c. equipment considerations

9. The candidates review the Category E freefall dive flow with the Examiner.

B. CANOPY

1. Instructor's level of understanding

  a. Candidates for the USPA Instructor rating should have a working knowledge of the aerodynamic principles of a ram-air canopy.

  b. During the course, discussion on these topics led by knowledgeable individuals is encouraged.

2. By Category E, the student should now have sufficient canopy experience to recognize the results of different flare entries (review the "nine flares" discussion in the Canopy outline in Category E).

3. The goal is for the student to learn how to assess the flare on any new or unfamiliar canopy before landing.

4. The student learns to evaluate the result of the flare by recognizing a dynamic stall following a flare on landing and to adjust flare height, flare rate, and flare depth for the next landing.

5. The candidates review the Category E canopy dive flow with the Examiner.

C. EMERGENCY PROCEDURE REVIEW

Two canopies out: Review the "Two Canopies Out" discussion in SIM Section 5-1.

D. EQUIPMENT

1. The student should be performing a pre-flight inspection on the equipment (USPA Flight Planner checklist) prior to each jump.

2. Characteristics of different canopy designs (overview)

3. A person with appropriate knowledge should introduce the student to the open parachute canopy, identifying and naming all the significant parts in preparation for packing.

T-2 | THE INTEGRATED STUDENT PROGRAM

E. RULES AND RECOMMENDATIONS

1. Detailed discussion on winds pertinent to the student's increased level of experience and to prepare the student to make informed decisions as a USPA A license holder
2. Discussion with pilot on portions of FAR 91 applicable to jump operations (Section 9 of the SIM)

F. SPOTTING AND AIRCRAFT

1. Category E aircraft briefing
   a. interaction between jumpers and aircraft control
   b. reading a winds-aloft report
   c. spotting procedures
2. The USPA Instructor should be sure the student has been trained for independent action in all aircraft emergency procedures (Category E aircraft briefing) before clearing the student to freefall self-supervision.
3. Technique for determining opening point by averaging the speed and direction of winds forecast at opening altitude and read at the surface on the drop zone

G. REVIEW CATEGORY E QUIZ

2-6: VERIFYING USPA LICENSES

1. A license
   a. Review SIM Section 3-2 for conducting the USPA A-license check dive and completing the USPA A license application.
   b. General review of the oral quizzes for the A license.
   c. Compare and contrast the two A license applications.
      (1) four-page A License Progression Card, designed for use with the ISP
      (2) two-page A License Proficiency Card for use with equivalent programs.
2. B and C license
   a. Review SIM Section 3-2 for instructions and procedures regarding the USPA B and C license, with particular attention to the license application checklist.
      (1) exam administration
      (2) verification of qualifications
   b. Review the USPA B-D License Application, available online at uspa.org/downloads.
   c. Only a USPA S&TA, Examiner or member of the USPA Board of Directors may approve D license applications.

3. Tandem Method

INTRODUCTION

1. The tandem method requires special knowledge both for preparation and use of the equipment.
2. The configuration of two jumpers harnessed together, one being new to skydiving, presents special challenges for the instructor.
3. Special FAA rules apply to the use of tandem equipment.

3-1: EQUIPMENT

A. TANDEM EQUIPMENT FAMILIARIZATION

Review with the Tandem Examiner the manufacturer's tandem equipment manual or video presentation and the actual equipment for the following:

1. System assembly and configuration
2. Drogue and drogue release operation
3. Fitting and adjustment
   a. instructor's harness
   b. student's harness
4. Reserve static line
5. Equipment checks
   a. before putting the equipment on
   b. student hook-ups and self-checks
6. Wear and maintenance
   a. inspection procedures and points of common wear (varies according to the type of equipment)
   b. manufacturer's component life or use limit recommendations
7. Equipment load limits

B. TANDEM PARACHUTE PACKING

1. The Examiner and staff teach the candidates how to pack the tandem equipment used for the course.
2. Refer to the manufacturer's tandem equipment manual for complete instructions on packing the tandem parachute.
3. Only a rigger or the "parachutist in command" (FAA term) making the next jump on the tandem parachute or a person under the direct supervision of an FAA rigger may pack the main (FAR 105.45.b.1).
   a. A tandem instructor is not approved to pack for another tandem instructor (unless the tandem instructor doing the packing is a rigger or under a rigger's direct supervision).
   b. A tandem instructor is not approved to supervise anyone to pack a tandem parachute, unless at least one of them is a rigger.

C. HANDLING AND USE OF THE TANDEM PARACHUTE

1. Refer to the manufacturer's tandem equipment manual for complete instructions on use of the tandem parachute.
2. Tandem parachutes are very heavy and should be handled with care.
   a. Avoid muscle strains.
   b. Reduce fatigue, which is a challenge of making multiple tandem jumps in one day.
      (1) Put the tandem rig on just before walking to the aircraft.
      (2) If a delay occurs, be seated comfortably in a cool area.
      (3) Find a comfortable position in the aircraft on the ride to altitude.
3. Tandem student hook-up procedures
   a. The Examiner demonstrates the correct hook-up method for the equipment being used in the course.
   b. The tandem instructor should follow the same hook-up procedure on each jump.
   c. The student should be trained and made responsible to check that the hook-up has been properly completed.

D. SOLO STUDENT EQUIPMENT

1. Review BSRs on student equipment.
2. AADs and audible altimeters are recommended for USPA instructional rating holders when making training jumps with students.

3-2: ROUTINE PROCEDURES

A. AIRCRAFT BOARDING AND IN-FLIGHT PROCEDURES

1. While approaching the aircraft for boarding, maintain a grip on the student as you approach the plane.
   a. A light grip on some part of the student harness works well to maintain control of the student in case the student inadvertently tries to walk in the direction of the propeller.
   b. If possible, place your own body between your student and the propeller as an additional barrier to prevent the student from walking into the propeller.
   c. Maintain this same practice regardless of whether the aircraft is running or sitting with the engine turned off.
   d. Assist the student as necessary with the seating position in the airplane.
2. Ensure the student is restrained either by seatbelt (for take-off or landing) or physically attached to the instructors harness during the climb to altitude.
3. The student should spend the remainder of the flight mentally rehearsing and self-calming.
4. Review the deployment altitude with the student at that point during ascent.
5. Just prior to jump run, the student and instructor should verbally rehearse the climb-out, exit, and canopy dive flow.
6. Following final rehearsal, the instructor performs the pre-exit equipment check.

B. EXIT AND CLIMB-OUT PROCEDURES

1. Use a procedure that enables the student and tandem instructor to get into position with minimal effort.
2. Protect all operation handles during movement of the tandem pair or by others in the aircraft.
3. Require the student to maintain both hands in a "safe position" throughout all movement in the aircraft, unless specifically told otherwise by the tandem instructor.
   a. In an aircraft with standing room, the student may—
      (1) sit in the harness, giving the instructor most of his or her weight, and cooperate during movement by keeping both feet ahead of the pair as they approach the door
      (2) stand and walk with the instructor toward the door (works better when the student is smaller than the instructor)
   b. In a smaller aircraft, the tandem student can move best by sliding from the seated position in the direction of the door as the tandem instructor either does the same or moves from a kneeling position (caution: this is hard on the knees).

T-3 | TANDEM METHOD

   c. Tandem instructors should guard against muscle straining and joint stress injury while moving about the aircraft with a heavy load attached.
4. Backing out is not recommended.
   a. The tandem instructor should never back out of any aircraft door, except a tailgate.
   b. Always exit with the student leaving first to minimize exposure of the backpack to the relative wind and prevent premature pack opening.
5. Aircraft exit by door type (discussion of techniques)
   a. strut (Cessna, Porter)
      (1) Take extra care to protect all operation handles when passing through any small door, especially when moving into position on a wheel strut.
      (2) Avoid contact between the back of the rig and the door, door frame, and overhead wing, which could cause a premature container opening.
      (3) Always perform a handle check just before the exit to ensure the drogue is in place and to ensure the tandem pair is free of any seat belts.
   b. large side door (Caravan, Twin Otter)
   c. small side door (King Air)
   d. tailgate (Skyvan, CASA)
6. Prepare for launch by pre-arching the student as much as possible in the door prior to exit.
7. Prepare the student for launch, for example, "Ready, set, go," with a rocking motion (which also helps the camera flyer anticipate the launch).
8. Launch in a position that—
   a. reduces unwanted momentum (to prevent tumbling)
   b. best faces the student into the relative wind

C. FREEFALL AND DROGUEFALL CONTROL

1. To facilitate control, the tandem instructor should wear a baggy, high-drag suit, and the student should wear tight-fitting, low-drag clothing.
2. Beginning tandem instructors should take students similar in size to the themselves until fully confident of control in all situations.
   a. Larger students can make certain climb-out exit, freefall, and landing procedures more challenging.
   b. Very small students can pose unexpected stability problems.
3. The student and instructor should exit in an arched position, with the student's hands in a safe position.
4. Drogue deployment
   a. within ten seconds if the tandem pair is stable
   b. by 8,000 feet (if at tandem terminal velocity), regardless of stability
5. The ability of the instructor to establish stability improves with additional airspeed.
   a. In the meantime while waiting for airspeed to develop, the instructor should coach the student verbally or by physically moving the student into a better body position.
      (1) The tandem instructor should maintain a flying position while moving the student into an arch to shorten the recovery time.
      (2) Keep the student's hands in a "safe position" while attempting to recover from instability.
   b. The additional time also gives the student time to become oriented and to relax, especially with verbal prompting by the instructor.
6. Throwing the drogue to gain stability is considered a serious failure of the tandem instructor.
   a. to exercise good judgment regarding—
      (1) student size
      (2) appropriate outerwear for the student and instructor
   b. to adequately prepare or supervise the student
   c. to adequately control the exit and freefall
7. The instructor should always keep both hands out of the student's grasp.
8. On every tandem skydive, once the drogue is deployed and while monitoring the student's activity, the instructor must touch each tandem system operation handle in the order it might be used. (This is a USPA BSR and a manufacturer requirement.)

D. UNDER CANOPY

1. If circumstances allow, the instructor should involve the student in as much of the canopy flight as possible, but consider—
   a. the actual opening altitude and time remaining
   b. traffic
   c. the spot
   d. the student's desire to be involved
2. After-opening procedures (good canopy)
   a. routine opening problems—line twist, slider, end-cell closure
   b. equipment check
      (1) canopy, lines, slider, and links
      (2) risers, canopy release system
      (3) operation handles in position
      (4) student's harness attachments
   c. traffic check
   d. spot check and altitude reading
   e. brake release and steering check (repeat traffic check before each turn)
3. Student comfort
   a. equalize inner-ear pressure
   b. harness
      (1) saddle position
      (2) chest and belly strap tension
      (3) hat and goggles
   c. queasiness (ask the student)
4. Canopy descent strategy
   a. Observe the opening point or current position (straight down).
   b. Find the landing area.
   c. Draw a line between the opening point and the target and divide it according to the remaining altitude to develop a flight plan.
   d. Fly the line, according to the plan.
5. Landing practice
   a. student's leg position
   b. flaring
6. Pre-landing check
   a. In windy landing conditions and once a cutaway is no longer a consideration, disconnect the RSL.
   b. Once a cutaway is no longer a consideration, loosen lateral straps.
   c. Pick up the flare toggles, if applicable.
7. Explain the canopy pattern points and altitudes.

E. LANDING

1. Prepare the student for landing.
   a. toggles full up
   b. leg position
2. Technique
   a. The instructor should practice with each size and type of tandem canopy to discover the best landing technique with experienced

jumpers prior to taking students on that canopy.

b. Maintaining maximum lift (prior to stall or sink) provides a softer landing, even when significant forward speed remains.

3. Slide landings are a good option for both instructors and students, especially in calm conditions.
4. Students should always land with their feet up and ahead in preparation for a slide landing.
5. All turns under canopy should be smooth and balanced, allowing the tandem pair to remain directly under the canopy in a coordinated turn.
6. The USPA BSRs prohibit turns under canopy greater than 90 degrees below 500 feet on any tandem skydive.
7. The final approach must be flown with the wing level with the flare at the correct altitude to help reduce the chances of an injury to the student or instructor.
8. PLFs and tandem
   a. Students should be advised that the tandem landing technique is not the best choice for solo jumping.
   b. Students should be trained for PLFs prior to making solo jumps.
9. Students who can't demonstrate the ability to lift their feet for a slide landing are at a greater risk for landing injury.
10. Windy conditions: Trained ground assistants should stand by for landings in winds strong enough to cause difficulty for the tandem pair after landing.
    a. The tandem instructor hands one toggle (or both toggles) to either or both ground assistants.
    b. If the student is assisting with the landing flare, the instructor will need to instruct the student to let go of the toggles once the ground assistant takes over.
    c. To collapse the canopy, each ground assistant should run forward and away to the outside of the tandem pair—never across the front—with the toggle in hand.
    d. Running across the front of the tandem pair with a steering line to collapse the canopy could cause line burns on the student, instructor, or the equipment.
    e. If the ground assistant does not run with the toggles, the canopy will not collapse and may, in fact, catch a greater amount of wind, pulling the tandem pair over.
    f. If ground assistants are unavailable, the tandem instructor should land and roll to his or her left side and either pull the steering line in to collapse the main canopy or release it.
    g. It is very difficult to access the cutaway handle when getting dragged right-side down in high winds.
    h. Even with ground assistance (canopy catchers) it is strongly recommended that the tandem pair land and sit down to decrease the possibility of being pulled off their feet and dragged by the inflated canopy.

F. SPECIAL NEEDS TANDEMS

1. Tandem jumps with disabled persons or even the elderly are very stressful to the Tandem Instructor and should only be done by very experienced instructors.
   a. The Tandem Instructor should have a minimum of 200 tandem jumps, 50 tandem jumps within the previous six months.
   b. The Tandem Instructor should receive personal instruction from another Tandem Instructor who has done these types of tandem jumps or seek the advice of a Tandem Examiner.
   c. The Tandem Instructor should never let their ego dictate the decision to take a disabled person on a tandem jump.
   d. Prior to taking a disabled person on a tandem jump, ensure that person has received advice from a physician.
   e. Wheelchair dependent persons may be at higher risk for injury from tandem landings and more prone to complications during recovery.
   f. United Parachute Technologies has published a document titled "Jumping with Wheelchair Dependent Persons" which is very informative.

G. REVIEW FARS CONCERNING TANDEM JUMPING

3-3: TANDEM PROBLEM SOLVING

A. INTRODUCTION

On any tandem dive, particularly a first jump, the instructor must choose the best course of action, based on the student's performance.

B. CLIMB-OUT AND EXIT

1. If there is difficulty walking with the student toward the door, have the student maintain both hands in a safe position and be seated in the harness, feet flat on the floor.
2. If the student grabs the door—
   a. Return the student's hands to a "safe position" with a reminder to keep them there.
   b. In a Cessna or seated exit from other small-door planes, students often reflexively use their elbows to brace themselves in the door.
3. If the student is in a poor body position in the door, remind the student to arch with his or her head back.
4. If the student assumes a poor body position on launch, remind the student to arch (shout into the student's ear).

C. FREEFALL AND DROGUEFALL

1. Instability
   a. Tumbling: The tandem instructor should attempt to control the student for at least ten seconds or until 8,000 feet, whichever comes first, before resorting to deploying the drogue to gain stability.
   b. Deploying the drogue while unstable may become necessary (by 8,000 feet) but is not an acceptable solution to instability.
   c. Side spin
      (1) Refer to the video on side spins available from Strong Enterprises for more information on this phenomenon.
      (2) If spinning drogue-side down and unable to establish stability, deploy the reserve by 8,000 feet.
   d. Flat spin (freefall)
      (1) Relax and allow time for opposite turn control to overcome the momentum of the tandem pair in the spin.
      (2) Monitor the altitude and deploy the drogue once regaining control or by 8,000 feet, whichever comes first.
2. The student may move his hands to a flying (open) position prematurely (before drogue deployment).
   a. If stability is compromised, tell the student to return both hands to a "safe position" ("Safety position!" or "Hands In!").
   b. If stable, deploy the drogue as normal.
3. Rocking in droguefall
   a. Check the instructor leg position, arch, and body tension (relax).
   b. Check student's leg position and coach as necessary.

T-3 | TANDEM METHOD

4. Droguefall turn
   a. Prevention
      (1) Before jumping, tighten the lateral straps of the student's harness according to the manufacturer's instructions to aid in freefall and droguefall control.
      (2) Overtightening the lateral straps can inhibit the student's ability to arch.
   b. Monitor the altitude and prepare to initiate drogue release higher to allow extra time to deal with the probable line twist.
   c. Situate the student in the harness for symmetry (grasp the student by the hips and move into position).
      (1) Situate both the student's legs between the instructor's.
      (2) High-drogue attachment (WT and SE): push the student forward and up to expose the instructor's legs for more control.
      (3) Low-drogue attachment (UV and SA): Push the student forward and down to expose the instructor's upper body for more control.
   d. Check the instructor body and leg position and relax.
   e. Check the student's body and leg position and coach as necessary.
5. Maintain altitude awareness throughout droguefall and deploy the drogue and parachute at the correct altitude, regardless of stability or control.

D. DEPLOYMENT

1. If the student appears distracted approaching 6,000 feet, tap the student's altimeter or present the circle of awareness signal.
2. If the student fails to wave off at 5,500 feet, carefully grasp student by the wrists and initiate the wave-off.
3. If the student fumbles or resists assistance with the drogue release handle, assist as necessary but deploy the primary or secondary (if available) drogue release handle by 4,500 feet.

E. UNDER CANOPY

1. If the student fails to steer—
   a. A tandem instructor should take students only as large as he or she is prepared to land without assistance.
   b. Continue the descent without the student's assistance.

2. If the student becomes airsick—
   a. communication
      (1) If a student is unusually quiet, it may indicate discomfort.
      (2) Continual communication with the student reduces the chance and severity of nausea.
   b. Once determining the student has become airsick—
      (1) Use minimal canopy control.
      (2) If possible, adjust the student in the harness to improve circulation.
      (3) If possible, remove the student's hat and goggles (replace the hat prior to landing).
   c. To prevent future problems, review the manufacturer's directions for harness adjustment.
3. If the student passes out in the harness or otherwise fails to lift his or her feet on landing—
   a. Rock the student back in the harness during the landing flare and position your legs under the student's legs.
   b. Execute a slide landing and protect the student, particularly his or her legs, from contact with the ground.
   c. To prevent future problems, review the manufacturer's directions for harness adjustment.

3-4: TANDEM EMERGENCIES

Also refer to specific tandem manufacturer guidelines for this section.

A. AIRCRAFT MALFUNCTION

1. Tandem parachutes open more slowly than personal parachutes, so emergency aircraft exit altitude plans must be raised accordingly.
2. Engine failure or other controllable aircraft malfunction below 1,500 feet AGL: Land with the aircraft.
3. Engine failure or other controllable aircraft malfunction from 1,500 to 4,000 feet AGL—
   a. Hook up the student's harness by at least one shoulder attachment.
   b. Scissors the student with your legs to secure and maintain the student's lower body tightly to yours.
   c. Exit and deploy the reserve.
4. Emergency exit under main (above 4,000 feet AGL): Because of the differences in the drogue collapse sequence, procedures for low-altitude exits vary among equipment:
   a. Types UV, US, and SA: Exit, deploy the drogue, then release the drogue.
   b. Types FO, PR and SE: Remove and discard the drogue release, exit, and deploy the drogue.
   c. On type PR, deploying the drogue will activate the main parachute system if the lower attachments are not hooked up.
5. Some automatic activation devices in common use for tandem jumping do not arm until 3,000 feet; check the owner's manual.

B. PREMATURE CONTAINER OPENING

1. Premature drogue or reserve deployment during the exit set-up: Get the student off the aircraft immediately.
2. Premature opening of the main container during climb-out—
   a. If possible, retrieve the bagged main and return to the aircraft cabin.
   b. If the main is deploying, jump, deploy the drogue, and release the drogue.
3. Premature container opening in freefall: Deploy the drogue, release the drogue and prepare for the likely malfunction.
4. Premature container opening in droguefall: Release the drogue, and prepare for the likely malfunction.

C. STUDENT

Student grabs the instructor's hand(s)

1. One hand: Shout "Let go!" close to the student's ear and attempt to free your hand for no more than 10 seconds or by 8,000 feet (whichever is first), then deploy the parachute available to the other hand.
2. Both hands
   a. Instruct the student to turn his or her head to facilitate hearing.
   b. Tell the student to let go and return his or her hands to a safe position.
   c. If unsuccessful, extend both hands forward as far as possible and then retract them using the shoulder muscles as aggressively as possible until at least one hand is free and a parachute can be deployed.

D. DROGUE EMERGENCIES

1. Failure to deploy the drogue: Deploy the reserve within ten seconds or 8,000 feet, whichever comes first.
2. Drogue entangled with the tandem pair: Attempt to clear twice, then deploy the reserve.
3. Failure of the deployed drogue (uninflated drogue in tow)
   a. Release the drogue (pull both release handles, if available).
   b. Attempt to deploy the main deployment bag until 3,500 feet;

- look hard over one shoulder to modify the burble.
- c. By 3,000 feet initiate cutaway and deploy the reserve.
4. Deployed drogue fails to release
   a. Primary drogue release failure: Activate secondary drogue release.
   b. Primary and secondary drogue release failure: Two possible solutions should be discussed, with the final decision determined by the Examiner according to the equipment being trained for.
      (1) Deploy the reserve (UV, US, SA, WT).
      (2) Cut away and deploy the reserve (FO, SE, PR).
5. Uninflated drogue in tow following drogue release
   a. Be sure both drogue release handles are extracted.
   b. Attempt to deploy main bag to 3,500 feet; look hard over one shoulder to modify the burble.
   c. By 3,000 feet
      (1) Deploy the reserve (FO, UV, US, SA, WT).
      (2) Cut away and deploy the reserve (SE, PR).
6. Detached drogue
   a. Attempt to deploy main bag to 3,500 feet; look hard over one shoulder to modify the burble.
   b. By 3,000 feet, initiate cut away procedures and deploy the reserve.
7. Skydiver (videographer) entangled in drogue or drogue bridle
   a. If altitude permits, give the skydiver some time to work free of the entanglement.
   b. Disconnect the RSL.
   c. Pull the cutaway handle.
   d. Pull the drogue release handle, which will release the drogue and pull the bagged main canopy out of the container and detach both risers immediately.
   e. The tandem instructor then needs to initiate a tracking position to gain horizontal separation from the skydiver above who is still likely entangled with the drogue bridle.
   f. Pull the reserve ripcord to deploy the reserve canopy by at least 3,000 feet.

E. TANDEM AAD CONSIDERATIONS

Refer to the manufacturer's instructions for all tandem AADs and adjust emergency procedure decision altitudes accordingly.

F. OTHER EQUIPMENT MALFUNCTIONS

1. In the event of a main canopy malfunction, decide and act by 3,000 feet to cut away and deploy the reserve.
2. Malfunction of the deployed main: Coach the student into the freefall position with arms in, cut away and deploy the reserve.
3. Riser release failure (one or both sides): Deploy the reserve by 2,000 feet.
4. Riser failure
   a. RSL side: Refer to manufacturer's instructions regarding the RSL and back-up devices (Collins lanyard on United Parachute Technologies equipment, etc.).
   b. Non-RSL side: Cut away and deploy the reserve
5. Both canopies deployed: Each situation needs to be assessed, and the correct response may be different from the following recommendations for a dual deployment.
   a. Main inflated, reserve deploying
      (1) Depending on altitude, attempt to contain the reserve or allow it to develop.
      (2) If the reserve inflates, assess the result and respond accordingly.
   b. Reserve inflated, main deploying
      (1) Cut away the main prior to inflation, if it appears likely to clear the reserve.
      (2) Retain the main if it appears to have gone through the reserve and could entangle if cut away.
   c. Biplane: Steer the front canopy using toggles; do not release the brakes on the rear canopy.
   d. Side-by-side
      (1) Determine controllability of the larger canopy and if the main can be cut away without fouling the reserve.
      (2) If the main will clear and there are control problems, disconnect the RSL and cut away.
   e. Downplane: Disconnect the RSL and cut away the main.
6. Main inflated, reserve entangled
   a. Attempt to control the main to the best landing option.
   b. Do not cut away, unless it is certain that releasing the main will result in full development of the reserve (very difficult to determine).
7. Reserve inflated, main entangled
   a. Attempt to control the reserve to the best landing option.
   b. Do not attempt cut away the main, unless it is obvious that the main is preventing further development or full function of the reserve.

G. HARD LANDINGS

1. In the event of a hard, vertical landing, e.g., from a malfunctioned canopy, a PLF for both instructor and student is probably the best choice, rolling the container toward the ground to protect the student.
2. In such extreme situations, consider large trees and soft fields as viable options.
3. Water provides another emergency option, but introduces the possibility of drowning.

H. WATER LANDINGS

1. A water landing during a tandem skydive is potentially a very dangerous situation for the tandem instructor and tandem student.
2. Practicing water landing procedures on the ground can help ensure correct actions are taken in the event of an actual water landing.
3. It is recommended that both the instructor and student wear approved flotation gear when the tandem jump is conducted within one mile of an open body of water in which a skydiver could drown.
4. If a water landing is unavoidable:
   a. Disconnect the reserve static line.
   b. Disconnect the student lower attachment points and student ripcord (if attached to the student harness).
   c. Disconnect the tandem instructor harness chest strap.
   d. Have the student inflate the student flotation device.
   e. Land near a shoreline or boat if possible.
   f. Fly a straight and level final approach facing into the wind, or in the case of a river with moving water, land in a direction that will allow the tandem main canopy to deflate in the water downstream of the tandem pair to help prevent the canopy and suspension lines from entangling around the student and instructor.
   g. Flare the main canopy at the appropriate altitude and be aware that judging height above water can be difficult.

T-3 | TANDEM METHOD

h. Once you have entered the water, pull the cutaway handle to release the main parachute and make sure the canopy and suspension lines remain clear of the tandem pair, or quickly work free of any lines or canopy fabric.
i. Disconnect the student upper attachment points to free yourself from the student.
j. Loosen your leg straps and swim out of the tandem instructor harness.
k. Inflate your own flotation device.

I. TANDEM EMERGENCY PROCEDURE PRACTICE

1. After reviewing the emergency procedures outlined by the manufacturer of the tandem system used for the rating, each candidate must demonstrate proper emergency procedures to the tandem instructor examiner.
2. The candidate must wear an actual tandem rig outfitted with auxiliary emergency handles, or a tandem training harness designed for practicing emergency procedures.
3. The candidate will attach a stand in student wearing a tandem student harness, to simulate a tandem skydive as closely as possible. Whenever possible, the tandem pair should be suspended in a training harness for the emergency procedure drills.
4. The tandem examiner will present each of the malfunctions outlined in the manufacturer guidelines for the tandem system used for the rating, to verify that the candidate responds correctly and pulls each handle in the correct sequence based on the specific malfunction scenario.
5. Candidates who do not respond correctly to each emergency procedure after three separate attempts may not continue any further with the tandem course. After acquiring 100 more skydives, the candidate may then attend another tandem instructor rating course.
6. After successfully demonstrating a proper response to each malfunction, the tandem instructor examiner may sign for this requirement on the tandem instructor proficiency card.

3-5: FREEFALL STUDENT EMERGENCIES

Review the student procedures for aircraft malfunction and open-parachute aircraft emergencies in the solo-method-specific emergency procedures in Category A and the Category B emergency procedure review section of the ISP.

A. AIRCRAFT MALFUNCTION

1. The correct response to a low-altitude emergency will always depend on circumstances, including the severity of the problem, the capabilities of the aircraft, the available terrain for landing the plane or parachute, and the abilities of the jumpers aboard.
2. Landing with the aircraft is usually required up to 1,500 feet.
   a. The student takes all direction from the instructor.
   b. Fasten seat belts and helmets on.
   c. For any aircraft descent, disarm the AAD as required (see owner's manual).
   d. Prepare for a hard landing (soft-field landing position).
3. Bailout: Exit and pull reserve (required only when below the altitude for a safe poised exit and when the situation makes landing the aircraft unsafe).
   a. The instructor positions the student in the door.
   b. The student places his or her left hand on the reserve ripcord and pulls immediately after exit.
   c. With sufficient altitude, the student may use a similar procedure with the main parachute.
4. A poised exit with a clear and pull on the main parachute whenever altitude allows.

B. PARACHUTE OPEN IN THE AIRCRAFT

1. If the parachute stays inside, first close the door.
   a. Main—disconnect the canopy release system and reserve static line, and all ride down with the aircraft.
   b. Reserve—remove the rig, if practical, and all ride down with the aircraft.
2. If the parachute goes out, the student must exit quickly without waiting for a command from the instructor.

C. SKYDIVER IN TOW

1. If the student is conscious and recognizes the problem and the parachute is the main parachute, the student should attempt to cut away and deploy the reserve.
2. If the student is unconscious or the parachute is a reserve parachute, the response will depend on the circumstances, including—
   a. controllability of the aircraft
   b. landing terrain or facilities available to the aircraft
3. If the student is in tow due to an entanglement with a seat belt or jump suit, cut the offending attachment.

4. Instructor's Duties

4-1: CONDUCTING THE JUMP

A. STUDENT PREPARATION

1. Introduction of student and instructor
   a. on the instructor's initiative
   b. familiarizes the two with each other
   c. sets the tone for the conduct of the training and jump
2. Administrative
   a. paperwork (registration, waiver)
   b. payment
   c. documentation available (logbook, A license application card)
   d. training and review complete
3. Personal
   a. water, food, restroom
   b. pockets cleared, jewelry off, gum disposed
   c. special considerations (medical)
4. Disposition
   a. behavior consistent and positive
   b. perspiration
   c. breath
   d. breathing rate
   e. rate of movement (nervous or jumpy?)
   f. voice

B. TRAINING

1. Each instructor is responsible for all previous training.
   a. thorough review of the student's performance records
      (1) logbook
      (2) A license application card
      (3) DZ master log
      (4) discussion with previous instructors
   b. student's subjective evaluation of the previous jump (What did the student think?)
   c. questions specific to the last skydive
   d. thorough review of the four emergency areas—aircraft, freefall, equipment, landing—using the appropriate training aids
      (1) aircraft mock-up
      (2) training harness
      (3) landing trainer
      (4) other
   e. the longer the interval between jumps, the more the student will have forgotten
2. Introduce the performance objectives of the next lesson and advancement criteria for the next jump.
   a. Use appropriate descriptions and demonstrations.
   b. Conduct informal rehearsals using the appropriate training aids to enhance realism.
3. Be sure the student is equipped correctly for the skydive (equipment check before rigging up).
4. Prepare the canopy flight plan.
5. Conduct a full-dress rehearsal or dirt dive until the student performs everything smoothly and correctly.
   a. without coaching or prompting
   b. real time
6. Perform the pre-boarding equipment check, including all personal items and the radio.

C. ABOARD THE AIRCRAFT

1. Monitor the student's equipment.
2. Coordinate exit position and planned interaction with other jumpers or groups during exit.
3. Review the deployment altitude with the student at that point during ascent.
4. Encourage self-reliance.
5. Conduct the pre-exit equipment check.
6. Supervise spotting, according to the student's level.

D. JUMP SUPERVISION

1. An instructor may be able to effectively observe a student making short freefalls (up to ten seconds) from the aircraft.
2. The instructor may jump with students making longer freefalls to observe and critique for retraining during the debrief.

E. POST JUMP

1. Verify that the student has landed safely and returned to the operations center.
   a. All equipment accounted for and put away.
   b. The student knows the debrief plan.
2. Debriefing
   a. The debrief provides instructors with an opportunity to facilitate the learning process by encouraging the student to recognize their achievements and what they did correctly, as well as help them realize what is needed to move forward in their skill development.
   b. The student must become more aware of their strengths and weaknesses and take responsibility for their training.
   c. The debrief process contains the following steps:
      (1) restate the goals
      (2) things that worked
      (3) things that need improvement
      (4) how to improve
      (5) make new goals
   d. Restate the goals
      (1) the student will most likely focus on the negative parts of the jump
      (2) restating the goals helps them open up their mind to the rest of the tasks whether it be the exit, break-off or canopy control tasks
   e. Things that worked
      (1) ask the student what went well on the jump, what he did well
      (2) the student will naturally want to focus on the negative; by having him state what he did well on the jump, it starts the debrief on a positive note
      (3) this process will need to be repeated on several jumps before the student typically starts to enter the debrief on a positive note stating what they liked about their performance then noting what they need to improve on
   f. Things that need improvement
      (1) ask the student what needs improvement
      (2) this lets you know if the student is aware of his errors
      (3) if the student overlooks a part of the skydive that should have been recalled, play through the video again and ask him how he felt about performing the skill to see if it jogs his memory
      (4) if it does not, this is the instructor's opportunity to restate the goals of the jump and provide guidance on how to improve

T-4 INSTRUCTOR'S DUTIES

g. How to improve
   (1) ask this question to the student
   (2) the student should have a good idea of what he needs to work on
   (3) if the student cannot see the answer, this is the opportunity for the instructor to review the correct techniques and assist him to see what is needed
   (4) patience and good listening skills of the instructor will help the student take charge of his learning and become further committed to his goals

h. Make new goals
   (1) ask the student what he would like to do on the next jump
   (2) if the goals and expectations of each jump are clear, the student should be quite realistic about his performance
   (3) if the environment has been set that "mistakes are OK" the student should have a realistic assessment of what he needs to do on the next jump, even if it means repeating the same jump
   (4) the Instructor's role during the debrief should be one of a facilitator
   (5) asking questions and directing the student to the right information through self-realization will be of greater benefit to the student

F. ADDITIONAL TRAINING

The instructor conducts or supervises the required training in equipment, rules and recommendations, and spotting and aircraft appropriate for the student's level of advancement (category).

4-2: PRE-JUMP CHECKS (SOLO JUMPS)

A. INTRODUCTION

1. One of the instructor's greatest responsibilities is equipment management.
2. Preparation before boarding prevents accidents.
3. Having an organized routine will make the operation run more smoothly.
4. Conduct three complete equipment checks.
   a. before rigging up
   b. before boarding
   c. before exit

B. EQUIPMENT PREPARATION

1. Always check the rig in a logical order, such as top to bottom, front to back.
2. A typical sequence (varies according to equipment configuration)
   a. automatic activation device
      (1) switched on
      (2) calibrated
   b. reserve ripcord
      (1) movement of the cable in the housing
      (2) pin in place at least halfway, but not shouldered onto the grommet
      (3) closing loop must have no visible wear
      (4) closing loop tight for properly closed container
      (5) reserve in date, seal intact
   c. main closing (hand deployment)
      (1) flap closing order and bridle routing correct
      (2) slack above the curved pin
      (3) pin fully seated
      (4) tight closing loop, with no more than ten percent visible fraying
      (5) pin secured to bridle with no more than ten percent fraying
      (6) collapsible pilot chute cocked (if applicable)
      (7) pilot chute and bridle with no more than ten percent damage at any wear point
   d. main closing (ripcord)
      (1) free movement of the cable in the housing
      (2) secure cable housing ends
      (3) ripcord end not kinked or nicked
      (4) closing loop with no more than ten percent fraying
   e. drogue movement in pocket and main deployment handle in place
   f. canopy release system and RSL
      (1) correct canopy release assembly
      (2) RSL connected and routed correctly
   g. chest strap and hardware
      (1) snap type connected and adjusted
      (2) friction adapter type: threaded correctly, adjusted, and running end secured to prevent slippage
   h. reserve ripcord handle
   i. canopy release handle
   j. harness adjustments
   k. leg straps and hardware
      (1) threaded properly
      (2) hardware function (snap operation)
   l. outer clothing (or jumpsuit)
      (1) free movement
      (2) adequate protection on landing
      (3) secure; can't impede handle access
      (4) pockets empty, jewelry removed
      (5) fall rate (if applicable)
3. Using the same sequence, check the equipment after the student is completely rigged and with everything adjusted, paying particular attention to the following:
   a. risers over the shoulder, not under the arm
   b. release handle clear from under the main lift web
   c. proper threading of harness hardware
   d. chest strap routed clear of the reserve ripcord
   e. twisted harness straps
   f. comfort pads in position
   g. overall adjustment and fit: On solo jumps, a loose harness may allow the container to shift in freefall, causing stability problems.
4. Student's personal equipment (SHAGGAR, explained below)
   a. **S**hoes
      (1) appropriate for the student jumping; sandals, heels, and leather (or synthetic leather) soles not recommended
      (2) hooks taped
      (3) laces double knotted
   b. **H**elmet
      (1) adequate protection
      (2) fit and adjustment
   c. **A**ltimeter
      (1) readable by student (farsightedness?)
      (2) zeroed
   d. **G**oggles
      (1) correct type for contacts or glasses
      (2) clear and clean
      (3) tight
   e. **G**loves
      (1) worn for jumps into 40 degrees or cooler

(2) light and flexible

(3) correct fit

f. **A**erial photograph for pattern planning (USPA Flight Planner)

g. **R**adio or other means of communication

(1) all required equipment in place and ready

(2) all required personnel coordinated

(3) entire team informed of the canopy flight plan

(4) "no-jump" signal prepared

(5) student's radio on

5. Perform another pre-jump inspection in the aircraft prior to exit.

C. AIRCRAFT PREPARATION

1. Inspect and prepare the aircraft.
   a. familiar with door operation
   b. protrusions removed
   c. smooth edges
   d. seat belts clear
   e. knife aboard
   f. paperwork for jump modifications
   g. pilot rig in date
2. Brief the pilot.
   a. spot
   b. routine procedures
   c. flap settings and airspeeds
   d. emergency procedures
      (1) aircraft malfunctions
      (2) premature openings
   e. flight plan and altitudes for the load

D. JUMP CONDITIONS

1. Up-to-date weather forecast
2. Surface winds and winds aloft
3. Daylight remaining

E. REFER TO SIM 5-4, PRE-JUMP SAFETY CHECKS AND BRIEFINGS

4-3: CURRENCY TRAINING

1. The Examiner and USPA Instructor rating candidates review USPA currency recommendations for students and experienced jumpers found in SIM Section 5-2.
2. Recommended currency training and jumps for most licensed skydivers may be conducted by a USPA Coach under a USPA Instructor's supervision.

4-4: TANDEM EQUIPMENT CHECKS

A. PERSONAL

1. Proper outerwear
   a. tight fitting to reduce drag
   b. won't interfere with handle operation or instructor's vision
2. Helmet: soft or hard (hard helmets for students only if instructor is wearing a full-faced helmet)
3. Tandem harness fitted and adjusted (see manufacturer's instructions)
4. Knife

B. TANDEM EQUIPMENT PREPARATION

1. Always check the tandem rig in order, top to bottom, back to front before putting it on.
2. A typical sequence (varies according to equipment configuration):
   a. automatic activation device
      (1) switched on
      (2) calibrated
   b. reserve ripcord
      (1) movement of the cable in the housing
      (2) pin in place at least halfway, but not shouldered
      (3) closing loop must have no visible wear
      (4) closing loop tight for properly closed container
      (5) reserve in date, seal intact
   c. main closing
      (1) correct bridle routing
      (2) tight closing loop
      (3) pin or cable secure to attachment, in place, and fully seated
      (4) cable coating intact with no cracks or dents
      (5) security locking devices in place
      (6) closing loop routed correctly and flaps in correct order
   d. drogue system
      (1) drogue cocked (window, if applicable)
      (2) release cables or lines routed correctly
      (3) handles in place and secured, if applicable
      (4) drogue pouch secure and drogue movable in pouch as one unit (does not telescope and jam when pulled)
      (5) pouch maintenance
   e. main canopy release system and RSL
      (1) correct canopy release assembly
      (2) RSL connected and routed correctly (frequently disconnected during descent to prepare for a cutaway on landing)
      (3) RSL back-ups (Collins lanyard routed correctly)
   f. riser covers: maintenance
   g. chest strap and hardware
   h. reserve ripcord handle
   i. canopy release handle
   j. harness adjustments
   k. leg straps and hardware
      (1) threaded properly
      (2) hardware function
      (3) ends secured
3. Special care required
   a. Tandem instructors must carefully manage their equipment throughout the flight to make sure nothing gets damaged or dislodged.
   b. Other jumpers in the aircraft may not be qualified to check tandem equipment, and other tandem instructors may not be able to move into position to check your equipment adequately.
   c. When taking a tandem student, it is not recommended for a tandem instructor to perform any additional duties or undertake any additional responsibilities on the aircraft.
4. Perform another pre-jump inspection in the aircraft just after hook-up.
   a. Check all available items.
   b. Have the tandem student assist with checking the harness attachments.
   c. A loose connection between the student's and instructor's harness may cause the student to shift in freefall, causing stability problems, including a side-spin.
5. Perform a complete handle check in likely order of use according to the manufacturer requirements—
   a. after hook up and prior to exit
   b. in droguefall after deploying the drogue
      (1) drogue release
      (2) secondary drogue release
      (3) cutaway handles

INSTRUCTOR'S DUTIES T-4

T-4 INSTRUCTOR'S DUTIES

   (4) reserve handle(s)

   (5) RSL shackle

   c. after main canopy deployment

      (1) cutaway handle

      (2) reserve handle(s)

C. GROUND CREW PREPARATION

Enlist the help of ground assistant for windy conditions.

4-5: VIDEO AND CAMERA

1. Video has proven to be an effective training and marketing aid, but the USPA Instructor must approve and brief the videographer prior to the jump.

2. Refer to the Skydiver's Information Manual, Section 6, for camera flyer recommendations, particularly those pertaining to student jumps.

3. Minimum experience qualifications

   a. 300 group freefall skydives

   b. 50 jumps flying camera with experienced jumpers

4. Considerations for jumpers photographing tandem jumps

   a. The camera flyer needs to remain clear of the tandem pair during and following exit until the drogue is deployed.

   b. The camera flyer must remain clear of the drogue and the area above the tandem pair at all times.

   c. Upon drogue release, the tandem pair accelerates downward abruptly (trap door effect).

      (1) The camera flyer must remain clear of the area immediately below the tandem pair.

      (2) The camera flyer should anticipate them dropping below during main parachute deployment.

5. The USPA instructor should correct any camera flyer actions that cause concern.

6. Use of handycam during tandem jumps is becoming more common. To ensure the Tandem Instructor is prepared to conduct handycam tandem jumps, USPA recommends the Tandem Instructor:

   a. Have a minimum of 200 tandems (required according to the Basic Safety Requirements)

   b. Have made at least 50 tandem jumps in the preceding six months

   c. Receive specific instruction in the safety and use of a handycam system

   d. Demonstrate emergency procedures with the handycam mounted and the student fully geared up and attached to the instructor harness. The procedures may be demonstrated standing on the ground or while suspended in a hanging harness.

   e. Should make two solo jumps using solo parachute equipment with the handycam mounted to become familiar with the effects of the camera in freefall and to become comfortable with the operation of the handycam.

   f. Should make one jump with the handycam using a tandem system with at least a C-licensed skydiver in the student position. A tandem instructor or tandem examiner familiar with handycam operation should be used whenever possible.

4-6: RELATIVE WORK ON TANDEM JUMPS

A. RISK CONSIDERATIONS

1. Under certain conditions, allowing other jumpers to join a tandem jump is possible with minimal increased risk to the tandem pair.

2. Once the tandem instructor and student are in droguefall, they have very limited range of vertical or horizontal movement.

3. The tandem pair must rely on those who may be making the jump with them to avoid collisions or other hazardous situations.

4. All added risks need to be considered by both members of the tandem pair, which requires that the tandem student be fully informed of any additional risks.

B. QUALIFICATIONS

1. Tandem parachutist in command

   a. USPA Tandem Instructor rating

   b. minimum of 100 tandem skydives as a tandem instructor or tandem parachutist in command

2. Other participants on the tandem jump should be approved by the USPA Tandem Instructor, the tandem student, and the camera flyer and should have the following minimum experience (either option):

   a. USPA Coach or higher rating

   b. 300 group freefall skydives

3. The USPA Tandem Instructor should personally know the skill level of all who are participating on the skydive.

C. BRIEFING

1. The USPA Tandem Instructor should thoroughly brief all the assembled participants.

2. Exit

   a. The tandem instructor must ensure that an exit is designed that keeps everyone involved leaving the aircraft in a safe order and prevents interference with the tandem pair or the drogue deployment.

   b. There should be no contact with the tandem pair on exit.

   c. No skydiver should ever be directly above or below the tandem pair.

   d. The tandem instructor needs to make sure the airspace above is clear prior to the drogue throw.

3. Freefall and droguefall

   a. Jumpers should approach in view of the instructor, never from behind, above, or below the tandem pair.

   b. Each participant should maintain visual contact with everyone in the formation, especially the tandem pair.

   c. fall rates

      (1) Tandem fall rates can be unpredictable, depending on the weight and body positions of the tandem pair.

      (2) Unless a skydiver cannot easily match the fall rate of the tandem pair there should be no attempt to dock.

   d. docking

      (1) No docks should be made on the instructor.

      (2) Jumpers docking on the student should be careful to prevent the student from taking too firm a grip.

4. Breakoff

   a. The USPA Tandem Instructor should wave off to signal the end of group activity at least 1,000 feet prior to planned drogue release.

   b. The tandem instructor may wave off one or more of the approaching skydivers at any time during the freefall or droguefall, and those jumpers should immediately stop their approaches towards the tandem pair.

   c. At the breakoff signal or by no lower than 1,000 feet prior to the planned drogue release, solo jumpers (except the camera flyer) should track clear of the tandem pair.

5. Under canopy, no jumper should attempt to approach the tandem pair; canopy formation activity with tandem equipment is prohibited.

6. Distractions: The USPA Tandem Instructor should adhere to his or her standard operating procedures at all times during the jump preparation and operations and not be distracted by the other jumpers—
   a. during the student preparation on the ground
   b. while approaching or boarding the aircraft with the student
   c. during the student hook-up procedure on the climb to altitude
   d. during the climb-out, exit and drogue deployment procedure

INSTRUCTOR'S DUTIES **T-4**

T-5 DEMONSTRATION AND GROUND PRACTICE FOR EVALUATIONS

5. Demonstration and Ground Practice for Evaluations

A. PURPOSE

1. After the classroom portion and prior to evaluations, the Examiner and staff demonstrate how to conduct the student training and jump activities for which the candidates are being rated and evaluated.
2. Candidates may practice the skills, supervised by the course staff, keeping in mind that course time is limited and evaluations must soon begin.

B. TANDEM SESSIONS

1. Prior-to-boarding sequence
   a. pre-jump training of tandem students in Categories A and B
   b. rigging the student's harness and other equipment
   c. jump preparation and pre-jump check
2. Aircraft emergencies
3. Pre-boarding, boarding, climb-to-altitude, and pre-jump sequence
   a. control of the student in the loading area and in the aircraft for boarding and the climb to altitude
   b. hook-up, student verification of hook-up, and equipment self-check procedures
   c. control of the student's movement in the aircraft during pre-exit
   d. spotting and pilot communications
4. Exit procedures, student observation, and coaching techniques in freefall and droguefall
5. Canopy descent, approach, and landing
6. Post-jump critique
7. Packing

C. DIVE FLOWS

EVALUATOR ACTING AS STUDENT

JUMP 1

Jump 1 and 2 may be made in either order.

1. Solo with tandem equipment or tandem with an evaluator (based on manufacturers requirements)
   a. maximum ten-second freefall prior to drogue deployment
   b. drogue inflation check
   c. handle accessibility check, in the order that they would be pulled in an emergency situation: primary drogue release, secondary drogue release, main cutaway handle then reserve ripcord, and where appropriate, the RSL attachment shackle on the riser
   d. droguefall turns
   e. wave-off and drogue release at 6,000 feet.
   f. post-deployment check
   g. post-opening check of cutaway and reserve ripcord, plus, where appropriate, the RSL attachment shackle on the riser
   h. practice landing flares
   i. pre-planned pattern to the landing area
2. Must be made prior to acting as instructor

JUMP 2

1. Candidate in the student position
2. Must be made as an instructional rating jump during the rating course

JUMP 3

Candidate in the instructor position

1. Qualified jumper in the student position (see introduction and orientation section of this rating course outline)
2. Stable exit followed by aggressive drogue deployment within 10 seconds of exit
3. Visual check of the drogue inflation, followed by a thumbs up to the jumper in the student harness
4. Handle accessibility check, in the order that they would be pulled in an emergency situation: primary drogue release, secondary drogue release, main cutaway handle then reserve ripcord, and, where appropriate, the RSL attachment shackle on the riser
5. 360-degree turns in both directions
6. Wave-off and drogue release at 6,000 feet.
7. Post-deployment equipment check
8. Post-opening check of cutaway and reserve ripcord, plus, where appropriate, the RSL attachment shackle on the riser
9. Practice landing flares
10. Pre-planned pattern to the landing area

JUMP 4

Unstable exit and recovery

1. Qualified jumper in the student's position (see introduction and orientation section of this rating course outline)
2. Unstable exit at 10,500 feet or higher
3. Drogue deployment by 8,000 feet
4. Visual check of the drogue inflation, followed by a thumbs up to the jumper in the student harness
5. Handle accessibility check, in the order that they would be pulled in an emergency situation: primary drogue release, secondary drogue release, main cutaway handle then reserve ripcord, and, where appropriate, the RSL attachment shackle on the riser
6. Two 360-degree droguefall turns
7. Wave-off and drogue release at 6,000 feet.
8. Post deployment check
9. Post-opening check of cutaway and reserve ripcord, plus, where appropriate, the RSL attachment shackle on the riser
10. Practice landing flares
11. Pre-planned pattern to the landing area

JUMP 5

1. Tandem freefall speed
   a. At solo terminal velocity, a jumper falls 1,000 feet approximately every 5.5 seconds.
   b. At tandem terminal velocity, the pair falls 1,000 feet in approximately 3.5 seconds.
   c. Both tandem instructor candidates and jumpers acting as students need to closely monitor altitude.
2. Recovery from instability; terminal velocity control.
   a. must have video if the Examiner is not on the jump
   b. unstable exit
   c. sufficient altitude to reach tandem terminal velocity (15-20 seconds) and deploy drogue by 8,000 feet
   d. depending on the manufacturer—360-degree turns to the left and right during tandem terminal
   e. drogue deployment at 8,000 feet
   f. system handles check once the drogue is deployed
   g. visual check of the drogue inflation, followed by a thumbs up to the jumper in the student harness

h. handle accessibility check, in the order that they would be pulled in an emergency situation: primary drogue release, secondary drogue release, main cutaway handle then reserve ripcord, and, where appropriate, the RSL attachment shackle on the riser

i. wave-off and drogue release at 6,000 feet.

j. post-deployment check

k. post-opening check of cutaway and reserve ripcord, plus, where appropriate, the RSL attachment shackle on the riser

l. practice landing flares

m. pre-planned pattern to the landing area

D. PRACTICE

1. Once the candidate has completed the five initial tandem training jumps under the direct supervision of a tandem instructor examiner, five additional tandem jumps are required for the USPA Tandem Instructor rating.

2. Jumper Acting as Student

    a. It is recommended that the Tandem Examiner complete each of the five practice jumps in the student position whenever possible.

    b. In the event the Tandem Examiner is not available, a USPA Tandem Instructor or a jumper with at least 100 skydives and a USPA B license or higher may jump in the student position, after a briefing from the Tandem Examiner to include the use of emergency handles and deployment altitudes and procedures.

    c. In the event that a non-tandem rated jumper is used for the student position, the Tandem Examiner or a USPA Tandem Instructor must supervise the practice jump and sign for the practice jump on the proficiency card.

3. The five practice jumps provide the tandem candidate a chance to become more experienced and comfortable with tandem procedures before earning the rating and jumping with actual tandem students.

4. The jumpers in the student position should conduct themselves as a good student, allowing the tandem instructor to focus on proper tandem techniques for the door position, launch, droguefall, deployment, canopy descent and landing.

5. The tandem candidate should conduct the first three practice jumps as a Category A tandem skydive.

6. The tandem candidate should conduct practice jumps four and five as a Category B tandem jump.

DEMONSTRATION AND GROUND PRACTICE FOR EVALUATIONS — T-5

T-6 CANDIDATE EVALUATION

6. Candidate Evaluation

A. INTRODUCTION

1. This section of the course is to be presented to the candidates with all evaluators for that course present.
   a. serves as the evaluator's briefing
   b. reassures the candidates that they are fully informed of all evaluation criteria and instructions
   c. provides a dialog and rapport between candidates and evaluators before testing begins
2. The Tandem Instructor Rating Course includes an evaluation of the first five tandem training jumps
3. The course also includes two written exams.
   a. the USPA Tandem Instructor Exam
   b. manufacturer's (equipment specific) exam
4. The initial five training jumps will vary slightly based on the tandem system used for the course.
   a. Either one solo, using the tandem harness and container system, or a tandem jump in the instructor position (follow the manufacturer requirements)
   b. One acting as a tandem student
   c. Three acting as tandem instructor

B. GENERAL

1. To ensure standardized procedures, each evaluation should be conducted in generally the same manner and to the same standards of performance.
2. For the tandem jump evaluations, the Examiner may divide the candidates into teams of two supervised by an evaluator, may switch team members, or the evaluator may act as tandem student.
3. The evaluator explains in detail what will be considered a satisfactory performance during the training and jump operations.

C. AREAS TO BE EVALUATED

TANDEM JUMPS

Each candidate is evaluated in all the following subject areas and sub-areas shown on the Tandem In-Air Skills Evaluation Form:

1. pre-jump equipment check
2. student hook-up and pre-exit check
3. exit control
4. heading control (no more than 90 degrees of unintentional heading change)
   a. droguefall
   b. freefall
5. deployment at the correct altitude
6. canopy descent
7. landing
   a. satisfactory landing
   b. accuracy
8. inspection and packing
9. ground training, supervision, and debriefing ("ground") evaluation: each tandem instructor candidate is evaluated in all the following subject areas:
   a. preparation – Lesson plans prepared, training aids available, and suitable teaching environment available
   b. explanation and demonstration on all required items
   c. student trial and practice – (vertical and Horizontal Training)
   d. Review and evaluation – check on learning concepts (feedback, questions, testing etc.)
   e. The use of whole part whole (why it's important, expectations, criteria to pass, breakdown of parts, recombine parts and practice until autonomous)
   f. category A
      (1) equipment
      (2) aircraft procedures
      (3) exit
      (4) freefall body position
      (5) deployment
      (6) canopy flight procedures
      (7) landing
      (8) freefall and canopy dive flows
      (9) hand signals
      (10) emergency procedures
   g. category B
      (1) review category A training
      (2) leg awareness
      (3) heading awareness
      (4) freefall turns
      (5) written flight plan
      (6) airport orientation
      (7) emergency procedure review
   h. supervision (equipment—three checks pre-boarding, boarding and pre-flight)
   i. climb to altitude
      (1) seat belt
      (2) view of airport
      (3) deployment altitude review
      (4) mental review
      (5) verbal review
      (6) hand signal review
   j. opening to landing
      (1) assisted student canopy control
      (2) student assisted flare
   k. debriefing
      (1) walk and talk
      (2) video reviewed, if available
      (3) corrective training
      (4) decision to advance
      (5) preview next dive
      (6) paperwork

D. EVALUATION SCHEDULE

TANDEM JUMP EVALUATION

1. The candidate is evaluated while acting as instructor during at least three practice tandem jumps with course candidates or staff.
2. The evaluations are combined with training sessions, with the evaluator offering advice and assistance as necessary.
3. The packing evaluation may be completed at any time during the course.
4. Tandem evaluation jump dive flows are in the demonstration and ground practice for evaluations section of this course.
5. Video is recommended for all evaluation jumps.

E. JUMPER ACTING AS TANDEM STUDENT (RESPONSIBILITIES)

1. Altitude monitoring
2. Verification of drogue deployment by 8,000 feet
3. If the candidate fails to deploy the drogue by 8,000 feet—
   a. Remind the candidate (prearranged signal) to deploy the drogue.
   b. Deploy the drogue by 7,000 feet.
4. Check of the main drogue release and safety handles (attached to the cutaway and reserve ripcord handles), followed by a thumbs up to the candidate
5. If the candidate fails to release the drogue by 6,000 feet—

a. Remind the candidate (prearranged signal) to release the drogue.

b. Release the drogue by 5,000 feet.

F. GROUND RULES FOR TANDEM EVALUATIONS

1. The pair conducts actual tandem jumps with the Examiner or an appointed tandem course evaluator observing.

2. During tandem jumping evaluations, the jumper acting as tandem student will cooperate and communicate as an experienced jumper during all phases of the jump.

    a. The evaluator may present or direct the candidate acting as student to present certain scenarios to challenge and enhance the experience of the candidate acting as instructor.

    b. In each case, the candidate acting as instructor must be fully informed of the scenario and reviewed on the expected response.

    c. By 8,000 feet, the evaluator or candidate acting as tandem student must cease all challenges and return to a stable position.

3. The evaluator determines who will be in charge during aircraft and jump operations; everyone must know who's in charge at any given time.

4. Tandem terminal velocity

    a. Each candidate, acting as tandem instructor, must demonstrate control during at least a 20-second freefall without a drogue.

    b. The Examiner or an appointed tandem course evaluator must accompany each candidate on at least one such jump.

    c. This will require an exit no lower than 12,000 feet, even if the jump is performed from a Cessna 182 or other single engine piston powered aircraft.

G. SCORING

TANDEM JUMPS

1. The candidate must obtain a score of Satisfactory in all areas of the USPA Tandem Instructor In-Air Skills and Instruction Evaluation Form.

2. Tandem jumps (evaluator riding or jumps alongside the tandem candidate pair)

    a. The candidate correctly and completely rigs a simulated student for a tandem jump and completes a satisfactory pre-jump check of all associated systems, meaning that everything is inspected and prepared as necessary for a safe jump under ordinary circumstances:

        (1) student's parachute equipment
        (2) student's personal items
        (3) tandem equipment
        (4) aircraft
        (5) pilot
        (6) ground support personnel

    b. The candidate performs satisfactorily during the tandem jumps—

        (1) a complete equipment check, including actively engaging the simulated student in checking the student harness attachments after hook-up
        (2) spots the aircraft correctly
        (3) establishes stability within five seconds of exit and maintains it throughout the jump
        (4) recovers from intentional, planned instability on exit
        (5) perform as a complete operation handle check during droguefall on each jump
        (6) demonstrates heading control during tandem freefall, including tandem terminal velocity and droguefall
        (7) demonstrates control of 360-degree turns in tandem freefall and droguefall
        (8) deploys and releases the drogue within 500 feet of the planned altitude
        (9) without assistance, steers the canopy to within 50 feet of the target on at least two tandem jumps while acting as instructor

3. Packing and equipment: Each candidate must demonstrate correct inspection and packing procedures using the tandem parachute system type for which the candidate is being rated (refer to the tandem equipment manual).

4. Unsafe performance

    a. The evaluator must advise the Examiner of any performance that, in the evaluator's opinion, creates a safety hazard during an evaluation jump.

    b. The Examiner may recommend additional training for the candidate or that the candidate not continue with the in-air practical evaluation of the course at this time.

    c. This also applies to freefall evaluation jumps.

5. Mandatory scores of Unsatisfactory

    a. missing attachment or forgetting lateral adjustment during hook-up (requiring evaluator prompt)

CANDIDATE EVALUATION | T-6

    b. failure to perform and verbalize pre-exit equipment check (requiring evaluator prompt)

    c. inability to recover stability within ten seconds after exit with the cooperation of the evaluator or another candidate acting as student

    d. initiation of drogue deployment below 8,000 feet

    e. failure to perform complete handle check after deploying the drogue

    f. inability to control heading in freefall or droguefall

    g. drogue release below 5,000 feet

    h. landing or canopy control that in the opinion of the evaluator or Examiner could lead to a student injury

    i. other

Note: "Other" is not meant as an open or broad interpretation of the reasons for a score of Unsatisfactory; rather, it is reserved for unforeseeable situations that in the judgment of the evaluator and the Examiner would compromise the safety of an evaluator or a real student.

H. RETESTING

1. Tandem jump retesting: A candidate who fails to obtain a score of Satisfactory in all areas of the Tandem In-Air Skills Evaluation Form must retake that portion of the USPA Tandem Instructor Rating Course at another time.

2. Written exam retesting

    a. USPA Exam

        (1) Each candidate will be provided a second opportunity to pass the test during the course.

        (2) Failure to answer 100 percent of the questions correctly on the second attempt will require the candidate to study, retake the classroom portion of a future Tandem Instructor Rating Course, and pass the written exam at that course.

    b. tandem equipment manufacturer's exam, according to the manufacturer

3. Retesting fees: All retesting and re-evaluation fees are at the discretion of the Examiner (and the manufacturer for its written exam).

4. All portional retesting must be accomplished within 12 months of the failed or incomplete course, or the candidate must retake the complete course.

TANDEM INSTRUCTOR RATING COURSE GROUND EVALUATION CHECKLIST

1. **Introduction (5 minutes)**
   a. Instructor
      - ☐ name
      - ☐ background
   b. student
      - ☐ motivations
      - ☐ physical condition: medical, vision, hearing, age, weight, dental, scuba, injuries, blood donations, prescription and non-prescription drugs, alcohol
      - ☐ USPA membership, waiver, etc.
      - ☐ appropriate clothing (pockets, jewelry)
      - ☐ non-jump background
      - ☐ procedure to prepare for jump (time frame, etc.)
   c. skydive
      - ☐ tie-in to previous experience
      - ☐ introduce objectives (emphasis on pull altitude)
      - ☐ brief description (concept, flow)
      - ☐ demonstration and video, if available
      - ☐ practice deployment (Category B)

2. **Training (10-15 minutes)**
   a. equipment
      - ☐ hook-up and check procedures
      - ☐ altimeter
      - ☐ drogue release handle
   b. aircraft
      - ☐ use of mock-up or aircraft
      - ☐ hand and foot placement
      - ☐ low altitude (landing with aircraft)
      - ☐ bail out
      - ☐ poised exit
   c. droguefall and freefall
      - ☐ hand placement
      - ☐ body position
      - ☐ hand signals (Category B)
      - ☐ altitude awareness
   d. landing
      - ☐ use of landing trainer mock-up
      - ☐ tandem landing
      - ☐ water
      - ☐ trees
      - ☐ wires
      - ☐ other obstacles, prevention, drag recovery

3. **Canopy Control (10 minutes)**
   - ☐ use of DZ photo or flight planner; walk in field
   - ☐ exit point
   - ☐ holding area
   - ☐ landing pattern from different directions
   - ☐ landing procedure: flare height, stall recovery
   - ☐ effect of low turn

4. **Meeting Student (20-Minute Call)**
   - ☐ pre-jump equipment check (student and instructors)
   - ☐ pre-boarding supervision
   - ☐ full-dress rehearsal at mock-up or aircraft
   - ☐ boarding

5. **Climb to Altitude**
   - ☐ helmet and seat belt
   - ☐ view of airport from aircraft
   - ☐ deployment altitude review (at correct altitude)
   - ☐ student hook-up
   - ☐ student verbal rehearsal with instructor
   - ☐ supervision during pre-exit and climb-out

6. **Opening to Landing**
   - ☐ canopy control
   - ☐ pattern, accuracy

SAMPLE EVALUATION FORM

Preparation ☐ Unsatisfactory ☐ Satisfactory

Individual knowledge. Organization, teamwork, instructional flow, preparation and control of training area, and use of training aids.

Explanation and Demonstration (Presentation) ☐ Unsatisfactory ☐ Satisfactory

Includes introduction. Objectives and flow of the dive, followed by a more detailed explanation of each point. It should be clear and understandable. Horizontal and vertical demonstrations.

Student Trial and Practice (Application) ☐ Unsatisfactory ☐ Satisfactory

Efficient and effective. Develops student performance to the degree that the student (after mastering each individual skill) can perform the dirt dives in real time without coaching. Emphasis on horizontal. Step by step.

Review (Evaluation) ☐ Unsatisfactory ☐ Satisfactory

Emphasis on requiring student demonstrations of skills with continual evaluation of progress. Effective written checklist with key questions. Complete (especially four emergency areas: aircraft, freefall, equipment, landing).

Supervision (equipment, pre-boarding, boarding, canopy descent) ☐ Unsatisfactory ☐ Satisfactory

Control during full-dress rehearsal, pre-boarding, and boarding. Canopy descent and landing pattern review. Equipment check—three required.

Climb to Altitude ☐ Unsatisfactory ☐ Satisfactory

Orienting the student to the DZ and ground winds, reviewing significant altitudes (no-more turns, lock-on, deployment), student's mental preparation, required description of the dive from the student, pre-exit equipment check, spotting (involving the student in the process and effectiveness), supervision while moving to the door and getting into position for exit.

☐ helmet and seat belt ☐ view of airport ☐ deployment altitude review ☐ mental review
☐ verbal review ☐ spotting ☐ climb-out

Exit, Freefall Observation, and Altitude Monitoring ☐ Unsatisfactory ☐ Satisfactory

Within range to observe, altitude aware, non-interference

Opening to Landing ☐ Unsatisfactory ☐ Satisfactory

Observe student canopy control and set good example.

Debriefing ☐ Unsatisfactory ☐ Satisfactory

Use of walk and talk technique (post dive with the student's story first). Thorough and accurate. Beneficial to the student. Positive and upbeat approach. Advancement decision. Corrective training. Paperwork (logbook, DZ records).

☐ walk and talk ☐ video reviewed ☐ corrective training
☐ advance decision ☐ lesson preview ☐ paperwork

SCORING AND CRITERIA EXAMPLES

Pre-Jump Equipment Checks (Three Required)	Pre-flight (observed), before boarding, before exiting. The candidate cannot enter an aircraft mis-rigged.
Student Hook-Up	Includes all points of attachment and pre-exit handle check
Exit Control	Stability and proper presentation to the relative wind within 10-seconds
Freefall	On heading able to execute stable turns to include drogueless scenario (Tandem Terminal)
Droguefall	Able to set the drogue in 5-10 seconds (stable) and execute turns with body control (not buffeting)
Heading Control	Able to maintain heading regardless of student body position
Deployment	On heading, stable, at the correct (assigned) altitude
Canopy Descent	Plan their strategy back to the landing area
Landing	Must be safe (can be seated or stand-up) and within 25-meters of the target
Inspect And Pack	In accordance with the manufacturers instructions
AUTOMATIC UNSATS	
Missed Attachment Or Lateral Adjustment	All points of attachment secured
Missed Pre-Exit Check	All attachment points and handles (in order)
Unstable More Than 10 Seconds	No drogue out or unstable drogue set
Unable To Control Freefall Heading	Lack of ability to maintain heading (no drogue Tandem Terminal)
Freefall Below 8,000 Feet	No drogue set by 8,000 ft AGL
Missed Droguefall Handle Check	Not checking handles in the proper order after drogue is set
Unable To Control Droguefall Heading	Lack of ability to maintain heading (after drogue is set)
Drogue Release Below 4,000 Ft.	Drogue must be released within 500 feet of the predetermined deployment altitude
Bad Canopy Control Or Landing	Creating a dangerous situation (potential injury) to the Tandem Instructor or Passenger/Student
Other	Safety; unstable drogue set, hazardous/dangerous landing approach, pulling the wrong handle or out of sequence response to emergency situations, etc.

TANDEM METHOD | T-3

EXAMINER RATING COURSE

ACKNOWLEDGMENTS

Lesson Design Format - "Essential Elements of Instruction", Madeline Hunter

Lesson Design - Lesson Conference Sequence by Instructional Training Co., Phoenix, AZ

Resolution Dimension – Allen Mendler

Resolution Mediation – "Discipline With Dignity", National Education Service

Lesson Design Image from www.lanecc.edu/fpd/resources/LENS/module6.pdf

Weston, Mc Alpine, and Bordonaro, (1995)

Hersey and Blanchard Situational Leadership

E-1 INTRODUCTION AND ORIENTATION

1. Introduction and Orientation

A. WHAT IS A USPA EXAMINER?

1. USPA Examiner (E) is the highest of the three instructional ratings USPA administers, preceded by Coach and Instructor.
2. A USPA Examiner may—
   a. Facilitate Coach or Instructor rating courses for any discipline of which he or she is qualified (Coach, AFF, IAD, SL or Tandem) After teaching three unsupervised and independent coach or instructor rating courses, an Examiner may begin the process of training new Examiner candidates under their supervision.
   b. Exercise all privileges of a Coach or Instructor for any discipline of which he or she is qualified (AFF, IAD, SL or Tandem)
   c. Verify any USPA license or rating and sign for all rating renewals, including other Examiner ratings.
3. Examiners may sign logbooks and other records with their signatures, rating and the current year, e.g. USPA AFF Examiner 2007, USPA CE 2007.
4. Expired Examiners can retain their signature authority by maintaining and keeping their instructor ratings (method-specific) current.

B. EXAMINER RATING COURSE BACKGROUND

1. The Examiner Rating Course was developed to address several key issues within the USPA rating structure:
   a. The original Examiner rating requirements and testing procedures did not fit the current rating program needs, and was placed on hold on January 1, 2006.
   b. Prior to the Advanced Instructor Course, USPA had never offered a formal training and evaluation process for candidates who desired to teach instructor rating courses.
   c. USPA needed a structured program to train instructors how to evaluate coach and instructor rating candidates, and facilitate rating courses.
   d. The rating structure needs to be as simple as possible, yet maintain high standards.
   e. A variety of courses were designed and tested beginning in 2002, called Advanced Instructor Courses.
   f. The Examiner Rating course was developed in 2007, based on input from many AIC course graduates and other members of USPA.
2. The goal of the course is to produce USPA Examiners who can train and evaluate USPA instructional rating holders to the same high level of proficiency.

C. WHAT IS REQUIRED TO ATTEND THIS COURSE?

1. This course may be attended by any member in good standing, who can read, write, and speak English, once all the following criteria have been met:
   a. Completed at least 100 actual freefall student training jumps.
   b. Conducted at least 15 solo student first jump courses

D. HOW TO BECOME A USPA COACH EXAMINER

1. A USPA Instructor who has been qualified as follows:—
   a. Current USPA Instructor rating in any discipline
   b. Completed at least 100 actual freefall student training jumps within the past 12 months or 300 freefall training jumps total
   c. Conducted at least 25 solo student first jump courses. You must also provide manifest records or other proof of conducting the solo first jump courses.
   d. Conducted at least 25 Coach air evaluation jumps under the direct supervision of a Coach Examiner (logged and verified on the Evaluation Jump Verification form). You must also include logbook or manifest records of the evaluation jumps when submitting the examiner proficiency card to USPA Headquarters.
   e. Conducted at least 25 Coach ground evaluations including the evaluation, scoring and debrief, under the direct supervision of a Coach Examiner (logged and verified on the Ground Evaluation Verification form), the ground evaluations for their requirement must be ground training on Category G1 or G2 as outlined in section C-6.
   f. Successful completion of the Examiner Rating Course (ERC)
   g. USPA D License
   h. Administered two complete Coach Rating Courses under the supervision of a current, appropriately rated Coach Examiner and received that Coach Examiner's recommendation after the examiner has verified all of the requirements have been met.
   i. When submitting a new examiner rating, the Safety and Training Committee must verify that all requirements have been met before the rating may be issued. The following items are required to be submitted:
      (1) Completed and signed Coach Examiner rating proficiency card that must be submitted to USPA by the endorsing instructor examiner
      (2) Logbook records showing at least 100 actual freefall student training jumps within the past 12 months or 300 freefall training jumps total
      (3) The Freefall Evaluation Jump Verification Form and the logbook records or drop zone manifest records showing at least 25 Coach evaluation jumps
      (4) The Ground Evaluation Verification Form showing at least 25 Coach ground evaluations
      (5) Logbook entries (or other evidence such as payment records or drop zone manifest records) of teaching at least 25 complete solo first jump courses
   j. Attended a biennial Coach standardization meeting within the last 2 years. (Effective February 1, 2020)
2. Evaluators
   a. The following is required for any course evaluators:
   b. USPA Instructor who has demonstrated to a USPA Coach Rating Course examiner the air skills required to pass the USPA Coach Rating Course
   c. Appointed by the course examiner
   d. Supervised by the course examiner, who is responsible for all evaluations.

INTRODUCTION AND ORIENTATION | E-1

E. **HOW TO BECOME A USPA AFF EXAMINER**

1. A USPA AFF Instructor who has met all the following requirements may attain the rating of Examiner to conduct this course and issue ratings:
    a. Completed at least 500 actual AFF jumps
    b. Conducted at least 50 solo student first jump courses. These must be logged and verifiable when submitting for the examiner rating.
    c. Conducted at least 50 AFF evaluation jumps used for candidate scoring. (Practice jumps may not be counted toward the required minimum number of 50 evaluation jumps, they must be actual course jumps that are scored for the certification course requirements.) Jumps must be logged and verified on the Evaluation Jump Verification Form and included with the AFF Examiner Proficiency card submitted for the rating. You must also include logbook or manifest records of the evaluation jumps when submitting the examiner proficiency card to USPA Headquarters.
    d. Conducted at least 25 AFF ground evaluations including the evaluation, scoring and debrief, under the direct supervision of an AFF Examiner (logged and verified on the Ground Evaluation Verification form).
    e. Successful completion of the Examiner Rating Course (ERC)
    f. Attended a biennial AFF standardization meeting within the last 2 years
    g. USPA D License
    h. Meets the current requirements for an AFF Designated Evaluator
    i. Administered two complete AFF Instructor Rating courses under the supervision of a current, appropriately rated Examiner and received that Examiner's recommendation
    j. When submitting a new examiner rating, the Safety and Training Committee must verify that all requirements have been met before the rating may be issued. The following items are required to be submitted:
        (1) Completed and signed AFF Examiner rating proficiency card that must be submitted to USPA by the endorsing instructor examiner
        (2) Logbook records showing at least 500 actual AFF jumps
        (3) The Freefall Evaluation Jump Verification Form and the logbook records or drop zone manifest records showing at least 50 AFF course evaluation jumps
        (4) The Ground Evaluation Verification Form showing at least 25 AFF ground evaluations
        (5) Logbook entries (or other evidence such as payment records or drop zone manifest records) of teaching at least 50 complete solo first jump courses

2. Evaluators
    a. The following is required for any course evaluators:
    b. must hold a USPA AFF Instructor rating and have conducted at least 100 actual AFF jumps
    c. attendance
        (1) must attend the entire classroom portion of the first course at which they evaluate
        (2) must attend the candidate and evaluator briefing of each course at which they evaluate
    d. are appointed by the instructor examiner
    e. are supervised by the instructor examiner, who is responsible for all evaluations
    f. must participate in one AFF Instructor Rating Course per year to maintain currency

F. **HOW TO BECOME A USPA STATIC-LINE OR IAD EXAMINER**

1. A USPA Static-Line or IAD Instructor may conduct this course if meeting all the following requirements:
    a. Current USPA IAD or Static-Line Instructor rating
    b. Completed at least 250 actual freefall student training jumps
    c. Completed at least 250 actual static-line or IAD student dispatches
    d. Conducted at least 50 solo student first-jump courses
    e. Conducted at least 25 method-specific static-line or IAD evaluation jumps under the direct supervision of a Static-Line or IAD Examiner (logged and verified on the Evaluation Jump Verification List form and include logbook or manifest records of the evaluation jumps when submitting the examiner proficiency card to USPA Headquarters)
    f. Conducted at least 25 static-line or IAD ground evaluations including the evaluation, scoring and debrief, under the direct supervision of a Static-Line or IAD Examiner (logged and verified on the Ground Evaluation Verification form)
    g. Successful completion of the Examiner Rating Course (ERC)
    h. USPA D License
    i. Administered two complete Static-Line or IAD Instructor Rating Courses (two courses required per method) under the supervision of a current, appropriately rated Examiner and received that Examiner's recommendation
    j. When submitting a new examiner rating, the Safety and Training Committee must verify that all requirements have been met before the rating may be issued. The following items are required to be submitted:
        (1) Completed and signed IAD and Static-Line Examiner rating proficiency card that must be submitted to USPA by the endorsing instructor examiner
        (2) Logbook records showing at least 250 actual IAD or static-line student freefall training jumps
        (3) Logbook records showing at least 250 actual IAD or static-line student dispatches
        (4) The Freefall Evaluation Jump Verification Form and the logbook records or drop zone manifest records showing at least 25 IAD or static-line course evaluation jumps
        (5) The Ground Evaluation Verification Form showing at least 25 IAD or static-line ground evaluations
        (6) Logbook entries (or other evidence such as payment records or drop zone manifest records) of teaching at least 50 complete solo first jump courses

2. Evaluators
    a. The following is required for any course evaluators:
    b. static-line or IAD evaluators: must hold a USPA Instructor rating in the appropriate method and have conducted 100 actual student jumps in that method where at least 25 are static line or IAD
    c. attendance

E-1 INTRODUCTION AND ORIENTATION

   (1) must attend the entire classroom portion of the first course at which they evaluate

   (2) for solo freefall evaluation jumps only, must attend all sections of the classroom portion, except those relating strictly to IAD or static-line jumping, of the first course at which they evaluate, but any USPA Instructor who has served as an evaluator at another USPA Instructor Rating Course has met this requirement

   (3) must attend the candidate and evaluator briefing of each course at which they evaluate

   d. are appointed by the Examiner

   e. are supervised by the Examiner who is responsible for all evaluations

3. Qualifications for individuals to act as simulated IAD or static-line students during practice and evaluation for a USPA IAD or Static-Line Instructor Rating:

   a. minimum 100 jumps and a USPA B or higher license

   b. briefed in the presence of a USPA Instructor rated in that method for all applicable equipment operation and emergency procedures

G. HOW TO BECOME A TANDEM EXAMINER

1. A USPA Tandem Instructor may conduct this course if meeting all the following qualifications:

   a. Current USPA Tandem Instructor rating

   b. Completed at least 500 actual tandem jumps

   c. Conducted at least 50 solo AFF, SL, IAD or solo student transition first jump courses

   d. Conducted at least 25 tandem air evaluation jumps, 15 of which must be made evaluating a Cat-A or Cat-B candidate training jump, under the direct supervision of a Tandem Examiner (logged and verified on the Evaluation Jump Verification List) and include logbook or manifest records of the evaluation jumps when submitting the examiner proficiency card to USPA Headquarters)

   e. Conducted at least 25 tandem ground evaluations, 15 of which must be made evaluating a Cat-A or Cat-B candidate ground training, including the evaluation, scoring and debrief, under the direct supervision of a Tandem Examiner (logged and verified on the Ground Evaluation Verification form)

   f. Current manufacturer examiner endorsement for the equipment type in use for the rating course

   g. Successful completion of the USPA Examiner Rating Course (ERC)

   h. USPA D license

   i. Administered two complete Tandem Instructor Rating courses under the supervision of a current, appropriately rated Examiner and received that Examiner's recommendation

   j. When submitting a new examiner rating, the Safety and Training Committee must verify that all requirements have been met before the rating may be issued. The following items are required to be submitted:

      (1) Completed and signed Tandem Examiner rating proficiency card that must be submitted to USPA by the endorsing instructor examiner

      (2) Logbook records showing at least 500 actual tandem jumps

      (3) The Freefall Evaluation Jump Verification Form and the logbook records or drop zone manifest records showing at least 25 tandem instructor rating course evaluation jumps

      (4) The Ground Evaluation Verification Form showing at least 25 tandem instructor ground evaluations

      (5) Logbook entries (or other evidence such as payment records or drop zone manifest records) of teaching at least 50 complete solo first jump courses

      (6) A current copy of the tandem manufacturer's examiner rating card or letter of designation

      (7) A copy of the FAA Third Class Medical or military or foreign equivalent

   k. Attended a biennial tandem standardization meeting within the last 2 years.

2. Evaluators

   a. The following is required for any course evaluators:

   b. Tandem jump evaluators must hold a USPA Tandem Instructor rating and have acted as an instructor on at least 100 tandem jumps.

   c. attendance

      (1) All tandem evaluators must attend the entire classroom portion of the first course at which they evaluate.

      (2) Evaluators must attend the candidate and evaluator briefing of each course at which they evaluate.

   d. Evaluators are appointed by the Examiner.

   e. Evaluators are supervised by the Examiner, who is responsible for all evaluations.

3. Individuals who may act as simulated students during the evaluation phases of this course—

   a. other candidates (each candidate is required to make at least one tandem jump in the student position)

   b. the Tandem Examiner

   c. evaluators designated by the Tandem Examiner

4. In the practice tandem phase, jumpers with at least 100 jumps who hold a USPA B or higher license may act as simulated students.

5. All jumpers acting as simulated students for tandem

   rating candidates need to—

   a. receive a briefing from a USPA Tandem Instructor on all phases of tandem equipment operation and emergency procedures

   b. under the supervision of a USPA Tandem Instructor, coordinate all decision and execution altitudes with the tandem rating candidate, in case the candidate fails to perform

   c. be trained on the location and use of examiner safety handles, if used

H. SUBMITTING AN EXAMINER PACKET

1. Upon completion of all requirements, the endorsing Examiner must submit the following to USPA Headquarters for verification by the Safety and Training Committee before the rating will be issued:

   a. Examiner candidates must not have any disciplinary action that resulted in a sanction for the previous 24 months, such timeframe subject to modification by the compliance group

   b. have completed the ERC in the last 24 months from submitting their examiner application

   c. A completed Coach Examiner/ Examiner Proficiency Card

   d. The Evaluation Jump Verification Form listing the evaluation jump dates, location and supervising examiner required for the rating

e. The Ground Evaluation Form listing the ground evaluation dates, location and supervising examiner required for the rating

f. Logbook records for the total jumps, student jumps, and evaluation jumps required for each examiner rating

g. Drop zone manifest records for the total jumps, student jumps and evaluation jumps for each examiner rating

h. Manifest records, payment records or other proof of completing the number of first jump courses taught for the requirement of each examiner rating

2. Examiner Rating Transition Requirements

a. Upon completion of the initial Examiner rating course, the candidate will receive an Examiner rating in each method specific rating for which he is qualified

b. In order to add the Examiner rating for a new discipline, a current Examiner must meet the following additional requirements for each rating:

(1) Actual student jump numbers for the specific discipline

(2) Additional number of required first jump courses taught, if any

(3) The number of method specific evaluation jumps required for each rating

(4) Any manufacturer endorsements (required for tandem)

(5) The additional requirements must be listed on the Examiner Proficiency card, then signed and verified by another current Examiner

(6) The completed Examiner Proficiency card must be submitted to USPA Headquarters with the appropriate rating fees for processing

I. THE NATURE OF THE COURSE

1. The Examiner Rating Course is conducted over a three-day period.

2. Course and testing arrangements

a. The host coordinates with the supervising Examiner for scheduling an Examiner Rating Course (ERC)

b. The course host negotiates the fees and accommodations with the Examiner (borne by the host and candidates).

3. The course must be held at a USPA Group Member drop zone, or USPA must receive a payment equal to the Category 3 Group Member fee.

4. Each candidate is required to arrive at this course with all prerequisites completed, as specified on the Examiner Proficiency Card.

5. The course is advanced in nature and should be attended only by qualified and prepared candidates.

6. There is no actual skydiving involved in this course.

7. The Rating fee paid to USPA Headquarters for each Coach and Examiner rating is $120.

J. WHO MAY CONDUCT THIS COURSE?

1. This course may be conducted by a USPA Examiner who meets the following qualifications:

a. Current USPA Examiner rating in at least two of the following USPA rating disciplines-Coach, AFF, IAD, Static Line and Tandem

b. Must assist in at least three Examiner Rating Courses, two of which are within the previous 12 months

(1) Assist in the first two courses

(2) Lead the third course under the direct supervision of a qualified Examiner responsible for administering the course

2. The Examiner candidate must obtain a letter of recommendation from a supervising Examiner.

3. The candidate must be approved and appointed by the USPA Board of Directors

K. WHAT IS REQUIRED TO PASS THIS COURSE?

Note: Review the Coach Rating syllabus Section Four within the Instructional Rating Manual, regarding Basics of Instruction. Each Examiner Candidate is expected to arrive at this course with a thorough understanding of this material, and no need for a review or retraining in the Basics of Instruction. Course candidates are expected to adhere to those principals during the evaluation process and during actual rating course evaluations and while training students.

1. Candidates for the USPA Examiner Rating must conduct several training sessions in order to be evaluated in the following areas:

a. Understands the course material

b. Conducts effective presentations

c. Effectively and objectively evaluates instructor candidate air skills using video or DVD footage of actual evaluation jumps

d. Use of available training aids

e. Understands and facilitates the learning process to take place during the training sessions

f. Ability to keep the training sessions specific, dynamic and positive

g. Demonstrates the ability to resolve conflicts and serve as a mediator to create the best possible resolution during contrived disputes using course candidates in role playing exercises.

2. The candidate must demonstrate satisfactory presentation and leadership ability during each of the practical sessions

3. Score 100 percent on the written exam, which must be completed prior to the course

4. The candidate must conduct three satisfactory ground training sessions during the course

a. The first training session must be a non-skydiving related topic.

b. The second and third training sessions must be from a discipline for which the candidate is attending the course to become a Coach or Examiner.

c. If the candidate is attending the course for more than one discipline, there must be two method specific training sessions completed for each discipline being sought.

d. One of the two required method-specific training session must include motor skills.

e. All three ground sessions must be scored as satisfactory by the supervising Examiner or course evaluator.

f. In the event of an unsatisfactory score, the candidate will be provided with one more chance to conduct a satisfactory training session.

g. If the second score is unsatisfactory, the candidate must retake the entire Examiner Rating Course at a later date.

5. Skill Analysis

a. Each candidate will review video footage of actual evaluation jumps and score the freefall performance.

b. The video footage will be method specific for each Coach Examiner

E-1 INTRODUCTION AND ORIENTATION

   or Examiner ratings being sought by the course candidate.

   c. In the event of an unsatisfactory score, the Examiner candidate will have one opportunity to score another video performance during the course.

   d. If the second score is unsatisfactory, the candidate must retake the entire Examiner Rating Course at a later date.

L. KEEPING A USPA EXAMINER RATING CURRENT

1. Examiners may annually renew their ratings with their USPA membership by paying the annual rating renewal fee, and meeting the following requirements:

   a. Within the previous 24 months, conducted or attend and assist in a full Rating Course and teach at least 50% of one Instructor Rating Course in each discipline for which the Examiner is qualified to conduct the course.

   b. Meets the annual renewal requirements for the appropriate instructional rating. (Teaching the academic portion of any IRC meets the annual FJC requirement for that instructor rating.)

   c. Attend a USPA biennial standardization meeting, within the last 2 years, for the appropriate examiner rating.

2. All examiner renewal requirements are tracked at headquarters. Providing all examiner renewal requirements have been met, the method-specific examiner rating will automatically update when the corresponding instructional rating is renewed.

M. PROCEDURES FOR RENEWING AN EXPIRED EXAMINER RATING

1. Ratings expire with USPA memberships.

2. Persons with an expired Examiner rating, up to two years, must attend and assist in an entire Rating Course and teach at least 50% in the appropriate discipline, under the direct supervision of the supervising Examiner and obtain the endorsement of the supervising Examiner

3. For persons with an expired Examiner rating of more than two years must requalify under the direct supervision of a supervising Examiner by successfully conducting an entire discipline-specific course and act as an evaluator for at least two air evaluations and two ground evaluations

4. Meet the annual renewal requirements for the appropriate method-specific instructor rating. For example, AFF Instructor rating renewal is required for the AFF Examiner Rating.

5. Attend a USPA standardization meeting, within the last two years, for the appropriate examiner rating.

2. Conducting Presentations

A. ADULT EDUCATION PRINCIPLES

1. Adults are normally physically and mentally mature, and should be treated as such
2. Adults tend to be more problem-centered than information-centered
3. Adults are responsible for their own learning
4. Adults are practical individuals who wish to apply the theory and knowledge learned to their current situation.
5. The audience is extremely varied in terms of experience and education
6. Adults usually have specific goals when signing up for a course
7. Adults may have not been in a classroom environment in a long time and should be made to feel at ease
8. Adults tend to link their new knowledge with their past and present experiences

B. MOTIVATION FOR LEARNING

1. Adults must be motivated to learn
2. You cannot motivate adults, they must be self-motivated
3. It is the educator's responsibility to discover the type of motivation that is driving the candidate
4. People want to learn for their own reasons, so the course information must be relevant and applicable
5. Create an environment in which the candidates are self-motivated and help them see how they will benefit from the information

C. INTRINSIC VERSUS EXTRINSIC MOTIVATION

1. Intrinsic motivation comes from within
   a. Intrinsic motivation is more effective than extrinsic motivation
   b. Intrinsic motivation occurs when people are internally motivated to do something because it either brings them pleasure, they think it is important, or they feel that what they are learning is significant
2. Extrinsic Motivation
   a. Extrinsic motivation comes into play when a person is compelled to do something from external sources
      (1) "I am getting a rating so I can get paid to jump."
      (2) "I am cleaning the house because my wife told me to."
   b. Extrinsic motivation is not as effective as intrinsic motivation

D. BARRIERS TO LEARNING

1. There are essentially four broad categories that make up barriers to learning
   a. Behavior, attitude and aptitude
   b. Skills, knowledge and understanding
   c. Intellectual capacity
   d. Environment
2. Use a small group workshop to expand upon each of the four categories that make up the barriers to learning

E. ACTIVE LEARNING

1. Active learning is based in the premise that adults tend to learn best when they are actively involved in the learning process
2. There are four basic assumptions related to active learning
   a. Significant learning takes place when the subject matter is perceived by the student as relevant to his purpose
   b. Much significant learning is acquired through doing
   c. Learning is facilitated by the candidate's responsible participation in the learning process
   d. Self-initiated learning involving the whole person—feeling as well as talent or intellect—is the most pervasive and lasting type of learning

15 BENEFITS OF ACTIVE LEARNING

1. Reinforces course content
2. Develops team building skills
3. Enhances candidate self-esteem
4. Promotes participative learning
5. Energizes and invigorates the candidates
6. Strengthens learner bonds
7. Offers variety that accommodates diverse candidate learning styles
8. Allows for practical application of course content
9. Enhances communications with diverse students
10. Offers an enjoyable and exciting learning environment
11. Helps improve student retention and motivation
12. Allows for creative problem solving
13. Promotes the concept of discovery learning
14. Provides an avenue for candidate recognition and reward
15. Promotes fun, fun, fun

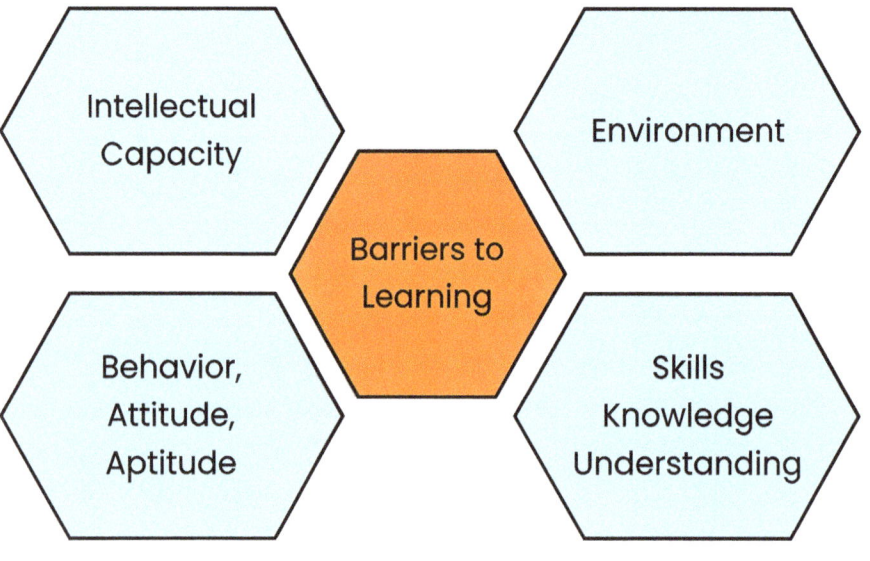

E-2 CONDUCTING PRESENTATIONS

F. USING SENSES

1. We learn by using all of our senses, sight, hearing, touch, taste and smell
2. Sight accounts for a large part of the learning process
3. From the chart below, visual material is obviously a large part of the learning process at 75%
4. Hearing, touch, taste and smell comprise the remaining 25%
5. Involving all of the senses will improve the learning process

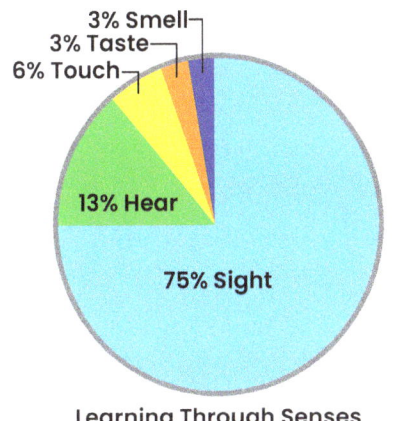

Learning Through Senses

G. EXPERIENCE AND LEARNING

1. The greater the involvement, the higher the retention level
2. Involving a candidate in an activity will help them retain the underlying concept for a much longer period of time than if the candidate had simply heard an explanation
3. Candidates should participate actively with their students by proposing situations in which they will be involved verbally, in written form, and physically.

H. REPETITION

1. Retention can be increased with frequent repetition and review of the subject material
2. Without repetition, up to 90% of the material can be forgotten in just 30 days
3. If six review sessions are conducted in a 30 day period, retention increases to more than 90%
4. Regular reviews and recaps during each training segment, focusing on the key concepts, will improve the retention rate Below are some sample reviewers:
   a. Summarize key points verbally
   b. Summarize key points by writing them on a flip chart
   c. Have the group come up with the key points
   d. Ask each candidate to write down the most salient key points for them, then share with the group
   e. Ask each candidate to formulate a question based on the contents of the module
   f. Distribute a written summary with a few "fill in the blanks"
   g. Use a creative reviewing strategy

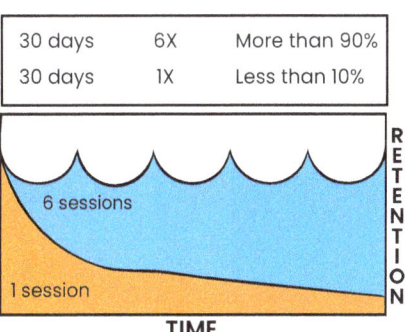

| 30 days | 6X | More than 90% |
| 30 days | 1X | Less than 10% |

YOU REMEMBER	YOU ARE ABLE TO
PASSIVE LEARNING	
10% OF WHAT YOU READ — Read	Define
20% OF WHAT YOU HEAR — Hear	List
30% OF WHAT YOU SEE — View Images	Describe/Explain
50% OF WHAT YOU SEE AND HEAR — Watch Videos	Demonstrate
— Exhibitions	Apply
— Watch a Demonstration	Practice
ACTIVE LEARNING	
70% OF WHAT YOU SAY AND WRITE — Participate in Hands-On Workshops	Analyze
— Design Collaborative Lessons	Define
90% OF WHAT YOU DO — Simulation of a Real Experience	Create
— Involvement in a Real Activity	Evaluate

3. Presentation Methods

A. LECTURE

The lecture (also called presentation) is undoubtedly the most controversial teaching method. Some experts in the field even suggest that this method be avoided altogether. This extreme point of view is based on a misunderstanding of the purpose of the lecture. It has no value as an application method, but it can be effective as a presentation or feedback method.

1. Advantages
   a. Quick and easy to prepare
   b. It can be implemented quickly
2. Disadvantages
   a. Ineffective method for learning if used alone
   b. Often overused or improperly used
   c. Frequently boring
   d. Requires good communication skills
   e. Lacks involvement of the group
3. Suggestions
   a. Use teaching points to establish a clear structure for the presentation
   b. Add audio-visual aids to supplement the lecture
   c. Write the key points down on a dry erase board to highlight a given concept
   d. Incorporate questions, examples, statistics, and comparisons to make it more dynamic
   e. Regularly introduce brief reviews or short recaps to improve retention
   f. Limit the lecture to 20 minutes or less
   g. Follow the lecture with an application exercise dealing with the same subject

B. READINGS

A large part of what we can learn comes from reading. This can be done before, during, or after a presentation. If done during the presentation, ensure that the person called upon can actually read the material.

1. Advantages
   a. Economical
   b. Reduces the time required for group sessions
   c. Provides a permanent reference for future referral
   d. All candidates receive the same information
2. Disadvantages
   a. Can be ineffective if the author lacks writing skills
   b. Concentration of the reader may be limited
   c. Information updates can be expensive
   d. Many candidates do not complete their reading assignments
   e. Readings must be accompanied with other training aids to be effective
   f. Many people are poor readers, requiring written literature to be written as simply as possible
3. Suggestions
   a. The readings should deal with the topics that the candidates need to know
   b. Explain the goal and justify the importance of the reading assignment
   c. Limit the reading to 20 minutes before interspersing it with a break or exercise

C. STRUCTURED DISCUSSION

A discussion is structured when the Examiner plays a predominant role in it by guiding the group through a series of prepared questions until everyone comes to a specific conclusion. Although the teaching points are generally provided by the group, the trainer is the one who "draws them out," so to speak, by skillfully managing the questions, answers and comments.

1. Advantages
   a. Leads to a high degree of participation
   b. Easy to provide and receive feedback
   c. Adaptable to individual differences
   d. Can be prepared relatively quickly
   e. Little equipment is necessary
   f. Excellent with small groups
   g. Encourages normally quiet individuals to participate in the discussion
   h. Topics that are controversial or that lend themselves to subjective opinions can be dealt with effectively
2. Disadvantages
   a. Requires a skillful Examiner or detailed lesson plan to cover all the possibilities
   b. Useful for certain abstract subjects (role of the Examiner) but not for others (motor skills)
   c. Requires a great deal of relevant knowledge or related experience on the part of the participants
   d. May not work in a group whose members are not used to speaking in public
   e. Some participants end up not wanting to speak or put them on the defensive if the discussion is not skillfully directed
3. Suggestions
   a. The outcomes discussed must be clearly understood by everyone
   b. Write down precise questions to be asked to initiate or refocus the discussion
   c. Write down the type of answers the group should normally provide
   d. Set or limit the discussion
   e. Tailor the questions to the experience level of the group

D. DEMONSTRATION

As previously stated "a picture is worth a 1000 words," then a demonstration is worth at least that, plus more. I cannot count how many times I have heard coaches or instructors attempt to verbally describe an action or body position rather than just "demonstrate it." With today's positive psychology and imagery, demonstrate only the correct techniques. If showing an example on video tape or DVD, show only the correct or model performances.

1. Advantages
   a. More effective than words
   b. Can be shown in stages or held for longer periods of time allowing the group to take it in
   c. Creates activity in the training area as well as changes the pace of the presentation
2. Disadvantages
   a. It may require facilities and equipment
   b. You may need to rearrange the classroom setting so everyone can see

E-3 PRESENTATION METHODS

   c. A demonstration should never be relied on alone, follow up with practice by the group
   d. Requires a perfect demonstration of the specific skill to the group
3. Suggestions
   a. Organize the activity so that everyone is able to participate
   b. Have the group act it out with you as you demonstrate
   c. Rehearse the skill ahead of time in the mirror or for another trainer
   d. If using an assistant, brief them well ahead of time
   e. Apply "whole-part-whole"
   f. Arrange the classroom ahead of time to be suitable for demonstrations

E. BRAINSTORMING

A small group activity where the candidates are given a subject or task in which they have some background experience in which they are list all of the ideas or thoughts that they think are relevant. The group would then report back to the class of there findings. The first step is to give the imagination free rein. No constraints are imposed on participants and they should provide as many ideas as possible, without analyzing them or evaluating them. The second step is to evaluate and discuss those ideas.

1. Advantages
   a. Encourages candidate participation
   b. Usually highly rated by participants
   c. Flexible and adaptable
   d. Can be used for groups of virtually any size
   e. Excellent for team building
2. Disadvantages
   a. Requires a good recap with the full attention of the candidate
   b. Time management
   c. Be prepared to fill in any gaps left by the group
3. Suggestions
   a. Have the questions, with clear parameters, ready ahead of time
   b. Provide clear instructions of what you want the candidates to achieve
   c. Have the groups appoint a reporter and a recorder
   d. Have lists of answers generated on handouts that can be passed out to the group following the assignment
   e. Apply necessary time management when recapping the groups work

F. CASE STUDY

A detailed description of an event or series of events which candidates must analyze on the basis of which they are to make decisions. The situations described must be as realistic as possible and should include all the relevant details. Participants must generally provide a diagnosis of the situation and prescribe a "treatment" or solution. Although many cases are fairly detailed, it is also possible to use mini-cases in which a situation is described in a few sentences or paragraphs.

1. Advantages
   a. Encourages candidate participation
   b. Usually highly rated by participants
   c. Flexible and can be adapted to many situations
   d. Can be used with groups of any size
   e. Effective in problem solving situations
2. Disadvantages
   a. Difficult to describe a completely plausible and realistic situation
   b. Requires an experienced leader who knows how to answer the participant's questions properly and take their actions into account
   c. There is rarely one correct answer, which can lead to a candidate feeling frustrated at the end of the case study
3. Suggestions
   a. Have experienced people read the case study who will be able to assess the realism and plausibility
   b. Base the case on facts rather than opinions
   c. Define the case on a basis of information that might be based from real life situations
   d. Make the situation seem realistic by describing the main characters (attitude, qualifications, experiences, and history) and including statements made by some of the characters
   e. Draw up a list of acceptable solutions and explain why they are acceptable
   f. Draw up a list of unacceptable solutions and explain why they are unacceptable
   g. Provide clear instructions on what you want the candidates to achieve

G. TUTORIALS

May be used when there is a candidate or small group of candidates who may need extra work on a particular subject or skill. The tutorial allows more personal time to be spent with the individuals as well as alters the pace and strategy of teaching.

1. Advantages
   a. Use to teach skills in a face to face individual situation
   b. Can be used following lecture to provide intended assessments and supplementary information to be discussed
2. Disadvantages
   a. Group size should be limited to anywhere from one to three
   b. Learners often regard these as too demanding
3. Suggestions
   a. Plan and prepare
   b. Ensure intention for tutorial is known to all before starting
   c. Keep the group size small
   d. Decide on several different approaches to presenting and applying the information

4. Application Methods

A. SMALL GROUP WORKSHOPS

Divide the participants into small groups for a short period of time. Each group has specified, defined outcomes, a leader and a recorder (secretary) who takes notes. All the group members must participate. The group leader or secretary then reports to an assembly of all the other small groups.

1. Small group workshops serve several useful functions
   a. Helps divide work among several different groups of people
   b. Develops ideas that might have been missed without any group input
   c. Helps course candidates bond with each other
   d. Fosters friendly competition between different groups
2. The groups can each work on the same project or each group can be assigned different tasks
3. How To Apply A Workshop
   a. Divide the class into groups of two to four candidates
   b. Assign each group a different task or discussion topic
   c. Assign a group leader, and a secretary to take notes
   d. The group leader or secretary then reports the outcome of the workshop to the other groups
4. Practice Application
   a. The Examiner candidates will use a small group workshop as a practical exercise
   b. Each group should be assigned a task for this exercise.
   c. Allow each group 15 minutes to collaborate for the assigned task

B. DEBATE DISCUSSION

Debate discussion of a controversial issue by participants who defend the reason for and against the attempt to gain the better of their opponents.

1. Advantages
   a. Encourages candidate participation
   b. Flexible and can be adopted to many situations
   c. Used with groups of any size
   d. Effective in problem solving situations
2. Disadvantages
   a. Difficult to describe a completely plausible and realistic situation
   b. Requires an experienced person to know how to answer candidate's questions properly and take their reactions into account

C. ROLE PLAYING

A small group activity in which the candidates must act out a scenario. This exercise is used for practice teaching (role play being a student), debriefing, skydiving aerial evaluations, conflict resolution, etc. The candidates playing out the role must keep it realistic and do their best to be sincere. A lot of people find it difficult to role play to their peers.

1. Advantages
   a. Encourages trainee participation
   b. Flexible and can be adopted to many situations
   c. Used with groups of any size
   d. Effective in problem solving situations
2. Disadvantages
   a. Difficult to describe a completely plausible and realistic situation
   b. Considerable research is sometimes required to make the cases sufficiently complete and realistic
   c. Some candidates may find the acting out of a role awkward
3. Suggestions
   a. Clearly define the parameters in which the role is acted out
   b. Define the role based on real life situations
   c. Focus on the process that is to be practiced rather than being overly creative or complex
   d. Provide clear instructions on what you want the candidates to achieve

D. APPLICATION WORKSHOP

Application methods are used to complement the presentation methods by providing participants with opportunities to apply the newly acquired knowledge. The application is a method in which participants work on a skill until they demonstrate that they have mastered it or fully understand it. This method may be used for psychomotor skills, mental processes, or for various kinds of cognitive skills.

1. Advantages
   a. Reproduces the tasks to be completed by the candidate
   b. Motivates the candidates because they can see the usefulness in the skill being taught
   c. The candidates "do" rather than "listen"
   d. Generally quick and easy to prepare
   e. Allows immediate practice for candidates
2. Disadvantages
   a. May require facilities and equipment
   b. May not always be feasible with a large group
   c. Candidates need feedback to be able to benefit from their practice
   d. It may take a great deal of time and require planned "choreography."
3. Suggestions
   a. Formulate aims and outcomes
   b. Organize the learning activity so that everyone is able to participate
   c. Carefully plan the various aspects of the practical exercise
   d. Make the exercise as realistic as possible
   e. Allow participants sufficient time to improve their performance during the practical exercise
   f. Provide specific, positive but constructive feedback to everyone
   g. Provide a diagram or description of the practical exercise in full
   h. Provide some flexibility with time allotments

E-5 | FEEDBACK METHODS

5. Feedback Methods

A. QUESTION AND ANSWER

A question-and-answer session during which the Examiner asks questions prepared in advance as a method of covering a particular subject. This may also be approached from the opposite direction. In this case, one group of candidates formulates questions and the Examiner provides the answers or assigns them to other groups so that they provide the answers.

1. Advantages
   a. Tests knowledge and review of past learning
   b. Stimulates interest and directs attention to important points
   c. Leads candidates to express thoughts
   d. Prompts candidates to come prepared
   e. Helps maintain candidate attentiveness during lectures
2. Disadvantages
   a. May be time consuming
   b. Can embarrass some candidates
   c. May stress unnecessary details
   d. May become superficial
3. Suggestions
   a. Write questions out in advance
   b. Check for clarity and support of session aim
   c. Encourage candidate questions
   d. Guide candidates to find answers
   e. Use proper question handling techniques

B. QUESTIONNAIRE, QUIZ, TEST

The candidates are asked questions or are given assignments to improve retention or evaluate what was learned.

1. Advantages
   a. It is economical
   b. Saves time
   c. Reduces the time required for group sessions when used with reading assignments and tasked prior to the start of the course
   d. Can be used to break up the pace of the class
   e. Holds everyone accountable to ensure learning
2. Suggestions
   a. Carefully design the questions and answers
   b. Multiple choice is excellent for standardization and quick, objective scoring
   c. Test "need to knows" only
   d. Practical tests are used for "show me"
   e. Written and oral tests are used for theoretical knowledge
   f. Assign the group to design questions for the recaps or closures

C. CONDUCTING RECAPS

Recaps are necessary following any workshop, group, or brainstorming activity to check the detail and quality of the findings. Recaps are usually facilitated by the Examiner with input coming from reporters in the groups.

1. Advantages
   a. Reviews and reinforces key points
   b. Works well after small group, brainstorming or topic closures
   c. Assists Examiner to achieve "optimal learning"
2. Disadvantages
   a. Time management
   b. Must apply proper question handling techniques
3. Suggestions
   a. List points on a white board or flip chart
   b. Avoid commenting on points during the report out
   c. Check for gaps
   d. Ask other groups to comment
   e. Fill in the gaps after all groups have had the chance to comment
   f. Ask specific questions of add comments at this time
   g. Have candidates write down summary questions they can ask other candidates later
   h. Distribute a written summary
   i. Trust your candidates to find similar conclusions
   j. Be patient during the recap
   k. Design questions to create deeper thinking of topics

6. Training Aids

A. GENERAL ADVANTAGES OR LIMITATIONS OF TRAINING AIDS

1. Benefits
   a. Holds the audience attention
   b. Encourages retention
   c. Facilitates learning
   d. Involves more senses
   e. Varies teaching method
   f. Focuses attention on important points
   g. Adds meaning and clarification
   h. Enables candidates to easily take notes
   i. Captures the attention of visually oriented people
   j. Encourages the use of imagination
   k. Review the material covered
   l. Serves as a memory aid for the Examiner

2. Limitations
   a. Requires time and work to prepare
   b. Can be of poor quality
   c. May become entertainment
   d. Sometimes requires expensive equipment
   e. Needs the correct environment

3. Suggestions
   a. Keep the session to aim
   b. Build a file or library of aids
   c. Become familiar with a variety of aids

4. General rules
   a. Spelling, grammar and language must all be impeccable
   b. Use different colors where possible
   c. Ensure diagrams, charts, tables and pictures are clear and organized
   d. Eliminate outside distractions
   e. Avoid turning your back to the group for too long
   f. Only use several aids in a single session
   g. Track the time for each presentation with a watch or stopwatch
   h. Avoid redundant information within different presentations
   i. Ensure everyone can clearly see the information
   j. Use proper positioning to avoid blocking the view of any candidate
   k. Arrive early to set up any equipment
   l. If you use a pointer or similar object, avoid excessive handling
   m. Pause when writing, then turn to the group to speak
   n. Maintain clutter-free visual presentations
   o. Breath, relax and pace your presentation, a pause is OK

5. Dry erase boards and paper blocks
   a. Write down only the main points "need to knows"
   b. Writing must be large and legible
   c. Use the top and center of the white board or flip chart, avoid using the bottom section unless the entire audience can see it
   d. Leave sufficient space between the words and letters
   e. Look from the board to the group and vice versa, avoid placing your back to the group for too long
   f. Use a flip chart for groups of two to twenty, larger groups may not be able to see the chart
   g. Use flip charts for small group activities where the group leader can present the information back to the rest of the class
   h. When erasing dry erase boards, use an up and down motion rather than side to side

6. Power Point, Transparencies (OHP), Slides
   a. Use aids only at the appropriate time, turn off the screen or projector when not in use
   b. Cover up parts that are not essential to the discussion
   c. Keep information on each slide to a minimum, no more than six words per line, or six lines per screen
   d. Project transparencies long enough for the candidates to take notes
   e. Use only five or six transparencies per each 30 minute session
   f. Ensure the equipment works and is in focus
   g. Use the "six foot law" and step back at least six feet from your transparency to make sure you can still read it from that distance
   h. Use sufficiently large characters of at least ¾ inches tall
   i. Avoid darkening the entire room, only turn off the lights directly above the screen

7. Video
   a. The size of the screen is determined as follows; allow one inch of screen per candidate
   b. Ensure the picture is clear and the volume is loud enough so that everyone can see and hear well
   c. Identify the points to watch before starting the video
   d. Use pause where appropriate to highlight a key point
   e. Interact with the audience, guide them to the key points
   f. Interject only on the "need to knows"

E-7 METHODS OF EVALUATION FOR GROUND AND AIR SKILLS

7. Methods of Evaluation for Ground and Air Skills

A. THE EVALUATION PROCESS

1. Each instructional rating includes evaluation of air and ground skills as part of the rating certification process
   a. Each Coach is evaluated on basic ground training skills and air evaluation skills necessary for coaching jumps
   b. Each USPA Instructor is evaluated on ground training and air skills necessary for a method-specific USPA Instructor rating
   c. Each Examiner is evaluated on the skills necessary to lead a coach or instructor rating course and evaluate candidate air and ground skills
2. Use of correct evaluation methods is critical for each coach, instructor and Examiner
3. Poor evaluation skills will lead to inconsistent and unfair scores for students or candidates.
4. Objective evaluations will provide a clear explanation of the expected outcome and the requirements to meet those goals.
5. Subjective evaluation leads to confusion, and may lack any supportive evidence for the student or candidate scores.

B. FORMATIVE AND SUMMATIVE EVALUATION

1. Each candidate evaluation must be fair and accurate.
2. Using both the Formative and Summative evaluation process will provide the most useful input to the candidate.
3. Formative evaluations are used as ongoing input to a candidate during a training session.
4. Formative evaluation can be used for helpful suggestions to the candidate, rather than being judgmental.
   a. Allows the Examiner or evaluator to point out the positive points of the evaluation and improve just the parts that need correcting.
   b. Provides immediate feedback throughout the candidate evaluation.
   c. Used to validate or ensure that the goals of the instruction are being achieved and to improve the instruction, if necessary, by means of identification and subsequent remediation of problematic aspects.
5. Summative evaluation should be used to identify larger patterns and trends in performance and judging these summary statements against criteria to obtain performance ratings.
6. Summative evaluations should be used during the mid-point of a course and at the end of a course.
7. Both summative and formative evaluations should be presented to the candidate in private, if possible.

C. EVALUATION BRIEFING

1. Prior to each classroom evaluation session, the evaluator will conduct a Pre-Evaluation Briefing with the candidate for all subjects of the evaluation process, to include:
   a. A brief review of the evaluation procedures
   b. Comprehensive detailed explanation of the scoring criteria
   c. The level of performance expected
2. A pre-lesson evaluation briefing between the evaluator and candidate to determine the following for each candidate acting as instructor during an evaluation:
   a. What do you want the students in the class to know? (This determines your main teaching points).
   b. How will you and I (the evaluator) know when the students have learned it?
   c. What should the examiner/evaluator look for during the lesson?
      (1) Training aids used
      (2) Presentation methods selected
      (3) Rules for handling questions
   d. Clarification and definition of the critical attributes of each part of the lesson structure used by the candidate/instructor i.e.; guided practice
   e. Are there any special requests or logistical concerns on the part of the candidate regarding the lesson before it begins?
3. Preparation for the post-lesson evaluation session
   a. The evaluator should take an anecdotal record of what the candidate/instructor said and did during the lesson.
   b. Label the candidate/instructor's actions on the script.
      (1) Do they fit the definition
      (2) Do they contain the critical attributes?
4. Post-lesson evaluation sequence
   a. Examiner displays or does the following during the lesson presentation:
      (1) Feeling line (honest statement of feeling about the observation, which should be used with caution because it can be subjective in nature.)
      (2) Introduction of the process
      (3) Examples of specific statements used during the feedback format
      (4) Discusses any concerns or questions about the teaching concept
      (5) Can explain rationale for the use of instructional techniques required
      (6) Can answer questions raised by the candidate/instructor as a result of teaching skills/concepts
      (7) Gives examples the candidate would have added/deleted or would have labeled differently (i.e. closure)

Formative Assessment
Given frequently to evaulate progress.
Requires feeback to be effective.
Activites
Homework
Discussion
Reflection
Practice Quizzes

Summative Assessment
Usually given at the end of instruction to assess mastery of learning objectives
Module Quizzes
Exams
Presentations
Final Project

8. Facilitation Methods

A. EFFECTIVE COURSE FACILITATION

1. Adults like to be actively involved in the learning process
2. The examiner should create a stimulating and non-threatening learning environment
3. Strong facilitation assets include:
   a. Having a thorough knowledge of the subject matter
   b. Knowing how to capture the group's attention
   c. Knowing how to make students feel at ease
   d. Providing clear expectations
4. The examiner must be familiar with the adult learning needs and adult motivation covered in Section 3 of this course

B. PRIOR TO THE COURSE

1. Knowledge
   a. The Examiner must have a thorough knowledge of the course material and subject matter
   b. Much of that knowledge and experience comes from assisting in courses and working beside experienced Examiners
   c. Work from a standardized curriculum to help ensure consistency with other courses and examiners
   d. Determine the main teaching points of each lesson and develop a thorough lesson plan
2. Start From The Learner's Prospective
   a. When working with adults it is important to be flexible and adjust your training methods and style to suit the group
   b. Use the learner's experience as the basis of learning outcomes
   c. Do not assume a prior level of experience or competence
   d. Consult with the student so they feel part of the learning experience
   e. Identify potential barriers to learning by asking what they find difficult
   f. Identify preferred styles of teaching
   g. Alter sessions to meet the needs of the students
   h. Change your own role from that of examiner to one of assistant
   i. Consider the wider issues of the student such as access, pace of learning, location, etc.
   j. Much of this information can be collected before the start of the course by using a pre-course questionnaire

C. OPENING THE COURSE

1. Ice Breakers
   a. Ice breakers help course participants become familiar with each other and work well as team building exercises
   b. They can be used at any time during the session, however they are usually used at the beginning of the course, or when new groups are formed
   c. Their primary purpose is to create a warm, relaxed environment so the participants can become familiar with each other
2. Introduce Your Neighbor
   a. Time required is approximately 10 minutes
   b. Materials required are a pen and piece of paper
   c. Explain to the participants that they are to briefly introduce their neighbor
   d. The participants group into pairs and conduct reciprocal interviews
   e. Each participant answers the following questions:
      (1) What is your name?
      (2) Where are you from?
      (3) How long have you been in the sport?
      (4) How many jumps do you have?
      (5) Do you hold any ratings?
      (6) Have you ever coached/instructed in any other sport?
      (7) What do you expect from the course?
   f. After the interviews, each participant briefly introduces his neighbor (one minute)
   g. Write each participants expectations on a white board or flip chart for reference during the course
   h. This exercise can be varied in a number of ways:
      (1) Change the questions
      (2) Instead of asking to interview the closest person, use someone across the room
      (3) Divide up the introductions over different parts of the day rather than all at once
3. My Favorite
   a. Time required is approximately 10-20 minutes
   b. Materials required are a handout sheet and pens
   c. Participants should fill in the blanks to the following statements:
      (1) My favorite color is
      (2) My favorite type of music is
      (3) My favorite month is
      (4) My favorite dessert is
      (5) My favorite sports team is
      (6) My favorite make of car is
      (7) My favorite type of movie is
   d. Next to each statement, find one other person in the room who lists the same answer
   e. Put that person's name next to the line and ask them to tell you something unique about themselves
   f. Make a note of the answers, and each participant reports out to the class
4. False Colors
   a. Time required is 10-15 minutes
   b. Materials needed are 3 x 5 index cards in four different colors
   c. Group size should be four to seven participants per group
   d. Part one
      (1) On four different colored individual index cards, list four statements about yourself, one on each card
      (2) Three statements should be true, one should be false
      (3) Example: "I own four German Shepherds" or "I have traveled to 12 countries since 1990."
   e. Part two
      (1) Each participant reads his statements out loud
      (2) The group members write down the color of the suspected false statement
      (3) In round-robin fashion, each – participant tells which color he selected and explains why he thinks that particular statement was false

E-8 FACILITATION METHODS

  (4) After hearing all the input, the individual then reveals the "false" color (the card containing the false statement)

D. CLEAR EXPECTATIONS

1. Prior to getting to the content of the course, take the time to discuss the course content, schedule and evaluation plan
2. This sets the tone for the course and ensures the candidates understand what is expected of them
3. Ask the candidates to list their expectations for evaluations and the behavior rules for the remainder of the course
4. The Examiner should repeat this process at the beginning of each program, topic introduction, learning day, and any exercises tasked to the participants

E. PERSONAL MANNER

1. Part of dynamic teaching is being a dynamic teacher
2. The Examiner should maintain personal contact with everyone in the group
3. Controlling voice and body language is an important ability
4. Listening
   a. Examiners must have excellent listening skills
   b. Be as present with the candidates as possible
   c. Listen with an open mind without being judgmental
   d. Be clear on any comments and reaffirm them with positive feedback
5. Confirmation and Correction
   a. There are three types of confirming or acknowledging your presence
      (1) verbally
      (2) non-verbally
      (3) extra verbally
   b. Verbally
      (1) use words that acknowledge you are listening
      (2) confirm a right answer, or that a correction or clarification is necessary
      (3) "Yes" or "Can you clarify" are two examples of verbal acknowledgment
      (4) Paraphrasing an entire sentence into just a few words is another form of acknowledging what was stated
   c. Non-verbally
      (1) Use body language or gestures to communicate a message
      (2) Head or hand movements
      (3) This works well when you do not want to interrupt a person who is speaking
      (4) Posture, physical appearance and facial expressions are other forms of non-verbal communication
   d. Extra verbally
      (1) Convey your opinion through sounds
      (2) "Uh-huh," "Ah-ha!" etc. are examples of extra verbal communication
      (3) This also works well when you do not want to interrupt the person who is speaking
6. Visual Contact
   a. Maintaining visual contact with the group allows the examiner to read the groups needs, feelings, actions, problems, attitudes, etc.
   b. Helps the examiner detect boredom, disagreement or interest
   c. Look at each participant, not just a select few
   d. Maintain eye contact when communicating directly with one participant
7. Voice
   a. Voice control is important for maintaining the interest of the group
   b. Volume is very powerful in helping to create the proper energy level for the material being taught
   c. Projecting at the correct volume ensures that everyone can hear what is being said
   d. Emphasis can be added to a point by speaking more slowly and adding volume
   e. Keep the pace of your speech reasonable, but avoid rushing through the information
   f. Changing the pace with intention can help to highlight key points
   g. Changing the tone of voice helps to avoid becoming boring and monotone
   h. Professional delivery of material requires the correct use of grammar and vocabulary
   i. Be aware of using acronyms or "jargon" and take the time to define any new terms
8. Body
   a. Nonverbal communication represents 80% of any communication
   b. Movement of the head, eyes, facial expressions, upper body and posture can all reflect mood, emotions and sincerity

F. DURING THE COURSE

1. Capture the group's attention
   a. Use of colors, visuals and the 90:20:8 rule as mentioned earlier in this syllabus will all help to keep the group's interest during a presentation
   b. Change the pace
      (1) Vary your teaching methods
      (2) Allow for sufficient breaks
      (3) Involve the group
      (4) Establish personal contact with the course candidates
      (5) Involve the group in physical tasks
      (6) Use handouts or transparencies with blanks that need to be filled out by the candidate
      (7) Ask open-ended questions
      (8) Make connections between subjects covered with real life experiences
      (9) Plan interesting and original review sessions
      (10) Ask the participants to write down one or two questions based on the material just presented then have the participants use small groups to come up with the answers
2. Creative Energizers
   a. Energizers can be used at any time during the learning process
   b. Energizers help to motivate the group and help participants refocus
   c. Top 10 is a quick and fun creative energizer
      (1) Time required is 10-15 minutes
      (2) Materials needed are a sheet of paper and a pen
      (3) Group size should be three to seven members per team
      (4) Ask each team to create a "top ten" of any list
      (5) The list should be something that can be verified
      (6) The group will score one point for each correct item on the list and one point for each item in the correct order on the list

d. Below are two "top 10" lists for use as a creative energizer

TOP 10 FRUIT CROPS IN THE WORLD
1. Oranges
2. Bananas
3. Grapes
4. Apples
5. Watermelons
6. Coconuts
7. Plantains
8. Mangoes
9. Tangerines
10. Pears

TOP 10 MOVIES OF THE '90S
1. Titanic 1997
2. Jurassic Park 1993
3. Independence Day 1996
4. The Lion King 1994
5. Forrest Gump 1994
6. The Lost World: Jurassic Park 1997
7. Men In Black 1997
8. Home Alone 1990
9. Ghost 1990
10. Terminator 2: Judgment Day 1991

3. Creative Content Reviewers
   a. Content reviewers may be used whenever the examiner wants to reinforce or review information
   b. The activities are beneficial to participants because they are sharing information with others in a fun and enjoyable way without realizing they are participating in a review session
   c. Below are two methods of reviewing, one is called "tree branching" and the next is called "name that term"
   d. Tree branching
      (1) Tree branching is based off of mind mapping, which takes advantage of the mind working in short intense "mind bursts" that allow you to dump your ideas onto paper in just a few minutes
      (2) Time required is 12-20 minutes
      (3) Materials needed are a flip chart or drawing paper and colored markers or pens
      (4) Participants are divided into teams of three to five
      (5) Each team is asked to creatively "tree branch" a certain topic
      (6) Each team then begins to create branches, then mini branches that relate to the topic
      (7) The "branches" should be sub-categories of the main topic, while the "mini-branches" should be information related to the sub-category
      (8) Designate a specific time period such as seven to nine minutes
      (9) When the time is up, look at each group's tree
      (10) Have a spokesman for each group explain the tree
      (11) An example of a topic might be "the role of a coach"
   e. Name that term
      (1) Time required is 12-20 minutes
      (2) Materials needed are colored 3 x 5 index cards and different color pens
      (3) Participants divide into groups of three to five
      (4) Each team is given three or four index cards of the same color
      (5) Each team should write their own definitions of specific terms, concepts, skills, etc. that were taught during that particular class session
      (6) Each definition will be listed on a separate index card
      (7) The color-coded index cards are then all placed in one basket
      (8) The teams then choose different color cards than the ones they used
      (9) Each team earns one point for each definition or answer that the other team is not able to identify the correct term or concept for

4. Creative Content Application Strategies
   a. Content application strategies are fun and enjoyable to use. Their primary purpose is to help students transfer the theories and concepts to real life, practical situations—regardless of the subject matter being taught.
   b. Windows of wisdom
      (1) Time required is 10-20 minutes
      (2) Materials needed are a flip chart, drawing paper and colored markers
      (3) Group size is four to seven participants
      (4) Participants are asked to draw a large window with anywhere from six to 15 window pains, depending on how much time there is for this activity
      (5) Participants are asked to brainstorm and identify as many ideas about how to apply a concept, or as many definitions of terms from a chapter, etc. as possible in the allotted time
      (6) A team spokesperson then present the different ideas generated by each team
      (7) Examples
         (i) Computers-use to introduce types of software, use terms/definitions in data communications, use to list administrator responsibilities
         (ii) Curriculum design-write 12 verb-object combinations that relate to student learning activities in the classroom
         (iii) Human development-use to minimize obstacle to being a successful student, resources available to improve the chances of success in school, possible ways to motivate employees, recruitment ideas
         (iv) Psychology-identify the rewards of becoming a better communicator, describe the various theories of psychology, use to teach the theories of motivation
         (v) Staff development-classroom uses of technology, teaching techniques, website ideas
         (vi) Workforce/life skills-Use in areas of personal budgeting, use in basic skills for motivation
   c. My relatives as teachers
      (1) This activity is used to help participants experience the power of course content application in a personalized manner
      (2) Time required is 10-20 minutes
      (3) Materials needed are paper, pens, and a flip chart or drawing paper
      (4) Each team member makes a list of the first names of one to three loved ones

E-8 FACILITATION METHODS

    (5) Each name should then be written vertically on a piece of paper

    (6) The team then identifies strategies (customer service strategies, computer technology strategies, English strategies, etc.) that can be used to reflect each letter in the name, using an action phrase

    (7) The following is an example for the name "Hattie" with regards to customer service:

        H (ear every customer's complaint)

        A (sk specific questions to get to the problem fast)

        T (ell the customer you understand their concern)

        T (ry to demonstrate empathy as much as possible)

        I (dentify ways to solve the problem)

        E (liminate judgmental attitudes about the customer)

    (8) After the allotted time, have the teams report their findings

    (9) Examples

        (i) Computers—can be used to review terms for tests; can also have them define terms when they repeat

        (ii) Human development—determine the characteristics of a good student, teach technical vocabulary, use in subject review, for use in reinforcement, introduction to a new topic, helps determine qualities of good communication, helps determine the qualities of healthy self-esteem

        (iii) Human resources—use to help in subject review, use for reinforcement, to introduce a new topic, teach technical vocabulary, human relation skills, use to determine leadership skills

        (iv) Life skills—use to identify factors an employer looks for in a new employee

        (v) Psychology—personal relations and interactions, identify the name of a relative and with each letter identify a type of communication or interaction that would improve personal relations; use relatives as teachers to teach parts of the brain; use to list and determine the characteristics of a mature person; list and determine the characteristics of a leader, counselor, parent

5. Links and transitions

    a. It is important to show relevance between different topics or how a specific topic relates to an actual task

    b. Using links and transitions can show how each training session is relevant and useful

    c. An example is how psychology relates to teaching, the teaching specifics provides the detail for skill analysis, and again psychology comes into play once again when we take the information from skill analysis to the debrief

    d. The examiner should apply links and transitions at the beginning and end of each course, the beginning and end of each day, and between session breaks or the start or end of learning sections.

6. Creating a conducive learning environment

    a. Build a team atmosphere

    b. Break down personal barriers

    c. Develop a supportive system for learning

    d. Define goals clearly and specifically

    e. Present information in a positive manner

    f. Present only correct techniques

    g. Identify the improvements in a performance first

    h. Consider mistakes as an opportunity to recognize and target areas for improvement

    i. Reprogram yourself and the candidates to see the successful, or model performances instead of only the problems

9. Psychology and Goal Setting

A. PSYCHOLOGY

1. The coaching process can be broken down into the following activities:
   a. Goal setting
   b. Positive presentations
   c. Practice perfect
   d. Skill analysis
   e. Debriefing

2. Goal setting
   a. Goals can be accomplished more easily with a specific plan
   b. Long term goals are established by your desire for an end result
      (1) A long-term goal might be obtaining a license, joining a team, or earning a rating
      (2) Long-term goals are goals in which you will not see immediate results
      (3) Progress can be measured by accomplishing a series of short-term goals
   c. Short-term goals should be designed to make up the steps necessary to achieve the long-term goal
   d. SMART Acronym with regards to goal setting
      (1) Specific-Make each goal specific, whether it is short or long term
      (2) Measurable—If each goal is specific it will be easy to measure the results and gauge progress
      (3) Achievable—Each goal must be realistic for a successful outcome.
      (4) Relevant—The short-term goals must work in a logical progression towards achieving the long-term goal
      (5) Timely—A time frame must be established for each goal so there is a sense of urgency.

3. Positive presentations
   a. Teach the correct technique only
   b. Demonstrating incorrect actions as a precautionary measure of "what not to do" only highlights the incorrect way to perform a skill
   c. If a mistake is made, bring the student's attention back to the correct method and retrain using only the correct method
   d. Identify the answer to the error and focus on the correct procedures necessary for the task
   e. When using video or other visual aids select only correct examples for demonstration

4. Practice perfect
   a. Eliminate distractions
   b. Clear mind
   c. Practice with concentration
   d. Use correct information only, focus on KISSS
   e. Make the practice realistic, develop proper mental pictures
   f. Concentration
   g. Relax
   h. Eyes closed
   i. Practice perfectly makes perfect permanent

5. Skill analysis
   a. Skill analysis is neither positive or negative, it is simply a matter of gathering facts
   b. The examiner is responsible for determining which facts are the most relevant or have the largest priority and focus on those facts
   c. Recognize the positive and draw them to the attention of the student
   d. Focusing on the positive will help to repeat the good parts of a performance done correctly
   e. Avoid pointing out the negative, which is inherent in most people

6. Debriefing
   a. The debrief is where examiners facilitate the learning process by encouraging the student to recognize their achievements and what they did correctly as well as help them realize what is needed to move forward in their skill development
   b. The student must become more aware of their strengths and weaknesses and take responsibility for their training
   c. The debrief process contains the following steps:
      (1) restate the goals
      (2) things that worked
      (3) things that need improvement
      (4) how to improve
      (5) make new goals
   d. Restate the goals
      (1) The student will most likely focus on the negative parts of the jump
      (2) Restating the goals helps them open up their minds to the rest of the tasks whether it be the exit, break-off or canopy control tasks
   e. Things that worked
      (1) Ask the student what went well on the jump, what he did well
      (2) The student will naturally want to focus on the negative, by having him state what he did well on the jump, it starts the debrief on a positive note
      (3) This process will need to be repeated on several jumps before the student typically starts to enter the debrief on a positive note stating what they liked about their performance then noting what they need to improve on
   f. Things that need improvement
      (1) Ask the student what needs improvement
      (2) This lets you know if the student is aware of his errors
      (3) If the student overlooks a part of the skydive that should have been recalled, play through the video again and ask him how he felt about performing the skill to see if it jogs his memory
      (4) If it does not, this is the examiner's opportunity to restate the goals of the jump and provide guidance on how to improve
   g. How to improve
      (1) Ask this question to the student
      (2) The student should have a good idea of what he needs to work on
      (3) If the student cannot see the answer, this is the opportunity for the examiner to review the correct techniques and assist him to see what is needed

E-9 PSYCHOLOGY AND GOAL SETTING

      (4) Patience and good listening skills of the examiner will help the student take charge of his learning and become further committed to his goals

  h. Make new goals

      (1) Ask the student what he would like to do on the next jump

      (2) If the goals and expectations of each jump are clear, the student should be quite realistic about his performance

      (3) If the environment has been set that "mistakes are OK" the student should have a realistic assessment of what he needs to do on the next jump, even if it means repeating the same jump

      (4) The examiner should act as facilitator during the debrief

      (5) Asking questions and directing the student to the right information through self-realization will be of greater benefit to the student.

10. Motor Skills Evaluation Methods

A. SKILL ANALYSIS

1. Skill analysis is the act of observing human movement and action to evaluate a performance for correct and incorrect actions.
   a. On the ground while dirt diving to practice for an actual skydive
   b. In freefall as a coach or instructor evaluating student training jumps
   c. In freefall as an evaluator or Examiner evaluating course candidates
   d. In a wind tunnel as a tunnel coach evaluating skydivers working on freefall skills
2. Accurate skill analysis techniques are essential for every coach, instructor and Examiner:
   a. For coaches and instructors evaluating student training jumps
   b. For Examiners and course evaluators scoring candidate ground training sessions and evaluation jumps
3. An understanding of how Newton's laws of motion apply to skydiving will help evaluators understand and correctly assess skydiving skills.
   a. Newton's First Law: An object will only change speed or direction when an external force is applied.
      (1) An object at rest will remain at rest, unless an external force is applied.
      (2) An object in motion will remain in motion in a straight line unless an external force is applied.
   b. Newton's Second Law: The relationship between an object's mass m, its acceleration a, and the applied force F, is F = ma. (Force equals mass times acceleration.)
      (1) If mass is constant, applying greater force will result in greater acceleration.
      (2) The applied force only creates a change in acceleration, it does not necessarily maintain the acceleration.
      (3) The longer a force is applied, the greater the acceleration
   c. Newton's Third Law: For every action there is an equal and opposite reaction.
   d. The external forces applied to skydivers come from three sources:
      (1) pushing or pulling on a solid object such as an aircraft or skydiver
      (2) pushing against the air
      (3) gravity
   e. Skydiving does not take place in a perfect, frictionless environment. Air resistance (drag) is an ever-present "external force" which must be taken into account. So, for example, even if a skydiver assumes a max-track body position, there is a limit to how fast he can go.
4. The seven Biomechanical Principles of skill analysis:
   a. Principle One: Factors that increase stability
      (1) Lower the center of gravity.
      (2) A larger base of support (wider stance)
      (3) Center of gravity at the center of the base
      (4) The greater the mass, the more stability increases
   b. Principle Two: The production of maximum force requires the use of all the joints that can be used.
   c. Principle Three: The production of maximum acceleration requires the use of joints in order from the largest to the smallest.
   d. Principle Four: The greater the applied force, the greater the increase in velocity.
   e. Principle Five: Movement occurs in the opposite direction of the applied force.
   f. Principle Six: Angular motion is produced by the application of a force acting at some distance from an axis, that is, by torque.
   g. Principle Seven: Angular momentum is constant when an athlete or object is free in the air.

B. OBSERVATION TECHNIQUES

1. Pre-observation plan
   a. Identify the purpose of the skill; e.g. forward motion for docking, tracking for separation
   b. Break the skill into phases; e.g. exit plan; door position and set up, launch, fly away
   c. Identify the key elements of each phase that need to be evaluated; e.g. specific body mechanics necessary to achieve the desired motion for forward movement; arms 90°-90°-90°, chin up, knees at shoulder width, legs fully extended.
   d. The characteristics of each movement must be fully understood in order to provide an accurate evaluation.
   e. Forward motion in skydiving is a good example of movement with several different purposes and actions required based on the desired type of movement.
      (1) Forward motion to dock on a formation
      (2) Diving towards a formation after exiting the airplane
      (3) Flat tracking away from the center of the formation at break-off
   f. Even though each of the above is a type of forward movement, each method is different and requires different body positions to achieve.
   g. The evaluator must establish a plan based on the specific type of motion that is being evaluated.
2. Observation plan
   a. Key elements to observe: Choose a priority for the following three elements to determine the best observation strategy to use.
   b. Choose a scanning strategy
      (1) Ground sessions can be more effectively viewed from a slight distance to allow for scanning all parts of the body.
      (2) Close, hands-on ground training is often necessary, but can make it difficult to scan the entire body.
      (3) In the air the evaluator must often remain in place, which may in some cases also limit the ability to see the entire body.
      (4) Use of outside video during freefall training jumps can help capture the necessary angles for use as an effective debrief following the skydive.
      (5) Canopy control is best observed from the target area using a video camera to film the landing while in front of and to one side of the candidate for the best view of the landing flare.
   c. Position planning
      (1) Establish the most valuable position for the planned

E-10 MOTOR SKILLS EVALUATION METHODS

   observation for each stage of the ground training or skydive

   (2) Positioning will change based on the type of training jump and the altitude

   (3) Videographers must be briefed to understand the required positioning and break-off procedures

   d. Decide on the number of repetitions or the expected maneuvers to observe

   (1) May be difficult to predict for skydiving maneuvers

   (2) Exit altitude and the type of maneuver will largely determine the number of repetitions that can be realistically expected

   (3) Different views may be required during the various stages of the freefall for air skills evaluations, depending on the maneuver

3. When observing or How to Apply

   a. Use whole-part-whole strategy

   (1) Review the entire performance

   (2) Break the performance down to phases of all the specific parts such as exit, freefall, practiced maneuvers, break-off procedure, deployment and canopy descent

   (3) Make a note of any areas that need improvement

   b. Identify the problems or weaknesses

   (1) Take note of any trends that continue throughout the skydive.

   (2) In general, the skydive should improve overall from start to finish.

   (3) Skydivers will often self-correct errors through repetition.

   (4) If the errors are eliminated as the skydive advances there is no need to focus on the error during the debrief.

   (5) Try to choose two major points of improvement to review, but no more than five.

   c. Correct the specific skill that needs to be addressed using a positive manner

   (1) The whole-part-whole method of evaluation allows the evaluator to point out as many correct aspects of a performance as possible.

   (2) The exact cause of the deficiency can then be examined and corrected, rather than focusing on elements which were performed correctly already.

   d. Practice again, training with the correct actions to strengthen the deficient skill.

11. Video Analysis Workshop

A. VIDEO EVALUATION

1. Each Examiner candidate will be provided with video footage of actual evaluation jumps.
   a. DVD footage is compiled from actual candidate evaluation jumps
   b. Footage is available for all USPA ratings
2. Each Examiner candidate must conduct two satisfactory video debriefs for each discipline sought.
   a. Each evaluation jump will include at least ten noteworthy actions that would factor into the scoring of the evaluation.
   b. Each score must include at least eight correction points (80%) in order to score as a satisfactory observation.
   c. The debrief must use the proper corrective measures for each point of retraining noted during the video observation.
3. Each candidate will be evaluated on overall observation skills and use of correct observation and debrief methods, as well as the correct use of objective evaluation techniques.

B. RETESTING

1. In the event of an unsatisfactory score, each Examiner candidate will be provided with a different video to use for an additional evaluation.
2. In the case of two unsatisfactory video evaluations, the candidate will be required to repeat the ERC and retest.

E-12 SITUATIONAL LEADERSHIP

12. Situational Leadership

A. LEADERSHIP STYLE

1. There are many different leadership styles
   a. Charismatic leadership
   b. Participative leadership
   c. Situational leadership
   d. Transactional leadership
   e. Transformational leadership
   f. The quiet leader
   g. Servant leadership
2. Situational Leadership provides a useful leadership model for coaches, instructors and Examiners
3. Independent study of different leadership styles is encouraged

B. SITUATIONAL LEADERSHIP

1. Leaders must adapt their style based on the development or maturity of the follower (student).
2. Four different styles are used to match the development of the follower
3. The four styles suggest that the leader should put greater or less focus on the task in question and/or the relationship between the leader and the follower, depending on the development level of the follower
4. S1: Directing
   a. Follower: R1: Low competence, low commitment/ unable and unwilling or insecure
   b. Leader is high task focus/ low relationship focus
   c. Leader takes a high directive role, telling the follower what to do while providing a working structure to follow
   d. Leader must discover what motivates the follower and if there are any limitations in ability
5. S2: Coaching
   a. Follower: R2: Some competence, variable commitment/ unable but willing or motivated
   b. Leader: High task focus, high relationship focus
   c. Follower can do the task but may be overconfident in abilities
   d. Leader "telling" the follower what to do will be ineffective, and possibly demotivate the follower or lead to resistance
   e. Leader must find other ways to effectively work with the follower
   f. The leader should listen, advise and help the follower to gain the necessary skills by coaching
6. S3: Supporting
   a. Follower: R3: High competence, variable commitment/able but unwilling or insecure
   b. Leader: Low task focus, high relationship focus
   c. The follower can now perform the task at hand but may refuse, showing insufficient commitment
   d. The leader does not need to worry about showing the follower what to do, but should instead focus on inspiring them to cooperate
   e. The leader must listen to the follower, and praise the follower and make them feel good when they have shown the necessary commitment
7. S4: Delegating
   a. Follower: R4: High competence, high commitment/able and willing or motivated
   b. Leader: Low task focus, low relationship focus
   c. The leader can now perform the task and the follower can leave them to it
   d. The leader will still need to keep a relatively distant eye on the follower to ensure the task is performed correctly
   e. The follower has less need for support or frequent praise, although occasional recognition is always welcome
   f. S3 and S4 are follower led

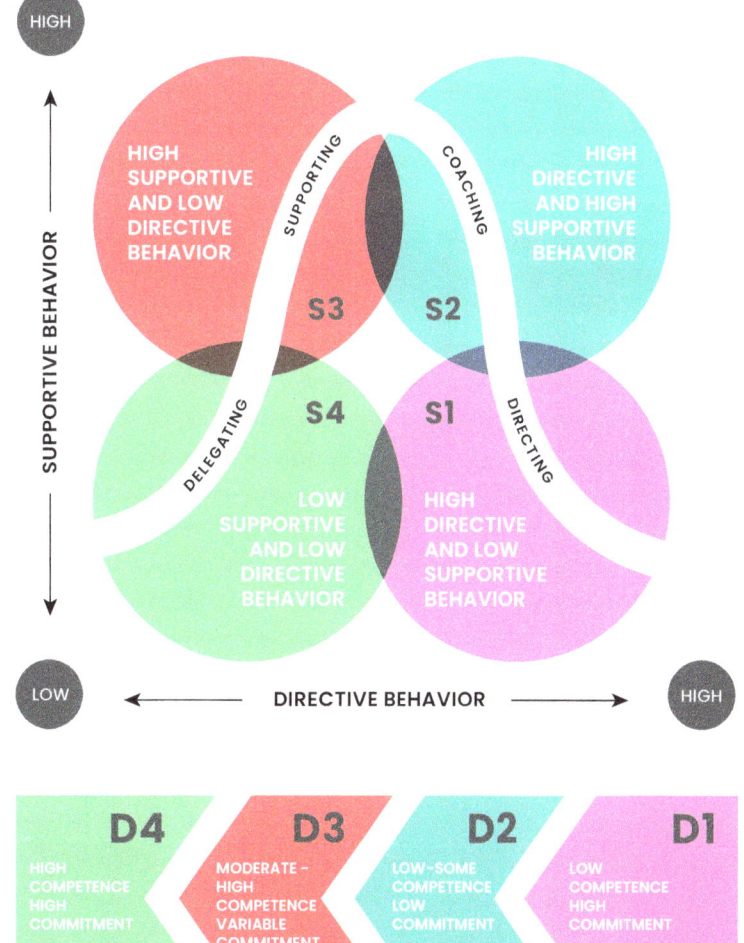

13. Administrative Duties of the Examiner and the S&TA

OVERVIEW

USPA can issue licenses and renew ratings only with complete and correctly submitted applications. USPA Headquarters returns rejected applications to the applicant.

Rejected applications can present a hardship for the USPA member, who may be traveling or otherwise inconvenienced in trying to get an S&TA to correct a mistake on an application.

Before signing any license or rating renewal application, verify that your own membership, ratings, and appointment as an S&TA are current.

USPA officials, including S&TAs, may not verify the requirements for renewing their own ratings.

LICENSES

A USPA Examiner or S&TA may administer the test and verify all qualifications for A, B, C and D licenses. Any USPA Instructor may administer the test and verify all qualifications for A, B, and C licenses. Refer to Section Three of the Skydiver's Information Manual for instructions regarding license verifications.

RATING RENEWALS

An Examiner or S&TA is required to verify renewal applications for instructional ratings and the PRO Rating. Refer to the renewal requirements for instructional ratings listed in the Introduction and Orientation section at the beginning of the training syllabus for each instructional rating, and duplicated in "IRM Essentials," available for free on the USPA website at www.uspa.org. For PRO rating and renewal, refer to the SIM Section 7. Rating renewal instructions also appear on the USPA membership and rating renewal form.

E-14 EXAMINER ADMINISTRATIVE RESPONSIBILITIES

14. Examiner Administrative Responsibilities

A. RESPONSIBILITIES OF THE EXAMINER

1. Before the course
   a. Coordinate course dates and hosting arrangements with the USPA Group Member drop zone
   b. Register the course with USPA Headquarters if desired. (USPA will list the course on its website calendar for instructional rating courses.)
   c. Courses registered 45 days in advance may also be listed in *Parachutist* magazine
   d. Registration may be accomplished by completing the online course registration form located in the rating course calendar on the USPA website.
   e. Each course must be planned to allow for an adequate number of days to run the course and complete the ground and air evaluations
   f. Ensure each candidate has completed any prerequisite course requirements
      (1) Proficiency card completed in required areas
      (2) Possesses a SIM and IRM dated within two years of the course
      (3) Acquired the necessary jump number and/or freefall time
      (4) Completed the written test prior to arrival at the course
   g. Arrange for adequate staffing for the course
      (1) Ensure the drop zone has arranged for the necessary aircraft and pilot support
      (2) Additional course evaluators will be needed for more than three course candidates
      (3) A ratio of one evaluator per three candidates will help the course run at the correct pace

2. Opening the course
   a. Introduction
      (1) Introduction of the Examiner and course staff
      (2) Establish the schedule for the course, providing a short explanation of the planned activities for each day of the course
      (3) Ensure that each candidate and course staff member has clear expectations of what is expected from the course candidates and staff
      (4) Introduction of the candidates to the course staff and each other
      (5) Determine why each course candidate is attending the course
      (6) Use of creative ice breakers as a fun and interesting way to handle course introductions and begin the team-building process
      (7) Collect course fees
   b. Creative Ice Breakers
      (1) Introduce Yourself
      (2) Introduce Your Neighbor (see facilitation section)
      (3) My Favorite (see facilitation section)
      (4) False Colors (see facilitation section)
   c. Confirm course requirements have been met by each candidate
      (1) Current regular member of USPA
      (2) Appropriate USPA license
      (3) Proficiency card requirements for any items required before the course have been completed
      (4) Verify the candidate has obtained the jump numbers or freefall time required
      (5) Candidate must be a USPA Coach or expired USPA rating holder for any USPA Instructor rating
      (6) FAA 3rd class medical or equivalent medical exam is required for the USPA Tandem Instructor rating
      (7) Section 1 of each rating course syllabus in the Instructional Rating Manual includes the course requirements for candidates, Examiners and the evaluation staff used for each course.
      (8) Be present and attentive for the entire course from start to finish.

3. During the course
   a. The supervising examiner must be present and attentive for the entirety of the specific course.
   b. Use the same principals of instruction reviewed with the candidates from the Coach Course syllabus while running the course
      (1) Keeps the course on track
      (2) Leads by example
   c. In addition to leading the course, each Examiner is expected to mentor the evaluators in the course
      (1) New course evaluators will need direct supervision and close guidance from the Examiner in order to learn the correct evaluation process
      (2) Evaluators who are seeking the Examiner rating should be given the opportunity to complete the required tasks listed on the Examiner proficiency card
      (3) The Examiner must ensure that the course evaluators apply the same standards to each course candidate

4. After the course
   a. Complete the after-action report
   b. Collect each evaluator information form
   c. Make copies of all successful candidate proficiency cards
   d. Complete any required letters of recommendation for any course evaluator who qualifies as a new Examiner
   e. For tandem instructor rating candidates, collect a copy of the FAA third class medical or equivalent
   f. Collect candidate course fees and USPA rating fees (if applicable)
   g. Send a copy of the above listed materials to USPA Headquarters, including any rating fees
   h. Only USPA Examiners may submit candidate rating proficiency cards and required course documentation for the candidates in their rating courses to USPA Headquarters for processing.

B. COURSE RECORDS

1. Each candidate should retain his original proficiency card (or a copy of it) for personal records
2. Items to be retained by the Examiner for at least two years
   a. After action report
   b. Candidate written tests
   c. Air skills evaluation forms
   d. Ground skills evaluation forms
   e. Copy of any letters of recommendations
   f. Copy of Proficiency cards

15. Conflict Resolution

A. TYPES OF CONFLICT RESOLUTION

1. Accommodate (I lose, you win)
2. Avoid (I lose, you lose)
3. Compromise (we both win, we both lose)
4. Compete (I win, you lose)
5. Collaborate (I win, you win)

B. RESOLUTION ISSUES BETWEEN CANDIDATES AND EVALUATORS

1. Why is it worth it to try to reach problematic candidates?
    a. Some candidates have been mislabeled and are waiting for someone to have faith in them
    b. Most of these candidates are reachable by a specific examiner who may be able to better relate with the candidate
2. Out of control candidates
    a. have experienced failure
    b. have been identified by negative labels
    c. have little hope for success
    d. associate with similar types who reinforce each other
    e. have low self concepts
3. Things to remember
    a. You and your candidate are on the same team
    b. Control your Anger
    c. Alter conditions to reach your highest goals
    d. Communication is better than force
4. Avoid
    a. Thinking in terms of winning and losing
    b. accepting excuses
    c. traps, diffuse power struggles
    d. excessive passive or aggressive behavior
    e. interpreting candidate behavior personally
5. Mediating Power Struggles and Disputes
    a. In some cases an issue between a course evaluator and a candidate will escalate to the point where outside mediation is necessary.
    b. Examiners and course evaluators should be trained to resolve these conflicts.
    c. The mediator's job is to develop a workable solution that best resolves the issues for both parties.
    d. The following series of steps can be used as a guideline for mediating disputes:
        1. The mediator should locate a quiet and private location to use for the mediation process.
        2. Once the group is isolated, the mediator should explain his role to the complainants and allow each person to tell his side of the story
        3. Each complainant should be asked to list the positive attributes of the other party, or what others have said they like about the other party
        4. Once the problem has been stated by both sides, the examiner should ask the individuals to restate the other person's issue to make sure each has understood what was stated by the other individual and that clear communication has been achieved
        5. Each party is then asked to state what he would like to see the other party to do differently to resolve the issue
        6. The mediator will then ask each complainant if he is willing to make those concessions in order to resolve the issue
        7. Once the resolutions have been agreed upon, each complainant re-states what he is willing to do and listens to the other complainant restate what he is willing to do to resolve the issue
        8. Once the agreement has been made, both parties shake hands and the agreement is recorded in writing along with a plan for follow up, to ensure the conditions continue to be met

C. CONFLICT RESOLUTION EXERCISES

1. Course candidates will use contrived scenarios to practice resolving arguments.
2. The candidates will split into groups of three for each exercise.
3. Two candidates will role play, with a third acting as a mediator.
4. The two candidates will represent opposing views of the contrived scenario.
5. The mediator works with the two candidates to resolve the issue as favorably as possible for both sides.
6. The following three examples are provided as topics to use for the evaluations, however course candidates may also fabricate different scenarios.

SCENARIO ONE

Two course candidates are having an argument about the value of the Integrated Student Program and why to implement it. Both are from the same drop zone, which does not currently use the ISP.

Candidate A viewpoint: Too complex, costly to the candidate, staff overload

Candidate B viewpoint: Modern program, complete training, safer, good for student progress, standardized.

SCENARIO TWO

An evaluator on your staff is a poor role model and exercising poor canopy control during his landings; he has performed downwind and crosswind approaches and beer line infractions.

The drop zone owner has approached the Examiner about the evaluator.

The Examiner has warned the evaluator once already, but he continues to land the same way.

The course is short staffed as it is and losing an evaluator will make it difficult to complete the course.

The conflict is between the DZO and the evaluator. The Examiner must mediate the argument.

SCENARIO THREE

During a freefall evaluation phase of your course you are approached by a candidate who is complaining about his score received from one of the evaluators. The evaluator has scored them with an automatic unsat for busting the hard deck. The candidate is challenging, saying he deployed the evaluator at the correct altitude. After consulting with your evaluator he stays firm on his score of automatic unsat based on what he observed. This was the candidate's last chance to receive a satisfactory score to pass the course and he will fail the course. There was no video of the evaluation. The evaluator claims the candidate was "just below" the hard deck.

One candidate plays the Examiner, one plays the candidate, and a third mediates the argument.

APPENDIX A: LESSON PLANNING

United States Parachute Association®
FLIGHT PLANNER

Name: _____

Date: _____

Category: _____ Jump: _____

EMERGENCY REVIEW (All students)

Topics to review: _____

Emergency training complete: ☐ **Initials:** _____ (Coach/Instructor)

EQUIPMENT (Category C students and up)

Main canopy: _____ Exit weight: _____ Wing loading (exit weight/sq. ft.): _____

Reserve: _____ Container system: _____

☐ shoes
☐ helmet
☐ altimeter
☐ goggles
☐ gloves

☐ reserve pin(s) and loop(s)
☐ reserve ripcord movement
☐ main pin and loop
☐ main ripcord movement (RC)
☐ bridle routing (throw-out)

☐ RSL attachment and routing
☐ riser covers
☐ chest strap and fastener
☐ cutaway handle
☐ reserve ripcord handle

SAMPLE
VISIT USPA.ORG/DOWNLOADS FOR THE MOST CURRENT VERSION

Gear pre-flighted and equipment training complete: ☐ **Initials:** _____ (Coach/Instructor/Rigger)

AIRCRAFT AND SPOTTING (Category F students and up)

Aircraft: _____ Jump run speed: _____

Winds aloft forecast		
Altitude	Direction	Speed (in knots)
3,000		
6,000		
9,000		
12,000		

Planned jump run heading: _____
Ground speed on jump run: _____
Estimated freefall drift: Direction: _____ Distance: _____
Spot (ex. 0.5 mile @ 120°): _____
Runway in use: _____
Time between groups: _____

Average: _____ _____

Aircraft & spotting training complete: ☐ **Initials:** _____ (Coach/Instructor/Pilot)

FREEFALL OBJECTIVES (Category D students and up)

Performance goals: _____

Planned exit altitude: _____ Planned pull altitude: _____ Estimated freefall time: _____

Freefall training complete: ☐ **Initials:** _____ (Coach/Instructor)

CANOPY OBJECTIVES

Performance goals: _____

Ground checkpoint (All categories)	Altitude
1.	Opening
2.	1,000
3.	600
4.	300

Spot (Category F students and up)		
Winds	Direction	Speed
Surface		
3,000		
Average:		

Canopy training complete: ☐   **Initials:** _____ (Instructor)

CANOPY FLIGHT PLAN (All categories)

Show the direction of the surface winds on the DZ photograph. Draw the planned wind line, spot, and landing pattern, including ground checkpoints and altitudes. Identify all significant landing hazards.

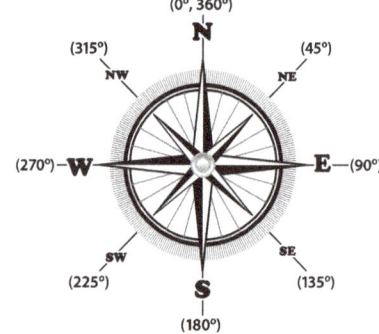

Runway length:

APPENDIX B: EXAMS

1. Administration (Course Examiners Only)

A. INSTRUCTIONS

1. Each candidate will answer only the questions pertaining to his or her rating.
   a. Coach—40 questions
   b. All USPA Instructor candidates—25 general questions, plus 15 method-specific questions (40 total)
   c. IAD and Static-Line Instructor candidates—
      (1) 11 method-specific questions in common
      (2) four questions specific to their deployment devices
   d. Examiner candidates —40 questions, use a blank sheet to write the answers.
2. Candidates should use one of the perforated answer sheets provided in this manual.
   a. Enough sheets are provided for testing and retesting to last the average candidate for several courses.
   b. If a candidate runs short, candidates with extras should share.
3. Each candidate writes his or her name on the answer sheet.

B. ANSWERING THE QUESTIONS

1. Instruct the candidates to choose the BEST answer for each question.
2. Questions are taken from the SIM and the IRM, and candidates may use refer to these references during the test (open book).
3. The Course Examiner may provide additional references for USPA Tandem Instructor candidates.

2. USPA Coach

USPA COACH EXAM | X-B

1. According to the ISP, by what altitude should a first-jump student decide on a safe landing area?
   a. 2,000 feet
   b. 1,000 feet
   c. jump altitude
   d. A student can't make this decision.

2. According to the ISP, what are the key altitudes of the landing pattern and what do they require the student to do?
   a. 1,000 feet, steer with the wind; 600 feet, fly a path perpendicular to the wind; 300 feet steer into the wind
   b. 2,500 feet, decision altitude; 500 feet into the wind and no more turns
   c. 3,000 feet, check position; 2,000 feet, determine landing pattern; 1,000 feet, determine wind speed
   d. 2,500 feet, decide to cut away; 2,000 feet, cut away; 1,000 feet, pull reserve without cutting away

3. How should a student steer into an alternate clear area?
   a. Face the drop zone, no matter what, until it's time to turn into the wind for landing.
   b. Face downwind until over the middle of the clear area, then face into the wind until landing.
   c. Steer a straight course and listen for radio commands before making any further corrections.
   d. Visually transfer the original planned pattern over the new field and fly it as trained.

4. What is the main purpose of the landing flare?
   a. to train students for landing smaller canopies
   b. to convert the forward speed of the parachute momentarily into lift
   c. to stop the canopy four feet above the ground
   d. to increase the effect of the Venturi principle

5. What are the five planned points of contact when performing a parachute landing fall?
   a. ground, leg straps (butt), container, helmet, hands
   b. feet, calves, thighs, hip (side of butt), across the back to the opposite shoulder
   c. eyes on the horizon, feet and knees together, chin tucked, cover the face, wait for help
   d. feet, knees, hands, shoulder, helmet

6. What happens when a student stalls a canopy while attempting to flare and then raises the brakes to full flight?
   a. The canopy returns to flying speed, allowing a smooth, diving landing.
   b. The radio operator will instruct the student to "Stop!"
   c. The canopy will remain in the stall and may begin to turn.
   d. The canopy will dive abruptly.

7. What is the student's best defense when landing in a stall?
   a. a PLF
   b. to steer quickly into the wind
   c. Students jump in winds that can't stall a canopy.
   d. Students don't know they will have a hard landing so are more relaxed and unlikely to get hurt.

8. What should a student do when landing in a tree?
   a. Aim for a tall, bushy tree and stall the parachute to drop straight down.
   b. Prepare for a PLF on the ground, flare halfway, protect the face and under the arms, find a secure perch, and wait for qualified help.
   c. Land with legs apart to assist with straddling the first available branch.
   d. Become as thin as possible to miss the tree.

9. What is the best ARM position for stable fall with the belly into the relative wind?
   a. the "crazy Y" position
   b. the "mantis" position
   c. upper arms positioned 90 degrees or less from the torso and relaxed; elbows bent 90-120 degrees, up, and relaxed
   d. hands flat, arms fully extended and relaxed

10. According to the ISP, what is one good way for a jumper to remain relaxed in freefall?
    a. self-actualization
    b. free association
    c. slow, rhythmic counting
    d. conscious breathing

11. At what three points should the student expect the USPA Instructor to check the student's equipment?
    a. before putting it on, before boarding the aircraft, before exit
    b. chest strap, leg straps, reserve ripcord (and pin)
    c. upon arrival at the DZ, when issued the rig, after the jump
    d. check-out area, dressing area, loading area

12. According to the ISP, what are the three stages of a parachute opening?
    a. activation, deployment, inflation
    b. deployment, inflation, rebound
    c. arch, look, reach, pull
    d. invitation, deployment, malfunction

13. Part of the DEPLOYED parachute is caught on the jumper or the jumper's equipment (horseshoe). Is that considered a total or a partial malfunction?
    a. total
    b. partial
    c. neither
    d. both

14. Describe the MOST IMPORTANT aspect(s) of a main canopy to determine if it can be landed safely.
    a. correct color, indicating the right size for that student
    b. cannot be stalled
    c. faced into the wind
    d. regular in shape; controllable for heading and flaring

15. What should a jumper do prior to reaching for any emergency operation handle?
    a. Look at it.
    b. Prepare for a PLF.
    c. Look at the other handle.
    d. Reverse arch.

X-B | USPA COACH EXAM

16. How should a jumper locate a hard-to-find main parachute deployment handle?
    a. Two tries, feeling the associated part of the harness or container.
    b. Begin the "arch-reach-pull" sequence again.
    c. Grab the reserve ripcord first, then look again for the main deployment handle.
    d. Try harder.

17. By what altitude should a student jumper decide and act when confronted with a problem main canopy?
    a. 1,800 feet
    b. 2,000 feet
    c. 2,500 feet
    d. 3,000 feet

18. For first-jump students, what is the ISP's recommended response to two canopies out that form a side-by-side?
    a. Release the outside steering line on each canopy and steer using just those two lines.
    b. Separate the canopies into a downplane, disconnect the RSL, and cut away the main canopy.
    c. Release the brakes on only the dominant (largest canopy most nearly overhead), steer it gently with the toggles, PLF; or if both canopies are clear, cut away.
    d. With canopies this size, the student can ignore the problem.

19. In the ISP, what is the recommended minimum deployment altitude for a student in Categories G and H?
    a. 3,500 feet for both categories
    b. 3,000 feet for both categories
    c. 3,500 feet for Category G; 3,000 feet for Category H
    d. 4,000 feet for Category G; 3,500 feet for Category H

20. After altitude awareness, which of the following is the student's MOST important priority when tracking?
    a. heading
    b. speed
    c. getting the arms into the delta position as soon as possible after the turn
    d. looking at the coach

21. If a student in Category G or H fails to break off at the assigned altitude and still fails to break off when the coach signals the break-off, what action should the coach take?
    a. Gain sufficient separation for safety and pull by 3,500 feet.
    b. Signal for the student to deploy.
    c. Deploy the student's parachute.
    d. Wait five additional seconds before taking action.

22. When teaching a student group exits:
    a. Advise the student against exiting too close to another jumper.
    b. Make sure that any grips taken can withstand an unstable launch, for example, on a chest strap or main lift web.
    c. Make sure the student understands and practices an exact exit position that enables the group to set up in the door efficiently.
    d. Tell the student to always allow ten seconds after the last group before beginning to climb into position.

23. To reduce tension on the formation after taking grips, a jumper should:
    a. extend both legs
    b. get "small" to increase fall rate
    c. extend both arms to allow other jumpers room to break in
    d. all of the above

24. To adjust fall rate on approach, a jumper should:
    a. get "small" to go faster and "hug the beach ball" to go slower
    b. push the hips forward to fall faster and cup the sternum to fall slower
    c. use the jumpsuit wings to increase and decrease drag
    d. grab the backpack to go faster and the chest strap to go slower

25. When observing a student's exit, the center of focus should be on the:
    a. head, then legs and arms
    b. arms and hands, then legs and feet
    c. hips (torso), then legs and arms
    d. legs, then head and butt

26. At breakoff, the USPA Coach should:
    a. Let the student initiate the breakoff at the planned altitude but remain in place to observe tracking.
    b. If the student fails to break off at the planned altitude, wave off, but remain in place to observe tracking.
    c. If the student fails to turn and track after the wave-off, turn and track for sufficient separation and deploy by 3,500 feet.
    d. all of the above

27. The minimum breakoff recommended for groups of five or fewer jumpers is:
    a. 3,500 feet
    b. 4,000 feet
    c. 1,500 feet above the highest planned deployment altitude, not counting camera flyers
    d. 2,000 feet above the planned deployment altitude

28. Breakoff should be planned higher—
    a. for larger groups
    b. for slow opening or high-speed canopies
    c. for dive plans with faster fall rates
    d. all of the above

29. The best teaching method to use when training skydivers is:
    a. preparation, presentation, application, evaluation
    b. lecture, analogy, theory, example
    c. objective, goal setting, recognition, meaningful
    d. stretching, exercise, cool down, review

30. Which of the following techniques would you find used in the best debrief?
    a. quick but accurate description of mistakes, warning in logbook
    b. review of objectives, positive reinforcement during review, compare performance to objectives, limit improvement points, retrain and practice improvement points, positive but factual record in logbook
    c. comfort student that everyone makes mistakes, avoid talking about the bad parts of the performance, say only good things in logbook, tell other instructors, "Look out for this one!"
    d. student debriefs while instructor remains silent, instructor logs jump using code to next instructor

31. "Primacy-recency" refers to:
    a. Students who arrive first should be the most recent ones to skydive.
    b. You have to start at the beginning to expect the student to remember anything.
    c. The most recent thing the student learned is the most likely one he'll forget.
    d. Students automatically tend to remember the first and last points made in the lesson.

32. The correct number of learning bits in a training session is:
    a. seven, plus or minus two
    b. one every eight minutes
    c. one every 20 minutes
    d. one every 50 minutes

33. The "90-20-8" rule refers to:
    a. no more than 90 students in a class, 20 for each instructor, eight per load
    b. limit training sessions to 90 minutes, change the pace or location of the course every 20 minutes, involve the student every eight minutes
    c. 90 jumps maximum, 20 average, and eight minimum to complete the ISP
    d. a total of 128 repetitions to develop muscle memory

34. Which of the following is the LEAST effective method of training motor skills?
    a. lecture
    b. guided practice
    c. visualization
    d. repetition

35. Who must supervise all student training conducted by a USPA Coach?
    a. an appropriately rated USPA Instructor
    b. a USPA Coach
    c. USPA Group Member drop zone owner.
    d. any USPA or FAA official

36. How often must a USPA Coach renew his or her rating?
    a. annually with membership renewal, including the first partial year
    b. No renewal is required.
    c. with the USPA PRO Rating
    d. every two years

37. Which of the following would be considered sufficient supervision of a USPA Coach during the solo first-jump course?
    a. The appropriately rated USPA Instructor has seen the USPA Coach teach the course more than a dozen times, remains at home by the phone, and will arrive later that afternoon after the general portion is complete.
    b. The USPA Coach teaches the general portion at his or her home and then meets the appropriately rated USPA Instructor at the drop zone for the method-specific portion of the course.
    c. The appropriately rated USPA Instructor is readily available and personally verifies that the students are taught in a satisfactory manner.
    d. The drop zone owner (no ratings) sits in on the entire class.

38. The USPA Basic Safety Requirements regarding wind limits for students apply to:
    a. all students, including tandem students
    b. only students jumping round reserves
    c. only students using solo equipment
    d. only students in Categories A-E

39. If exiting at under a 13,000-foot ceiling MSL over an airport with a field elevation of 1,000 feet MSL, the planned exit can legally be no higher than:
    a. 9,000 feet AGL
    b. 11,000 feet AGL
    c. 13,000 feet MSL
    d. 12,000 feet AGL

40. Regarding jumps with students after sunset:
    a. Each student must be equipped with a light visible for at least three miles from exit to opening.
    b. Each student must be equipped with a strobe light visible for at least five miles from opening to landing.
    c. Each student must be equipped with a strobe light visible for at least three miles from exit to landing.
    d. None of the above. According to the USPA Basic Safety Requirements, all student jumps must be completed by sunset.

X-B USPA GENERAL INSTRUCTOR EXAM

3. General USPA Instructor

1. Each student should expect a complete equipment check by the instructor:
   a. before gearing up on the ground
   b. before boarding the aircraft
   c. before exiting the aircraft
   d. all of the above

2. Whose job is it to protect the student's parachute operation handles during boarding of the aircraft and the ride to altitude?
   a. Student are expected to remember everything they were taught in the first-jump course.
   b. Students are taught to protect their handles, but instructors must monitor them closely on the first few jumps.
   c. Experienced jumpers know to watch out for students' handles when boarding and moving about the aircraft.
   d. Handle protection isn't necessary with modern student skydiving equipment.

3. Students should be taught to fly a straight in approach without S-turns to prevent:
   a. stalling the canopy
   b. collisions with other canopies
   c. 180-degree hook turns
   d. off-field landings

4. In the Category A first jump course, who may teach the student emergency procedures?
   a. a USPA Coach
   b. any USPA Instructor
   c. both A and B
   d. neither A nor B

5. The Category A student should understand the canopy descent well enough to:
   a. make a dead-center accuracy landing
   b. handle a landing at the airport only
   c. jump a canopy with a 1.3:1 wing loading
   d. solve contrived problems from opening to landing

6. The emergency procedure review in Category B serves to:
   a. review the first-jump-course emergency procedures
   b. review for all returning solo first-jump students who did not get the chance to jump on the same day as their training
   c. review for students and experienced jumpers making currency jumps
   d. all of the above

7. How a parachute opens is best taught by:
   a. watching parachutes from the ground
   b. making drawings on a board
   c. classroom lecture
   d. using an open parachute on the ground

8. One of the student's freefall objectives for Category C is:
   a. two 90-degree turns
   b. two 360-degree turns
   c. barrel rolls
   d. hover control

9. Regarding canopy training, Category C ISP students are introduced to:
   a. front-riser turns
   b. rear-riser turns
   c. low-turn recovery techniques
   d. wing loading and its effects on canopy flight

10. A Category D AFF student who wishes to make solo freefall jumps in the IAD or static-line freefall progression must first:
    a. continue in AFF through Category E.
    b. make a static-line jump supervised by a USPA AFF Instructor
    c. demonstrate 360-degree turns
    d. under the supervision of an appropriately rated instructor, perform a stable IAD or static-line jump with a practice deployment

11. If a student attempts to initiate a turn, but the response is sluggish or the turn goes the other way, the student should:
    a. put more effort into the turn
    b. extend the arm opposite the intended direction of the turn
    c. return to neutral arch, relax, extend legs, and attempt the turn again, provided altitude allows
    d. retrain for center-point turns before the next jump

12. In the event of an uncontrolled spin, the student should be taught to:
    a. Track out of the spin.
    b. Apply aggressive opposite turn input.
    c. Arch as hard as possible.
    d. Know the altitude, arch, check leg position, and relax.

13. Emergency procedure review with Category D students should include:
    a. review in a training harness
    b. review of procedures for landing on a building
    c. both A and B
    d. neither A nor B

14. Once a student has demonstrated stability recovery, a USPA Instructor may clear the student to:
    a. freefall self-supervision
    b. jump in groups with any skydiver
    c. a USPA A License
    d. none of the above

15. By Category E of the ISP, each student should be able to perform the following without assistance:
    a. a complete main parachute pack job
    b. a complete preflight inspection of the gear
    c. a complete reserve repack
    d. three-ring maintenance

16. The initial focus for the student's first tracking dive should be:
    a. distance
    b. flat tracking
    c. diving steep to gain speed
    d. heading

17. From which altitudes are the clear-and-pull jumps in Category F

176 | Exams

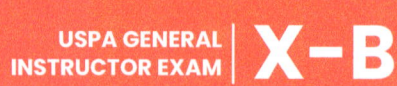

USPA GENERAL INSTRUCTOR EXAM — X-B

performed?
a. 2,500 and 2,000 feet
b. 4,500 and 3,500 feet
c. 5,500 and 3,500 feet
d. 6,500 and 4,500 feet

18. In Category G of the ISP, the student should be practicing which of the following maneuvers under canopy?
a. using front risers
b. rear riser stalls
c. basic CRW docks
d. performance turns above 2,500 feet

19. In Category H of the ISP, the student should be practicing which of the following maneuvers under canopy?
a. using front risers
b. rear riser stalls
c. basic CRW docks
d. performance turns above 2,500 feet

20. In Category G of the ISP, the student should receive detailed instruction on what subject area?
a. flying a canopy pattern
b. CRW docks
c. front riser performance landings
d. canopy collisions

21. Where should a USPA Instructor get instructions on how to conduct the USPA A license Exam and check dive?
a. the Skydiver's Information Manual section, "License Exam Instructions"
b. drop zone owner
c. the A-License Proficiency Card
d. Parachutist articles

22. What level of supervision is required over candidates working in the first-jump course to meet their pre-course requirements for the USPA Coach Rating Course?
a. direct supervision, with the supervising USPA Instructor present and attentive
b. direct supervision, with a USPA Coach present and attentive
c. supervision with a USPA Instructor available
d. supervision with a USPA Coach available

23. The USPA Basic Safety Requirements must be followed:
a. according to the needs of the school owner
b. by all USPA instructional rating holders, regardless of location
c. only at USPA Group Member drop zones
d. only if students are trained according to the ISP

24. The upper winds from 12,000 feet to 3,000 feet are averaging 180 degrees at 20 knots. The expected freefall drift from 13,000 feet is approximately:
a. one third of a mile to the south
b. one third of a mile to the north
c. two thirds of a mile to the south
d. two-thirds of a mile to the north

25. A jumper with 35 jumps and a USPA A license has come to the drop zone. He hasn't jumped in 75 days. He should:
a. make at least one jump under the direct supervision of a USPA instructional rating holder
b. complete an entire first jump course and Category A jump
c. make a jump in Category B
d. make an unsupervised solo jump after a review and pre-briefing from a USPA Instructor

PROCEED TO THE APPLICABLE METHOD-SPECIFIC SECTION OF THE EXAM FOR QUESTIONS 26–40.

X-B USPA AFF INSTRUCTOR EXAM

4. USPA AFF Instructor
Complete questions 1-25 of the general instructor exam.

26. Regardless of aircraft used, the design of the exit should PRIMARILY allow for:
    a. a good video shot
    b. keeping the instructors from fighting the prop blast
    c. allowing the student to make the best presentation to the relative wind
    d. all of the above

27. The recommended opening altitude for AFF students in Category A is:
    a. 5,500 feet
    b. 4,500 feet
    c. 3,500 feet
    d. 3,000 feet

28. During an AFF exit using two instructors from a Cessna (right-hand door and wing strut), the reserve-side instructor is primarily responsible for what actions?
    a. checking the front of the student's equipment
    b. making sure the student has enough room on the step
    c. assisting the student with the climb-out
    d. none of the above

29. AFF student exits should:
    a. allow the instructors to make a clean launch
    b. allow the student to exit hips into the wind
    c. allow for the instructors to follow the students count
    d. all of the above

30. What is the minimum number of jumps recommended for AFF students to complete Category C of the ISP?
    a. one
    b. two
    c. three
    d. No specific number is recommended.

31. During a side-door exit with an AFF student leaving from inside, the "point of no return" is:
    a. when the student lets go of the airplane with one hand
    b. When the student finishes the exit count
    c. when the student gets into the exit position
    d. when the student's hips break the plane of the door

32. Regarding AFF student jumps, the reserve-side instructor should deploy the student's main parachute, if necessary, by what altitude?
    a. 2,000 feet
    b. 5,000 feet
    c. 3,500 feet
    d. 4,000 feet

33. If the exit tumbles, the instructors should:
    a. deploy the student as soon as more than two revolutions occur
    b. roll with the tumble and get the student facing into the relative wind
    c. both let go and quickly re-grip as the student faces the relative wind
    d. each let go with one hand and face the relative wind

34. If the student does not start the practice deployments, the main-side instructor should:
    a. continue the skydive and pull for the student at pull altitude
    b. shake the student and yell "practice pulls!"
    c. guide the student's hand to the handle while the reserve-side instructor signals the student to start them
    d. tap on the student's helmet

35. What is considered the lowest safe altitude for an initial release of the student in freefall?
    a. 7,000 feet
    b. 8,000 feet
    c. 9,000 feet
    d. 6,000 feet

36. A Category D student overshoots the turn and continues spinning. The instructor should:
    a. allow the spin to continue until pull altitude
    b. re-dock immediately if the spin accelerates and give corrective hand signals
    c. hold up a "legs out" signal every time the student's head comes around in the turn
    d. grab a hand or foot as it passes by to stop the spin

37. If a Category D student is still attempting turns at the wave-off altitude, the instructor should:
    a. signal for wave off or deployment, depending on altitude
    b. give the student the "no more turns" signal
    c. deploy for the student immediately
    d. tap the student's deployment device

38. Re-docking with a student after release requires:
    a. grips be taken with the student's hands
    b. use of hand signals and an immediate re-release, regardless of the situation
    c. a good reason
    d. all of the above

39. According to the BSRs, a USPA Instructor who holds only the AFF rating may conduct jumps in which of the following training disciplines?
    a. static-line
    b. harness hold
    c. instructor-assisted deployment
    d. all of the above

40. To keep his or her rating current, a USPA AFF Instructor must annually:
    a. make 15 jumps acting as an AFF Instructor
    b. teach or assist with one first-jump course or first-jump course review
    c. attend a USPA Instructor seminar
    d. all of the above

5. USPA SLI/IAD Instructor
Complete questions 1-25 of the general instructor exam

USPA SLI/IAD INSTRUCTOR EXAM | X-B

26. In case the student's main container opens during climb-out, the instructor should brief the pilot as follows:
    a. be prepared to skid the aircraft to get the horizontal stabilizer (tail) out of the way of the deploying parachute
    b. to always carry a knife aboard the aircraft
    c. be particularly aware and prepared for the possibility of a premature deployment during climb-out
    d. all of the above

27. According to the BSRs, how many successive stable exits with successful practice deployments must an IAD or static-line student make prior to freefall?
    a. No minimum number specified in the BSRs, but three are recommended.
    b. three
    c. as many as necessary to complete the practice deployment before the parachute inflates
    d. two

28. What is the number of jumps recommended for IAD and static-line students to complete Category C of the ISP?
    a. one
    b. two
    c. three
    d. There are no recommended number of jumps in any category.

29. A Category D student in the AFF program wants to jump today, but the ceiling is at 6,000 feet AGL. What do the BSRs state is necessary for that student to jump under the supervision of an IAD or Static-Line Instructor?
    a. demonstrate a stable practice deployment on an IAD or static-line jump before performing freefall jumps under the supervision of a USPA IAD, Static-Line, or Tandem Instructor
    b. be briefed on the IAD and Static-Line harness-hold exit method prior to jumping with a USPA IAD or Static-Line Instructor
    c. continue in Category D, since the student has already made a freefall
    d. The student must wait for another day when the weather is better.

30. If an IAD or static-line student while climbing out is unable to get into position in time for a good spot, the instructor should:
    a. Push the student off the step.
    b. Tell the student to go before fully in position.
    c. Open the student's parachute to clear the step.
    d. Retrieve the student, if possible, and ask the pilot to go around.

31. Assisting with a freefall student's deployment:
    a. may be done by only a USPA AFF Instructor
    b. may be done by any USPA Instructor once the student has been cleared to self-supervise in freefall
    c. is allowed through Category D
    d. is the responsibility of the USPA Instructor in that student's discipline

32. IAD and static-line students may freefall with:
    a. BOC throw-out
    b. pull-out
    c. leg mounted throw-out
    d. none of the above

33. What is the minimum recommended deployment altitude for Category A and B IAD and static-line students?
    a. 2,000 feet
    b. 2,500 feet
    c. 3,000 feet
    d. 3,500 feet

34. Students with insufficient strength to hang from the strut of a Cessna before their exit:
    a. should not be allowed to jump
    b. will always back loop during their exit
    c. should make a diving exit towards the tail
    d. should be trained for a step exit

35. The instructor should anticipate IAD and static-line students to take as long as to climb out:
    a. 15 seconds
    b. 30 seconds
    c. 60 seconds
    d. 90 seconds

36. On ISP Category D jumps with an IAD or static-line trained student, a USPA IAD or Static-line Instructor:
    a. should always stay in the plane and observe the freefall from the door
    b. may exit with harness grips on the student
    c. may dock with the student and deploy for them if necessary
    d. is encouraged to exit the airplane and observe the freefall to critique the student later

IAD CANDIDATES ONLY (SKIP TO NEXT PAGE FOR STATIC-LINE QUESTIONS)

Note: Answer these questions only if you are applying for the USPA IAD Instructor rating.

37. Which of the following is true?
    a. Hand deployment provides the most reliable means of opening a parachute.
    b. A safety device to secure the bridle during IAD operations could result in a pilot-chute-in-tow malfunction.
    c. The instructor should throw the pilot chute up and out as the student exits.
    d. The instructor should never allow the pilot chute to get outside the aircraft cabin while the student is climbing into position on the strut.

38. During IAD operations, the instructor must make sure the pilot chute—
    a. is never out of the student's control
    b. is loose in its pouch to ensure easy extraction
    c. is not stuck in the pouch when the student exits
    d. is thrown under the horizontal stabilizer (tail) of the aircraft as the student releases from the aircraft

39. Before climbing out, the IAD student must verify—
    a. that the pilot has lowered the wing flaps
    b. that the tailwheel of the aircraft has been taped to reduce the possibility of snagging the pilot chute
    c. that the instructor has extracted the pilot chute and is ready to control it while the student climbs out
    d. that the curved pin is inserted no more than halfway into the closing loop

X-B USPA SLI/IAD INSTRUCTOR EXAM

40. Which of the following is true?
    a. During IAD operations, the IAD instructor may need to step partway out of the aircraft to keep the pilot chute out of the windstream and in the burble behind the student.
    b. The IAD instructor throws the pilot chute down and away as soon as the student's body has dropped clear of the aircraft.
    c. If the container opens on the step, the IAD Instructor must immediately deploy the pilot chute below the aircraft's horizontal stabilizer.
    d. all of the above

STATIC-LINE CANDIDATES ONLY

Note: Answer these questions only if you are applying for the USPA Static-Line Instructor rating.

37. Which system requires an assist device (FARs)?
    a. Stevens static line
    b. pilot-chute assist static line
    c. direct bag static line
    d. hand-deployed static line

38. The following is true of a static-line attachment:
    a. Attaching the static line to a seat belt or hardware may result in the failure of the seat belt assembly.
    b. Attachment to the pilot's seat could result in its sudden removal from the aircraft.
    c. Static-line attachments need to be inspected regularly by an aircraft mechanic.
    d. all of the above

39. Holding the static line high during the student's climb-out and exit will help—
    a. prevent the student from seeing the static line and getting a false sense of security
    b. maintain tension on the closing loop
    c. prevent deployment under the student's inboard arm
    d. allow the instructor to get under the static line more easily if the student needs help

40. A static-line instructor should—
    a. never allow any part of his or her body to get between the load path of the static line and the aircraft
    b. always wear gloves
    c. wearing gloves, practice operating the static line many times in the actual aircraft to be used prior to supervising static-line jumps with actual students
    d. all of the above

6. USPA Tandem Instructor
Complete questions 1-25 of the general instructor exam.

USPA TANDEM INSTRUCTOR EXAM | X-B

26. The FAA class 3 medical certificate:
    a. is required only for completing the initial tandem certification course
    b. is no longer a requirement for tandem instructors
    c. must be kept current by any USPA Tandem Instructor making tandem jumps
    d. is required for all USPA instructional ratings

27. Who may legally pack a tandem main parachute according to FAR part 105?
    a. an experienced packer with instructor supervision
    b. the parachutist in command making the next jump on the tandem parachute
    c. any USPA Instructor
    d. any USPA Coach or Instructor

28. The drogue should be deployed within how many seconds after exiting the aircraft?
    a. five
    b. ten
    c. 20
    d. 25

29. Throwing the drogue to gain stability is considered:
    a. standard procedure
    b. acceptable for new tandem instructors
    c. necessary for exits with large students
    d. a serious failure of the tandem instructor to control the freefall

30. The proper response to a serious aircraft emergency at 3,000 feet would be:
    a. land with the airplane
    b. hook up the student, exit, deploy the drogue, then release the drogue
    c. hook up the student, exit, and deploy the reserve
    d. hook up the student, pull both drogue release handles, exit, and deploy the drogue

31. Exit stability is more easily achieved:
    a. if the tandem instructor conducts ground training effectively
    b. if the tandem instructor exits with the student facing into the relative wind
    c. if the tandem instructor wears a baggy suit and the student wears low-drag clothing
    d. all of the above

32. The instructor cannot find the drogue handle in freefall. The proper response should be:
    a. Continue looking for the drogue handle if above 5,000 feet.
    b. Pull the drogue release handle.
    c. Pull the cutaway handle.
    d. Deploy the reserve within ten seconds of the exit if the drogue handle cannot be located.

33. The drogue bridle entangles with the tandem pair. The correct response should be:
    a. Attempt to clear it twice, then deploy the reserve.
    b. Pull the drogue release handle.
    c. Pull the cutaway handle.
    d. none of the above

34. During droguefall, the main container opens prematurely. The tandem instructor's first response should be:
    a. Deploy the reserve.
    b. Pull the cutaway handle.
    c. Pull the drogue release handle.
    d. Grab the main bag if possible.

35. Once the drogue is deployed, the tandem instructor should on every jump:
    a. Turn the student's face away from the sun to improve visibility.
    b. Remind the student of his or her responsibilities during parachute deployment.
    c. Touch each tandem system operation handle in the order it might be used.
    d. Adjust the fall rate to match the video flyer.

36. The Airtec Tandem Cypres AAD will not arm unless the airplane climbs above approximately what altitude?
    a. 750 feet
    b. 1,800 feet
    c. 2,000 feet
    d. 3,000 feet

37. In the event of a main canopy malfunction, the tandem instructor should decide and act by what altitude to cut away and deploy the reserve?
    a. 1,800 feet
    b. 2,000 feet
    c. 3,000 feet
    d. 3,500 feet

38. What qualifications are required for experienced jumpers acting as tandem students during the probationary stage or for jumps to regain currency after a period of tandem inactivity of less than 180 days?
    a. USPA B license plus 100 jumps
    b. received a briefing from a USPA Tandem Instructor on all phases of tandem equipment operation and emergency procedures
    c. under the supervision of a USPA Tandem Instructor, coordinated all decision and execution altitudes with the tandem rating candidate in the event that the candidate fails to perform
    d. all of the above

39. Concerning landings, a tandem student should be trained:
    a. Never make a downwind landing.
    b. The instructor's feet should never touch first.
    c. The legs-up-and-forward position for a tandem landing is not suitable for landing solo.
    d. Landings under tandem canopies are so fast, the student should never jump a seven-cell parachute.

40. Before taking a student with disabilities on a tandem jump, a USPA tandem instructor should verify that:
    a. The student is capable of executing a legal contract.
    b. The student can perform all functions of an able-bodied jumper.
    c. The student has received the advice of a physician.
    d. The student is really sure that he'll be OK.

X-B USPA EXAMINER EXAM

7. USPA Examiner

1. Candidates must have a SIM and IRM dated within how many years of your course date in order to be considered valid manuals?
2. What are the three levels of the USPA rating structure?
3. What are requirements for the USPA Coach rating?
4. What are the requirements for the USPA AFF Instructor Rating?
5. What are the requirements for the USPA Tandem Instructor Rating?
6. What are the jump number and experience requirements for the USPA Static Line or IAD Instructor Rating?
7. How long is the grace period for candidates to use the new rating before it must be issued in the USPA database?
8. According to the BSR's, at what point may a Coach supervise a static line or IAD student in the airplane and in freefall?
9. What is the purpose of an ice breaker?
10. List two different ice-breakers.
11. What is subjective evaluation?
12. What is objective evaluation?
13. What is formative evaluation?
14. What is summative evaluation?
15. What are the four parts of a lesson design?
16. Define the acronym SMART with regards to goal setting.
17. Define whole-part-whole with regards to presentation strategies.
18. Define forward chaining with regards to presentation strategies.
19. Define backward chaining with regards to presentation strategies.
20. How many bites of information should be included in one learning session?
21. What is required regarding the location of any USPA rating course?
22. What is the recommended ratio of candidates to evaluators for a USPA rating course?
23. What needs to be checked with each candidate at the start of the course?
24. What needs to be sent to USPA Headquarters at the completion of each course?
25. How long must each Examiner retain copies of all course materials?
26. What are the major points of a pre-observation plan?
27. What are the four main points of an observation plan?
28. What is the number of improvement points that should be provided to candidates during a debrief?
29. How many biomechanical principles are applied to the skill analysis process?
30. What is the overall objective of Skill Analysis?
31. Define intrinsic motivation:
32. Define extrinsic motivation:
33. What are the four barriers to learning?
34. List the percentages of each of the five senses regarding the learning process:
35. What percentage of material can be forgotten within 30 days if there is no repetition of the training material?
36. How many repeat sessions are required in a 30-day period to increase the retention to more than 90%?
37. What are two disadvantages of lecture as a training method?
38. What are two advantages of structured discussion as a training method?
39. Describe Facilitation.
40. What is the definition of Conflict Resolution?

www.ingramcontent.com/pod-product-compliance
Lightning Source LLC
Chambersburg PA
CBHW042018090526
44590CB00029B/4329